The Trinitarian Ethics of Jonathan Edwards

COLUMBIA SERIES IN REFORMED THEOLOGY

The Columbia Series in Reformed Theology represents a joint commitment of Columbia Theological Seminary and Westminster John Knox Press to provide theological resources for the church today.

The Reformed tradition has always sought to discern what the living God revealed in scripture is saying and doing in every new time and situation. Volumes in this series examine significant individuals, events, and issues in the development of this tradition and explore their implications for contemporary Christian faith and life.

This series is addressed to scholars, pastors, and laypersons. The Editorial Board hopes that these volumes will contribute to the continuing reformation of the church.

Columbia Theological Seminary wishes to express its appreciation to the following churches for supporting this joint publishing venture:

Central Presbyterian Church, Atlanta, Georgia

First Presbyterian Church, Franklin, Tennessee

First Presbyterian Church, Nashville, Tennessee

First Presbyterian Church, Quincy, Florida

First Presbyterian Church, Spartanburg, South Carolina

First Presbyterian Church, Tupelo, Mississippi

North Avenue Presbyterian Church, Atlanta, Georgia

Riverside Presbyterian Church, Jacksonville, Florida

Roswell Presbyterian Church, Roswell, Georgia

South Highland Presbyterian Church, Birmingham, Alabama

Spring Hill Presbyterian Church, Mobile, Alabama

St. Simons Island Presbyterian Church, St. Simons Island, Georgia

St. Stephen Presbyterian Church, Fort Worth, Texas

Trinity Presbyterian Church, Atlanta, Georgia

University Presbyterian Church, Chapel Hill, North Carolina

COLUMBIA SERIES IN REFORMED THEOLOGY

The Trinitarian Ethics of Jonathan Edwards

WILLIAM J. DANAHER JR.

Westminster John Knox Press
LOUISVILLE • LONDON

© 2004 William J. Danaher Jr.

Book and cover design by Drew Stevens

First edition
Published by Westminster John Knox Press
Louisville, Kentucky

This book is printed on acid-free paper that meets the American National Standards Institute Z39.48 standard. ∞

PRINTED IN THE UNITED STATES OF AMERICA

04 05 06 07 08 09 10 11 12 — 10 9 8 7 6 5 4 3 2 1

Library of Congress Cataloging-in-Publication Data

Danaher, William J., 1956–
    The Trinitarian ethics of Jonathan Edwards / William J. Danaher, Jr.
        p. cm. — (Columbia series in Reformed theology)
    Includes bibliographical references and index.
    ISBN 0-664-22737-6
    1. Edwards, Jonathan, 1703–1758—Ethics.   I. Series.

BX7260.E3D26 2004
241'.0458'092—dc22   2003061614

CONTENTS

PREFACE

For several years Jonathan Edwards has fascinated me. Like many others, my first contact was through reading, but not completely understanding, *The Nature of True Virtue*. There I encountered a brief sketch of the moral life that was at once puzzling and moving. Edwards's arguments and language are complex, and I subsequently developed some fluency with the philosophy and theology of Edwards's day so that I could better understand them. But even with this knowledge there seemed to be a deeper point of coherence that Edwards refers to only indirectly. For Edwards, Christian ethical reflection must begin with the character of God, in whom we live and move and have our being. Therefore, to know what true virtue is, we must know ourselves properly, and to know ourselves properly, we must know God. Yet who is this God we must know?

Consequently, I turned to those passages in Edwards's other writings where he reflects on the character of God. What I found in these passages surprised me. As many have noted, Edwards cared a great deal about divine attributes such as beauty or sovereignty. But on my reading, Edwards's doctrine of the Trinity appeared to condition everything he says about God and humanity. Indeed, Edwards's doctrine of the Trinity seemed to provide a perspective on his theological ethics that could incorporate other writings in his corpus into an overarching vision of the moral life. This book, then, develops the connection between Edwards's Trinitarian reflection and his theological ethics.

A deep paradox lies at the heart of writing. In the midst of writing, no pursuit feels as lonely; at the same time, no pursuit depends so radically on community. In my case, three communities made this book possible. The first community I would like to thank is intellectual. I owe a great debt to Gene Outka, who directed the dissertation on which this book is based. I benefited greatly from the comments and encouragement Gene offered throughout the writing process. Another important influence was Robert Jenson, who provided guidance that was essential to the general direction of the book. Harry Stout also urged me to explore new avenues in Edwards's thought. In addition, I would like to thank my professors in

Christian ethics, Margaret Farley and Richard Fern, as well as the staff, past and present, of the *Works of Jonathan Edwards* at Yale, in particular Kyle Farley, Douglas Sweeney, Ava Chamberlain, and Ken Minkema. Finally, I wish to thank the colleagues and friends that I met during my time as a graduate student at Yale, in particular Kaari Reierson, Matthew Weiler, Amy Laura Hall, Jennifer Beste, David Clough, Lauris Kaldjian, Eric Gregory, William Inboden, Jesse Couenhoven, Chris Steck, and Brian Stiltner.

The second community is ecclesial. As a teenager, I was fortunate to encounter two priests of the Episcopal Church, Philip Lyman and Charles Tait, who nurtured and shared with me a passion for Reformed theology and the Puritans. Shortly after college, David Stokes taught me to see theological reflection as a form of worship. While in seminary, Walter Eversely helped channel my energies toward Edwards, and Gerald McDermott reviewed my first attempt to write about Edwards. More recently, there are those who have little interest in Edwards but who have faithfully supported me during the time I wrote this book. I am grateful to my colleagues at the University of the South, in particular Guy Lytle, Christopher Bryan, Robert Hughes, Don Armentrout, Allan Parrent, Rusty Goldsmith, James Turrell, Bran Potter, John Willis, and Jill Hendrickson. I am also grateful to my students, especially William Carroll, Glenda Curry, and Carl Badgley. Finally, I would like to thank Jeff Hoppa and Curtis Almquist, SSJE, for walking with me along some difficult paths.

The most important community is familial—my daughter, Phoebe, and my wife, Claire. Through Claire and Phoebe I have received innumerable joys and blessings. When I am with Phoebe, I am rich even if my pockets are empty. And of all the persons I have mentioned, by far my greatest debt is to Claire. When I am with Claire, I know that God is love. To draw from the last words Edwards spoke to his beloved wife, Sarah, I believe that the "uncommon union" between us is of a "spiritual nature" and therefore "will continue forever." To Claire, I dedicate this work.

ABBREVIATIONS

Due to frequent citation the following works are abbreviated. All but the last are from *The Works of Jonathan Edwards*.

Y1   Vol. 1, *Freedom of the Will*, ed. Paul Ramsey, 1957.

Y2   Vol. 2, *Religious Affections*, ed. John Smith, 1959.

Y3   Vol. 3, *Original Sin*, ed. Clyde A. Holbrook, 1970.

Y6   Vol. 6, *Scientific and Philosophical Writings*, ed. Wallace E. Anderson, 1970.

Y8   Vol. 8, *Ethical Writings*, ed. Paul Ramsey, 1989.

Y9   Vol. 9, *A History of the Work of Redemption*, ed. John F. Wilson, 1992.

Y11   Vol. 11, *Typological Writings*, ed. Wallace E. Anderson, 1993.

Y13   Vol. 13, *The "Miscellanies,"* ed. Thomas Schafer, 1994.

Y18   Vol. 18, *The "Miscellanies" 501–832*, ed. Ava Chamberlain, 2000.

Y20   Vol. 20, *The "Miscellanies" 833–1152*, ed. Amy Plantinga Pauw, 2002.

Y21   Vol. 21, *Writings on the Trinity, Grace, and Faith*, ed. Sang Hyun Lee, 2003.

H   *Treatise on Grace and Other Posthumously Published Writings*, ed. Paul Helm, 1971.

INTRODUCTION

The purpose of this study is to examine the theological ethics of Jonathan Edwards from the perspective of his doctrine of the Trinity. In studies of Edwards's theological ethics, three interpretations currently prevail on the connection between Edwards's Trinitarian and moral reflection. The first interpretation allows that a connection exists between Edwards's moral and Trinitarian thought but attributes the source of this connection to a wider metaphysics of beauty that comprehends both Edwards's ethical and Trinitarian reflection. Thus, Roland Delattre writes in *Beauty and Sensibility in the Thought of Jonathan Edwards* (1968) that Edwards's "concept of spiritual beauty provides the platform upon which he erects his doctrine of the Trinity." While the "unity of the Triune God" is "the fountain of all being and beauty," beauty stands behind Edwards's "speculations about the internal structure and life of God" as "preeminent among the divine perfections" and informs Edwards's understanding of the "meaning and structure of moral selfhood."[1] Delattre reiterates this interpretation in two recent articles on Edwards's ethics, in which he argues that for Edwards the "religious life is a life made new by participation in the divine life," a "participation" which enters "into the very center of the divine life." Such "a life is, first of all, made new" by "a sense of the beauty of God." Therefore, although "Edwards was a decidedly Christian theologian," his "central convictions are—or can be—fairly expressed, without sacrificing anything of their distinctively Christian features, in language addressed to a wider circle of religious believers and spiritual seekers."[2]

The second interpretation admits of a connection between Edwards's moral and Trinitarian thought, but refers to this connection only occasionally in analyzing the main themes in Edwards's theological ethics. Thus, in his extensive introduction and appendices to volume 8 of the *Yale Edition of Jonathan Edwards* (1989), Paul Ramsey turns to aspects of Edwards's doctrine of the Trinity to illuminate his conception of conscience, secondary beauty, and the nature of heaven as a "progressive state" of asymptotic union and participation in God.[3] For the most part, however, Ramsey speaks at length of concepts and relations that figure in both Edwards's

1

Trinitarian and ethical reflection—such as self-love, consent, benevolence and complacence, happiness, knowledge of God, and communication of the divine nature—without considering the connection between them as necessary.

A third interpretation asserts a strong connection between Edwards's moral and Trinitarian thought, but devotes little space to exploring or explaining this connection. Thus, in his work of comparative moral philosophy, *Jonathan Edwards's Moral Thought and Its British Context* (1981), Norman Fiering argues that "the Trinity for Edwards" is "never an inert dogma." Edwards's "entire moral theology," in particular his "moral psychology" and his "model of a morally ideal human society" are "logically deducible from his theory of the Trinity alone." Despite the promising nature of these remarks, however, Fiering offers only a brief excursus on Edwards's doctrine of the Trinity, and he places this excursus in a chapter on Edwards's estimation of human understanding unaided by grace rather than in his chapter on Edwards's "synthetic ethics" or "moral theology."[4] Similarly, in "The Ethics of Jonathan Edwards" (1964), Henry Stob contends that Edwards's writings on the Trinity reflect "an interest that is more than casual." Edwards's thought concerning the "doctrine of the Trinity" is something "he is brought to consider" by "the exigencies of his ethical theory." The Trinity offers Edwards a vision of God as "three persons consisting in some mysterious and ultimately inexplicable way a oneness of being and unity of perfection" that is "both moral and absolute." Thus, "morality is essentially social and as such presupposes relations," and "since these relations exist pure and perfect within the very Godhead," Edwards can articulate an "infinite" ethics of "love" displaying an "unconquerable optimism" that asserts "what ought to be will be, for in God it already is."[5] Like Fiering, however, Stob devotes little space to exploring this connection, and he analyzes Edwards's doctrine of the Trinity mainly in order to reconcile Edwards's idealism with his ethics.

In this study, I offer a fuller account of this third line of interpretation suggested by Stob and Fiering. With them, I take Edwards's writings on the Trinity as the paradigm through which to view his theological ethics. In the process of doing so, I hope to cast doubt on the adequacy of the lines of interpretation offered by Ramsey and Delattre. One may comprehend Edwards's theological ethics from the standpoint of his aesthetics rather than his doctrine of the Trinity, as Delattre contends. Unquestionably, beauty has a unique place in Edwards's theological ethics. Edwards uses the experience of beauty as a means of integrating the moral and spiritual life, and he employs beauty as an analytical concept for identifying the nature of true, as opposed to illusory, virtue. But if beauty is Edwards's favored theological *definiens*, the Trinity is the *definiendum* of his theological ethics. The all-encompassing nature of Delattre's conception of Edwards's aesthetics threatens to confuse this distinction, and he fails to recognize the extent to which Edwards's aesthetics stem from the doctrine it ostensibly systematizes.

To cite the most obvious example, early in *Beauty and Sensibility* Delattre offers a "preliminary definition" of Edwards's conception of beauty or "excellency" as "consent" or the "cordial agreement" that "consists in concord and union of mind and heart." This definition identifies the category of "primary" or "spiritual" beauty, which in turn, according to Delattre, establishes the aesthetic foundation upon which Edwards develops his doctrine of the Trinity and his ethics.[6] Here Delattre cites Edwards's own notation in "The Mind," entry 1, "this is a universal definition of excellency: The consent of being to being, or being's consent to entity" (Y6:336). Delattre fails, however, to mention the extent to which consent is a Trinitarian concept. Later in "The Mind," entry 45, Edwards writes that "we were obliged to borrow the word 'consent' from spiritual things" (Y6:362). The "consent of spirits consists in their mutual love one to another, and the sweet harmony between the various parts of the universe is only an image of mutual love" (Y6:337–38). Now "God is the prime and original being, the first and last, and the pattern of all, and has the sum of all perfection. We may therefore doubtless conclude that all that is in the perfection of spirits may be resolved into that which is God's perfection, which is love." The pattern of all beauty and consent is God's own love in the Trinity. God's "excellence" consists in "the mutual love of the Father and the Son" that generates "the personal Holy Spirit," who is God's "infinite beauty, and this is God's infinite consent to being in general" (Y6:364). Consequently, while Delattre considers beauty the "platform" upon which "Edwards erects his ontological doctrine of the Trinity," the textual evidence suggests the opposite to be the case.

One may also comprehend Edwards's ethics from the standpoint that Ramsey adopts, that is, to speak generally of the theological "principles" operating in Edwards's theological ethics, such as the "love of God," our "participation in the divine love," and God's "communication" of God's self to intelligent creatures (Y6:12–33). The broad discussion of the principles at work in Edwards's "ethical" writings fits Ramsey's genre, where as an editor he introduces and comments on a selection of texts. Yet such a discussion serves inadequately as a basis for Ramsey's implicit attempt to present his own interpretation of Edwards. As I have noted, Ramsey's analysis of Edwards's theological principles avails itself of Edwards's doctrine of the Trinity only at key points. This reliance on Edwards's doctrine of the Trinity is particularly evident in his most important work of analysis in volume 8, the appendix "Heaven Is a Progressive State." Here Ramsey sees the culmination of Edwards's ethics as the moment, in Edwards's words, when the saints are "admitted into the society of the blessed Trinity" (Y8:736).[7] If this is the case, however, an orderly analysis of Edwards's ethics begins where Ramsey ends. Accordingly, I start with Edwards's doctrine of the Trinity as the foundation upon which he builds his understanding of the moral life.

Perhaps the main reason for the different interpretations noted above is that those who argue for a strong connection between Edwards's Trinitarian and moral reflection consider Edwards's specific writings on the Trinity as paradigmatic statements of his theological ethics. The primary source of Edwards's Trinitarian thought are several entries from his "Miscellanies" notebooks, a set of notebooks of miscellaneous theological reflections that he compiled throughout his life.[8] Edwards also addressed specifically Trinitarian themes in three essays: the "Discourse on the Trinity," later known as the "Essay on the Trinity," which Edwards began in early 1730 and intermittently revised until the mid-1740s; the "Treatise on Grace," which Edwards wrote sometime during the Great Awakening (1740–1742); and "Miscellanies" entry 1062, titled "Observations concerning the Scripture Economy of the Trinity and the Covenant of Redemption," which Edwards wrote sometime in 1743.[9]

Admittedly, the seminal nature of these texts is not obvious. In an influential set of articles, Edwards Amasa Park, who was the most prominent interpreter of Edwards in the nineteenth century, asserted that Edwards pays only "occasional" and "incidental attention" to the doctrine of the Trinity, and that his remarks are uncharacteristically "inconsistent" and "undigested." According to Park, the impression one receives after reading Edwards's writings on the Trinity is not of encountering a long lost masterpiece but a kind of artist's study, akin to "one of Michelangelo's unfinished statues."[10] To a certain extent, Park's image of an artist's study has merit. Edwards never published an account of the Trinity, and his entries on the Trinity are sporadic rather than systematic. Furthermore, as we will see, in his writings on the Trinity Edwards uses concepts and categories that he refines and changes in his later writings.

In his "Miscellanies" entries, however, Edwards recounts an awareness of the centrality of the doctrine of the Trinity. In "Miscellanies" entry 181, he reports a transformation in his thought concerning the theological and ethical relevance of the Trinity: "I used to think sometimes with myself, if such doctrines as those of the Trinity" are "true, yet what need was there of revealing them in the gospel? What good do they do towards the advancing of holiness?" But "now I don't wonder at all at their being revealed, for such doctrines as these are glorious inlets into the knowledge and view of the spiritual world, and the contemplation of supreme things; the knowledge of which I have experienced how much contributes to the betterment of the heart" (Y13:328). Later in entry 343 of the "Miscellanies," Edwards wrote under the heading of "moral law" that "duties are founded on doctrines." The "revelation we now have of the Trinity," as the chief doctrine of the Christian faith, makes "a vast alteration with respect to the reason and obligations to many amiable and exalted duties, so that they are as it were new" (Y13:416).

Trinitarian themes and relations are evident in other significant writings. In "God Glorified in Man's Dependence," a sermon published in 1731, Edwards writes that regeneration is "a kind of participation of God," in which the saints "are made partakers of the divine nature" through the Holy Spirit becoming an "inhabitant," or "vital principle," in the "soul" (Y17:208). Hence, there exists a "dependence on each person in the Trinity" in the work of regeneration: "[W]e are dependent on Christ the Son of God, as he is our wisdom, righteousness, sanctification, and redemption"; we "are dependent on the Father who has given us Christ, and made him to be these things to us"; and "we are dependent on the Holy Ghost, for 'tis of him that we are in Christ Jesus," for "'tis the Spirit of God that gives us faith in him, whereby we receive him, and close with him" (Y17:201). In Edwards's recollection of his own experience of regeneration, which he wrote in 1740, these Trinitarian themes and relations reappear. One of the results of having "a new sense" of the "glory of the divine being" is that "God has appeared more glorious to me, on account of the Trinity"—"it has made me have more exalting thoughts of God, that he subsists as three persons; Father, Son, and Holy Ghost" (Y16:800).

While brief, the most significant passage where Edwards indicates the importance of the Trinity to his theological and ethical reflection is a short resolution he recorded in an outline for a proposed treatise of philosophical theology titled "A Rational Account of the Main Doctrines of the Christian Religion":

> To explain the doctrine of the Trinity before I begin to treat of the work of redemption; and of their equality, their equal honor in their manner of subsisting and acting, and virtue. But to speak of their equal honor in their concern in the affair of redemption afterwards, after I have done with all the doctrines relating to man's redemption. (Y6:396)

Although Edwards never completed the treatise, the place he assigned to explaining the doctrine of the Trinity is striking. Not only does the Trinity precede all discussion of the work of redemption, which in "Miscellanies" entry 702 Edwards describes as the "great end and drift of all God's works and dispensations" (Y18:284), but all reflection on the work of redemption culminates in a reconsideration of the Trinity. In short, Edwards envisioned the doctrine of the Trinity as the alpha and omega of the "Rational Account."

1. THE STUDY IN OUTLINE

Consequently, to develop a Trinitarian account of Edwards's theological ethics requires two steps. The first is to gather Edwards's entries and writings into an organized presentation of his Trinitarian doctrine. Edwards follows a longstanding practice in Western Christian theology that develops models for the Trinity based on the activities in the mind, traditionally known as the *psychological analogy,* and the desire to live in relations of love, traditionally known as the *social analogy.* Edwards's depiction of both the psychological and social analogies displays affinities with those of prominent patristic, medieval, and modern theologians. However, at the same time, Edwards's articulation of the psychological and social analogies is remarkably original, which in turn affects the relation he draws between these analogies and the moral life.

Following Augustine (354–430), traditional articulations of the psychological analogy depict it in terms of substance metaphysics. In contrast, Edwards articulates his psychological analogy within an idealist metaphysics that he appropriates from the French philosopher Nicholas Malebranche (1638–1715). This shift in metaphysics allows Edwards to generate not only a different account of the processions in the Godhead, but also a new perspective of what it means to participate in the divine life through the indwelling of the Holy Spirit. Through the psychological analogy, Edwards envisions the moral life as one of *divinization* or *theosis,* that is, the self-communication of God to the regenerate through the indwelling of the Holy Spirit. Thus, true "saving grace," which provides the foundation of all true virtue and charity, "is no other than that very love of God—that is, God, in one of the persons of the Trinity, uniting Himself to the soul of the creature, as a vital principle, dwelling there and exerting Himself by the faculties of the soul of man, in His own proper nature" (H:72–73).

A similar level of originality is evident in Edwards's reworking of the social analogy. Traditionally, the social analogy has played a minor role in Western Trinitarian reflection. Following Richard of St. Victor (d. 1173), articulations of the social analogy carefully distinguished the relations between the divine persons from human participation in these relations. The social analogy, then, typically offered an eternal template of divine love that human love could only imperfectly approximate. In contrast, for Edwards the primary teaching of the social analogy is that the "love and society" of the Godhead has been poured out on humanity through the work of redemption (H:64). In other words, for Edwards the social analogy reveals the depth of communion into which humanity has been invited through the missions of the Son and the Spirit: "Christ has brought it to pass . . . that those that the Father has given him should be brought into the household of God, that he and his Father and they should be as it were one society, one family; that his people should be in a sort admitted into that society of the three persons in the Godhead" (Y18:110). Thus, the Spirit, which the saints participate in through *theosis*, is an interpersonal love. The Spirit, which is the "perfect and intimate union and love" between the Father and the Son, is the "bond" of "all holy union between the Father and the Son, and between God and the creature, and between the creatures among themselves" (H:64). Further, the social analogy provides Edwards with a way to describe the missions of the Son and the Spirit as manifestations of God's triune love.

Perhaps the most distinctive moment in Edwards's articulation of the Trinitarian analogies concerns the role of personhood in the moral life. Where Western Trinitarian theology traditionally conceived of personhood as an individual substance of a rational nature, Edwards conceives of a person as a dynamic state of relationality in the self-consciousness, which is modeled after God's own triune personhood. Moreover, in humanity self-consciousness is not merely self-knowledge, but for Edwards we are fully persons to the extent our minds participate in the mind of God. All knowledge of God derives from God's knowledge of God's self. True knowledge, and by extension true love, is Triune, and to know and love ourselves fully, we must know and love God. The social analogy also provides an essential aspect of personhood. Given that God is a society of three persons, the desire to live in communion with another represents one of the most basic expressions of love in the universe. Therefore, we are realized as persons to the extent we live in relations of mutuality and self-giving. This inclination to love another, of course, is perfectly fulfilled when God is the source and end of our interpersonal love. Nonetheless, there is a sense in which love in any form bears a resemblance to the triune love of God.

Another distinctive moment in Edwards's Trinitarian thought arises during his treatment of the social analogy. To say that humanity's end is to live in communion with the triune God addresses not only the nature of things to come but the nature of things on earth. That is to say, the social analogy establishes an interplay between the created order and its eschatological fulfillment. For Edwards, the church is the fundamental eschatological society that experiences the triune love of God, and it is the proper locus for living the moral life. Through "partaking of the Holy Ghost," the community of the saints "have communion with the Father and the Son and with other Christians: this is the common excellency and delight in which they are all united: this is the bond of perfectness, by which they are one with the Father and the Son, as the Father is in the Son and the Son is in the Father" (Y13:448). Nonetheless, relations of mutuality and self-giving pervade the created order and bear the image of the divine community. Edwards often emphasizes the discontinuity between the created order and its eschatological fulfillment. The decisive question in the moral life is not whether one participates in the social relations that pervade the created order, but whether one participates through the Spirit in the church's eschatological communion with Christ. The created order, however, also provides insight into the nature of this eschatological reality. Particularly in friendship, marriage, and in the experience of beauty, one sees a glimpse of the spiritual communion that saints experience in part now but in full in the new creation.

A final distinctive moment in Edwards's Trinitarian writings concerns the incarnation of Christ. For Edwards, Christ is the visible manifestation of the triune love of God, and this love is perfectly expressed in his atoning death on the cross. The "divine excellency of Christ and the love of the Father to him, is the life and soul of all that Christ did and suffered in the work of redemption" (Y13:524). The incarnation of Christ also represents the realization of the divine participation in humanity: "Christ took on himself man's nature" to enable "a more familiar conversation than the infinite distance of the Divine nature would allow of" (Y18:108). Thus, "one glorious end of the union of the human to the Divine nature" is "to bring God near to us," so that "Jehovah, who is infinitely distant from us, might become familiar to us" (Y13:248). Finally, Christ is the promise of humanity's aspiration to participate in the life and love of God. The incarnate Christ initiates "the transcendent advancement of men in their union with God, whereby they partake of the beauty, life, honor and joy of the eternal Son; and so are made as gods by communion of his Spirit, whereby they are partakers of the Divine nature" (Y18:288). As a result of this spiritual communion, human love in every form is assumed and transformed.

The second step in this study is to provide a Trinitarian interpretation of Edwards's major writings, specifically *A Treatise concerning Religious Affections* (1746), *Freedom of the Will* (1754), *Original Sin* (1758), *Two Dissertations* (1765), and *Charity and Its Fruits* (1738). As I hope to show, viewing these works from the perspective of Edwards's Trinitarian thought is essential to assessing what each contributes to Edwards's theological ethics. To sketch this task in brief: While commentators often view the *Religious Affections* as an exercise in religious psychology or as a repudiation of enthusiasm, a Trinitarian interpretation of the *Religious Affections* retrieves the sense in which it is equally a constructive work of ethics. Specifically, in the *Religious Affections* Edwards develops a theological anthropology that places communion with God at the center of the moral life, which in turn informs his understanding of the nature of virtue, duty, and practice.

Similarly, a Trinitarian interpretation of *Freedom of the Will* and *Original Sin* connects Edwards's theories of the will, sin, and evil to his Trinitarian commitments regarding divine and human agency, as well as to his understanding of the redemptive mission of the incarnate Christ. Commentators typically view these works as intricate defenses of positions that are no longer tenable. When viewed from the perspective of his Trinitarian thought, however, Edwards's proposals in *Freedom of the Will* and *Original Sin* acquire an explanatory power that eludes other theories that proceed on the basis of autonomy.

In the same manner, a Trinitarian interpretation of the *Two Dissertations* provides a fuller account of love that can support Edwards's claims in these writings concerning the priority of benevolence. Commentators typically view these writings as summary statements of Edwards's theological ethics, and on this account find Edwards's proposal too abstract and austere. But a Trinitarian interpretation of these writings suggests that these works are best viewed as apologetical efforts that seek to engage moral sense philosophy and therefore must be viewed against the background of the different aspects of love generated by Edwards's Trinitarian reflection.

Finally, a Trinitarian interpretation of *Charity and Its Fruits* helps identify the distinctive teaching in this sermon series on the relation between ethics and ecclesiology. For Edwards, living the life of love provides the primary point of contact between the church's present reality and its eschatological fulfillment in heaven. Moreover, God's triune love animates the interpersonal relations in the church and establishes an ethos that is transformative of the surrounding society.

In addition to identifying the individual contribution each of these writings makes to Edwards's theological ethics, the Trinitarian interpretation I propose also provides a way to integrate Edwards's major writings into a coherent whole. As I just noted, commentators on Edwards generally view the *Two Dissertations* as the definitive articulation of Edwards's theological ethics.[11] This impulse is understandable, for Edwards's other major writings are occasional, apologetical, and pastoral works deeply embedded in the moral and theological controversies of his day. Such an approach, however, tends to generate an interpretation of Edwards's theological ethics that not only neglects the Trinitarian themes present in Edwards's thought, but fails to appreciate the ethical insights of these other writings.[12] As we will see, when Edwards's Trinitarian thought provides the prism through which to conceive Edwards's theological ethics, it becomes possible to integrate Edwards's major writings into a comprehensive account of the moral life. While this account is not free of complications and tensions, it does offer a compelling portrait of ethics in a Trinitarian key.

The greatest advantage that a Trinitarian interpretation of Edwards's theological ethics offers is that it provides a new perspective from which to consider Edwards's contribution to contemporary theological ethics. As Gene Outka observes, in recent philosophical and theological ethics there has been a shift in paradigm away from "universalist" accounts that transcend particular beliefs and practices, and toward "particularist" accounts that proceed from within a specific historical and theological context.[13] Consequently, most of the recent writings in contemporary philosophical and theological ethics emphasize a given tradition's formative narratives, canonical texts, signal virtues, and general conception of human nature and the human good. Accordingly, a Trinitarian interpretation of Edwards's theological ethics allows for substantive comparisons between Edwards and some of the more prominent figures in contemporary philosophical and theological ethics. In particular, in the following chapters I compare different aspects of Edwards's proposal with those of Alasdair MacIntyre, Richard Swinburne, William Wainwright, John Hick, Gene Outka, Timothy Jackson, Edward Vacek, and Stanley Hauerwas, among others.

2. THEOLOGY AND ETHICS

The guiding presupposition of the interpretation I offer in this study is that Edwards's theological reflection deeply informs his ethical reflection, or in Edwards's words, that "duties are founded on doctrines" (Y13:416). Consequently, my interpretation develops in conversation with theological studies of Edwards's Trinitarian thought. Although often overlooked, the dissertations on Edwards's doctrine of the Trinity by Herbert Richardson and Krister Sairsingh are considerable.[14] In addition, Robert Jenson, Sang Hyun Lee, Stephen H. Daniel, Stephen Holmes, Bruce Stephens, and Janice Knight offer significant discussions and essays on Edwards's Trinitarian thought.[15] Finally, Amy Plantinga Pauw offers an important discussion of Edwards's psychological and social analogies, as well as of the anticipations of Edwards's Trinitarian reflection in seventeenth-century Puritan piety.[16]

At points, these studies provide helpful insights that inform my interpretation of Edwards's doctrine of the Trinity. In addition to specific disagreements, however, my interpretation departs from these previous assessments in the following ways. The clearest difference between these preceding studies and my own is that I attend to the ethical themes and concepts in Edwards's doctrinal reflection. For example, none of these studies recognize that Edwards's psychological analogy turns on "self-love" and the "conscience," two ethical topics that Edwards engages throughout his Trinitarian reflection, as well as in his major writings (Y13:257, 260). Further, none of these studies recognize the extent to which Edwards's social analogy generates an account of "benevolence," "complacence," and "mutuality," aspects of love that Edwards also engages throughout his Trinitarian reflection and in his major writings (H:49; H:108). As we will see, Edwards himself is deeply aware of the implications of using these ethical concepts as vehicles for Trinitarian reflection.

Indeed, one essential way that Edwards connects his Trinitarian reflection to the Christian life is precisely through appropriating these concepts and thereby changing their meaning and role in both theological and ethical discourse. Certainly, the attention I pay to the ethical terms and concepts at work in Edwards's Trinitarian reflection is due to my interest in providing a Trinitarian interpretation of Edwards's theological ethics. But I also hope to demonstrate that what is *theologically* unique about Edwards's Trinitarian reflection is that he places these moral concepts at the very center of his thought. Indeed, to overlook these ethical terms and concepts is to miss one of the original moments in Edwards's doctrine of the Trinity. For what is distinctive in Edwards's writings on the Trinity is that he integrates the moral life with the life of the Trinity such that understanding the nature and character of God is inseparable from understanding the nature of morality.

Another point of difference concerns the particular synthesis I offer of Edwards's Trinitarian writings and his major writings. Specifically, I draw out the implications Edwards's Trinitarian reflection has not only for theological questions such as Christology and ecclesiology but for questions such as the nature of personal identity, divine impassibility, and the connection between the created order and its eschatological fulfillment. For the most part, I do this by casting a wider net into Edwards's "Miscellanies" notebooks in order to develop a more inclusive account of Edwards's theology. Admittedly, at times such a synthesis pushes the borders of Trinitarian reflection beyond its traditional focus on the processions and relations of the divine persons. Nonetheless, such a synthesis is in line with the direction of recent Trinitarian thought, in which, as Catherine LaCugna writes, "all theological reflection" is "potentially a mode of Trinitarian theology."[17]

A third point of difference concerns the comparisons I draw between Edwards and other theologians and philosophers. Where the preceding studies note the *continuities* between Edwards's Trinitarian thought and its anticipations in patristic, medieval, and modern theology, I also emphasize the *discontinuities* between Edwards's account and those which precede it. To do so requires a closer reading both of the specific contours of Edwards's Trinitarian theology and of the Trinitarian approaches and philosophical movements that precede and inform it. But noting these differences is essential for fully appreciating Edwards's account.

A final point of difference concerns the emphasis most of these previous studies place on locating Edwards's Trinitarian reflection within the Reformed tradition. While such an exercise is certainly legitimate, my emphasis is more on the extent to which Edwards's Trinitarian ethics provides a bridge for Reformed theologians to recover a part of their heritage that resonates with central themes in catholic theology and ethics. Indeed, what is remarkable in Edwards's Trinitarian thought is not the extent to which he preserves and extends the Reformed tradition, but the extent to which he anticipates many of the major themes in recent Trinitarian theology. As we will see, Edwards's Trinitarian thought and its ethical implications display affinities with recent work by Catherine LaCugna, Jürgen Moltmann, and John Zizioulas, among others. In this contemporary discussion, I argue that Edwards holds his own. To quote a well-known statement by Perry Miller, Edwards is "so much ahead of his time that our own can hardly be said to have caught up with him."[18] Although Miller's intellectual portrait of Edwards as a Lockean and Puritan *Übermensch* has undergone substantial revision, the veracity of this comment remains. It is the nature of theological genius as we encounter it in Edwards that we find in his writings new facets and insights that continue to engage us, even as our theological questions change and evolve.

3. FURTHER PREFATORY REMARKS

The portrait I offer of Edwards in this study is unabashedly sympathetic and, in the classic sense, apologetic. Edwards is too often overlooked in contemporary theology and ethics, for reasons too numerous to enumerate. Consequently, this study is what Edwards would have called a "vindication," a reasoned attempt to reassert the validity of a particular person, position, or doctrine. Although Edwards's theological ethics is not without difficulties and points of tension, the same may be said of every other theologian of significance in the Christian tradition. And even where Edwards falls short, his Trinitarian reflection has within it resources that address these deficiencies.

In a small way, what I hope to offer in the course of this study is a demonstration of the type of theology that Hans Frei attributes to Edwards in his *Types of Christian Theology* (1992). Frei suggests that in Edwards's thought, "Christian doctrinal statements" have "a status similar to that of grammatical rules implicit in discourse." As such, these doctrinal statements are prior to more "formal" and "universal" philosophical structures, and the appropriation of these broader philosophical structures to redescribe these doctrinal statements is always selective and fragmentary. Thus, the theological task is an "unsystematic *ad hoc performance* of subordinating explanatory theory more generally, as a tool in Christian communal self-description." To engage in such a performance requires that one remains open to new insights and that one "constantly restate doctrinal statements in the light of cultural and conceptual change."[19]

Unfortunately, Frei died before he could substantiate this suggestion, and few have taken the time to explore to what extent this is in fact the case for Edwards. Indeed, commentators on Edwards have been quick to impose a governing ontology and metaphysic on his thought,[20] and even to find fault with Edwards when elements of such an "ad hoc" approach surfaces.[21] Consequently, it is my hope in the course of this study to offer a new approach to Edwards's thought that confirms Frei's thesis.

That said, there are certain limitations in the lexical approach to Edwards's Trinitarian theology and ethics that I attempt in this study. The first concerns the status of theological language for God, in particular the traditional Trinitarian formula of "Father, Son, and Holy Spirit." One of the implications of approaching Christian doctrinal statements as a set of grammatical rules is that it prioritizes the role the traditional formula plays in establishing the nature and relations of God's triunity. In this sense, as George Lindbeck suggests, the traditional formula has a lexical priority that is indispensable, or "unconditionally necessary," as one of the "general regulative principles" of the Christian faith.[22] Consequently, though well intentioned, attempts to substitute a symbolic construct for the traditional formula that is gender inclusive run the risk of unconsciously importing a different set of grammatical rules into the doctrinal lexicon, as well as bypassing the economy of salvation to which the traditional formula refers.

Nonetheless, as Rowan Williams notes, though "real immersion in the Christian tradition" is appropriate and necessary, this immersion is incomplete without the recognition that "our own words and stories may carry sin and violence in their telling, even as they provide the resource for overcoming that sin and violence." Therefore, every engagement with the traditional formula should be set "side-by-side" with an awareness of how one might "focus doctrinal language in a new way" that can respect the concerns raised by those who object to the gender exclusiveness of the traditional formula.[23]

Accordingly, in the following study of Edwards, I retain his use of the traditional formula for the triune God. At the same time, I also emphasize the ways in which Edwards's Trinitarian thought reflects some of the concerns expressed in feminist critiques of the traditional formula.[24] Although Edwards draws patriarchal comparisons between the triune relations and human relations in a few passages, much more prevalent in his theology and ethics are visions of God that call forth relations of mutuality, friendship, freedom, and love that resonate with contemporary feminist and liberation theologies. As Paula Cooey notes, though Edwards uses the traditional formulation of God as Father, Son, and Holy Spirit, there are passages in his devotional writings that suggest the motherhood of God.[25] Edwards also frequently describes the nature of conversion as akin to childbirth, in particular the Virgin Mary's role as *theotokos* in the incarnation. Edwards writes in the *Religious Affections* that the "conception of Christ in the womb of the blessed Virgin, by the power of the Holy Ghost, seems to be a designed resemblance of the conception of Christ in the soul of a believer, by the power of the Holy Ghost" (Y2:347). Moreover, as I show in more detail, in Edwards's Trinitarian writings there is a strong theme that accords with the emphasis in contemporary feminist ethics on the positive role of erotic love and intimacy.[26] Not only do relations of erotic love provide an important way to live in light of the church's eschatological destiny, but Edwards describes the "intimacy" between Christ and the saints in terms of erotic love. In Edwards's vision, Christ invites the saints to receive "the kisses of his mouth" (Y18:370).

Finally, throughout this study I make an effort to use those passages in Edwards's writings where he uses gender inclusive language for humanity, and to limit the quotation of those passages where he does not. While there are moments in Edwards's writings where in the interest of accuracy I quote the terms "man" and "mankind," in many passages Edwards himself uses the word "person."

The second limitation concerns the historical nature of this study. Inherent in the lexical approach that I take of Edwards's Trinitarian theology and ethics is a deep awareness of the historicity of Edwards's thought. Not only do I carefully note the contours of the Trinitarian thought that precedes Edwards in patristic and medieval theology, but I treat with care the specific vocabulary and reasoning of those modern theologians and philosophers with whom Edwards interacts. In my analysis of Edwards's Trinitarian reflection, I compare Edwards's proposal with John Locke (1632–1704), Nicholas Malebranche (1638–1715), Francis Turretin (1623–1687), George Berkeley (1685–1753), and Cotton Mather (1663–1728), among others. And when I turn to offer a Trinitarian interpretation of Edwards's major writings, I compare Edwards's positions with those of Samuel Clarke (1679–1729), John Taylor (1694–1761), and Francis Hutcheson (1694–1746). Such comparisons are essential for correctly understanding Edwards's Trinitarian thought, as well as for identifying what Edwards offers to contemporary theology and ethics. As William Babcock notes, historical studies of the Trinity typically skip the seventeenth and eighteenth centuries, moving from a review of "patristic formulation and medieval elaboration" straight to "subsequent nineteenth- and twentieth-century discussions of the Trinity."[27] Therefore, it is necessary to retrieve a sense of the issues Edwards faces, as well as his response to them.

Nonetheless, the task of this study is to explore Edwards's theological ethics rather than to establish the precise writers who anticipate or influence Edwards. I introduce these figures from Edwards's milieu in order to interpret, clarify, or emphasize what Edwards says at a given point. I do not attempt to locate Edwards's direct sources or determine his stature and influence in American religious history. Such a task is not only another topic but another field—intellectual history rather than theological ethics.[28]

While I hope historians find my efforts informative, my task is one of theological and ethical interpretation, and when I engage Edwards's texts, I maintain the present tense as a reminder to the reader of this perspective.

4. ORGANIZATION

This study is organized into five chapters. Chapter 1 examines Edwards's development of the psychological analogy, and chapter 2 examines Edwards's development of the social analogy. I then turn in chapter 3 to offer a Trinitarian interpretation of the *Religious Affections*. In chapter 4, I focus on *Freedom of the Will* and *Original Sin*, and in chapter 5, I focus on *Two Dissertations* and *Charity and Its Fruits*.

1

"PARTAKERS OF THE DIVINE NATURE":
TRINITARIAN AND MORAL REFLECTION
IN EDWARDS'S PSYCHOLOGICAL ANALOGY

> TRINITY. It may be thus expressed: the Son is the Deity generated by
> God's understanding, or having an idea of himself; the Holy Ghost is
> the divine essence flowing out, or breathed forth, in infinite love and
> delight. Or, which is the same, the Son is God's idea of himself, and the
> Spirit is God's love to and delight in himself.
>
> Edwards, "Miscellanies" entry 405 (Y13:468)

The doctrine of the Trinity is never a purely speculative or dogmatic concern, but it bears profound implications for theological ethics. Without
question, a prime motivation behind Trinitarian reflection is to provide a
coherent account of the inner life of God that corresponds to the soterio-
logical affirmation that God redeems through Jesus Christ in the power of
the Holy Spirit. But the images and analogies one uses to approach the
mystery of the Trinity provide models, either implicit or explicit, of what
it means to be unified and complete persons and communities in God. The
connection between Trinitarian and moral reflection is particularly clear in
the psychological analogy, that is, the exploration of the Trinity that conceives of the being of God as analogous to the activities and nature of the
mind or soul. The descriptive search for the image of God in the soul
inevitably yields a normative account of what it is for the soul to live in
right relation to God. The concepts and relations we use to describe the
unity, plurality, and personhood of God define in large part the unity, plurality, and personhood of human beings. Further, the parts of the soul we
privilege in the psychological analogy identify those parts of human
nature that are constitutive of human dignity and value—those parts we
must protect and promote in every person.

As I noted in the introduction, in entry 343 of the "Miscellanies,"
Edwards writes under the heading of "moral law" that "duties are
founded on doctrines." The "revelation we now have of the Trinity," as the
chief doctrine of the Christian faith, makes "a vast alteration with respect
to the reason and obligations to many amiable and exalted duties, so that
they are as it were new" (Y13:416). In this chapter, I will begin the process
of retrieving the connection Edwards posits between the doctrine of the

Trinity and his theological ethics by examining his development of the psychological analogy. In viewing the Trinity through the lens of the soul, Edwards follows a long tradition of inquiry established by Augustine in *The Trinity*. The founding premise of this approach is that the mind is made in the image of God and that consequently the relations and properties in the mind disclose what are traditionally known as the "processions" within one God of three persons. That is to say, the unified soul and its different mental activities reveal how the Father begets the Son in total equality of nature and how the Holy Spirit proceeds from Father and Son as from one principle or origin. Throughout, the central task is to develop a conception of unity in God that accommodates the essential equality and integrity of the divine persons. In Augustine's words, one seeks "to understand as far as it is given us the eternity and equality and unity of the Trinity" by examining "ourselves" and our "minds."[1] Likewise, Edwards considers the "soul" as the "image of God," and he believes "one of the more eminent and remarkable images of the Trinity" is "the mind, and its understanding or idea, and the will or affection or love" (H:126; Y13:435).[2]

Although Edwards follows Augustine in his use of the psychological analogy, he conceives of the soul and the mind differently. In the first part of this chapter, I argue that Edwards develops his account of the psychological analogy in the context of idealism, rather than, as Augustine does, in categories of substance, accident, and relation drawn from classical metaphysics. This difference of metaphysical context yields different conceptions of the unity, plurality, and personhood that pertain to God and human nature. By doing so, Edwards avoids some problems that Augustine's psychological analogy incurs, particularly regarding the accommodation of plurality and the conception of personhood, concepts that are problematic for Augustine but foundational for Edwards.

In the second part of this chapter, I explore how Edwards uses the psychological analogy in his writings on the Trinity to portray the moral life in terms of *theosis*—human nature reaches its fulfillment only when it is incorporated into the inner life of God. This vision of participation in God, I argue, departs from typical depictions of the moral and religious life in Western Christianity in both Protestant and Roman Catholic traditions. "True saving grace," Edwards writes, "is no other than that the very love of God—that is God, in one of the persons of the Trinity, uniting Himself to the soul of the creature" (H:72). Thus, the "new nature" wrought by God's Spirit in conversion *is* the "divine nature" which "dwells in the soul and becomes there a principle of life and action" (Y13:462). The divine nature is not a communication of the divine "essence," but rather the "love" and "holiness" of the Spirit to the mind, and it is in this sense that the "nature" or "character" of the saint is transformed and renewed by the

Spirit (Y8:639). Therefore, Edwards believes that the moral life hinges upon personal transformation; the relationship each person has individually with God is as decisive in Edwards's theological ethics as the relationship persons have with each other. "Hence persons, by being made partakers of the Holy Spirit, or by having it dwell in them, are said to be 'partakers of the fullness of God'" (H:65).

While compelling, Edwards's account of the psychological analogy and its relation to the moral life is not free of tensions and complications. In the third part of this chapter, I analyze the issue of individuality as it operates within a conception of the psychological analogy that sees *theosis* as the proper end of the moral life. I also explore Edwards's problematic use of concepts from moral theology and philosophy—namely, the conscience and self-love—to define the unique participation of the regenerate soul in God. These problems indicate points for further development that Edwards will address through the social analogy and his occasional and pastoral writings. All the same, despite these difficulties, the psychological analogy is essential to Edwards's theological ethics, not only because it provides Edwards with his central vision of the moral life as a life of *theosis*, but also because it is integral to his theological anthropology and social ethics. The connections Edwards draws between the psychological analogy and the moral life recur in his pastoral and apologetical writings, albeit with some revision and modification.

Moreover, as I suggest throughout this chapter, the psychological analogy has limitations as a mode of Trinitarian and moral reflection. To speak of God and human nature only in terms of intrapersonal relations and the act of self-consciousness shortchanges those aspects of God and human nature that are actualized in interpersonal relations and acts of self-donation. Further, the psychological analogy has difficulty accommodating the witness to God's triune nature evident in the economy of salvation. It is apparently in light of these limitations that Edwards develops the social analogy of the Trinity, which I examine in the next chapter.

1. THE PSYCHOLOGICAL ANALOGY

"Though the divine nature be vastly different from that of created spirits," Edwards writes at the beginning of the "Essay," "yet our minds are made in the image of God, we have understanding and will, idea and love as God hath, and the difference is only in perfection or degree and manner." Therefore, the proper way to proceed is to examine that which bears the marks of the divine mind in our own minds. Because God is omnipotent, there is no difference between the volitional activities of "habit" and "inclination" and between the cognitive activities of "perception or idea" and "reasoning and judgment." God is a being of "one simple act" and one "perfect idea" (H:99–100). Yet while "simple" and "perfect," the divine knowledge and will, like all knowledge and will, presuppose an object that serves as their end. For this reason, "there must be a duplicity" within the mind of God, "God and the idea of God," and because such an idea is necessarily perfect, it must be equal and essentially identical to the God that conceives it. Therefore, the "Deity" is "truly and properly repeated by God's thus having an idea of himself" and the "idea of God is truly God, to all intents and purposes" so that "by this means the Godhead is really generated and repeated" (H:99–100).

In addition, the *act* of affirming a perfect idea from one's mind is also perfect, that is, it perfectly loves, accepts, and appreciates the object that the mind conceives. Thus, God's mind, in having an idea of God's self, generates not only the perfect corresponding idea, who is the Son, but a perfect act that loves the idea generated, who is the Spirit. From the "Godhead being thus begotten by God's loving an idea of Himself and showing forth in a distinct subsistence or person in that idea, there proceeds [a] pure act, and an infinitely holy and sacred energy." This act is "yet another manner of subsistence" in the "third person of the Trinity, the Holy Spirit, viz. the Deity in act" (H:108). Therefore, in terms of the "image of the soul," the Trinitarian structure of the processions within God are the following: "The Father is the Deity subsisting in the prime unoriginated and most absolute manner, or the Deity in its direct existence. The Son is the Deity generated by God's understanding, or having an idea of Himself and subsisting in that idea. The Holy Ghost is the Deity subsisting in act, or the divine essence flowing out and breathed forth in God's infinite love to and delight in Himself" (H:118).

1.1. Modes of Apprehension

At first read, the compressed nature of Edwards's thought may suggest that he intends no novel formulation of the psychological analogy as he has received it.[3] The innovative nature of his use of the psychological analogy, however, unfolds as we unpack his terminology, particularly God's "perfect idea" and the concept of the Deity "repeated."

According to Edwards, there are two modes of intellectual apprehension.[4] The first, which Edwards draws from John Locke, is the mind's perception through the senses of the relations and properties that exist in the physical world. These relations, Edwards writes in "The Mind," are that of "equality," "likeness," and "motion," and these properties are principally "size," "figure," and "color," which are categories of a basic "solidity" or "resistance" that pertains to all material things. Together these relations and properties compose the external world of "bodies," and to apprehend the "solidity" or "resistance" in a given "body" is not, as classical meta-physics had argued, to encounter an individual "substance," but a partic-ular and persistent circumstance or "place" where these relations and properties exist.[5]

This first mode of apprehension, Edwards writes in the "Essay," is by far the most common mode through which persons negotiate everyday life. Through using it, we generate ideas that are "representations" or "something *like*" reality in our minds, and "such kind of ideas very com-monly serve us, though they are not indeed real ideas of the thing itself." They are mental images of "external circumstances" that "we have learned by experience, and it has become habitual to us to govern our thoughts" as "though we conceived of the thing itself" (H:100–101).[6]

But the problem with this mode of apprehension is that it can provide no true knowledge of reality per se—only mental images that rational beings produce as they parse experience (Y6:349, 355, 361). This is so, for the habitual association of ideas in our minds that corresponds to reality is essentially disconnected from the reality it represents. The apprehension of color, for example, is an idea or perception born of the senses and expe-rience, and does not identify an objective property in a given body. Thus, Edwards concludes that "it is now agreed upon by every knowing philoso-pher that colors are not really in the things, no more than pain is in the nee-dle"; they are "merely mental existences, because all these things with all their modes do exist in a looking glass, where all will acknowledge they exist only mentally" (Y6:350). While there is a fair degree of consensus con-cerning color, because it is a "merely mental" mirror of existence, the idea is artificial, in the sense of being the product of human artifice. And as arti-ficial, the ideas we construct are limited by our material (i.e., our senses) and our skill (i.e., our experience).[7]

The first mode of apprehension is also unable to penetrate the nature of what Edwards calls in both the "Essay" and "The Mind" ideas of "thought" and "reflection," such as "love" and "understanding" (H:102). Asks Edwards rhetorically in entry 2 of "The Mind," "How large is that thing in the mind they call thought? Is love square or round? Is joy an inch, or a foot in diameter? These are spiritual things." To conceive of "spiritual things," in other words, requires that we leave "our common way of con-ceiving," which is "very gross and shadowy and corporeal, with dimen-sions and figure, etc.; though it be supposed to be very clear, so that we can see through it" (Y6:338).

Therefore, Edwards develops a second mode of apprehension, one that he believes directly sees reality as it is, rather than constructing a complex and unsteady picture of what it appears to be. "If a person has truly and properly an idea," Edwards writes in the "Essay," "things must be ordered and framed in his mind that he must for that moment have something of a consciousness" of it "that is *pro re nata*, thither referred and as it were transposed." And "this consciousness" is the "idea itself," and "if it be perfectly clear and full it will be in all respects the very same act of mind of which it is the idea, with this only difference that the being of the latter is to represent the former" (H:102).

In using the term *pro re nata* ("of the occasion" or "for the affair born"), Edwards signifies that he is drawing from Nicholas Malebranche's theory of ideas in *The Search for Truth* (1674–5, 1712). In this account, apprehension is not defined in terms of a correspondence between ideas—either innate intuitions or concepts developed through experience—and an external object. Rather, ideas exist in the mind as souls exist within God. Ideas are therefore discrete occasions of immediate and immanent "communications" in one's consciousness of the simple, transcendent idea that is in God, and not a corresponding mental picture of what exists externally.[8]

On the basis of this theory of ideas and their communication, in "The Mind" Edwards posits an ideal universe. All reality and existence is not only attended by consciousness, but the "secret" hidden from many who see the world only in terms of the first mode of apprehension is that all existence is fundamentally ideal, existing first and foremost in God's consciousness and then in ours. All existence is nothing but "the infinitely exact and precise and perfectly stable idea in God's mind, together with the stable will that the same shall gradually be communicated to us, and to other minds, according to certain fixed and exact established methods and laws" (Y6:344).[9]

The second mode of apprehension, therefore, is consciousness, and consciousness is "the mind's perceiving what is in itself—its ideas, actions, passions, and everything that is perceivable" (Y6:345). Through consciousness one is able to experience the "ideas of reflection" such as "love" and "joy" that elude the first mode of apprehension. And not only does one experience them, but one experiences them as exact repetitions rather than replications. Edwards writes in "Miscellanies" entry 238, "Those ideas which we call ideas of reflection—all ideas of the acts of the mind, such as the ideas of thought, of choice, love, fear, etc.—if we diligently attend to our own minds, we shall find that they are not properly representations, but are indeed repetitions of those very things, either more fully or faintly." They "are not properly ideas" in the sense of the first mode of apprehension, for in the second mode, " 'tis impossible to have an idea of a thought or of an idea" and not have "that same idea repeated" (Y13:353).

Through consciousness, one is able to put oneself in the place of another. In the beginning of the "Essay," Edwards writes that persons are able to share ideas of thought or reflection, such as love, by substituting something or someone we love. "So if we think" of "the love of others that we have not," we "frame things in our imagination, that we have for a moment a love to that thing, or to something we make to represent it and stand for it" (H:101). In this way, Edwards writes in entry 238, we can evoke ideas of "our own past love" or "the love of others which we have not." Therefore, by putting ourselves in the place of others, we can "have an idea of a judgement not of our own," for "we have the same ideas . . . repeated in our minds" which gives rise to "something in our minds that is really our judgement" as well (Y13:353–54).

Most importantly, in the second mode one is able to experience self-reflection and self-consciousness, a "reflex or contemplative idea." As Edwards writes in the "Essay," "There is a great difference between a man's having a view of himself," or "mere direct consciousness," and a "reflex or contemplative idea of himself so as to delight in his own beauty or excellency." Indeed, "consciousness" in its fullest sense refers not only to the apprehension of thoughts and feelings, but also to "a power by reflection to view or contemplate what passes" in our minds concerning ourselves as a whole, our deliberations, decisions, and actions (H:102). In this fullest sense of self-consciousness, the mind itself is the object of its thought, and the repetition is, for all intents and purposes, exact. Therefore, self-consciousness is definitive of the second mode of apprehension, that is, it is the proper model of the kind of cognition where the image in the mind is an exact repetition of the mind that generates the image, where one "is twice fully and perfectly" (H:102–3).

A final difference between the first and the second modes of apprehension concerns their respective conceptions of reason. In the first mode, reason is a kind of instrumental rationality that pertains to "direct consciousness," "rational actions," and "judgments" one makes from "experience." As such, reason is "passive," or merely reactive to external stimuli and essentially "involuntary," that is, incapable of its own determination to "bring its ideas into contemplation." Reason in this mode is not distinctively human, and Edwards sees no difficulty in "allowing" this sort of "reason to beasts." Reason in the second mode, however, is a kind of intellectual sensation of the immaterial through contemplation. Reason in this mode is "abundantly active," that is, free to reflect on what passes in our "own minds," and to choose which ideas to ponder. Thus, the "main difference between men and beasts" is that animals only have reason in the first mode, "nothing but direct consciousness." But human beings "are capable of viewing what is in themselves contemplatively." Moreover, it is through having reason in the second mode of apprehension that humans become "capable of religion." "Man," Edwards writes, "was made for spiritual exercises and enjoyments, and therefore is made capable by reflection to behold and contemplate spiritual things" (Y6:373–74). In other words, self-consciousness is a distinctively human trait, and through the proper exercise of self-consciousness, humans realize their capacities and experience union with God.

Edwards provides two examples of self-consciousness in his writings on the Trinity. The first is an extraordinary instance of déjà vu, the "perfect" apprehension of an "idea" from our memory of our past affections, deliberations, and actions. If someone "could have an absolutely perfect idea of all that passed in his mind, all the series of ideas and exercises in every respect perfect as to order, degree, circumstance, etc., for any particular space of time past, suppose the last hour, he would really to all intents and purpose be over again what he was that last hour." That person would, by having a "perfect reflex or contemplative idea" be "indeed double, he would be twice at once. The idea he has of himself would be himself again" (H:102).[10] The second, less remote, example describes the operation of the self-consciousness as it functions within the moral context as the conscience:

> Man is as if he were two, as some of the great wits of this age have observed. A sort of genius is with man, that accompanies him and attends wherever he goes; so that a man has a conversation with himself, that is he has a conversation with his own idea. So if his idea be excellent, he will take delight and happiness in conferring and communing with it; he takes complacency in himself, he applauds himself; and wicked men accuse themselves and fight with themselves, as if they were two. And man is truly happy then, and only then, when these two agree, and they delight in themselves, and in their own idea and image, as God delights in his. (Y13:260)

While the example of self-consciousness in the form of total recall is reminiscent of the use of memory in other explorations of the Trinity through the psychological analogy, the example of self-consciousness as a peaceful and integrated conscience better fits Edwards's own approach to the Trinity. For the "approval," "complacency," "happiness," and "delight" that accompanies the mind's apprehension of the perfect idea's excellence when it operates as the conscience corresponds to the "triplicity" he asserts of God. In the conscience, we not only see ourselves as a perfect "duplicity," but we evaluate ourselves through self-reflection. And the approval we experience as a result of our own self-reflection leads to the "triplicity" that constitutes the love that comprises the Holy Spirit in Edwards's psychological analogy. Hence, it is not merely self-consciousness, but self-consciousness operating as the conscience that provides the model for Edwards's articulation of how the soul is an image of the Trinity. That is to say, when Edwards develops his account of the Trinity in terms of the mind's generation of its perfect idea, his implicit understanding of self-consciousness is in terms of the conscience: "I think it really evident from the light of reason that there are these three distinct in God. If God has an idea of himself there is really a duplicity; because if there is no duplicity, it will follow that Jehovah thinks of himself no more than a stone. And if God loves himself and delights in himself, there is really a triplicity, three that cannot be confounded, each of which are the Deity substantially" (Y13:262).

The dialogical "conferring and communing" through the conscience is also important to note in order to see the nuance of Edwards's understanding of the nature of God's self-love. Edwards first refers to God's self-love as a commonplace of rational theology, specifically in its Neoplatonist mold as the source and sum of cosmic *exitus* and *reditus*: "'Tis often said that God is infinitely happy from all eternity in the view and enjoyment of himself, in the reflection and converse love of his own essence, that is, in the perfect reflection he has of himself, infinitely perfect" (Y13:257). All creation therefore serves the purpose of magnifying God's love for God's self. In typical Neoplatonism, God's self-love derives from the inherent unity, perfection, and value of the divine essence, and is the supreme motivation in the universe. It is the source of *eros*, or what Edwards calls the love of "complacence," a love that appraises value in a beloved object. And in the framework of desire that all creatures possess, self-love is a logically necessary and unavoidable desire that accompanies any attraction, that is, all love is a reflexive desire and need for something that we find lovely, worthy, valuable, pleasant, or beautiful.

Edwards's thought retains vestiges of Neoplatonism, both conceptual and semantic, and he admits that "there is no other affection in God essentially, properly and primarily, but love and delight—and that in himself, for unto this is his love and delight in his creatures resolvable" (Y13:299). For Edwards, however, God's complacence and self-love is not merely unitive but generative and comprehensive. Indeed, in God it is social. For just as a person achieves happiness through the dialogical "conversation" he or she has with a peaceful conscience, so too does God's own happiness exist not merely in admiration of God's good qualities but in actual "communion" or the "bond of union" between Father and Son: "God's love is primarily to Himself, and his infinite delight is in Himself, in the Father and the Son loving and delighting in each other. We often read of the Father loving the Son, and being well pleased in the Son, and the Son loving the Father. In the infinite love and delight that is between these two persons consists the happiness of God" (H:61).

Edwards's understanding of the second mode of apprehension therefore provides the foundation upon which he builds his account of the generation of the Son as the "perfect idea" of the Father. In "Miscellanies" entry 94, Edwards writes, "I will form my reasoning thus: if nothing has any existence any way at all but in some consciousness or idea or other," then "God's idea, being a perfect idea, is really the thing itself. And if so, and all God's ideas are only the one idea of himself," then God's idea "must be a substantial idea, having all the perfections of the substance perfectly;

so that by God's reflecting on himself the Deity is begotten, there is a sub-stantial image of God begotten. I am satisfied that though this word 'begot-ten' had never been used in Scripture, it would have been used in this case: there is no other word that properly expresses it" (Y13:258).

But self-consciousness also evokes an act of self-approbation, self-approval, and self-transcendence. And God's act of self-approval, after God figuratively speaking examines his own conscience, "is certainly dis-tinct from the other two," that is, the mind and its idea, for "the delight and energy that is begotten in us by an idea is distinct from the idea. So it can-not be confounded in God, either with God begetting or with his idea and image, or Son. It is distinct from each of the other two, and yet it is God; for the pure and perfect act of God is God, because God is pure act." There-fore, the "Holy Spirit is the act of God between the Father and the Son infi-nitely loving and delighting in each other" (Y13:260).

As with any dualistic metaphysics, reconciling these two modes of apprehension is a complex and delicate task. Though distinct, Edwards sees the two modes of apprehension as continuous. Because God is a self-reflective being, all creation, or being in general, is the product of God's mind. The "world exists only mentally," Edwards writes in "Miscellanies" entry 247. Creation is essentially Trinitarian, for all created existence emanates from God's contemplation of God's perfect idea, and the "very being of the world implies its being perceived" (Y13:360). In addition, Edwards notes in "Miscellanies" entry 332, created existence is essentially the self-communication of God: The "great and universal end of God's cre-ating the world was to communicate himself," for "God is a communica-tive being" (Y13:410).

Nonetheless, because all existence emanates from the mind of God, the different properties, relations, and categories which compose the material universe also have integrity, as a "shadow" of God's triune being (Y13:262). While the first mode of apprehension in the human mind does not deliver a "real" idea of a given object, the coherence and reality of the physical order is intact, for it is truly perceived and maintained by the divine mind. Edwards writes in entry 34 of "The Mind" that his idealism does not "make void natural philosophy, or the science of the causes and reasons of cor-poreal changes," for "to find out the reasons of things in natural philoso-phy is only to find out the proportion of God's acting." Although "we suppose that the existence of the whole material universe is absolutely dependent" on God's idea, God in the beginning created "a certain num-ber of atoms, of such a determinate bulk and figure, which they yet main-tain and always will; and gave them such a motion, of such a direction, and of such a degree of velocity; from which arise all the natural changes in the universe forever in a continued series" (Y6:353–54). Therefore, Edwards concludes in "The Mind" entry 40, "there must be an universal attraction in the whole system of things from the beginning of the world to the end." The "series of ideas in all created minds" follows the "order and course settled by the supreme mind" (Y6:357).

Certainly, Edwards's "objective idealism" is not without tensions or possible points of objection.[11] Commentators on Edwards debate the adequacy of his synthesis of Locke and Malebranche.[12] This discussion, however, fails to recognize the extent to which the psychological analogy provides the basis and point of integration of these two seemingly different epistemologies in Edwards's thought, as well as the theological and ethical ramifications of the innovative, synthetic epistemology he proposes. On one hand, Edwards privileges self-consciousness and self-reflection in his development of the psychological analogy. As we will see later in this chapter, the psychological analogy provides Edwards with an essential lens through which to conceive of the moral life. But on the other hand, the apprehension of external objects and relations also plays an important role in moral and religious reflection. Because God's self-communication is expressed in material as well as mental existence, all creatures have transfigurative and sacramental qualities as *vestigia trinitatis*, that is, as vestiges of the Trinity, that reveal God's Triunity. Thus, as we will see in more detail in chapter 2, Edwards accepts Augustine's teaching that "as we direct our gaze at the creator by understanding the things that are made, we should recognize the Trinity, whose mark appears in creation in a way that is fitting."[13] The world we encounter through our senses, in short, can provide mediations of God's knowledge and love, so long as we know and love God truly. "The system of created beings," Edwards writes in "Miscellanies" entry 1069, "may be divided into two parts." There is the "typical world," or the "inferior and carnal," the "more external and transitory part of the universe." And there is the "antitypical world," or the "superior, more spiritual, perfect and durable part," which is "as it were the substance and consummation of the other." In this way, "the material and natural world is typical of the moral, spiritual and intelligent world, or the City of God" (Y11:191).[14]

1.2. Unity, Plurality, and Personhood

By basing his psychological analogy within the framework of an idealism that he draws from Malebranche, Edwards offers a unique approach to a problem that had vexed previous articulations of the processions in the Godhead—how to articulate a conception of God's unity that could accommodate God's plurality.[15] Traditionally, Western Christianity had followed Augustine's articulation of the psychological analogy in *The Trinity*, although with some restatement. Augustine first conceives of the unity and plurality of the Godhead in terms of the categories of *substance* and *relation* that he appropriates from classical metaphysics. God's substance, according to Augustine, is identical to God's essence and pertains to God's ineffable nature as simple, immutable, eternal, and impassible. All composite or accidental categories such as "color," all modifications such as "growth" or "diminishment," and all relative changes in a state of being such as "rest" are excluded from God, or else God is not God. God's relations, however, represent a discrete category that pertains to the ontological reality implied by the linguistic connection in the names of the divine persons, principally "Father" and "Son." For in the case of these relations as they pertain to God, one does not predicate something of God that is accidental or subject to modification. Therefore with God, Augustine concludes, "some things are said in reference to something else, like Father with reference to Son and Son with reference to Father."[16]

On the basis of the distinction between substance and relation, Augustine asserts that the divine persons are one God in regard to substance, but *relationally* plural. The divine attributes such as wisdom, power, or goodness pertain to God substance-wise and apply to all three equally and identically. "But as for the things each of the three in this triad is called that are proper or peculiar to himself, such things are never said with reference to each other or to creation, and therefore it is clear that they are said by way of relationship and not by way of substance."[17] Thus, the relations of the three persons of the Godhead are constituted by their processions: The Son is begotten of the Father, and the Holy Spirit is the "Gift" that proceeds from the Father to the Son.

By his own admission, Augustine finds the distinction between substance and relation in God unsatisfying. The category of relation reveals virtually nothing about the subsisting relations within the Godhead other than their origin. As such, Augustine's conception of unity in God does not accommodate plurality as a meaningful constituent of the divine nature. Moreover, Augustine's depiction of the relations in God tends to obscure and minimize the conception of person as it applies to the Father, Son, and Spirit individually. The attenuated sense of relation leaves little room for those aspects of personhood that normally apply, such as agency, or the capacity to will and consent to being and action. Augustine's implicit understanding of a person follows that of classical metaphysics: A person is an individual substance of a rational nature, and with such an understanding it is hard to conceive of personhood in a God who is one substance but three persons.[18] For this reason, when he speaks of God as a person, he tries to play it both ways. In one passage, Augustine says the Father "is called person in reference to himself, and not with reference to the Son or Holy Spirit," which suggests he understands person as an individual substance; in another he writes that "person" is merely a "word for signifying what we mean by trinity" in order to answer the question, "Three what?"[19] Personhood therefore occupies an ambiguous place in Augustine's theology of the Trinity, for it is too substantial a concept to assign to God's plurality and too dynamic to apply to God's unity.

Nonetheless, Augustine's conception of substantive unity regarding the divine essence and relational plurality regarding the divine persons provides the foundation through which he articulates his psychological analogy. Augustine's premise for exploring the nature of the Trinity through the psychological activities of self-awareness is that the mind is created in the image and likeness of God (Gen. 1:26). The mind is a mirror that reflects—truly but imperfectly—the being of God. Therefore, a correlation exists between knowledge of oneself and knowledge of God. To know oneself fully, one must know God and know oneself in God. For Augustine, the movement of the mind inward is also a movement upward. What we believe about God is "what we experience in ourselves."[20]

Throughout the second half of *The Trinity*, Augustine discusses different psychological triads that might serve as the proper analogy of the Trinity.[21] Three analogies in particular stand out. The first is the triad of "the lover, what is being loved, and love."[22] "You see a trinity when you see charity," because in the relations of love there is a dynamic interlocking of lover, beloved, and love.[23] Hence, the Father loves the Son, and the love of God that is the "Holy Spirit is something common to Father and Son, whatever it is, or their very commonness or communion, consubstantial and coeternal."[24] While illuminating, this triad is problematic. The terms, lover and beloved, pertain to distinct individuals, and the relation of love between persons has complex and external aspects. Consequently, these categories violate the categorical framework of subject, accident, and relation that he appropriates from classical metaphysics. The second is the triad of the *mens, notitia sui, amor sui*, or the "mind," its "self-knowledge," and its "self-love."[25] Although this triad is better than the previous one, it still does not provide an adequate portrait of the psychological analogy, for Augustine believes that human self-knowledge and self-love are inherently limited and flawed. Therefore, Augustine's final draft of the psychological analogy, which provides a "clearer trinity," is that of *memoria sui, intelligentia sui, voluntas sui*, or "memory and understanding and will."[26] Augustine finds this triad the most sufficient of all the psychological analogies he introduces in *The Trinity*, for it guards the substantive unity of God best. "These three," Augustine writes, "memory, understanding and will, are not three lives but one life, nor three minds but one mind. So it follows of course that they are not three substances, but one substance."[27]

Augustine's development of the psychological analogy and its accompanying substance metaphysics initiated a general trend in Western Trinitarian reflection of treating the doctrine of the Trinity, particularly the processions of the Godhead, as primarily a speculative concern. But this was not Augustine's intention. For Augustine, to reflect on the image of the Trinity in the mind is essentially an act of prayer that is morally and spiritually transformative. At the end of *The Trinity*, Augustine confesses that even his final draft of the psychological analogy is ultimately insufficient, for in God "there are three persons of one being, not, like any single man, just one person."[28] But through self-reflection, the mind contemplates God and is united with God. Augustine's belief is that, by the grace of God, our knowledge of God, or *scientia*, will move in us to *sapientia*, or wisdom. The latter not only identifies the deeper knowledge that comes through experience, but also a kind of "relish," or active savoring, of our participation in God.[29]

On these matters, Edwards shares Augustine's sensibilities. Indeed, although he did not have direct access to Augustine's writings, Edwards's development of the psychological analogy appears to be a conscious attempt to retrieve and restate Augustine's central insights on the psychological analogy. As we observed in the previous section, Edwards disavows the sense of substance as an individual entity.[30] Although Edwards continues to use the word "substance," speaking of God's "substantive idea" as the "spiritual substance" that exactly repeats the divine mind, it is clear from his writings that he considers the term to possess little ontological significance, particularly in comparison to the term "perfect idea." For example, Edwards writes in "Miscellanies" entry 194 that it is better to speak of the "increated Spirit" of God's being in terms of the "comprehensiveness of idea" and not "as if it was a sort of unknown thing that we call substance" (Y13:335). And in "Miscellanies" entries 370 and 396, Edwards deleted the phrase "spiritual substance" and in its place wrote "mind."[31]

Accordingly, Edwards conceives of unity in terms other than that of an invisible and undifferentiated substance. And the benefit of doing so is that it provides him with a conception of unity that accommodates God's plurality, relation, and personality. Edwards's fundamental understanding of unity is in terms of the self-reflection that occurs in the second mode of apprehension, in the mind's contemplation of its "perfect idea." Unity for Edwards refers to *identity* rather than simplicity. To have unity is to share an identical idea, or the immediate "repetition" of an idea in the mind. In "Miscellanies" entry 260, Edwards reiterates this position to remove any sense of mediation between mind and idea:

> Seeing the perfect idea of a thing is to all intents and purposes the same as seeing the thing; it is not only equivalent to seeing of it, but it *is* seeing of it, for there is no way of seeing but having an idea. Now by seeing a perfect idea, so far as we see it we have it; but it can't be said of anything else that in seeing it, we see another, speaking strictly except it be the very idea of the other. (Y13:368)

As these last remarks indicate, however, Edwards's conception of unity as identity in the second mode of apprehension *presupposes plurality and relation*, because we achieve identity precisely in the act where "we see another" or the "very idea of the other." For self-consciousness is definitive of the second mode of apprehension, and the relation between mind and idea set the condition for unity as identity. Thus, Edwards is careful to remark that mere "similitude," or identity alone, does not constitute unity in the second mode of apprehension, but there must be also a sense of relation or "representation." In the "Essay," Edwards writes, "The design of an idea is to represent, and the very being of an idea consists in similitude and representation." If it does not "actually represent to the beholder, it ceases to be. And the being of it is immediately dependent upon its pattern: its reference to that ceasing, it ceases to be its idea" (H:104). Edwards sharpens this distinction in "Miscellanies" entry 260: "There is no properly spiritual image but an idea; although there may be another spiritual thing that is exactly like, yet one thing being exactly like another" does not "make it the proper image of that thing." To be the "image" of a mind requires a specific relation between that mind and its own perfect idea, and it is in this sense—of begetting an idea that perfectly reflects the mind that generates it—that constitutes unity in the second mode of apprehension. For it is only in this sense that the mind or soul discloses the Triune mystery that "Christ is the spiritual image and idea of God" (Y13:368).

Finally, unity for Edwards not only presupposes plurality and relation, but the essential structure of unity and plurality in the self-consciousness is *triadic, objective, and dynamic*. As Jürgen Moltmann argues, the general trend of the idealism that Edwards draws from developed into a "logic of identity" and a corresponding theology that predicated an "Absolute Subject" that transcends any objects, evolving into a general feeling of dependence.[32] But Edwards's idealism emphasizes the objective "happiness," "complacency," "delight," and "love" that exists between the mind and its idea as equally vital coordinates in the soul. As we have seen, Edwards believes all knowledge and will presuppose objects of apprehension and affection. Conversely there is no self-consciousness separate from a mind that generates it. Therefore, it is not self-consciousness alone that reflects the Trinity, but the self-consciousness operating as a peaceful conscience that serves as the ground for seeing God's self-transcendent "triplicity, three that cannot be confounded, each of which are the Deity substantially" (Y13:262). This "triplicity" serves as the distinctive point through which we gauge a person's true nature. For the "disposition" that a mind and idea generate is not only reflexive but, like a good conscience, also serves as the basis for subsequent thought and action. Hence, Edwards writes that the "sum of God's temper is love," and love represents at once the perfect reflexive nature of God and the active nature of God. For God "is infinite love, and as I have observed before, here there is no distinction between habit and act, between temper or disposition and exercise" (H:110).[33]

Foundational to Edwards's conceptions of unity, plurality, and relation in the self-consciousness is his conception of personhood in the Godhead. Where Augustine speaks of the divine personhood and the psychological analogy after developing his categories of substantive unity and relation, for Edwards *personhood is the fundamental ontological principle.* Edwards articulates his psychological analogy within an idealism that considers consciousness integral to existence. All reality is ideal and therefore personal; at the basis of existence is God's generation of God's infinitely comprehensive idea, which upholds all categories and relations, both material and spiritual. Thus, Edwards writes in the "Miscellanies" entry 383 that the "first supreme and universal principle of things, from when results the being, the nature, the powers and the motions, and sweet order of the world, is properly an intelligent willing agent, such as our souls only without our imperfections." Indeed, "man's soul only seems to be in the image of that supreme universal principle" (Y13:452). Just as "the greatness of a soul consists not in any extension, but in its comprehensiveness of idea and extendedness of operation. So the infiniteness of God consists in his perfect comprehension of all things and the extendedness of his operation equally to all places" (Y13:335).[34]

Because God's personhood upholds all relations in the nature of things, all reality reflects the nexus of relations in God's self-consciousness. The attributes of God such as infiniteness, eternity, or immutability do not, as Augustine holds, apply to God substance-wise, but conform to the relations within a single personality. In the "Essay," Edwards writes that what confirms his conception that the psychological analogy "is the true Trinity" is that "reason is sufficient to tell us that there must be these distinctions in the Deity, viz. of God (absolutely considered), and the idea of God, and the love and delight, and there are no other real distinctions in God that can be thought." For whatever "else can be mentioned in God are nothing but mere modes or relations of existence." The "attributes of infinity, eternity, and immortality" are mere "modes" of God's absolute being. God's "understanding, His wisdom and omniscience" are "the same with his idea." God's "will" is "not really distinguished from His love, but is the same but only with a different relation." All predications of the divine intelligence and will or power resolve into the triadic relation where "the sum of God's understanding consists in His having an idea of Himself" and "in His Loving Himself" (H:118).[35] Indeed, Edwards believes that the usual "maxim among divines that everything that is in God" must conform to the usual attributes such as "immutability," "omniscience," and "authority" yields an abstract and vacuous theology. "If a man should tell me that the immutability of God is God or that the omnipresence of God and the authority of God is God, I should not be able to think of any rational meaning of what he said." But "if it be meant that the real attributes of God, viz. His understanding and love are God, then what we have said may in some measure explain how it is so, for Deity subsists in them distinctly, so they are distinct divine persons." Further, "We find no other attributes of which it is said that they are God in Scripture or that God is they, but *Logos* and *Agape*, the reason and love of God" (H:119).

By resolving the attributes of God into God's triune relations, Edwards conceives of the generation of all things as bearing the image of the Trinity. All things external to the Godhead disclose God's inner life to the creation: "For the perfect energy of God with respect to himself is the most perfect creation of himself, of which the world is but a shadow" (Y13:262). Therefore for Edwards, all metaphysical relations, values, laws of nature, or aesthetic categories that operate in creation, and all human capacities, dispositions, and virtues, stem from Edwards's conception of the unified personhood of God subsisting as Trinity and manifesting itself in creation (Y18:191–92). As Herbert Richardson notes, "Edwards starts with a Trinitarian conception of God and a Trinitarian conception of reality. There is no abstract conception of being as the *fons et origo* to which the other persons are 'raised.'"[36] Rather, God's triune personhood is the sum and source of all existence.

Most importantly, for Edwards personhood is not an individualistic concept. That is to say, he does not define a person in isolation from all relations, for to be a person is to exist in a kind of community. Edwards conceives of a person in terms of self-consciousness, but self-consciousness itself is a kind of self-transcendence—one sees oneself from the perspective of another, and one's happiness culminates in the union and communion that exists. The "Father" is the "fountain of the Godhead" or "Deity without distinction." And yet the Father cannot exist as the infinite mind without having a "perfect idea" that is "begotten," yet "coeternal." Therefore, "it is easy to conceive how this image, this thought, reason or wisdom of God, should be eternally begotten by him, and yet begotten by him from eternity and continually through eternity; and so how the Holy Spirit, that personal energy, the divine love and delight, eternally and continually proceeds from both." Hence, "God the Son," unlike God the Father, is "spoken of with a distinction" and "called the Son of God; and so the Holy Spirit, the Spirit of God" (Y13:298–99). But these distinctions in God do not entail that God the Father is independent of God the Son or God the Holy Spirit: "For though one proceeds from another, and so may be said to be in some respects dependent on another, yet it is no dependence of one on the will of another. For it is no voluntary, but a necessary proceeding; and therefore infers no proper subjection of one to the will of another" (H:78). In short, the Father's begetting of the Son and procession of the Spirit are necessary to the Father's self-actualization. Although "the Son as it were depends on the Father, as the Father as it were his principle, yet in other respects the Father depends on him as his object. The Father has good, and though the Son receives the infinite good, the Holy Spirit, from the Father, the Father enjoys the infinite good through the Son" (Y21:146). It is in view of Edwards's conception of the person as a dynamic and relational state of being rather than as an individual entity that the most salient difference between the psychological analogies of Edwards and Augustine arises. For Edwards and Augustine identify different psychological triads as the most appropriate image of the divine processions. Augustine initially favors the triad of the mind, its self-knowledge, and self-love, as the best of those triads that explore relations of love. But Augustine subsequently develops another psychological triad, which he believes offers a "clearer trinity," of memory, understanding, and will.[37] As I have already noted, Augustine prefers memory, understanding, and will because he believes they guard the substantive unity of God best. But another reason Augustine prefers his final draft of the psychological analogy is that the earlier triads that work from the relations of love portray the Holy Spirit as a mere relation in the Godhead, rather than either a substance or person. Augustine therefore is careful to assert that in God, charity "too is substance because God is substance, and 'God is charity' as it is written."[38] At the same time, to speak of the Holy Spirit as a relation that proceeds from the Father and the Son diminishes the personhood of the Holy Spirit. For while the names "Father" and "Son" imply a relation, "Holy Spirit" is not likewise determinative, and only determines what is "common to them both."[39] Finally, in his initial formulation of the psychological triad based on love, the implicit relation of love and beloved suggests a state of need or want in God the lover, for underlying Augustine's understanding of love is the residual Neoplatonist conception of love as the creature of need. Therefore, Augustine admits late in *The Trinity* that "when we came to charity, which is called God in holy scripture, the glimmerings of a trinity began to appear, namely lover and what is loved and love. However, that inexpressible light beat back our gaze, and somehow convinced us that the weakness of our mind could not yet be attuned to it."[40]

Unlike Augustine, Edwards finds the psychological analogy of the mind, its self-knowledge, and self-love sufficient. He does so because the relation of love between one's mind and idea is as constitutive of personhood as the other coordinates of self-consciousness. For as we have noted, the love or delight in self-consciousness determines the nature of one's "disposition," or the overall bent of a person. No one, not even God, is an island of absolute self-sufficiency or aseity in Edwards's understanding, but each person is a vital web of identity, mutuality, contemplation, and affection. To be is to be in love. As we proceed to develop Edwards's Trinitarian ethics, the radical nature of this statement will continue to unveil itself.

Furthermore, because he defines personhood as a nexus of identity, relationality, and love in the self-consciousness, Edwards can ascribe personhood to the Holy Spirit, even though he considers the Spirit the "reflex act" of God's love generated as God "views himself and so loves himself" (H:130). He writes in the "Essay" that "one of the principle objections that I can think of against what has been supposed" concerns "the personality of the Holy Spirit—that this scheme of things don't seem well to consist with the fact that a person is that which hath understanding and will" (H:120). But the integrity of God's personhood consists in the perfect love that unites God and God's idea in an "ineffable" union of mutual inherence, permeation, and interdependence. Thus, Edwards argues in a massive sentence that the love that integrates God's self-consciousness perfectly integrates the persons of the Trinity:

> In order to clear up this matter let it be considered that the whole divine office is supposed truly and properly to subsist in each of these three, viz. God and His understanding and love, and that there is such a wonderful union between them that they are, after an ineffable and inconceivable manner, one in another, so that one hath another and they have communion in one another and are as it were predicable one of another; as Christ said of Himself and the Father, I am in the Father and the Father in me, so may it be said concerning all the persons of the Trinity, the Father is in the Son and the Son is in the Father, the Holy Ghost is in the Father, and the Father is in the Holy Ghost, the Holy Ghost is in the Son and the Son is in the Holy Ghost, and the Father understands because the Son who is the divine understanding is in Him, the Father loves because the Holy Ghost is in Him, so the Son loves because the Holy Ghost is in Him and proceeds from Him, so the Holy Ghost or the divine essence subsisting is divine, but understands because the Son the divine idea is in Him. (H:120)

In other words, God's personhood culminates in the Trinitarian doctrine of *perichoresis*, that is, that there is perfect coinherence, love, union, and mutual participation between the persons of the Godhead, yet without any loss of their individual uniqueness.[41] Any part of God's self-consciousness partakes in the others completely, such that to speak of one necessarily evokes the others. Thus, Edwards emphasizes in the "Essay" that the love of the Holy Spirit is "not a blind love." The "understanding may be predicated of this love," because "God loves the understanding and that understanding also flows out in love so that the divine understanding is in the Deity subsisting in love." Even "in creatures there is consciousness included in the very nature of the will or act of the soul, and though perhaps not so that it can properly be said that it is a seeing or understanding will, yet it may truly and properly be said so in God, by reason of God's infinitely more perfect manner of acting." Thus, the "Spirit may be said to know and to search all things, even the deep things of God" (H:120–21). The Spirit as the love of God, however, is distinct from God and God's idea and "cannot be confounded in God, either with God begetting or with his idea and image, or Son" (Y13:260).

Still, Edwards's psychological analogy encounters limits. For the question concerning the Spirit's "personality" is not merely whether one can predicate consciousness of the Spirit, but whether the Spirit interacts with the Father and the Son as a discrete person. Even if one grants Edwards his conception of the person as a nexus of self-consciousness, the psychological analogy does not reveal how the three persons of the Godhead cohere as a community united in love. Edwards accepts that personhood entails agency, or the possession of understanding and will, but these characteristics manifest themselves more clearly interpersonally rather than intrapersonally, in acts of self-donation rather than self-reflection. Such a limitation seems inherent in any attempt to see the soul as an image of the Trinity. And for this reason, as we will see in chapter 2, Edwards also approaches the Trinity through the social analogy.

2. PSYCHOLOGICAL ANALOGY AND MORAL REFLECTION

Throughout Edwards's development of the psychological analogy, he carries on a parallel exercise in moral reflection to complement his Trinitarian reflection. As we have seen, Edwards comprehends the second mode of apprehension in terms of an idea that perfectly repeats the mind that generates it. The existence of this mode of apprehension supposes an ideal universe. That is to say, all true ideas are the immediate and immanent communications in created minds of the perfect idea of God.

Edwards views the mind, however, not as a physical entity but a spiritual entity. The mind is not the same as the brain, nor is it somehow contained in the brain, but is more accurately equated with the soul. Although God creates soul and body so that they are always conjoined—and to this extent it is accurate to say that the soul has "its seat in the brain"—the brain represents merely an organ of the body (Y6:368–69). Further, while there is an affinity between the activities of the mind and brain, the origin of thought and movement in the body is not the brain, but "every action of the mind." As a result, "our perceptions, or ideas that we passively receive by our bodies, are communicated to us immediately by God while our minds are united with our bodies," even though it is difficult to explain "the rule" why this is so (Y6:339).

Consequently, Edwards's account of the relation between ideas and the consciousness not only serves as an analogy for the inner life of the Trinity, but it also reveals the Trinitarian nature of the "spiritual knowledge" or "spiritual ideas" that indwell the minds of the regenerate. Edwards devotes several entries in the "Miscellanies" to the exploration of these terms, but it is only when he develops his understanding of the processions of the Godhead according to God's "perfect idea" of God's self that he is able to articulate "wherein spiritual knowledge consists" (Y13:354). This connection between spiritual knowledge and the psychological analogy is clear at three points in the "Miscellanies."

2.1. The New Nature Is the Divine Nature

In "Miscellanies" entries 238 and 239, Edwards approaches the subject of spiritual knowledge and ideas as he continues to sharpen his distinction between the first and second modes of apprehension. "Those ideas we call ideas of reflection" are "not properly representations," or complex depictions of reality in the second mode, "but are indeed repetitions of those very things." As we have seen, one construal of ideas as repetitions pertains to the processions of the Godhead, "that idea which God hath of the divine nature is really and fully the divine nature and essence again." But another construal pertains not merely to God's nature, but more broadly to the nature of "spiritual ideas." For as God's generation of the Son comes by way of God's perfect idea, "so certainly it is, in all our spiritual ideas." They "are the very same things repeated, perhaps faintly and obscurely, and very quick and momenteously, and with many new references, suppositions, and translations." But "if the idea be perfect, it is only the same thing absolutely over again" (Y13:353–54). Spiritual ideas, in other words, are not impressions, imprints, or replications of something that is different in *kind* from the perfect idea of God. For such is the nature of knowledge in the first mode of apprehension, and as we have seen, knowledge in this mode is unable to see things as they really are. But spiritual ideas occur in the second mode of apprehension and are actual instantiations and repetitions of God's idea in the mind. They differ from God's own idea of God's self only in their *degree* of perfection, not in the manner of their existence. Hence, Edwards writes in entry 135 that the mind of God differs from human minds only in terms of greatness: "If we should suppose the faculties of a created spirit to be enlarged infinitely, there would be the Deity to all intents and purposes" (Y13:295).

Edwards therefore finds in the second mode of apprehension the key expression of the vital and decisive nature of communion with God in regenerate persons. In an earlier "Miscellanies," Edwards records a deep intuition he has concerning the nature of spiritual knowledge:

> I, for my part, am convinced of an immediate communication between the Spirit of God and the soul of a saint; because when a person is in the

most excellent frame, most lively exercise of virtue, love to God and delight in him, he naturally and unavoidably thinks of God as kindly communicating himself to him, and holding such a manner of communion with him, as much as if he saw God smiling on him, giving to him, and conversing with him. (Y13:296)

With the understanding of the second mode of apprehension in mind, however, it is clear that this intercourse and communication between God and persons has its basis in the Trinity. Indeed, Edwards reiterates this entry in the "Treatise on Grace" as an example of how the soul participates in the life of the Trinity through the indwelling of the Holy Spirit (H:52).

God's knowledge of God's perfect idea therefore forms a lens through which Edwards reiterates Augustine's understanding of the psychological analogy: All knowledge of God derives from God's knowledge of God's self through God's perfect idea. We know God in the same way we know ourselves—that is, through ideas of reflection—and God knows us through the same ideas of reflection. All our knowledge of ourselves ultimately derives from the knowledge of God. Indeed, all spiritual knowledge is nothing other than the communication of the knowledge of God's self. And to know ourselves fully, we must know God.

Because knowledge of God in the second mode of apprehension is decisive, the difference between natural and regenerate humanity hinges upon the nature of God's operation in the self-consciousness. Edwards writes in entry 239 (which serves as a corollary to 238), "From what has been said under the foregoing head, we learn wherein spiritual knowledge consists." For in order to have "the knowledge of spiritual things, there must be those things in the mind." And this being the case, "sinners must be destitute even of the ideas of many spiritual and heavenly things and of divine excellencies, because they don't experience them." Therefore, "'tis impossible for them so much as to have the idea of faith, trust in God, holy resignation, divine love," and "Christian charity." For these "things" are repetitions of "the excellencies and beauties of God and Christ" (Y13:354–55).

Though he compares the "spiritual knowledge" of regenerate persons to that of "sinners," Edwards does not mean that regenerate persons are without sin or transcend the normal conditions of human finitude, so to attain a higher heaven where all the ideas of God are crystal clear. For as we have seen, spiritual knowledge is itself faint and obscure (Y13:354). Rather, Edwards's point is that the relation between spiritual knowledge and God is something like the relation between a photocopy and an original rather than, say, that between a signet ring and sealing wax. In the former analogy, the image on the photocopy differs from the original in terms of its resolution—it is either clear or blurry, too dark or too faint. Nonetheless, it is essentially the same image, now repeated.[42] In the latter relation, however, the image of the ring that is left in sealing wax is not the same, but is merely *like* the ring; our knowledge of the ring is something we know only because of what the wax looks like.

In "Miscellanies" entries 396 and 397, Edwards develops his account of "spiritual knowledge" to show how it, like God's own knowledge of God's perfect idea, leads to the expression of the "disposition" or "affection" of "infinite love." In entry 396, Edwards reiterates his position that the "Holy Spirit of God" is the "divine temper" that flows from God's being. "As God's understanding is all comprehended in that, that he understands himself, so his temper or disposition is perfectly expressed by that, that he infinitely loves himself." This "holy temper, or disposition, or affection of God" is "another spirit" (Y13:462).

Given the Spirit's proceeding from the perfect idea of God, Edwards continues in entry 397 to argue that the reception of the "divine light" in a human mind reaches fruition in the communication of the divine dispositions. "The first act of the Spirit of God" is in "spiritual understanding," in the "ideas it has of divine things." The operation of the Spirit of God on the mind comes "before any acts of the will." But the "inclination of the soul" is "immediately exercised in that sense of the mind which is called spiritual understanding," or the "intellect." For it is "not only the mere presence of ideas in the mind" that represents spiritual understanding, but "it is the mind's sense of their excellency, glory and delightfulness." That is to say, just as God's idea evokes the disposition of love and delight and happiness, so too do our ideas or "spiritual knowledge" evoke "infinite love." In this way, the "prime alteration that is made in conversion, that which is first and the foundation of all, is the alteration of the temper and disposition of the Spirit of the mind." Further, this alteration is "nothing but conferring the Spirit of God, which dwells in the soul and becomes a principle of life and action." The "new nature" wrought by God in conversion and which forms the "principle" of the moral life *is* the "divine nature." And "whenever the Scripture speaks of the Spirit of God dwelling in us, or our being filled with the Spirit, it will signify much the same thing if it be said, a divine temper or disposition dwells in us or fills us" with "infinite love" (Y13:462–63).

These points of connection between the psychological analogy and the epistemological experience of regenerate persons provide the structure through which Edwards conceives of the ontological operation of the "Spirit of God" in the soul. "Man's reason and conscience seem to be a participation of the divine essence," Edwards writes. "The giving of the Holy Spirit, therefore, in sanctification, is a sort of adding a new soul to this that is come to nothing, or is making a new soul of this: whence we may explain the manner of the Spirit's operation" (Y13:342). The nature of this participation therefore concerns not only the immediate communication of the idea of God to the mind, but also the soul's fullest attainment of human capacities—the greatest extent to which we become persons is as persons in God.

Crucial to the connection Edwards draws between epistemology and ontology is his understanding of participation, which differs from the understanding of "participation" that theologians within the Augustinian tradition typically appropriate from Platonism. Platonism understands the knowledge we have by way of "participation" (*kata methexin*) as that of imitating the pattern set by universal and infinite "forms" or ideas. Thus, our knowledge of what is "beautiful" or "good" conforms to what is beautiful or good, and to this extent the properties of beauty and goodness inhere in us. This knowledge, however, does not mean one is beautiful or good intrinsically, but only by participation or resemblance to what is beautiful and good itself.[43] For Edwards, however, "partaking" and "participation" apply in the idealist sense of identity and repetition, rather than a Platonic sense of representation. Thus, while Edwards will continue to speak of being conformed to God, the way one is conformed to God is by experiencing in one's mind the actual repetition of God's idea and love. Participation therefore represents a relation that is equally epistemological and ontological—to know God is to have something "added to the soul."

2.2. Partakers of the Divine Nature

In the "Treatise on Grace," Edwards makes a preliminary attempt to extend the connection he draws between the psychological analogy and regenerate humanity into the sphere of ethics. Edwards's ostensive task is to reiterate the standard, specifically Puritan, apologetic for Christian ethics against those who argue for *autonomous* morality, that is, that ethics and moral philosophy should be independent of religious concepts, particularly regeneration and the biblical imperatives and virtue of love.[44]

In the first two chapters of the "Treatise," Edwards makes quick work of this assignment. In terms of regeneration, a fundamental difference exists between "*common* grace," that is, the "religious or moral attainments" that are common to both "saints and sinners," and "*special or saving* grace," that is, the immediate "operation or influence of God's Spirit, whence saving actions and attainments do arise in the godly" (H:25). The saints, unlike "natural men," have experienced the "new birth," in which the "divine principle" produces an "immediate" change or "conversion" in their nature, akin to "resurrection" or God's creation *ex nihilo* by which "something is brought out of nothing in an instant" (H:34). Hence, "special or saving grace" is "not only different from common grace in degree, but entirely diverse in nature and kind," such that "natural men not only have not a sufficient degree of virtue to be saints, but that they have no degree of that grace that is in godly men" (H:26). And "it is impossible for men to convert themselves by their own strength and industry, with only a concurring assistance" of the Spirit (H:37–38).

In terms of the biblical imperatives and virtue of love, Edwards argues that "the Scripture" is "frequent, express, and particular" in "teaching us that all duty is comprehended in love." This is so, whether one takes the term "Law" to signify "the Ten Commandments, or the whole written Word of God" (H:41–42). Scripture is also clear, in terms of virtue, that virtue does not signify a set of distinct "habits" or character traits, but a unified, single virtue of love, of which more particular virtues such as justice are mere "denominations." Every "Christian disposition of mind and heart" consists "in divine love, and may be resolved into it," though "it may be diversified" with respect "to its kinds and manners of exercise and its appendages." Thus, it is "manifest that love or charity" is "the very essence of all Christianity," the "quintessence, life and soul of all religion," and "comprehends all holy virtues and exercises" (H:42–45).

As an apology for Christian ethics against autonomous morality, the "Treatise" is perfunctory and unoriginal. Edwards's strategy is essentially to assemble the relevant passages in Scripture that buttress the doctrine of regeneration and that identify love of God and neighbor as the summary of the law. As we will see in the following chapters, Edwards handles the challenges of autonomous morality to Christian ethics with greater care and subtlety in his apologetical writings.

What is unique about the "Treatise," however, is Edwards's exploration of the question "What is the nature of this divine principle in the soul that is so entirely diverse from all that is naturally in the soul?" (H:39). This question is implicit in Edwards's argument against autonomous morality, for Edwards must justify the stress he places on regeneration and love as distinctive and irreplaceable aspects of Christian ethics. In forming his answer, Edwards returns to his statements about regeneration and obligation. The Christian life consists in "divine love." Christian love to God and Christian love to neighbor do not present different forms of charity or obligation; they are not "two distinct principles in the heart." Rather, "Christian love to God and Christian love to men" are "radically the same; the same principle flowing forth towards different objects, according to the order of their existence." God is the "first cause of all things," the "fountain and source of all good," and human beings "are derived from him." Therefore, "the first and supreme object of divine love is God." Human beings are loved as "the children of God," for they "are in his Image," are "the objects of his mercy," or are "in some respects related to God" as "partakers of his loveliness" and "capable of happiness" (H:47–48).

Divine love consequently operates according to the following phenomenology. Because the Christian moral life consists "radically" in the divine love, the "first effect of the power of God in the heart in Regeneration, is to give the heart a divine taste or sense; to cause it to have a relish of the love-liness and sweetness of the divine nature." The imparting of the divine love begins in a love of "complacence," or the appreciation of God's inher-ent excellency and desire to be with God, from which arises a love of "benevolence," or the inclination that God "should be glorified" and that God's "will should be done in all things." This progression follows the "order of nature" according to which "love is commonly distinguished," for "a person must first relish" the goodness and excellence of someone "before he can wish well to him on the account of that loveliness, or as being worthy to receive good." But phenomenology aside, the *"main ground* of true love to God is the excellency of His own nature, and not any benefit we have received, or hope to receive, by His goodness to us" (H:50). This excellency "which we have shown does radically and summarily con-sist in divine love, comes into existence in the soul by the power of God in the influences of the Holy Spirit, the third Person of the Trinity" (H:51). Not only is the divine love that forms the "divine principle" of saving grace "from the Spirit of God," but "it is of the nature of the Spirit of God" (H:55). "So that that holy, divine principle" or "divine love, is no other than a com-munication and participation of that same infinite divine love, which is God, and in which the Godhead is eternally breathed forth; and subsists in the third person in the blessed Trinity" (H:73).

What begins then as apparent reiteration of the rejection of autonomous morality by Christian ethics now evolves into a more profound, if not unique, integration of the moral and religious life. Edwards's main argu-ment in the "Treatise" is not merely that morality is inseparable from piety, but that the life of virtue is one of *actual participation* in the spiritual life of the triune God. Throughout the "Treatise," Edwards weaves a central pas-sage of Scripture (2 Pet. 1:3–4) that he sees as the definitive statement of the Christian moral life: "According as his divine power hath given unto us all things that pertain unto life and godliness, through the knowledge of him that hath called us to glory and virtue: whereby are given to us exceeding great and precious promises; that by these ye might be partakers of the divine nature, having escaped the corruption that is in the world through lust" (KJV). The weight of this passage leads Edwards to make the follow-ing statement:

> The Scripture therefore leads us to this conclusion, though it be infinitely above us to conceive how it should be, that yet the Son of God is the per-sonal word, idea, or wisdom of God, begotten by God, being an infinitely perfect, substantial image or idea of Himself, (as might be very plainly proved from the Holy Scripture, if here were proper occasion for it); so the Holy Spirit does in some ineffable and inconceivable manner pro-ceed, and is breathed forth from Father and Son, by the divine essence being wholly poured and flowing out in that infinitely intense, holy, and

pure love and delight that continually and unchangeably breathes forth from Father and Son, primarily towards each other, and secondarily towards the creature, and so flowing forth in a different subsistence or person in a manner to us utterly inexplicable and inconceivable, and that this is that person that is poured forth into the hearts of angels and saints. (H:63)

While "ineffable" and "inconceivable," Edwards draws on the connections he makes between the psychological analogy and spiritual knowledge to explain the saints' participation in God through becoming "partakers in the divine nature." The "divine principle" in the "heart" is "spiritual understanding" (H:54). This "spiritual understanding" is "not merely nor chiefly" called spiritual because "it is from the Spirit of God, but that it is of the nature of the Spirit of God." Although the Spirit of God operates on all hearts and minds, and therefore "natural men may have common grace, common illuminations, and common affections," spiritual understanding "partakes of the nature of that Spirit," while "no common gift of the Spirit doth so" (H:56).

Spiritual understanding therefore results in *theosis*, whereby the love of God that is the Holy Spirit "indwells" in the saints. For the Spirit "is the Deity wholly breathed forth in infinite, substantial, intelligent love: from the Father and Son first towards each other, and secondly freely flowing out to the creature, and so standing forth a distinct personal subsistence" (H:63). In this way, creatures experience the "fullness" of God, that is, the happiness and joy that exists in the inner relations of the Trinity. "God's fullness does consist in the Holy Spirit," who is the "holiness and happiness of the Deity" that exists between "the Father and the Son." "Hence persons, by being made partakers of the Holy Spirit, or having it dwelling in them, are said to be 'partakers of the fullness of God' or Christ" (H:65). Thus, "we may understand how the saints are said to be made 'partakers of God's holiness,' not only as they partake of that holiness that God gives, but partake of that holiness by which He himself is holy," in "that divine love in which the essence of God really flows out." The Spirit of God "properly lives, acts, and exerts its nature in the exercise of their faculties." So that "true saving grace is no other than that very love of God—that is, God, in one of the persons of the Trinity, uniting Himself to the soul of the creature, as a vital principle, dwelling there and exerting Himself by the faculties of the soul of man, in His own proper nature, after the manner of a principle of nature" (H:72–73).

To experience spiritual understanding is to experience the highest attainment of human capacities as well as incorporation into the spiritual life of the Godhead. The "Holy Spirit is the *summum* of all good"—that is, the "sum of all good"—both divine and human. The "holiness and happiness of the Godhead consists in it; and in communion or partaking of it consists all true loveliness and happiness of the creature" (H:66). This personal transformation is not merely the decisive point in personal fulfillment, but also the decisive ethical relationship—all ethics depends on the state of our souls in God. For "as we have already proved, all creature holiness consists essentially and summarily in love to God and love to other creatures; so does the holiness of God consist in His love, especially in the perfect and intimate union and love there is between the Father and the Son. But the Spirit that proceeds from the Father and the Son is the bond of this union, as it is of all holy union between the Father and the Son, and between God and God's creatures, and between the creatures among themselves" (H:64).

As we will see in the next chapter, Edwards further explores the connection between the relations in the Trinity and human society, particularly the goodness and love that serve as the measure of all societies, divine and human. Here it is important to notice that the psychological analogy underlies Edwards's arguments concerning the difference between Christian ethics and autonomous morality. In "Miscellanies" entries 238 and 239, Edwards asserts that the difference between saints and sinners is that the latter have minds that are "destitute" of "spiritual ideas." While Edwards makes this point in the "Miscellanies" to emphasize personal transformation, in the "Treatise" personal transformation, or lack thereof, determines the difference he draws between "common" and "special" grace, and between "natural" and "regenerate" persons.

As we have observed, Edwards distinguishes between ideas in the first and second mode of apprehension on the basis of whether they can truly reflect reality as it is. In the first mode, ideas are mere representations of reality in the mind through the deliverance of the senses and experience. In the second mode, however, ideas are repetitions of reality as it is through the communication to the mind of the idea of God. The second mode differs from the idea of God only in degree, while the first mode is a different kind of knowledge altogether. Edwards all but repeats this dichotomy to show the difference between common and special grace. Common grace differs from saving grace not merely "in degree," but it is "entirely diverse in nature and kind" (H:26). Likewise, "the sense of religion that a natural man has, is not only not to the same degree, but nothing of the same nature with that which a true saint has" (H:29). It is only with spiritual understanding that the saints experience the "vital union" between God and "the soul of a believer," whereby the "Spirit is actually united to the faculties of their souls" (H:73).

Indeed, the moral capacities of "natural" persons are analogous, if not roughly equivalent, to the epistemological limitations of the first mode of apprehension. However sophisticated knowledge in the first mode becomes, it will nevertheless remain artificial, uncertain, and ultimately secondhand. "All that men can do by their own strength and industry is only gradually to increase and improve . . . qualities, principles, and perfections of nature that they have already." Just as "the qualities and principles of natural bodies, such as figure or motion, can never produce anything beyond themselves," even if "infinite comprehensions and divisions be eternally made," so "nothing can be produced" in the soul "by only those qualities of figure and motion, beyond figure and motion." Therefore, Edwards concludes, saving grace "can't be produced in man by mere exercise of what perfections he has in him already, though never so much assisted by moral suasion, and never so much assisted in the exercise of his natural principles, unless there be something more than all this, viz., an immediate infusion or operation of the divine Being upon the soul" (H:38–39).

Although he places considerable stress on personal transformation to the exclusion of self-determined, incremental changes in the soul, Edwards does not see the moral experience of natural persons as God-forsaken. Edwards calls the experience of natural persons that of "common grace," whereby the Spirit of God "assists" rather than "indwells" the souls of the unregenerate. And Edwards allows that "the Spirit of God may operate and produce effects upon the minds of natural men that have no grace, as He does when he assists natural conscience and convictions of sin and danger." But these operations of the Spirit of God are indistinct, ontologically speaking, from God's influence over "inanimate things" (H:69). The problem, in a word, with "natural" persons is that they are radically incomplete; their knowledge of God and their self-consciousness is largely the product of the first mode of apprehension. The "natural man is perfectly destitute of any sense, perception, or discerning of those things of the Spirit"; "he is a perfect stranger, so that he does not know what the talk of such things means; they are words without meaning to him; he knows nothing of the matter any more than a blind man of colors" (H:29). Perhaps, given Edwards's broader point concerning the intimate communication between God and the soul through the second mode of apprehension, it is better to amend this metaphor in the following way: "Natural" persons are not strangers to God or God's preserving love, but God is a stranger to them.

2.3. Comparisons and Clarifications

Certainly, Edwards is not the first to make the triune God and the indwelling of the Holy Spirit in the saints the distinctive starting point in Christian ethics. We find anticipations of Edwards's ideas not only in Augustine but also in more immediate predecessors in both Reformed and Roman Catholic traditions, specifically Francis Turretin (1623–1687) and Thomas Aquinas (1225–1274).[45] For both Turretin and Thomas, participation in God through the communication of the Spirit of God are essential aspects of what it means to live according to God's will and love. Both Turretin and Thomas, however, distinguish the exploration of God's triunity through the psychological analogy from their respective articulations of the moral life. Further, both maintain the Platonic sense of "participation" in their descriptions of the nature of the communication of the Spirit in order to preserve essential aspects of the ontological divide between Creator and creature.

In his *Principles of Elenctic Theology* (1679), Turretin, whom Edwards refers to as the "great Turretin" in the *Religious Affections* (Y2:289), touches upon ethics in his extensive treatment of the Trinity. In speaking of the communication of the attributes of God, Turretin introduces a distinction regarding communication between God and creatures. Communication is not a univocal term; its meaning is twofold: There is "formal and essential" communication, by which one receives the "intrinsic being" of another; and there is communication by "resemblance and analogy," by which one reflects in one's own being the "effects and works" of another. The former type of communication is impossible between God and creatures and exists only between the divine persons, for otherwise "the properties of God," such as simplicity, "would cease to be properties." But "the latter we confess can be granted since God produces in creatures (especially in rational creatures) effects analogous to his own properties, such as goodness, justice, wisdom, etc." "In this sense," Turretin writes, "God alone is said to be good, i.e. originally, independently, essentially; but concerning creatures only secondarily, accidentally, and participatively." Therefore, although one reads in 2 Peter 1:4 that "believers are said to be partakers in the divine nature," Turretin believes that the proper understanding of the sense of participation in this passage is "not univocally (by a formal participation of the divine essence), but only analogically (by benefit of the regeneration which impresses upon them the marks of holiness and righteousness most properly belonging to God, since they are renewed after the image of their Creator)." Only the incarnate Son of God receives the "essential" and not "analogical" communication of the attributes of God.[46]

Later in the *Principles*, when he speaks directly to the nature of the moral life, Turretin returns to this distinction regarding communication and speaks of the Christian life as a life of outward "conformity" to God as the necessary prism through which to view ethics: "God is ours in respect of conformity." That is to say, God is "not satisfied with pouring out upon us the salutary effects of his properties, but wishes further to impress upon us their mark and likeness (as far as a finite creature can bear it) that we may be 'partakers of the divine nature.'" Hence, "no communion can be held with God except on the basis of conformity to him." Yet conformity in this sense refers to a likeness or resemblance, rather than instantiation, of God.[47]

In the *Summa Theologiae*, Thomas offers an articulation of the Christian moral life that in its emphasis on love or charity appears closer to Edwards's than Turretin's, particularly at the point in the *Summa* where Thomas speaks of the nature of the virtue of charity. Charity is the "creaturely" reception of the gift of the Holy Spirit.[48] "Charity is not something created in the soul," nor does it represent merely a precondition or disposition of the soul toward God, but it is "the Holy Spirit himself dwelling there." Humanity, according to Thomas, "leads a double life" regarding its nature and happiness. The first life is "outward" involving the happiness available through "the world of body and senses"; the second is "inward" and spiritual, and it is here that we have the happiness that comes through "communion" or "intercourse with God and the angels."[49] Charity, given this double nature and in terms of the divine indwelling, is a "certain participation in the Holy Spirit."[50]

Yet while Thomas defines charity as the indwelling of the Holy Spirit, he does not consider charity identical to the Holy Spirit. On this point, Thomas departs from the position of Peter Lombard, who concludes that charity "is not something created in the soul, but the Holy Spirit himself dwelling there."[51] Thomas offers two reasons why this cannot be the case. One reason is that, like Turretin, Thomas comprehends our participation in God through charity in a Platonic sense: "The divine essence itself is charity even as it is wisdom and goodness."[52] As Thomas writes earlier, only God is good "by nature," and all other creatures are merely good in terms of their "participation" or "resemblance" to God. Therefore, Thomas concludes, one may "calls things good and existent by reference" to the perfect goodness of God, which is "existent and good by nature, in as much as they participate and resemble it." In this way, the "divine goodness" is the "pattern, source and goal of all goodness."[53] Likewise, the "charity by which we formally love our neighbor is a sharing in the divine charity." Rather than a creaturely instantiation of God, then, charity is a creaturely representation of the pattern of love as it exists within the Trinity. This "way of speaking," Thomas writes, "was customary among the Platonists" and identifies the proper understanding of the virtue of charity.[54]

The other reason, related to the previous one, is that Lombard's position makes the indwelling of the Spirit equivalent to quasi-demonic possession in which the Spirit takes control of a soul and acts as an efficient cause "like a body which is set in motion by an outside force." Such a depiction of the Spirit's activity would eliminate the agency and freedom that constitutes human individuality. For Thomas, the Spirit's indwelling is "connatural." God "moves all things to their appropriate ends," and charity therefore in human terms is a sacramental "sharing in the divine charity," of the love that is the Holy Spirit.[55]

As we have seen, Edwards comprehends participation in terms of the idealism connected to the psychological analogy, rather than in a Platonic sense. Participation for Edwards comes when our minds repeat, rather than merely replicate or represent, the perfect idea of God. In this way, the regenerate person lives a life of actual participation in the triune life of God through sharing the idea and love that animates the divine mind. Edwards believes that the regenerate persons' "reason and conscience seem to be a participation of the divine essence" (Y13:342).

Consequently, in the "Treatise" we find that Edwards eschews the concept of the moral life as one of conformity and disallows any equivocation of God's self-communication to the soul. On these points, Edwards is explicit: "That holy and divine principle, which we have observed does radically consist in divine love, is no other than a communication and participation of that same infinite divine love, which is GOD, and in which the Godhead is essentially breathed forth; and subsists in the third person in the blessed Trinity." Therefore, "saving grace" is "no other" than the "very love of God—that is God, in one of the persons of the Trinity, uniting Himself to the soul of a creature as a vital principle." For this reason, Edwards continues, one of the points implicit in the Scripture passage, "partakers of the divine nature," is to signify that the regenerate "are not only partakers of a nature that may, in some sense, be called divine, because 'tis conformed to the nature of God." But the "very Deity does, in some sense, dwell in them," that is to say, "that holy and divine love dwells in their hearts, and is so united to human faculties, that 'tis become a principle of new nature" (H:73).

Indeed, Edwards writes in the "Treatise" that he thinks "no good reason can be given" why persons "have such an inward disposition to deny any immediate communication between God and the creature, or to make as little of it as possible." The upshot of this "unreasonable disposition" is that "men have tried to thrust God out of the world": "Many schemes have been drawn to exclude, or extenuate, or remove at a great distance, and influence of the divine being in the hearts of men, such as the schemes of the Pelagians" (i.e., those who stress the freedom of the will) and "the Socinians" (i.e., those who deny that God has three persons). At the same time, those systems that ascribe to the "immediate influence of the Spirit" are labeled as the product of "enthusiasm, fanaticism, whimsy, and distraction" (H:53).

While Edwards believes his own scheme to be utterly reasonable, he would have to admit it departs from even fellow idealists such as George Berkeley and Malebranche. As we have seen, Malebranche inspired Edwards to develop his own conception of ideas as the immediate and immanent communications of the divine mind, which became central to Edwards's articulation of the second mode of apprehension and the psychological analogy. Malebranche restricts, however, his own reflections on the Trinity to its *economic* operation rather than its *immanent* relations, that is, to the work or missions of the Trinity in created existence rather than to the processions of the Godhead in eternity. At points in *The Search for Truth*, Malebranche construes from his occasionalism a conception of the operations of the Trinity in the redemption of humanity. For "it is through this dependence, this relation, this union of our mind with the Word of God, and of our will with His love, that we are made in the image and likeness of God." Though this image is "greatly effaced through sin," if "we follow the impulses of the Holy Ghost, this union of our mind with the Word of the Father, and with the love of the Father, will be reestablished and made indelible." We shall be "like God," for "God will be entirely in us, and we in Him."[56]

Malebranche is reluctant to use his occasionalism to disclose the mystery of the immanent Trinity, or to suggest that the union humans experience in their minds through the communication of the divine idea is the *actual* repetition of the Holy Spirit. Concerning the immanent Trinity, he allows that the implications of his idealism suggest that "if these ideas were clear, one could by attending to them, perfectly understand these mysteries and explain them to others" so that they ceased to be "ineffable mysteries." But the mystery of the Trinity admits of only a limited amount of disclosure. Therefore, at other points in *The Search for Truth*, Malebranche dissociates himself from any further attempt to use his occasionalism to mine the mysteries of the inner relations of the Godhead: "We believe the mystery of the Trinity, although the human mind cannot conceive it." It is better that "the mind should not be employed except on subjects suited to its capacity, and that our mysteries should not be scrutinized lest they benumb us." "I say here," declares Malebranche at one point—as if to remove the possibility of any contrary allegation—"that we have no ideas of our mysteries." Malebranche even admits that at its core the word "idea" is equivocal—it tells us only what we know concerning our perceptions, and not the deeper mysteries of the universe. Although Malebranche adheres to an account of the processions of the Godhead that is similar to Edwards's, he believes that "only the saints in heaven see by an evident light that the Father begets His Son and that the Father and the Son produce the Holy Spirit." For "God assures them of it by revealing His will to them in a way unknown to us." Malebranche's reticence concerning the viability of his occasionalism as a means for disclosing the inner life of the Trinity may underlie his retention of the Platonic sense of participation in his depiction of the moral life. "That which makes a Man Just," writes Malebranche, "is that he loves Order, and *conforms* his Will to it in all things."[57]

Like Edwards and Malebranche, Berkeley is an idealist and an occasionalist, though his own interests are philosophical rather than theological. With Malebranche and Edwards, Berkeley argues that all our ideas are participations in the idea of God. Berkeley also introduces a distinction between ideas in the mind of God and the ideas that reside in human minds. Ideas in God's mind compose "archetypal and eternal existence," and ideas in the minds of humans compose "ectypal or natural existence."[58] Further, Berkeley holds that not only God but all mental entities, persons included, are capable of communication, both causal and intellectual.[59] Nonetheless, despite these distinctive points in his idealism, Berkeley also describes the moral life in terms of the Platonic sense of participation. "Moral goodness," Berkeley writes in *Passive Obedience*, consists "in a conformity to the laws of God." This conformity accords with the "eternal rules of reason" and is evident in the "laws of nature" that the "Author of Nature" has "stamped on the mind" and "engraven on the tablets of the heart" through the conscience.[60]

3. DIFFICULTIES AND POINTS FOR FURTHER DEVELOPMENT

Although brief, the "Treatise" represents the most extended attempt in Edwards's Trinitarian writings to draw a connection between the moral life and the psychological analogy. In comparison to the above theologians and philosophers, Edwards's system appears unique in the emphasis he places on participation in the divine nature as the culmination of the moral and religious life. From unique approaches, however, come unique problems, and the brevity of Edwards's remarks in the "Treatise" entails that there are several issues he does not cover adequately and must revise in later writings. Primarily, these problems concern two points of departure Edwards makes from the traditional depictions of the relation between the Trinity and the moral life.

3.1. Individuality and Personal Identity

The first is the coincidence Edwards creates in his development of the psychological analogy between God's consciousness and human consciousness in regenerate persons. As we have seen, Trinitarian theology traditionally presupposes an ontological divide between divine and human minds in its development of the psychological analogy. Underlying Augustine's use of the soul as an analogy for the Trinity is his understanding that all our analogies for God are equivocal. That is to say, they are useful for understanding God as far as such inquiries into the nature of God are possible, but in the end we see only in a glass darkly, not face to face. "I know that I am alive," writes Augustine, but "it is not the same thing to be as to know." Our knowledge of ourselves is not knowledge per se, even if it is a kind of wisdom or faint awareness of the divine mind. Only God's knowledge and wisdom and being are one.[61]

In respecting the ontological divide between God and humanity, traditional articulations of the psychological analogy maintain that there are important differences between divine and human nature. Prominent among these differences is the negative burden of human sinfulness and finitude, a topic we return to in chapter 4. But equally important, if not normally as prominent, are the positive differences between God and human beings, specifically human individuality and personal distinctiveness. The latter are not only good but are particular blessings and special gifts of God. From this perspective, there are important respects in which our loves and lives are *unlike*, as well as *like*, God's life and love.

In the previous section, the concern to protect the positive gifts of human individuality and personal distinctiveness is most evident in Thomas, but it is possibly an implicit concern for the others (Turretin, Malebranche, and Berkeley) as well. And perhaps it is for this reason, and not for any inherent attractiveness of classical metaphysics, that the figures we have examined find the Platonic sense of participation in some way congenial to Christian beliefs and ethics. On one hand, the concern for individuality and personal distinctiveness expresses a well-founded prejudice in Christian theology against schemes that entail metaphysical merger with God, or that collapse human knowledge into divine knowledge. On the other hand, the concern for individuality recognizes that individuality is an intrinsic good that has profound implications for the moral life. As Thomas's remarks indicate, tied to the conception of individuality and personal distinctiveness is human agency and voluntariness, that is, the capacity to love and obey God as an individual and not as one who has lost all sense of personal identity. Moreover, personal distinctiveness in the form of one's unique and unrepeatable nature constitutes the whole notion of human dignity and value; we are worthy of respect and love because we are children of God.

Therefore, while the other figures we have examined tend to minimize, if not eliminate, the relation between the psychological analogy and ethics, Edwards's conception of the moral life through the prism of the psychological analogy tends to leap the ontological divide between Creator and creature in a single bound. For as it stands, Edwards's account of the coincidence of divine and human consciousness and his account of the moral life as participation in God through the repetition in one's mind of the perfect idea of God suggests that there is no meaningful sense of human individuality and personal distinctiveness.

In later correspondence, Edwards argues that his proposal regarding the Holy Spirit's indwelling the saint in no way suggests "God's communicating his essence" to the regenerate, but rather the "Spirit of God's communicating himself is his proper nature," that is, "holiness" and "love." For the biblical name for the third person of the Trinity, *Holy* Ghost, identifies the nature of what the Spirit communicates to humanity, namely, the "nature" of "holiness." Holiness therefore is a "communicable attribute," such that "the saints are made partakers of his holiness" without "imparting to them his essence" (Y8:638–39). Similarly, in "Miscellanies" entry 396, Edwards distinguishes "two senses" for the word "spirit." On one hand, "spirit" identifies the "mind" that exists in an "angel, or human soul, or divine essence." On the other, "spirit" identifies "the temper," "disposition," "inclination, or will" of an entity. Consequently, when speaking of the "divine essence," both senses of the word "spirit" apply. But when speaking of the "Spirit of God's dwelling in us," only the second sense applies. Therefore, the proper understanding of "our being filled with the Spirit" is that "a divine temper or disposition dwells in us or fills us" in the form of "infinite love." And it is in this sense that the divine nature is spoken of in 2 Peter 1:4 (Y13:461–62).

Moreover, at several points in the "Treatise," Edwards insists that the indwelling of the Holy Spirit completes, rather than obliterates, human nature. The "divine principle in the hearts of the saints," which is the "third person of the Trinity," is "united to the soul, living and acting in it, and exerting itself in the use and improvement of its faculties" (H:71). The Holy Spirit is "so united to human faculties, that 'tis itself become a principle of new nature." But the "divine love exerts itself in its own nature in the exercise of those faculties, after the manner of a natural or vital principle in them" (H:72–73). That is to say, the work of the Holy Spirit is *restorative* of human nature. The Holy Spirit neither adds anything to human nature that is extraneous nor possesses human nature as an external force, but returns to human nature the proper faculties and integrity it had originally, were it not for sin. In the context of the second mode of apprehension and Edwards's understanding of spiritual knowledge, Edwards's argument therefore is that to see God as God is leads us to see ourselves as we are, and ought to be.

These qualifications, however, do little to resolve the problem of individuality inherent in Edwards's depiction of the coincidence of divine and human consciousness. If, as Edwards believes, God's "idea" of God's self and "spiritual knowledge" differ only in degree and not kind, how is it that our minds are not absorbed into the Godhead? While Edwards acknowledges the difference between the divine mind, understood as the "essence" of God, and humanity's participation in the divine "inclination and disposition," it is hard to see where this distinction exists within his idealism. Although Edwards does not address this question further in his Trinitarian writings, he returns to it in other "Miscellanies" entries when he incorporates insights from his development of the psychological analogy into his account of the economic missions of the Son and the Spirit in the world.

Concerning the mission of the Son, the idealism of the psychological analogy provides an important way to conceive of the incarnation. In "Miscellanies" entry 184, Edwards writes, "What insight I have of the nature of minds, I am convinced that there is no guessing what kind of union and mixation, by consciousness or otherwise, there may be between them. So that all difficulty is removed in believing what the Scripture declares about spiritual unions—of the persons in the Trinity, of the two natures in Christ, of Christ and the minds of the saints" (Y13:330). That is to say, in all of these different dimensions of relations in God, the concept of unity that operates in all of them is that of identity, of experiencing an identical idea that perfectly repeats the mind that generates it.

As we have seen, unity is not the only criterion in Edwards's idealism; there is also a necessary plurality, dynamism, and objectivity in each of these relations that make self-consciousness in the second mode of apprehension what it is. Subtle but essential differences attend each dimension in God. Operative in these differences is the subject or agent who is generating the perfect idea as an act of self-consciousness, as well as the place within the hierarchy of being that self-consciousness occurs. Accordingly, in the unity that pertains to the persons of the Trinity, the Father is the agent whose self-consciousness is composed of his "perfect idea" and "perfect act" of love and delight. Within this dimension, the Son, as the second person of the Trinity, is internal to God's own self-actualization as a person, for the "*Logos*" is "God's idea" (Y13:393).

In the "work of redemption," the Son is the perfect "idea" or self-consciousness of the concrete person of Jesus Christ: "The man Jesus Christ, being the same person with the eternal Son of God, has a reminiscence or consciousness of what appertained to the eternal *Logos*, and so of his happiness with the Father." As a human being with a finite mind, Jesus Christ did not have an infinite mind that encompassed all possible communication of the mind of God. "For the idea of the Creator cannot be communicated to the creature as it is in God," and a finite mind could not hold the things that the Son "remembered" from "all eternity in the *Logos* after the manner of God." Rather, "the man Christ Jesus was conscious to himself" after "the manner of a creature." Thus, Christ was conscious of himself as the Son of God, but his "consciousness" of God accords with human nature. Edwards admits that he is uncertain about "the particular manner of this consciousness," or "how far the ideas of a creature can be after the manner of the divine," but he believes "in general" this scheme of "necessity to be" (Y13:340–41).

In "Miscellanies" entry 487, Edwards returns to the topic of the incarnation, and he further distinguishes between having an idea in the consciousness that represents a human being's "personal union," or individuality, and the consciousness of God that is definitive of human persons in general. Through God's communication of God's knowledge and will through the Holy Spirit, each human being receives its personal identity. For it is "not just any communication of understanding and will that makes the same person, but the communion of understanding is such that there is the *same consciousness*." God holds each person together as a vital nexus of mind, idea, and disposition, so that each is unified and unique, so that we have individuality. Each person, in other words, is unrepeatable to the extent that he or she represents a distinct nexus of self-consciousness.

Within the context of this "personal union," the "man Christ" is united to the "*Logos*" in two ways." The first is "by the respect which God hath to this human nature," that is, "God hath respect to this man and loveth him as his own Son." This "man hath communion with the *Logos*, in the love which the Father hath to him as his only begotten Son." Second, the incarnate Christ is united with the *Logos* "by what is inherent in this man, whereby he becomes one person, which is only by the communication of understanding and communion of will, inclination, spirit or temper" (Y13:528–29). In other words, all of us have a God-given individuality through self-consciousness. The difference between other persons and Jesus Christ is that Christ, as an individual person with a discrete self-consciousness, possesses the distinct personhood and identity of the Son and *Logos*, who in turn is the self-consciousness of God the Father. Thus, Christ's individuality as a person is complete, as well as ours.

Nonetheless, what Edwards gains concerning personal individuality as he considers the mission of the Son, he gives back in his description of the mission of the Spirit. For as we have seen, within the confines of his psychological analogy, Edwards strains to represent the Spirit as a distinct person, as well as a state of love and relation between the Father and the Son. This relative paucity of personhood on the part of the Spirit leads to an attenuated sense of individuality. Although the Spirit occupies a crucial role in the work of redemption as the "energy" or "principle" that indwells the souls of the saints and makes possible their personal transformation and participation in God, Edwards does not ascribe to the Spirit a distinctive locus of communion. Edwards emphasizes that he believes the Spirit is a "person" in the same sense as the Father and the Son are persons, but the main expression of the Spirit's personality is as the "bond of union" between the Father and the Son (H:57–58). Thus, the individuality of the Spirit is largely subsumed by the Spirit's role as conduit of the divine love.

From this attenuated sense of individuality in the Spirit arises an attenuated sense of individuality in the saints. In "Miscellanies" entry 94, Edwards writes that the saints, as they further experience the indwelling of the Spirit, are transformed not into perfect individuals but into "perfect action." Edwards observes, "[H]ow frequently do we say that the saints of heaven are all transformed into love, dissolved into joy, become activity itself, changed into mere ecstasy?" While Edwards describes these remarks as "metaphorical," they represent the logical ramifications of his idealist definition of unity transposed into the sphere of action, for "it is true that the more perfect an act is, the more it resembles the infinitely perfect act of God in this respect" (Y13:260–61).

Even when Edwards *does* use the psychological analogy to speak of the Spirit in discretely individual terms, as a kind of agent, it is often under the auspices of the Son, as the "Spirit of Christ." For while regenerate persons participate in God when their minds repeat God's "idea," in "Miscellanies" entry 487 Edwards reflects that this "idea" is perfectly manifest in the person of Jesus Christ. Believers therefore are united with God not merely by experiencing the repetition in their self-consciousness of the consciousness of God, but when they experience this consciousness as the distinct "Spirit of Christ." Edwards writes, "There is a likeness between the union of the *Logos* with the man Jesus Christ and the union of Christ with the church." For both, there is an indwelling of consciousness: "Christ dwells in believers as his temple" and the "*Logos* dwells in the human nature of Christ." The only difference Edwards sees between the communion of believers and Christ follows the somatic image of the church as the "body of Christ" in the Scripture (Eph. 1:23; 1 Cor. 12:12): "God dwells in the man Christ as the head, and in us as the members, as the head is the seat of the soul after a peculiar manner." Christ has a distinct consciousness toward God as a "Son," and God dwells in Christ as the "Spirit of the Son." Believers experience a "vital union" and have a "filial spirit, or spirit of children." The shape of the regenerate saints' participation in God therefore is fundamentally christological, even as it is essentially Trinitarian: "The great thing purchased by Jesus Christ for us is communion with God, which is only in having the Spirit; 'tis participation of Christ's fullness, and having grace for grace, which is only in having of the Spirit which he has without measure; this is the promise of the Father" (Y13:466).

Concerning the missions of the Son and the Spirit as they extend central insights from Edwards's psychological analogy, then, we find a conception of personal individuality that exists alongside a corresponding conception of anonymity. Edwards's exaltation of individuality in his depiction of the incarnation matches his exaltation of the saints' utter incorporation—and loss of personal distinctiveness—into the perfect love and Spirit of God. Given Edwards's difficulty with the personality and individuality of the Holy Spirit, combined with his idealist understanding of unity, one could conclude that, at its core, Edwards's scheme renders the whole concept of individuality problematic.

But in a more sympathetic light, it appears that Edwards is trying to articulate a conception of individuality in the moral and spiritual life that follows the model of God's own individuality in the persons of the Trinity. As we saw earlier in this chapter, Edwards's answer to the problem of the Spirit's personality is to assert that the persons of the Trinity exist in *perichoresis*. There is, to reiterate, a relation among the persons and attributes of God so that each permeates and penetrates the other, yet without a loss of distinctiveness. In the same way, the saints through their participation in God receive their individuality. In this scheme, one is not an individual on the basis of one's autonomous capacity to choose or to love for oneself, but one becomes an individual only through partaking in the love of God in Christ. We become complete persons, in short, through surrendering that which we hold dearest. We find our true individuality only when we lose it.

In the "Miscellanies" and in the "Essay," Edwards hints at this conception of individuality in his image of the sun, which he sees as providing a "lively image" in the physical world of the psychological analogy of the Trinity (Y13:434).[62] For just as the Trinity in the soul is composed of the mind, its idea, and its love, so there is a Trinity in the sun, its light, and its heat. In the "Essay," Edwards writes that the Father "is as the substance of the sun"—not in "a philosophical sense" of substance, but "as to its internal constitution." The Son "is as the brightness and glory of the disk of the sun or that bright and glorious form under which it appears to our eyes." The Spirit, "as it is God's love to Himself and happiness in Himself, is as the internal heat of the sun, but, as it is that by which God communicates Himself, it is as the emanation" or "the emitted beams of the sun" that "enlightens, warms, enlivens, and comforts the world" (H:126).

Edwards's use of the sun as a metaphor for the relations within God is not original, for at the very beginning of Trinitarian theology Tertullian speaks to the unity and equality between the persons in the Godhead in terms of the "sun and its ray."[63] Edwards's acquaintance with scientific textbooks and his own experiments with light, however, showed him that light not only is unified but also differentiates according to the spectrum.[64] Therefore, the sun is not only an image of God's unity but also of the diversity and individuality the saints achieve in God. Edwards thinks "the various sorts of rays of the sun and their beautiful colors do well represent the Spirit, or the amiable excellency of God, and the various beautiful graces and virtues of the Spirit" (Y13:442). Not only is there diversity among the virtues the saints possess, but the saints themselves, transformed by the light and heat of God, are as individual, and yet as similar, as the different rays of the sun. For as "Moses was changed by God's glory shining upon him," so "we are changed by God's Spirit shed as bright beams on us" (Y13:442).

Although intriguing, Edwards's conception of individuality and unity in God, like his previous account of the personhood of the Holy Spirit, struggles within the confines of the psychological analogy and leaves basic aspects of individuality and personal distinctiveness uncovered. For although Edwards has established that individuality and personal distinctiveness is something of value in God's eyes, he has not yet shown adequately how individuality and personal distinctiveness are rooted in God's own triune nature. What shape does individuality take interpersonally, and not merely intrapersonally? Is there a sense in which our fullest expression of individuality and personal distinctiveness comes only in the self-donation and mutual love we experience when we participate in a community or society? Certainly Edwards's understanding of the psychological analogy presupposes the value of self-transcendence and sociality, but as we have seen, Edwards finds it difficult to articulate these things within the psychological analogy itself. In addition, Edwards has not yet offered an account of how agency and voluntariness are integral parts of the Godhead and the Christian moral life. In the next chapter, we will explore how Edwards expands his account of individuality from the perspective of God's excellency or beauty, which stems from the benevolence, agency, and voluntariness of the social analogy. Edwards's fullest answers to these questions, however, come only in his occasional writings, particularly the *Religious Affections*, *Freedom of the Will*, and *Original Sin*.

3.2. Moral Concepts: Conscience

The second point where Edwards incurs difficulties stems from the concepts and terms he uses from moral philosophy and theology to depict the integration of the psychological analogy and the moral life. As we have seen, Edwards assigns to unregenerate persons moral capacities roughly in accordance with their experience of reality. The unregenerate experience reality largely through the lens of the first mode of apprehension; they have no spiritual "idea" of God, and thus have no real participation or meaningful experience of themselves or God in the second mode of apprehension. Hence, the moral knowledge and the moral capacities of unregenerate persons are essentially deformed, even if occasionally correct. Throughout his writings, Edwards will continue to characterize natural morality and unregenerate persons in this way.[65] Nonetheless, the depiction as it now stands is too neat. Edwards uses commonplace principles or concepts from moral philosophy to construct the second mode of apprehension and his depiction of spiritual knowledge, and he must therefore account for why or how these same principles exist in both natural and regenerate persons.

The most immediate concept is the conscience. As we have seen, the conscience provides Edwards with the primary image through which to envision God's triadic and dynamic relations, specifically God's delight or love of God's excellency. The delight one experiences when one has a peaceful conscience reveals the relations of the Trinity in God's own consciousness. Moreover, the conscience is not only a model for the relations of the Trinity, but it is a medium through which the regenerate experience "sanctification"; "man's reason and conscience seem to be a participation of the divine essence" (Y13:342). Conscience, therefore, in Edwards's writings on the Trinity operates as an integral part of the second mode of apprehension. It is not merely a capacity or function within the mind that perceives the will of God or the moral state of one's soul, but, as Fiering puts it, it is a kind of "innate and instinctive craving for participation in the Trinity."[66] Hence, we read in "The Mind" that Edwards defines the "conscience" as "that sense the mind has" of God's "love of himself in his own Holy Spirit," which is the supreme model and source of all beauty and unity in the world (Y6:365).

But if conscience is integral to the second mode of apprehension, and by extension properly only resides in the hearts of the regenerate, in what form does it exist in the unregenerate? In Edwards's milieu, the conscience was defined as a principle inherent in all persons, both regenerate and unregenerate, as a kind of general knowledge of the moral law. Although there was considerable disagreement over what exactly constituted the conscience—whether it was innate or acquired, veracious or spurious, the voice of God or of reason, located primarily in the intellect or in the will— on this point there was wide agreement in the wider philosophical and theological marketplace.[67]

Edwards's awareness of the need to create space in his account of the moral capacities of unregenerate persons for "natural conscience" presents itself in "Miscellanies" entries 471 and 472. In entry 471, Edwards assigns to unregenerate persons a discrete "natural" conscience that is different from the conscience he assigns to the regenerate. Where the conscience in the regenerate is a means of apprehending and participating in the life of the Trinity, "natural conscience" provides "an apprehension of right and wrong" that "suggest to the mind the relation that there is between right and wrong and a retribution" (Y13:513). The "natural conscience," then, differs from the conscience proper in that it is a means of general revelation—a way God reveals "right and wrong" to persons through the "assistance" of the Holy Spirit, rather than being a unique means of participation in the Godhead. Natural conscience in this sense approximates the traditional conception of the conscience as *synteresis*, as an innate or connate grasp of the principles of the moral law apart from biblical revelation.[68]

In entry 472, however, Edwards appears to contradict his previous understanding of "natural" conscience. Rather than assigning to the unregenerate a true apprehension of right and wrong, Edwards now writes that "natural men in strictness see *nothing* of the proper deformity of wrong," but only develop an acquired *sense of desert*. The unregenerate merely develop a rudimentary conception of rewards and punishments on the basis of experience, as a kind of abstraction or "association of ideas" akin to the first mode of apprehension. The unregenerate therefore see the moral law only as it appears and not as it is, given their familiarity with the world and their self-interested desire to live happily. They see "an agreeableness" or "an equality, proportion and likeness of nature" between a person's "causing his neighbor to suffer and suffering himself," and "not from a sense of the deformity of causing his neighbor to suffer" (Y13:514).

Commentators on Edwards often attribute the difference between 471 and 472 to ancillary concerns, such as his dissatisfaction with the Puritan doctrine of the preparatory work of the Holy Spirit, or his growing engagement with works of autonomous moral philosophy. Thus, the progression from defining the "natural" conscience as a kind of *synteresis* in entry 471 to a *sense of desert* in 472 represents a gradual shift in Edwards's thought away from the conscience as a special means of God's revelation.[69]

These interpretations, however, overlook the extent to which Edwards's Trinitarian reflection establishes the context for the development of his theory of the conscience, as well as the extent to which Edwards's Trinitarian reflection continues to influence even his "mature" theory of conscience. In fact, what is striking about Edwards's ostensively mature theory of conscience is not that he privileges the *sense of desert* over *synteresis*, but that he considers the formerly regenerate sense of conscience to be part of the "natural conscience." In a chapter devoted to the "natural conscience" in *The Nature of True Virtue*, a treatise I will explore in chapter 5, Edwards reiterates his conception of conscience in the second mode of apprehension. He argues that persons have a general capacity for consciousness through which they are able to put themselves "in the place of another" by "recalling and exciting the ideas of what we ourselves are conscious of" in "our own minds." This consciousness yields a desire for "self-union," a desire to "act as in agreement with ourselves, or as one with ourselves," so to have "what is called peace of conscience." Therefore, it pertains to "all moral things we conceive of in others, which are called mental and not corporeal things; and everything that we conceive of, belonging to others, more than shape, size, complexion, situation, and motion of their bodies."[70] Not only does consciousness provide a means through which persons are "intelligent moral agents," but "this is the only way that we come to be capable of having ideas of any perception or act even of the Godhead," or of "conceiving of anything in the Deity" (Y8:589–92).

Edwards's mature theory of conscience, then, does not privilege one conception of the conscience over another.[71] If anything, Edwards tries to reconcile each of these apparently contradictory conceptions of the conscience into a unified account that maintains the conscience as a unique mode of apprehension and participation in God. Edwards considers conscience in every sense, the formerly regenerate sense included, as part of the "natural conscience." Therefore, the conception of conscience that is definitive of the second mode of apprehension and an image of the Trinity *no longer* is the exclusive means through which the regenerate participate in the inner life of God, or through which God indwells the soul of the saint. Rather, now saints and sinners alike possess a natural conscience and therefore bear in their souls the image of the Trinity.

Consequently, as we observe Edwards's more developed moral anthropology in ensuing chapters, two related questions need further explication. The first concerns the nature of spiritual knowledge. If the consciousness that perceives the Trinity is merely a natural capacity, in what way do regenerate persons participate in the inner life of God? Edwards must find another way to articulate his belief that "the Spirit of God" immediately "communicates and exerts itself" to "the soul" (Y13:513). The second concerns the moral capacities of unregenerate humanity. If the unregenerate have a natural conscience that accurately apprehends right and wrong, what role does it play in the moral life? Why do the unregenerate fail to see the love and goodness of God?

3.3. Moral Concepts: Self-love

Another problematic moral concept for Edwards is self-love. As we have seen, self-love is integral to understanding how the love of God derives from God's self-consciousness, and the fullest expression of God's self-love is God's self-transcendence in the form of God's "triplicity." Moreover, there is a corresponding emphasis on the saints' love of happiness and desire for well-being that sees God as the "*summum* of all good" and the source of "all the true loveliness and happiness of the creature" (H:66). The saints experience real and authentic happiness and "joy" when they encounter God in their consciousness. Therefore, the love of God and the love of self, taken as merely a desire for one's own happiness, are ontologically correlated; to experience true happiness and by extension true satisfaction, one must love God.

But in the moral theology and philosophy of Edwards's day, self-love possessed multiple and contradictory connotations: as a positive and prudential concern for personal happiness, as a neutral mortar of society, and as a negative instance of sinful self-interest.[72] In the face of these different connotations of self-love, in what way does Edwards's sense of self-love apply? In "Miscellanies" entry 530, Edwards articulates a conception of self-love that is positive and reflects his writings on the Trinity. Edwards poses the question "Whether or no a man ought to love God more than himself." He answers that self-love and love of God "are not things properly capable of being compared with one another: for they are not opposites, or things entirely distinct; but one enters into the nature of the other." Self-love "in the most extensive sense"—that is, a "capacity for enjoyment or suffering"—is necessarily implicated in any description where God is the supreme good and the fulfillment of human desires. Thus, "'tis improper to say that our love to God is superior to our general capacity of delighting in anything. Proportionate to our love of God is our disposition to delight in his good." There is no comparison, logically speaking, between an object one loves and the delight one feels in relation to that object. The "delight in a particular thing, and the degree of love to pleasure or delight in general" are "not entirely distinct, but one enters into the nature of the other." Moreover, self-love is necessarily implicated in any love of "benevolence." For "evermore equal to the inclination or desire anyone has of another's good, is the delight he has in that other's good if it be obtained, and the uneasiness if it not be obtained."

The real question, Edwards continues, is whether one defines self-love merely as a person's narrow focus on the delight one experiences in relation to a good, or includes in self-love a desire for the well-being of the beloved object. The first definition, which Edwards calls "simple mere self-love," is "entirely distinct" from the love of God, and in this sense, each love does not "enter into the nature of the other at all." The second, which Edwards calls "compounded self-love," arises from the delight of simple self-love but evolves into a "principle uniting this person to another, that causes the good of another to be its good." This "second sort of self-love is not entirely distinct from love to God, but enters into its nature."[73]

A clear relation seems to exist between Edwards's Trinitarian reflections and his conception of "compounded self-love." As we have seen, God's self-love is not merely a force of unity motivated by a love for what is best, but is generative, comprehensive, and properly social. Thus, self-love in God is as much an act of self-transcendence as it is an act of self-esteem. Likewise, compounded self-love yields a love that desires not only one's own private pleasure but a love that desires the union with, and the well-being of, another. Self-love, in short, has not only a positive connotation in Edwards, but his definition of compounded self-love derives from his conception of God's love as a dynamic and relational state of communion between the persons of the Trinity.

Indeed, the difference between simple and compound self-love operates in "Miscellanies" entry 117, one of Edwards's early entries on the Trinity. "Love is certainly the perfection as well as happiness of a spirit. God, doubtless, as he is infinitely perfect and happy, has infinite love," or simple self-love. God's love, however, encompasses more than "that which some call self-love, whereby even the devils desire pleasure and are adverse to pain." For in and of itself, simple self-love "is exceedingly improperly called love, and is nothing at all akin to that affection or delight which is called love." Proper love is compounded self-love, and for this reason "there must have been an object from all eternity which God infinitely loves." Therefore, "there must be a plurality in God" (Y13:283–84).

Implicit in Edwards's depiction of compounded self-love, however, is a conception of self-love that is negative and pertains to fallen nature. Edwards's elevation of compounded self-love is correlated to his designation of simple self-love as unremarkable and pervasive in all creation— something which God and "devils" have in common. In "The Mind," Edwards cautions, "We shall be in danger, when we meditate" on the "love of God to himself," of "some alloy to the sweetness of our view by its appearing with something of the aspect and cast of what we call self-love." For God's "love includes in it, or rather is the same as, a love to everything, as they are all communications of himself" (Y6:365).

Simple self-love alone, in short, is alien to the love of God. Edwards further argues in "Miscellanies" entry 301 that without compounded self-love, simple self-love becomes the root of all "sinful inclinations." Commending his grandfather Solomon Stoddard, who offers "the best philosophy" of original sin, Edwards reflects "that it is self-love in conjunction with the absence of the image and love of God" from which proceed "thousands of unlovely and hateful actions." Therefore, "there is nothing new put into the nature that we call sin, but only the same self-love that necessarily belongs to the nature" of human persons "without regulation from that superior principle"—that is, the love of God—"that primitively belongs to our nature and that is necessary in order to the harmonious existing of it" (Y13:387). Simple self-love, in other words, is the predominant concern of unregenerate humanity. In fact, simple self-love perfectly depicts the diminished state of fallen, sinful human beings. For simple self-love is not inherently an inordinate or sinful concern, but only when humans suffer from the "absence of that influence of God's Spirit, whereby love to God" maintains the proper equilibrium in the soul. Minus "God's continual and immediate influence every moment," the natural inclination of simple self-love predominates, and the soul becomes "blind and dead" to "spiritual things" and loses those "holy inclinations" that are necessary to its "regular existence" (Y13:387–88).

To these depictions of self-love in positive and negative lights, Edwards adds a further depiction that is neutral and considers self-love as the mortar of friendships, communities, and society. In "Miscellanies" entry 473, Edwards writes that "many things arise" from "a principle of self-love," which Edwards here defines in terms of simple self-love—as "a love of pleasure and a love of being loved," or affirmation, "and a hatred of pain and an aversion to being hated." From self-love "may arise the affection of gratitude" toward another for favors and services one receives. This gratitude may generate other-regarding love in the form of "complacence" or "benevolence," and may even yield "strong desires of a person's friendship" seeking "union with him." There may even arise "many virtues" such as a "love of justice" and a "love of generosity" that tend "directly to men's good," for the perpetuation of these virtues contributes to the common good. All of these shades of self-love, Edwards emphasizes, are useful but not commendable. "'If Ye love them that love you, what reward have ye? Do not even the publicans the same?'" (Y13:514–16; Matt. 5:46).

Along with the positive and negative depictions of self-love, Edwards also refers to self-love in neutral terms in his writings on the Trinity. In the "Treatise," Edwards writes that "it is possible that natural men, without the addition of any further principle than they have by nature, may be affected with gratitude by some remarkable kindness of God to them, as that they should be so affected with some great act of kindness of a neighbor. A principle of self-love is all that is necessary to both." This is not to equate self-love with the love of God, for the two cannot be compared; "divine love is a principle distinct from self-love, and from all that arises from it." But "after a man is come to relish the sweetness of the supreme good there is in the nature of God, self-love may have a hand in an appetite after the enjoyment of that good. For self-love will necessarily make a man desire to enjoy that which is sweet to him" (H:50–51). One must only be clear about the difference between a simple desire for pleasure alone, and the simple desire for God that comes from one's conscious contact with God.

Commentators on Edwards have not failed to notice the connection between Edward's doctrine of the Trinity on his treatment of self-love. Nonetheless, these commentators attribute the different connotations Edwards assigns to self-love to an evolution in his attitude, from positive to neutral and even negative, as a result of experiences like the Great Awakening and his dialogue with the wider currents of moral theology and philosophy.[74] As a result, they miss the extent to which Edwards's psychological analogy is responsible for the complexity that surrounds Edwards's thinking on self-love.

As we will see in the ensuing chapters, self-love presents Edwards with an enduring problem that he examines from a number of perspectives. Part of this preoccupation with self-love is due to the conflicting accounts of self-love operating in his philosophical and theological milieu. But the central deficiency in self-love is clear. In a word, self-love cannot yield a total account of love for either God or human nature. As we have seen, even within the limitations of the psychological analogy, self-love is wanting. God's own self-love is essentially an act of self-transcendence—by conceiving of another, God exercises God's own self-actualization. Thus, God's love is a love of self, but it is also a love of another. For love is as much an interpersonal act of self-donation and mutuality as it is an intra-personal state of happiness or well-being one experiences through self-reflection. Hence, Edwards's need, as we will see in chapter 2, of another model of God's being and love that is social rather than psychological.

Self-love is not only inadequate as a depiction of the love of God, but it is similarly inadequate as a description of human love. Self-love is an irreplaceable part of human nature, but it is unable to disclose those aspects of human nature that are irreducibly interpersonal and social. Although self-love operates as a negative principle in unregenerate humanity and is most godlike when it evokes the love for another, self-love exists across the continuum of existence. The inadequacy of self-love therefore has nothing to do with whether or not it is essentially good, neutral, or negative, but with its inability to provide humanity with an unequivocal sense of divine love. Self-love, defined as either compounded self-love or as mere delight in those persons and things that make one happy, does not provide Edwards with any clearer notion of what it means to experience God in one's consciousness. For if self-love exists across the continuum of existence, then it can no longer identify the crucial difference that pertains to the regenerate and unregenerate. Nor can self-love provide a ladder in the chain of being through which persons may follow their apprehensions of beauty and their pursuit of happiness to God.

In the end, then, self-love is only able to make hazy distinctions on the horizon of the moral and religious life, for it provides only one part of Edwards's more developed spiritual anthropology and his fullest understanding of Christian love. As we proceed to examine Edwards's social analogy of the Trinity and his ethical writings, these points on the horizon will become clearer.

4. EDWARDS'S PSYCHOLOGICAL ANALOGY AND RECENT TRINITARIAN THEOLOGY

In recent Trinitarian theology, the psychological analogy has not fared well as a vehicle for theological reflection, primarily for two reasons. The first is the general trend of approaching the inner relations of the Trinity, commonly referred to as the "immanent" Trinity, through the scriptural witness of God's triune work of redemption, commonly referred to as the "economic" Trinity. Many attribute this shift to Karl Rahner, specifically to Rahner's principle that "the 'economic' Trinity is the 'immanent' Trinity and the 'immanent' Trinity is the 'economic' Trinity."[75] But Rahner's insight is anticipated and more extensively analyzed by Karl Barth. For Barth, God's triune witness is definitively manifested in the ministry, death, and resurrection of Jesus Christ, who is the revelation of God's perfect "Word" to humanity. Therefore, the triune God is properly understood as three dimensions of God's self-disclosure through Jesus Christ as "Revealer, Revelation, and Revealedness." Consequently, the psychological analogy represents an effort to articulate "a second and different root of the doctrine of the Trinity side by side with revelation," which leads to a distrust of "revelation in respect of its self-evidential force." The psychological analogy, then, at best should occupy a minor role as an ultimately unimportant outgrowth of the tradition of *vestigia trinitatis*. As such, it provides "an interesting, edifying, instructive, and helpful hint towards understanding the Christian doctrine," but one which is "supplementary and non-obligatory." Far more central is the economy of salvation revealed in Jesus Christ, who is "the true *vestigium trinitatis*" assumed "by God in revelation."[76]

The second reason the psychological analogy has fallen into theological disfavor is that it yields an inappropriate understanding of both God and humanity, particularly in the form it takes in Augustine's thought. Thus, where Barth considers the psychological analogy a pious irrelevancy, Colin Gunton views it as a main cause for the "crisis" in theology in Western Christianity. Not only does Augustine neglect the "economy of salvation," but his understanding of the "divine threeness" is so indebted to "Neoplatonic philosophy" that Augustine develops a view of God as "an unknown substance *supporting* the three persons rather than *being constituted* by their relatedness." As a result, "he is precluded from being able to make claims about the being of the particular persons, who, because they lack distinguishable identity tend to disappear into the all embracing oneness of God." Further, Augustine's development of the psychological analogy suffers from "individualism" and "intellectualism." Augustine's individualism is evident in his tendency to illustrate the nature of the Trinity not as "persons in relation" but as an "individual human mind." Augustine's intellectualism is evident in his aversion to "materiality," his portrayal of the "eternal Word" of God as an "abstract relation" rather than a "concrete person," and his tendency to "think of God as a kind of supermind." Consequently, Augustine's psychological analogy fails to continue the "revolution achieved by the Cappadocians," namely, the insight that the relations of the three persons of the Trinity constitute the "ontological foundation of the being of God," rather than "some*thing* other than the God made known in the economy."[77]

Admittedly, there is some truth in both of these criticisms. As we will see in the next chapter, one of the main benefits of the social analogy is that it provides a fuller depiction of God's triune economy of salvation than the psychological analogy alone can provide. The social analogy also provides an additional lens through which to conceive of persons in relation that uses communal acts of self-donation and mutuality as its model. But in light of what we have discussed in this chapter, these criticisms are not as applicable to Edwards's development of the psychological analogy as they are perhaps to Augustine's development of it. Although Edwards's psychological analogy cannot account for every facet of the economy of salvation, it certainly has economic implications. As we have seen, Edwards directly connects the psychological analogy to the experience of God in regeneration, and the psychological analogy informs Edwards's understanding of the missions of the Son and the Spirit. In addition, where Augustine's psychological analogy, on account of his adherence to substance metaphysics, might be appropriately described as individualistic and overly intellectual, these terms are not fairly applied to Edwards's proposal. As we have seen, Edwards's development of the psychological analogy views the relational nature of personhood as the fundamental ontological category. Moreover, through his idealism Edwards generates a conception of personhood that views plurality and relationality as equally fundamental as unity.

Indeed, despite the difficulties we have identified in the previous section concerning individuality, conscience, and self-love, the psychological analogy is essential to Edwards's theological ethics and underlies much of what he writes concerning the moral life. Edwards's vision of the moral life as a life of *theosis* and actual communication and participation in God—the "great and precious promise" of being "partakers of the divine nature" that Edwards reads in 2 Peter 1:4 and takes at face value—represents a major theme in his writings. For example, it recurs in the first sermon of *Charity and Its Fruits* and provides the basis for all that follows concerning the nature of the moral life:

> The Spirit of God is a spirit of love . . . and therefore when the Spirit of God enters into the soul, love enters. God is love, and he who has God dwelling in him by his Spirit will have love dwelling in him. The nature of the Holy Spirit is love; and it is by communicating himself, or his own nature, that the hearts of the saints are filled with love or charity. Hence the saints are said to be "partakers of the divine nature." (Y8:132)

Edwards's understanding of the personhood of God he develops through his psychological analogy will also continue to provide a central way to comprehend the personhood of human beings. Where traditional articulations of the psychological analogy have the soul providing only an equivocal image of God, Edwards's psychological analogy is nearly univocal. Indeed, at one point in his writings on the Trinity Edwards indicates that, rather than seeing the soul as an analogy for the relations in the Godhead, he believes exactly the opposite—the relations in the Godhead provide an analogy for the faculties of the soul. God is a being composed of "God, and his idea, and his love or delight," and there "is a resemblance to this threefold distinction in God a threefold distinction in a created

spirit, namely the spirit itself, and its understanding, and its will or inclination or love; and this indeed is all the real distinction there is in created
spirits" (Y13:367). In short, for Edwards, personhood is a concept one
develops "from above" rather than "from below." Edwards considers personhood a state of being, where each person is a settled "place" of identity
and self-consciousness that mirrors the dynamism of God, and the nature
and goal of Christian ethics is the recreation in human nature of personhood as it exists in the Godhead. The moral life is not something that pertains narrowly to our actions and obligations, but to our whole persons.
Normative in each act, in each decision, in each movement of the heart, is
not merely to pursue what is good or to do what is right, but to become
complete persons.

Finally, through his psychological analogy, Edwards conceives of a God
whom the saints experience as a complete and unified person, who invites
them into a personal relation through the act of self-communication. The
personhood of God is important to underscore, for other interpretations of
Edwards's theology rightly emphasize that Edwards articulates a "dispositional ontology" that sees God and God's relation to God's creation as a
"dynamic and never-ending activity of self-communication."[78] But standing behind this ontology of self-communication is an actual "self" that is
actualized through communion, who brings persons into ever-increasing
participation in the divine nature and gives the gifts of true personhood.
Edwards conceives of a triune God of "great and precious promises,"
whose nature is personal. In "Miscellanies" entry ff., Edwards asserts that
believers truly do "possess all things" by virtue of their union with Christ.
And by "possessing all things," he means that "God three in one, all that
he is, and all that he has, and all that he does, all that he had made or
done . . . are as much the Christian's as the money in his pocket, the clothes
he wears, or the house he dwells in, or the victuals he eats. . . . [I]t is all his"
(Y13:183–84).

2

"THE SOCIETY OR FAMILY OF THE THREE": TRINITARIAN AND MORAL REFLECTION IN EDWARDS'S SOCIAL ANALOGY

> TRINITY. It can no other way be accounted for, that in I John 1:3 our fellowship is said to be "with the Father, and with his Son Jesus Christ," and that it is not said also "with the Holy Ghost," but because our communion with them *consists* in our communion of the Holy Ghost with them. 'Tis in our partaking of the Holy Ghost that we have communion with the Father and Son and with Christians: this is the common excellency and delight in which they are [all] united; this is the bond of perfectness, by which they are one in the Father and the Son, as the Father is in the Son and the Son in the Father.
>
> Edwards, "Miscellanies" entry 376 (Y13:448)

We observed in chapter 1 that Edwards's psychological analogy represents more than a means to comprehend the processions within the Trinity. Through his psychological analogy, Edwards develops a vision of the moral life that views persons as fulfilled to the extent their self-consciousness participates in the self-consciousness of God. All true knowledge and love of God is a form of God's self-communication. Thus, to know ourselves fully and experience true love and happiness, we must know and love God. Two weaknesses, however, were also apparent in Edwards's construal of the psychological analogy and its correlative vision of the moral life. The first concerns its ability to account for interpersonal relations of love among the three persons of the Trinity. As a result of the psychological analogy's emphasis on self-reflection, the entry point for speaking of God's love in the Trinity is self-love. Edwards's understanding of self-love is generative, comprehensive, and, after a fashion, social. But even in this expansive form, self-love does not do justice to the love that the persons of the Trinity express in their acts of self-donation and mutuality. The second weakness is the inability of the psychological analogy to provide an account of the order and manifestations of God's triune creation and redemption of the world through the missions of the Son and Spirit. The primary focus of Edwards's psychological analogy is on the "immanent" Trinity, or the relations within the Godhead itself—also referred to as God's triune relations *in se*—and not on the "economic" Trinity, or God's triune relations outside of the Godhead—also referred to as God's triune relations *ad extra*.

Edwards therefore turns to explore the Trinity from the perspective of the "love and society" of the Godhead (H:64). Where the psychological analogy conceives of the Trinity in terms of self-consciousness, the social analogy conceives of the Trinity in terms of interpersonal participation. Consequently, the social analogy conceives of the love of God in terms of self-donation, mutuality, and inclusion. Love is transposed from a governing "disposition" within the mind of the Deity into an interpersonal relation that is diffusive and overflowing—a love that seeks the welfare of, and communion with, others. Further, as a result of this understanding of love, the social analogy provides the inner logic and dynamism behind Edwards's depiction of the nature and order of the "economy of the persons of the Trinity" and their respective roles in the "work" of "Redemption" (H:122; H:84). Through the social analogy, Edwards conceives of the cross of Christ and the indwelling of the Spirit as the principal moments in which God reveals and gives God's love to the world. Indeed, the prime motivation behind the incarnation of the Son and the indwelling of the Spirit is so that humanity can participate in the love of the Trinity. "Christ has brought it to pass," Edwards writes, "that those that the Father has given him should be as it were one society, one family, that his people should be in a sort admitted into that society of the three persons of the Godhead" (Y18:109). The "Spirit," in turn, "that proceeds from the Father and the Son is the bond of this union, as it is of all holy union between the Father and the Son, and between God and the creature, and between the creatures among themselves" (H:63–64).

Like the psychological analogy, Edwards's development of the social analogy occurs within a long tradition of inquiry. As we will see, anticipations of Edwards's understanding of the social analogy are evident in the thought of Augustine, Richard of St. Victor (d. 1173), Bonaventure (1217–1274), and Thomas Aquinas (d. 1274), among others. But where these figures generally limit the purview of the social analogy, in Edwards's thought the social analogy plays a distinctive role in the moral life, specifically in his vision of the church, and in his understanding of love, beauty, and society. The church represents the fullest embodiment of the Trinity and provides the primary locus for living the Christian life. At the same time, even preferential relations such as friendship and marriage provide essential ways to embody the benevolence of God. Finally, every society bears the imprint of, and participates in, the heavenly society of God to one degree or another; the love of the Trinity underlies sociality in any form.

Where the complexity of Edwards's development of the psychological analogy is due to the synthesis he creates out of different epistemologies operating in his milieu, the complexity of the social analogy is due to its multivalency. Conceptually, in Edwards's theological ethics the social analogy serves as the hub around which he connects the most daring and creative spokes of his thought. While the psychological analogy provides a metaphysical framework for Edwards's theological ethics, the social analogy provides his ethics with its dynamism and center of gravity. Nonetheless, as with his development of the psychological analogy, Edwards's social analogy is not free of tensions and difficulties that recur in his major writings.

1. THE SOCIAL ANALOGY

Edwards develops two arguments for the social analogy. The first concerns the nature of goodness and takes place in "Miscellanies" entries 96 and 97. In God "there must be more than a unity in infinite and eternal essence," Edwards writes, "otherwise the goodness of God can have no perfect exercise." Goodness is not a state of absolute sufficiency or simplicity, but an inclination to "delight in making another happy in the same proportion as it is happy itself" (Y13:263). For "no reasonable creature can be happy, we find, without society and communion, not only because he finds something in others that is not in himself, but because he delights to communicate himself to another." Further, goodness as it exists in God must be a "delight as much in communicating happiness to another as it is in enjoying of it himself," as well as "an inclination to communicate *all* his happiness," for in God happiness and the inclination to make another happy must be perfect (Y13:263–64). Therefore, God's Trinitarian relations must be the direct result of God's need to express goodness and happiness. "No absolutely perfect being can be without absolutely perfect goodness, and no being can be perfectly happy which has not the exercise of that which he perfectly inclines to exercise" (Y13:264). As an infinite being, God cannot "communicate all his goodness to a finite being." Hence, God "must have a perfect exercise of his goodness, and therefore must have the fellowship of a person equal to himself" (Y13:264). The "Father's begetting of the Son," then, "is a complete communication of his happiness, and so an eternal, adequate and infinite exercise of perfect goodness, that is completely equal to such an inclination in perfection" (Y13:272).[1]

In addition to this argument concerning goodness, Edwards develops an aesthetic argument in terms of "excellence" or "excellency" in his notebook "The Mind." Although everyone desires excellence in one form or another, nothing is more "without definition than excellency" (Y6:332). Clearly, "excellence, to put it in other words, is that which is beautiful and lovely," or that which exhibits symmetry and proportion (Y6:344). But it explains nothing to say, "all excellency is harmony, symmetry, or proportion," for the prior question is "why proportion is more excellent than disproportion." We find the clue to the nature of excellency, then, not in observing it wherever it exists, but where it exists in its most sublime form. The "highest excellency" is "the consent of spirits one to another," in "their mutual love one to another"(Y6:332, 337). Indeed, when viewed from the standpoint of relations of mutual love, all other instances of beauty and excellency appear as loving societies in miniature. The "beauty of figures and motions" is "very much the image of love in all the parts of society united by sweet consent and charity of heart." In "notes of music," the "notes are so conformed and have such proportion to one another that they seem to have respect one to another, as if they loved each other." Likewise, "the beauty of figures, as of flowers drawn with a pen, and the beauty of the body, and of the features of the face" all "appear like a society of so many perceiving beings, sweetly agreeing together" (Y6:380, 382). "I can conceive of no other reason why equality and proportion should be pleasing," Edwards confesses, "but only that it has the appearance of consent" (Y6:382). Edwards therefore concludes:

> One alone, without any reference to any more, cannot be excellent; for in such a case there can be no manner of relation no way, and therefore, no such thing as consent. Indeed, what we call "one" may be excellent, because of a consent of parts, or some consent of those in that being that are distinguished into a plurality some way or other. But in a being that is absolutely without plurality there cannot be excellency, for there can be no such thing as consent or agreement. (Y6:337)

As an infinite being, God must be infinitely excellent and the paradigm of all excellency. And if excellency is necessarily social, the source of God's excellency must be God's triune relations—that is, the "mutual love of the Father and the Son," from which proceeds "the personal Holy Spirit" (Y6:364). Thus, the "divine excellence" is God's "Spirit" or God's "infinite general love." Further, the excellence "cast abroad upon the whole earth and universe" derives from the Spirit's "general love and delight, everywhere diffused" (Y13:365). In other words, the Trinity must be the ultimate source of beauty and excellence in the created universe.

Edwards reiterates this aesthetic argument in "Miscellanies" entry 117, only now using love rather than excellency as his point of departure. "Love is certainly the perfection" as well as the "happiness of a spirit." Therefore, "God, doubtless, as he is infinitely perfect and happy, has infinite love." God's love cannot be merely "self-love," for "even the devils desire pleasure and are averse to pain." Rather, God's love must consist in mutual "consent." Accordingly, there must exist "an object from all eternity which God infinitely loves." And "that object which God infinitely loves must be infinitely and perfectly consenting and agreeable to him; but that which infinitely and perfectly agrees is the very same essence, for if it be different it don't infinitely consent" (Y13:283). "Again," Edwards concludes, "we have shown that one alone cannot be excellent, in as much as, in such case, there can be no consent." Therefore, "if God is excellent, there must be a plurality in God; otherwise, there can be no consent in him" (Y13:284).

Though implicit, Edwards's development of his social analogy mirrors the development of his psychological analogy. Recall that in developing the psychological analogy, Edwards conceives of unity in terms of a single mind's self-reflection, from which he further supposes relation and plurality. In contrast, his development of the social analogy begins with plurality, sociality, and relation. Thus, Edwards's argument from the nature of goodness presupposes that goodness requires others toward whom one can be good. Similarly, in his aesthetic argument, excellence describes a state of relation that exists as a result of mutual love and consent between a plurality of persons.

1.1. The Social Analogy and God's Triune Love

The most immediate implication Edwards draws from the social analogy concerns the love that exists in the immanent Trinity. As we have seen, the psychological analogy portrays the love of God as a form of self-love. Moreover, the primary form self-love takes in the psychological analogy is that of *complacence*. In the "Treatise," Edwards defines complacence as a "delight in the presence and possession of the beloved" (H:50). As such, Edwards reflects elsewhere, complacence is "not entirely distinct" from "simple" self-love, or the love of "one's own proper, single, and separate good." The "difference is only this, that self-love is a man's desire of or delight in his own happiness, and this love of complacence is a placing of his happiness, which he thus desires and delights in, in a particular object" (Y18:76). Accordingly, in the psychological analogy God "takes complacency in himself" in the "converse love of his own essence" (Y13:260, 257).

In contrast, the social analogy portrays love as the desire to make another happy. "That in John," Edwards writes in the "Essay," we read "God is love (I John 4:8), shows that there are more persons than one in the Deity." For "this supposes that there is an eternal and necessary object, because all love respects another, that is, the beloved. By love here the apostle certainly means something beside that which is called self-love: that is very improperly called love and is a thing of an exceeding diverse nature from the affection or virtue of love the apostle is speaking of" (H:100). In the "Treatise," Edwards defines such love as *benevolence*, as a "desire" for "the good of the beloved" that "rejoices" or is "glad" that the beloved is "happy" (H:49). Elsewhere, Edwards writes that the "love of benevolence to any person is an inclination to their good," or that it is a "delight that a man has in the good of another" and "the value that he sets upon that delight." Unlike complacence, then, benevolence finds "the good of another to be its good" (Y18:73–76).

Benevolence reveals, in a way that complacence does not, the other-regarding aspect of God's triune love. Nonetheless, Edwards refuses to subordinate the place of complacence within the Godhead, and by extension the place of complacence in the moral life. Within the relations of the Godhead, the reason for this symmetry is clear: To assign different values to the manifestations of the love of God would undermine the principle of divine perfection. God's love, in any form it takes, is not only perfectly expressed but perfectly appropriate and merited. Edwards writes in the "Treatise" that the love of benevolence "the Father and the Son have in each other is not to be distinguished from their love of complacence one in another, wherein love does most essentially consist" (H:64). In addition, as we noted in the previous chapter, Edwards holds that both complacence and benevolence derive from a form of self-love that rightfully motivates persons. Indeed, in the ordinary framework of desire, benevolence completes an already existing complacence. In the "Treatise," Edwards writes that complacence "comes before" benevolence and is the "foundation and reason for it" (H:49). Metaphysically speaking, this precedence is an undeniable part of what it means to be a person, either human or divine. Moreover, while benevolence desires the good of another, benevolent action is an expression of, and cause for, complacence. "God takes complacence in communicating felicity, and he made all things for this complacence" (Y13:256). Thus, Edwards writes in "Miscellanies" entry 1182 that when God "acts from benevolence" God "makes his happiness his ultimate end," for it is the "very nature of benevolence" to "have pleasure or happiness in the pleasure of another."[2]

In addition to emphasizing benevolence, the social analogy also magnifies the equality and mutuality of God's triune love, particularly as it is appropriated to the Spirit. As we have seen, in the psychological analogy Edwards defines the Spirit in terms of the dialogical "conversation" or relationship of "communion" that takes place in an integrated soul. The social analogy, however, enables Edwards to speak of communion in its proper sense as the union among persons who share a common life. Thus, the "happiness of the Deity, as all other true happiness, consists in love and society." Viewed from this perspective, the Holy Spirit is the "bond of union" created by the "Father loving the Son" and the "Son loving the Father" (H:64). The Spirit is an "infinitely holy energy" that "arises between the Father and the Son in mutually loving and delighting in each other, for their love and joy is mutual"; "this is the eternal and most perfect and essential act of the divine nature, wherein the Godhead acts to an infinite degree and in the most perfect manner possible" (H:108). In other words, through the social analogy, the Spirit no longer conforms to the limits of self-reflection, as the disposition that determines the personhood of God, and is transformed into an interpersonal relation of self-donation that is generated by the mutual love of the Father and the Son.

As with his development of the psychological analogy, Edwards does not assign to the Holy Spirit a discrete locus of communion in the relations of the Godhead. Nonetheless, on the basis of the Spirit's role as the principle of mutuality in the Godhead, Edwards stresses that each of the divine persons is "every way equal in the society or family of the three" (H:122–23). For viewed from the perspective of the social analogy, the Spirit represents the perfection of the Godhead—the Father's and Son's mutual participation in goodness, excellence, and love. As such, the Spirit occupies an ontological position that is as central as the other divine persons. The "honor of the Father and the Son is that they are infinitely happy and are the original and fountain of happiness," Edwards writes in the "Essay," but "the honor of the Holy Ghost is equal for He is infinite happiness and joy itself" (H:122).

Edwards further expounds on the theme of the Spirit's equality in a short essay titled "The Equality of the Persons of the Trinity." There he argues that the "equality" between the three divine persons is not only one of "essence," but also an equality of "personal glory." The "Father" is "the first person from whom the others proceed, and herein has a peculiar honor." The "Son has his peculiar glory" also, for "though the Son as it were depends on the Father, as the Father is as it were his principle," yet "the Father depends on him as his object." The Father, in other words, "through the Son receives infinite good." And the "Holy Ghost," while being "the last that proceeds from the other two," yet "has this peculiar dignity: that He is as it were the end of the other two, the good they enjoy, and the end of all procession." Existing alongside the personal glory of each member of the Trinity is a mutual subordination in the Godhead. For "in one sense the Father has superiority: He is the fountain of Deity, and He begets the Son." But "in another respect the Son has superiority, as He is the first and great object of divine love." And "in another respect the Holy Ghost, that is, divine love, has the superiority, as that is the principle that as it were reigns over the Godhead" and "wholly influences both the Father and the Son in all they do" (Y21:146–48). In other words, between the Father, Son, and Spirit, there is a relationship of self-donation and mutuality that distinguishes the Godhead as a society of equals.

1.2. The Social Analogy and the Economy of the Trinity

The next implication Edwards draws from the social analogy concerns the "economy of the persons of the Trinity" (H:122).[3] In using the word "economy," Edwards follows in part the normal terminology of Trinitarian reflection. "Economy" has its roots in the Greek word *oikonomia*, which translates as "dispensation," "administration," "plan," or "order of acting," and originally applied to the management of a household. But where the "economic" Trinity typically refers to the manifestations of God's activity *ad extra*, Edwards includes in his understanding of "economy" the interaction, deliberation, and organization of the persons of the Trinity *prior* to the work of redemption.[4]

Edwards's longest essay on the economic Trinity is found in "Miscellanies" entry 1062, titled "Observations concerning the Scripture Economy of the Trinity, and the Covenant of Redemption." Edwards wrote this entry to respond to "some,"[5] who held that "the second person of the Trinity consists *only in the relation He bears to the Father in his mediatorial character*; and that His generation or proceeding from the Father *as a Son*, consists only in His being appointed, constituted and authorized by the Father to the office of mediator" (H:93). In other words, Edwards intended to refute the heresy of *subordinationism*, that is, the belief that an ontological subordination exists between the persons of the Trinity, either of the Father over the Son, or of the Father and the Son over the Spirit.

Instead of his favored apologetic technique of refuting the logical underpinnings of a particular doctrine or position, Edwards offers a rival account of the "economy" of the divine persons that is more in line with orthodoxy. He acknowledges that the New Testament speaks of a "subordination of the persons of the Trinity, in their actings with respect to the creature" and "particularly in the affairs of man's redemption." Hence, "the Father acts as head of the Trinity, and the Son under Him, and the Holy Spirit under them both."[6] But an acceptable description of the processions of the Trinity must also hold "that the persons of the Trinity are not inferior one to another in glory and excellency of nature." While the Father has "priority of subsistence" as the font of Deity, "yet this is more properly called priority than superiority." For "there is dependence without inferiority" in the Godhead, because in the Son and the Spirit "everything in the Father is repeated, or expressed again, and that fully: so that there is properly no inferiority" (H:77).

The question, then, is not *whether* there is subordination between the persons of the Trinity, but *what kind*. Although no ontological subordination exists in the Trinity, Edwards does acknowledge an economic subordination. The "other persons' acting under the Father does not arise from any natural subjection." But it is "in some respect established by mutual free agreement, whereby the persons of the Trinity, of their own will, have as it were formed themselves into a society, for carrying out the great design of glorifying the Deity and communicating its fullness" (H:78). "This agreement," Edwards stresses, "is not to be looked upon as merely arbitrary, founded on nothing but the mere pleasure of the members of this society" (H:78). Rather, it is an arrangement that is founded in the nature of things and therefore "in itself fit, suitable, and beautiful." The "order of the acting of the persons of the Trinity" is agreeable to "the order of their subsisting." Just "as the Father is first in the order of subsisting," so "he should be first in the order of acting." The Father is "the fountain of all the acts of the Deity," and the "other two persons" act "from Him and in a dependence on Him" (H:79).

Edwards's account of the economic hierarchy of the Trinity frames his discussion of the missions of the Son and Spirit. From the beginning, before designating any actions or offices among the divine persons, the Father "acts as the head of the society of the Trinity, and in the capacity of supreme Lord"; the Father is the "one that sustains the dignity and maintains the rights of the Godhead" (H:81). Likewise, at the "ultimate consummation," after "the work of redemption is finished," the "economical order of the persons of the Trinity shall yet remain, whereby the Father acts as Head of the society and supreme Lord of all, and the Son and the Spirit shall be subject to Him." Following the Pauline vision of the resurrected Christ handing over the kingdom of God to the Father "so that God may be all in all,"[7] Edwards writes that "this economical order shall not only remain, but shall then and on that occasion become more visible and conspicuous" (H:82, 90).

The hierarchy established in the economic Trinity, however, does not determine the content of the Trinity's acting *ad extra*. The Father and Son establish an additional "covenant of redemption," a "particular new agreement" that concerns the "redeeming" of humankind (H:80). Like the decision to form the economic hierarchy, a basic condition of the covenant is that each party freely "consents" to its establishment. The Father, exercising his "right" as head of the Trinity, "chooses the person that shall be the Redeemer," namely, the Son. But the Son "acts as one wholly in his own right, as much as the Father," and is "not under subjection or prescription in His consenting to what is proposed to Him." This condition is necessary, because the affair of redemption, with its concomitant suffering and humiliation of the Son, is below the Son's dignity and economical character as God. As a result, the "Father has no right to prescribe to Him with regard to those things, unless as invested with a right by free covenant engagement with his Son" (H:85).

Therefore, the covenant of redemption represents a "new kind of subordination and mutual obligation" between the Father and the Son that incurs new obligations and reaps new rewards (H:86). In the covenant of redemption, the Son "puts himself under a new kind of subjection to the Father far below his economical station." The Son lays "aside the divine glory" and places himself under the Father's "Law" and becomes, after the manner of creatures, absolutely dependent on God for his being. At the same time, the "Father also comes under a new obligation to the Son." The Father promises the Son, in exchange for his "subjection and obedience," "a kind of rule and authority" that "does not belong to Him in His economical character"—that of "Lord and Judge of all" (H:88). The Father confers authority to the Son so that the Son may reign in glory until the time "when the work of redemption will be finished, and the ends of the covenant of redemption obtained." Then the Son, in return, will "resign the new dominion that He then is invested with over the universe," and "things will return to be administered by the Trinity . . . according to their economical order" (H:88–89).

On account of the precise nature of the shared obligations and rewards, Edwards holds that "the covenant of redemption is only between two persons of the Trinity," between "the Father and the Son." The fact, however, that the Holy Spirit is not "party" to the covenant does not mean that the Spirit is an uninvolved participant or passive observer. The Holy Spirit "is infinitely concerned in the affair of redemption, as well as the Father and the Son, and equally with them." For "the affair was," Edwards explains, "concerted among all the persons" of the Trinity, "and determined by the perfect consent of all." And "there was a joint agreement between them all" regarding the covenant, even if there was "not properly a covenant between them all" (H:93).

In addition to agreeing with the covenant, the Spirit plays an active role in the work of redemption. The Spirit is the greatest reward that the Father promises to the Son in exchange for his humiliation and suffering. "Not only does the Son, by virtue of the covenant of redemption, receive a new dignity of station," but the Son also receives "the dispensation and disposal of the Holy Spirit committed to Him." By doing so, the Father gives to the Son "His own divine, infinite treasure, to dispense of it as He pleased to the redeemed"; "He has made Him Lord of His house, and Lord of His treasures" (H:89). This reward, like all the rewards the Son receives when the Father exalts "Jesus Christ, God-man," are eventually resigned at the fulfillment of the covenant. The Son even relinquishes his authority over the Spirit, but the Spirit, at the Father's bidding, remains for eternity subordinate to the Son so that the Son as Jesus Christ continues to preside as the spiritual "husband, and vital head of the Church." Throughout the process of being given and received, the subordination of the Spirit involves "no humiliation or abasement" and therefore does not require any covenant agreement (H:91). All "that is new in this subjection" is that "where as by the economy of the Trinity the Spirit acts under the Son as God or as a divine person, He now acts in like manner under the same person in two natures united, or as God-man," who is "the husband and vital head of the Church." For the Spirit is "the inheritance that Christ, as God-man, purchased for Himself and His church, or for Christ mystical; and it was the inheritance that He, as God-man, received of the Father, at His ascension, for Himself and them" (H:90).

Clearly, Edwards's articulation of the covenant of redemption reflects his theological family of origin. Traditionally, in Puritan theology this doctrine holds that before the foundation of the world there was a transaction between the Father and the Son regarding the redemption of the elect. Although it engaged concepts from Trinitarian theology, its primary aim was to ensure, through the logic of contract, the individual "covenant of grace" between Christ and the believer; in the context of double predestination, the covenant of redemption assuaged lingering questions concerning the believer's personal salvation. Thus, the doctrine is fundamentally not so much an exercise in Trinitarian theology as it is an attempt to mitigate troubling implications of Puritan soteriology.[8]

In contrast, Edwards's appropriation of the covenant of redemption is expressly an exercise in Trinitarian reflection along the lines of the social analogy. Indeed, the social analogy serves as the motivation for God's tripersonal decision to assume the economic hierarchy as well as to seal the covenant of redemption. "God's determining to glorify himself and communicate Himself must be conceived of as flowing from God's nature," rather than any specific determination on the part of God concerning the order and method of redemption. "We must look upon God" from the standpoint of "the infinite fullness and goodness of his nature, as naturally disposed to cause the beams of his glory to shine forth, his goodness to flow forth." We must "conceive of God's natural inclination as being exercised before wisdom is set to work to find out a particular method to gratify that natural inclination." Therefore, the "particular constitution or covenant among the persons of the Trinity" must be "looked upon as in the order of nature after that disposition of the Godhead to glorify and communicate itself" (H:79).

Further, Edwards's articulation of the economic Trinity is notably egalitarian. Based on the "order of subsisting," the economic hierarchy is not established arbitrarily, or as the mere exercise of divine will. At the same time, however, the decision *is* "established by mutual free agreement" (H:78). To this relation of mutuality and freedom, the covenant of redemption adds a contract of interpersonal promises and subordination. Not only do the Father and Son come to a decision regarding the redemption of humanity as equals, but one of the conditions of the covenant is that the Father yields his own economical authority to the Son. The Son receives the authority to judge the world, yet in the end returns it to the Father when, as the glorified Christ, he receives the church as his spouse. The Spirit, while not party to the covenant, is integral to the community of "consent," concurs in the divine decision, and is the greatest "gift" and "treasure" that the Father gives the Son and that the Son gives to the church. And the Spirit personifies the self-giving love of God, through dwelling in the souls of humanity so that the church may be the "body" and the "spouse" of Christ.

1.3. The Social Analogy and the Missions of the Son and the Spirit

Given that his intent is to refute ontological subordinationism, Edwards spends little time in the "Observations" exploring the missions of the Son and the Spirit. As a result, the "Observations" leaves the impression that the specific missions of the Son and Spirit reveal little that is new in comparison to the general description of God's communicative nature. Indeed, in several "Miscellanies" entries, Edwards describes God's goodness and love as the independent attributes of a solitary being utterly distinct from the form they take within the triune missions. For example, in entry 314, Edwards writes that "God has in his own nature a propensity to communicate goodness and make happy," and "having created creatures for that end," God's love for the saints derives from an "absolute inclination to goodness in his own nature." Thus, God loves the saints "for nothing at all in them, and without being inclined thereto by any of their perfections natural or moral." As Edwards notes, such a vision of God's absolute benevolence reinforces the "free" nature of God's love for the saints (Y8:395). But it says little of the love that is expressed specifically through the cross of Christ or the indwelling of the Spirit.

In several other "Miscellanies" entries, however, Edwards explicitly connects the diffusive love of God revealed through the social analogy with the missions of the Son and the Spirit. Concerning the mission of the Son, Edwards writes in "Miscellanies" entries 327a and 483 that the Christ's redemptive love for humanity manifested on the cross represents the temporal manifestation of the mutual love and self-donation between the Father and the Son. "The infinite love which is from everlasting between the Father and the Son is the highest excellency and peculiar glory of the Deity." Accordingly, "God saw it therefore meet that there should be some bright and glorious manifestation made of it to creatures, which is done in the incarnation and death of the Son of God" (Y13:406). Therefore, "the divine excellency of Christ and the love of the Father to him, is the life and soul of all that Christ did and suffered in the work of redemption." God pardons the sins of humanity on the basis of the fact that, through the union of human nature with the "divine excellency of Jesus Christ," the "Father is willing for his sake to accept" those "that have deserved infinite ill at his hands." For Christ's love is "such a love as is sufficient to cause the lover to place himself in the beloved's stead for his sake in the most extreme case," namely, the "beloved's loss of his all, and his utter destruction." Through his love, Christ "sets a value upon the beloved's welfare or life equal" to the value he places on his own; therefore, "the lover by his love is thoroughly united to the beloved, and becomes as himself." Christ is a "lover that from love is not averse to bear the beloved's destruction," or "his own suffering equivalent to it," so that the beloved "may be free and may enjoy his welfare." Edwards therefore concludes that the "death of Christ was needful for our salvation" not merely because Christ had to make an "expiation for sin" and thereby satisfy what "justice requires," but because "the foundation of our acceptance is Christ's love for us." The death of Christ is more fundamentally the "manifestation" of God's "sufficient love to us," through which Christ, by "uniting himself with us," provides the means of "our being accepted as in him, and upon his account, and for the sake of his excellency and dearness to the Father" (Y13:525–27).

Consequently, the mission of the Son manifests two facets of the divine love. The first reinforces the distinction between the persons of the Trinity regarding the mutuality and particularity of the divine love expressed in the economy of salvation. "The infinite love of the Father to the Son is thereby manifested, in that for his sake he would forgive an infinite debt, would be reconciled with and receive into his favor" those "that had rebelled against him." The Father's love for the Son is also manifest in the Father's "exalting" of the Son to his position of "mediatorial glory." In return, "Christ showed his infinite love to the Father in his infinitely abasing himself for the vindicating of his authority and the honor of his majesty." Thus, "Christ infinitely laid himself out" so that the Father's "glory might be advanced" (Y13:406).

The second facet of the love of God the incarnation reveals is that God's desire to communicate happiness to the creature entails a willingness to experience loss for the sake of the beloved. Edwards writes in "Miscellanies" entry 197 that it is "exceeding congruous" for God, "a being of infinite goodness and love" to "give to the creature the highest sort of evidence or expression of love." The "highest sort of manifestation and evidence of love," however, "is expense for the beloved." For no matter how much "the lover gives or communicates to the beloved, yet if he is at no expense himself, there is not that high and noble expression of love, as if otherwise." Therefore, through the mission of the Son, God reveals a love that suffers on behalf of the beloved. "Now I can clearly and distinctly conceive, how the giving of Christ" is the perfect "expression of love, as the greatest expense in a lover." For the incarnation expresses the love of God "in a way that is exceeding noble and excellent, and agreeable to the glorious perfections of God" (Y13:336).

When he writes that the love of God manifested in the person of Christ is a suffering love, a love willing to experience expense, Edwards skates onto what traditionally represents the thin ice of Trinitarian reflection. A major problem in the history of Trinitarian theology concerns how it is that God, a being who is "impassible" or beyond suffering, is incarnate in the person of Jesus Christ, who suffers all things so that humanity may be reconciled to God. Particularly as the creedal affirmations concerning the Trinity developed in the fourth and fifth centuries, the principle of divine impassibility was broadly accepted as axiomatic. To suffer is not merely to experience limitation, constriction, or pain, but to be acted upon, to be beholden to another. In order for God to be God, God would have to be beyond the power of anything or anyone else. Yet the Scriptures amply attest to the fact that Jesus Christ, the Son of God, suffered. Hence, the question arises: In what way does God in Jesus Christ suffer? To protect itself from heresy, while at the same time remaining faithful to its proclamation of Jesus Christ as the Son and Logos of the Father, the church developed the doctrine that only the human nature of Christ suffered and that the divine nature did not. Cyril of Alexandria (d. 444) established this doctrine according to the principle of *communicatio idiomatum*, or "the communication of attributes." Briefly, this principle states that the attributes of the divine and human nature, while distinct, may be predicated of the same person, Jesus Christ, by virtue of the incarnation. This is so, on the basis of the argument that predications can be equally true of someone, even though they are distinct. Just as one can say of a scientist, for example, that "this is a mathematician" and "this is a physician," one may also say of Jesus Christ that "this is God" and "this is a human being."[9] Christ is both "true God" and "true man," for "each nature is agent of what is proper to it, working in fellowship with the other: the Word doing what belongs to the Word and the flesh what belongs to the flesh. The one shines forth in miracles, the other submits to the injuries."[10]

Although he is certainly aware of Cyril's predicational logic, Edwards does not use it to articulate his understanding of the two natures of Christ.[11] As we observed in chapter 1, Edwards believes that the idealism that he articulates in the course of his development of the psychological analogy largely cracks the code concerning the union of natures in Christ. From "what insight I have of the nature of minds," he writes in entry 184, "all difficulty is removed in believing what the Scripture declares about Spiritual unions—of the persons of the Trinity" as well as "of the two natures of Christ" (Y13:330). Thus, in entry 738, Edwards writes that "the *Logos*," in assuming the "humanity of Christ did not merely make use of his body as its organ, but its soul" by "such a communication with his understanding as we call identity of consciousness" (Y18:738). Further, Edwards specifically rejects the implications of the traditional position of the *communicatio idiomatum* concerning suffering. In entry 180, Edwards notes the inherent contradiction between our appreciation for the "death of Christ," which tends to "inflame our hearts with a sense of his love," and the traditional doctrine that "the *Logos* felt nothing, no pain, and suffered no disgrace, but 'twas the human nature that suffered." Faced with this antinomy, Edwards replies, "But I answer, the love the human nature had to mankind, and by which he was prompted to undergo so much, it had only by virtue of its union with the *Logos*; 'twas all derived from the love of the *Logos*, or else they would not be one person" (Y13:327).

Ultimately, Edwards's response to the problem of the suffering of the Logos is that it is *precisely through the benevolent love of God* that the Logos takes on suffering so that the person of Christ expresses the inner love of the Trinity. Edwards writes in entry 183 that Christ's love originates in the love the "Son of God" had for human nature: "Such was the love of the Son of God to the human nature, that he desired a most near and close union with it, something like the union in the persons of the Trinity, nearer than there can be between any two distinct beings." This love "moved him to make the human become one with him, and himself to be one of mankind that should represent all the rest, for Christ calls us brethren and is one of us" (Y13:329). And it is precisely *because Jesus Christ is the God-man* that he loves the world in the way he does. In "Miscellanies" entry z, Edwards grants that the "Love of God, as it is in the divine nature, is not a passion, is not a love as we feel." Yet "by the incarnation" Christ has "really become passionate to his own, so that he loves them with such a love as we have to him or to those we most dearly love." Therefore, the assumption of human nature by Christ not only effects the transformation of human nature, but also magnifies the love of the divine nature by translating the infinite love of God into temporal terms. The "passionate love of Christ, by virtue of the union with the divine nature, is in a sort infinite" (Y13:176–77). For this reason, Edwards writes in entry 213, "God's love to the saints may be said to be infinite," for "Christ, who is infinitely holy, loves the saints infinitely" (Y13:343).

The genius of his position is that, strictly speaking, Edwards articulates a conception of suffering that still honors the doctrine of divine impassibility. For through the incarnation, the Son voluntarily accepts the limitations inherent in human nature and is not beholden to any superior person or force.[12] Nor does Edwards hold that the Son resigns a measure of divinity in order to experience suffering, which would place the Logos in a class of its own, as the heresy of Arianism holds.[13] Rather, Edwards argues that the fullest revelation of the infinite love that is expressed in the social analogy is temporally manifest in the suffering love of Jesus Christ. For the social analogy defines love as an interpersonal act of self-donation, of communicating goodness to another, of giving oneself freely to another, of participating in another person's life and joy. Thus, it is only through the cross that one gains a vision of God's diffusive goodness and benevolence that is total and complete, for the cross represents the temporal manifestation of God's infinite triune love. In short, Edwards offers a new way to conceive of the *communicatio idiomatum*: The proper correlate to the love of the divine nature in the person of Christ is a human nature in which love is expressed in self-sacrifice.

Although Edwards spends considerable time exploring the nature of the divine love expressed through the mission of the Son, in other passages of the "Miscellanies" he argues that the mission of the Son and the mission of the Holy Spirit are interdependent: "Jesus was conceived by the power of the Holy Ghost, so that he was anointed as united to the divine nature when he first began to be" (Y13:530). The Spirit inspired Christ throughout his earthly ministry. It was the Spirit "by which not only Christ offered up himself in sacrifice, but it was the Spirit by which he did all he did when on earth." For it was "by the Spirit that he taught, it was by the Spirit that he cast out devils, it was by the Spirit that he wrought all his miracles." The "Spirit" resurrected "Christ in the grave" (Y13:531). Finally, the indwelling of the Spirit is the goal of the mission of the Son: "The great thing purchased by Jesus Christ for us is communion with God, which is only in having the Spirit" (Y13:466). The "Spirit is the sum of all that" the saints "have from the Father through the Son," and "all that the Father doth through the Mediator, to and for the saints, terminates in the Spirit." On the other hand, "all that by which they come to the Father through the Mediator is the Spirit, and all that they do or transact through the Son, towards God, is through the Spirit" (Y18:359).

In addition to playing an indispensable role in the mission of the Son, the cross reveals the love of the Spirit as much as it does the love of the Father and the Son. Thus, "if it be said that more glory belongs to the Father and the Son because they manifested a more wonderful love, the Father in giving his Son infinitely dear to him, the Son in laying down his life; yet let it be considered that the Holy Ghost *is* that wonderful love." The Father and the Son, "by showing the astonishing greatness of their love and grace" glorify "that love and grace, who is the Holy Spirit." Not only does the Spirit personify "God's giving of his dear Son, and the Son's suffering so much," but these manifestations demonstrate "the worth of the Holy Ghost, that the Father should give his Son, and the Son pay so great a price that the Holy Spirit might be purchased" (Y13:466–67).

In several "Miscellanies" entries, Edwards also describes the Spirit's own distinct ministry as the common bond that unites the saints to God and to each other. Edwards identifies three biblical images that particularly signify the Spirit's mission as "being shed forth" and "poured out" (H:115–16). The first is the dove. In "Miscellanies" entry 98 Edwards notes that the image of the dove illustrates well how "the Holy Spirit is nothing but the infinite love and delight of God." The dove is a "symbol of love," a "bird beyond all other irrational animals in the world" that "is remarkable for its love to its mate, both in expressions of it by billing together and the like while together, and for its mourning for the loss of its correlate." Under "this representation," the "Holy Spirit descended on Christ at his baptism, signifying the infinite love" between "the Father and Son, which is further illustrated by the voice which came with the dove, 'this is my beloved Son, in whom I am well pleased'" (Matt. 3:17). And "when Christ says to his Father (John 17:26) that he would declare his name to his disciples, 'that the love wherewith thou hast loved me may be in them,' I can understand nothing else" but "that the Holy Spirit might be in them and dwell in them, which is the love of the Father to the Son" (Y13:265).

The second image is oil. In the Scriptures, oil "is often used as a type of the Holy Ghost and may well represent divine love from its soft, flowing, and diffusive nature," Edwards writes in the "Essay." Like the dove, there is a natural propriety to this signification: "oil is from the olive tree which was of old used to betoken love, peace, and friendship." The olive branch held in the dove's mouth when it returned to Noah in Genesis 8:11 "was a token for and sign of God's love and favor, after so terrible a manifestation of his displeasure as the deluge." Finally, the "holy anointing oil, the principle type of the Holy Ghost, represents the divine love and delight" (H:114–15). The oil poured "upon Aaron's head" in Psalm 133, Edwards writes in "Miscellanies" entry 330, signifies how "the Spirit which Christ our head has without measure is communicated to his church and people" (Y13:409).

The third image is "the river of the water of life" mentioned in the Gospel of John (7:38–9) and Revelation (22:1). This river, Edwards notes in entries 334 and 336, "proceeds from the throne of the Father and the Son" and "is called the 'river of God's pleasures' (Ps. 36:8)," in order to confirm "that the Holy Ghost is the infinite delight and pleasure of God." As with oil and the dove, it represents the "perfectly active flowing affection, holy love of God" that is "poured out and shed forth" and "shed abroad in our hearts" (Y13:411–12). The image also helps retrieve the Pauline promise that the saints "drink into one Spirit" (1 Cor. 12:13) and are "to be filled with all the fullness of God" (Eph. 3:19). "For the way we know the love of Christ is by having that love dwelling in us" which "consists in the Holy Spirit." In this way, the saints "have communion or fellowship" with the Father and Son through partaking "of their good in their fullness in union and society with them" (H:65).

Throughout his depiction of the missions of the Son and the Spirit, Edwards holds that each acts in concert with the other divine persons in the work of redemption. Traditionally in Western theology, articulations of the operations of the Son and Spirit follow Augustine's doctrine of appropriations, which asserts that the works of the Trinity in the economy are indivisible (*opera trinitatis ad extra indivisa sunt*), such that, strictly speaking, the Trinity creates, the Trinity redeems, the Trinity sanctifies.[14] So important did maintaining the unity between the operations of the Trinity seem to Thomas that he went so far as to assert that any one person of the Trinity could have become incarnate or indwell human beings.[15] The Son's work of incarnation and the Spirit's work of sanctification are merely activities arbitrarily appropriated by the Godhead to a given person.[16]

Edwards argues, however, that while the missions of the Son and the Spirit follow "one design," they are distinct works by distinct persons in which "all the members of it" are "mutually dependent and subservient" and "help one another and mutually forward each other's ends" (Y18:191). Hence, as "the persons of the Trinity are equal among themselves, so there seems to be an exact equality in each person's concern in the work of redemption, and in our concern with them in that great affair; and the glory of it equally belongs to each of them." There is, in other words, a necessary self-differentiation that manifests itself in the missions of the Son and the Spirit. The "benefits and blessedness of redemption are wholly and entirely from each of them"; "it is wholly originally from the Father; the Son is the medium of it all; the Holy Ghost immediately possesses us of it all, or rather is the sum of it all." God "is he of whom the purchase is made, God is the purchase and the price, and God is the thing purchased: God is the Alpha and the Omega in this work" (Y13:466–67).

1.4. The Social Analogy and Ecclesiology

Finally, the social analogy shapes Edwards's ecclesiology. As we have seen, in the "Observations" Edwards views the union between Christ and the church as the end of the covenant of redemption, as the moment when "God may be all in all" (H:82). Edwards uses two biblical images to describe this union: Christ is the "husband and vital head of the church" (H:91). The former refers to the spousal image of Christ as the "husband" and the church as his "bride" that appears at several points in the New Testament, examples of which are Matthew 9:15, John 3:29, Ephesians 5:30–31, and Revelation 21:2. The latter refers to the somatic image of Christ as the "head" and believers as his "body" that appears in the Pauline literature, examples of which are 1 Corinthians 12:12–31 and Romans 12:4–8.

Of these two images, the spousal image is more central to the connection Edwards draws between the church and the economic Trinity. In "Miscellanies" entry 103 Edwards writes that "heaven and earth were created that the Son of God might be complete in a spouse." Accordingly, the church is the "spouse of the Son of God, the bride, the Lamb's wife, the completeness of him who filleth all in all" and "that for which all the universe was made" (Y13:271–72). The church, then, was central to God's triune deliberations before the foundation of the world and plays an integral role in the fulfillment of the economy of salvation. "There was," Edwards writes in entry 741, "an eternal society or family in the Godhead, in the Trinity of persons," and "it seems to be God's design to admit the church into the divine family as his son's wife" (Y18:367).

The profound nature of this ecclesiology is most apparent in "Miscellanies" entry 702, where Edwards explores the *Hexaemeron*—the biblical account of the creation of the universe in six days (Gen. 1:1–31; 2:18–24)—to argue that the church was evident "in the beginning." As the Word of God, the mission of the Son is creative as well as redemptive. "God made the world by Jesus Christ," for God brings creation into being by speaking the Word (Gen. 1:3). The work of creation therefore is "properly the work of the Son" and "belongs to him" (Y18:289). Moreover, throughout the work of creation, including even the "creation of the angels," the Father maintained "an eye to the Son of God" and "his mediatorial kingdom." Hence, "the state and circumstances of the world of mankind shadow forth" the work of redemption and "point to them in many ways" (Y18:284).

God's redemption through Christ, then, is not only implicit in the created order, but the creation narratives themselves foreshadow the redemption of the world, both in the particular context of an individual soul's sanctification and in the universal context of the church's glorification. In the first creation narrative, the six-day, progressive nature of the first creation is analogous to the new creation wrought by Christ through the indwelling of the Spirit (Gen. 1:1–2:3). For as there are six days of creation until "the seventh day, the day of holy rest," so the work of redemption in individual souls and in the church is a progressive evolution toward wholeness, completeness, and peace. The "work of grace" in the soul "is gradually carried on, till it is brought to its perfection without any remains of sin or misery in the heavenly rest and eternal Sabbath." Likewise, the "work of redemption is gradually carried on in the world, till the church shall be brought to the most perfect and glorious and happy state on earth, to a state of rest" (Y18:285).

In the second creation narrative (Gen. 1:26–27; 2:4–25), Edwards writes that "the creation of man in particular seems to have been in such a manner, as it was, that it might shadow the manner of his greater creation, viz. his new creation." The creation of humanity is accompanied by a "consultation of the persons of the Trinity about it, as there was about redemption." This, Edwards believes, is the proper interpretation of the divine discourse that precedes the decision to create humanity "in our image, according to our likeness" (1:26). Further, the figure of Adam is a "type," or foreshadowing, of Christ. Christ achieves and fulfills for humanity what Adam lost—the blessedness of communion with God. Indeed, the "blessedness that Adam would have received if he had stood for himself and his posterity was but a type of the blessedness that Christ obtained for himself and his seed by his obedience." The nature of this blessedness is evident in the union of human nature and the divine nature of Christ. "The man Christ Jesus being made in union with the divine nature" experienced "in a sense the Godhead communicated to him" (Y18:287). The incarnation of the Word, in other words, represents the realization of the divine participation in humanity, as well as the fulfillment of humanity's aspiration to participate in the life and love of God. Jesus Christ is the living promise of "the transcendent advancement of men in their union with God, whereby they partake of the beauty, life, honor and joy of the eternal Son of God; and so are made as gods by communion of his Spirit, whereby they are partakers of the divine nature" (Y18:288).

Edwards's comparison between Adam and Christ recalls that of Irenaeus of Lyon (130–200), specifically the doctrine of recapitulation or *anakephalaiosis*, that is, that God's plan for humanity is recapitulated in Christ, who is the "concluding summary" of God's work in creation, in such a way that the end restates the beginning. Thus, Irenaeus writes that "the Word, fashioner of all, preformed in Adam the future divine plan for humanity around the Son of God."[17] Edwards goes beyond Irenaeus, however, when he insists on an explicitly ecclesiological interpretation of the creation narratives, specifically the marriage between Adam and Eve as a type of Christ's relation to the church. For Irenaeus, Eve foreshadows the Virgin Mary; in particular, Mary fulfills Eve's frustrated virginity.[18] In contrast, Edwards believes that the marriage of Adam and Eve itself reveals an important teaching concerning the church. As Eve came from Adam's rib, "even from near his heart, bone of bone, and flesh of his flesh," so Christ is "he out of whom the church is, as it were, taken, from his transcendent love and by the deep sleep of death." And as Adam is the "natural father" and "federal head" of humanity, so Christ is the "spiritual father" and "federal head of all his seed," that is, the church. Further, "when God created man, he created them male and female and united them in marriage." Marriage is one of the few blessings that precedes and survives the fall, for "it was even before the fall that God said, 'A man shall leave his father and mother, and shall cleave to his wife: and they shall be one flesh,'" which is a sign that the intimacy in marriage "is a mystery or type representing the relation that there is between Christ and his church" (Y18:288–89).

Where the comparison of Adam and Christ reveals the "transcendent advancement of men in their union with God," the marriage of Adam and Eve reveals the "transcendent love" of Christ for his church, which finds its "greatest manifestation" in the Father "sending his only begotten Son into the world to die" for the church (Y18:299). Nonetheless, the foundation of this self-sacrificial love is the communication of the mutual love and happiness of the Trinity itself. Accordingly, the "end of the creation of God was to provide a spouse for his Son Jesus Christ that might enjoy him and on whom he might pour forth his love." And "the end of all things in providence are to make way for the exceeding expressions of Christ's love to his spouse and for her exceeding close and intimate union with, and high and glorious enjoyment of, him" (Y18:289). Thus, the "last thing and the issue of all things is the marriage of the Lamb. And the wedding day is the last day, the day of judgment, or rather that will be the beginning of it. The wedding feast will be eternal; and the love and joys, the songs, entertainments and glories of the wedding never will be ended. It will be an everlasting wedding day" (Y18:298).

Although the spousal image is central in the "Miscellanies" entries we have examined, the somatic image provides a different perspective from which to view this connection in new light. As we have just seen, Edwards weaves the somatic image into his discussion of the eternal wedding of the church, particularly in the typological interplay between Adam and Christ. In other entries, Edwards places the somatic image at the center in order to highlight new teaching. Thus, to the seminal vision of the church being implicit in creation, in "Miscellanies" entry 371 Edwards adds a final vision of the church's fulfillment in the "resurrection," when both the bodies of believers and the church as the body of Christ will be "perfectly free from sin and sorrow." In the resurrection, Edwards writes in entry 371, the souls of the saints will no longer be bound to bodies that suffer from sin and death, but to "glorious bodies, bodies perfectly fitted for the uses of a holy glorified soul." Similarly, the church as the body of Christ will also be "perfect" and "complete," with "all the parts of it in a perfect state, all the parts of it together, no longer mixed with ungodly men." Then "the church will exceedingly rejoice." The church is now only "growing and preparing for that state," for "all things" that "are now done in the world are but preparations for it" (Y13:443).

Jesus Christ, the "Mediator" and "God-man," Edwards continues in entry 736, "will to all eternity continue the medium of communication between God and the saints" so that "the whole family in heaven, and on earth, good angels, and redeemed men, are named of Christ." In Christ "all the members of this family are united, and in him they forever abide." Through "his Spirit," Christ "is eternal head of the whole family," and "there is a strict union and conjunction, all having one heavenly necessary bond of union, as one of the ancient writers [i.e., John Chrysostom (347–407)] has expressed it" (Y18:363).[19] The nature of this "union" is an eternal image of Jesus' meeting with his disciples after the resurrection: "When the saints get to heaven, they shall not merely see Christ," Edwards writes in entry 571, but "Christ will most freely and intimately converse with them as friends and brethren." For in heaven, "Christ neither will call his disciples servants, but friends," as he did "here on earth." Therefore, "though Christ be in a state of exaltation at the right hand of God," appearing in the "height of glory, yet this won't hinder his conversing with his saints in a most familiar and intimate manner" (Y18:107–8). For the "glory" of Christ is "not as a private person only," but consists in "the greatest nearness, intimacy, and communion of good," which the saints have with "their representative" and "brother" Christ (Y18:108–9). This intimacy and communion the saints have with Christ includes the other divine persons: "Christ has brought it to pass, that those that the Father has given him should be brought into the household of God, that he and his Father and they should be as it were one society, one family; that his people should be in a sort admitted into that society of the three persons in the Godhead" (Y18:110).

1.5. The Social Analogy and Western Christian Thought

Like the psychological analogy, Edwards's development of the social analogy occurs within a significant tradition of inquiry. The social analogy originates in the thought of the Cappadocians—Basil (330–379), Gregory of Nyssa (330–395), and Gregory of Nazianzus (329–389)—who argued that God's triunity must be conceived as a relation of three equal persons (*hypostases*) rather than as an undivided essence (*ousia*).[20] Within Western Christian thought, the social analogy provides an additional lens through which to envision the relations between the divine persons, as well as the significance these relations have for human bonds and communities. In general, however, Western theologians were also aware of significant problems inherent in the social analogy, and therefore most often subordinated it to the psychological analogy.

The social analogy initially appears in Augustine's *The Trinity*. Although Augustine prefers the psychological analogy, when he discusses the relation between the economic Trinity and the church he argues that a moral or spiritual unity flows from the substantial unity of the Trinity in the form of "friendship" or "harmony of wills." In heaven, "the will of God presides, as in his house or his temple, over the spirits who are joined together in the highest concord and friendship, fused indeed into one will by a kind of spiritual fire of charity."[21] Contemplating Jesus' prayer, "that they may be one as we are one" (John 17:22), he writes, "as Father and Son are one not only by equality of substance, but identity of will," the church, "for whom the Son is the mediator with God," should also "be bound in the fellowship of the same love."[22] Friendship also describes the specific mission of the Son in the redemption of the world. The "Son of God did not disdain to become our friend in the companionship of death," for "our redeemer said himself, 'greater love has no one than to lay down his life for his friends' (John 15:13)."[23] And the Son, incarnate as Jesus Christ, represents the diffusive "outflow of the glory of almighty God" like "light flowing from light."[24] Aspects of the social analogy also appear when Augustine discusses the procession of the Spirit from both the Father and Son. The Spirit is the mutual "gift" or love that the Father and Son give to each other. The "Holy Spirit is a kind of inexpressible communion or fellowship of Father and Son." Indeed, the name "Holy Spirit" designates not only the third person of the Trinity, but also indicates what is common to both Father and Son, for "both Father and Son are holy and both Father and Son are spirit." And "to signify the communion of them both by a name that applies to them both, the gift of both is called the Holy Spirit."[25] Regarding its mission, the Holy Spirit is "the gift of God who is love," for "the love which is from God, and is God, is distinctively the Holy Spirit; through him the charity of God is poured out in our hearts, and through it the whole triad dwells in us."[26]

Nonetheless, while Augustine allows that the social analogy discloses aspects of the economic Trinity, he is reluctant to use the social analogy to explore the immanent Trinity. The external and complex nature of social relations such as friendship undermines the principle of divine unity understood in terms of simplicity. As we observed in chapter 1, in his development of the psychological analogy and his appropriation of substance metaphysics, Augustine excludes any accidental or relative terms for God, as these imply change or modification of God's infinite, immutable essence. Excluded then is "everything that can be lost or diminished," such as "sizes and qualities, and whatever is said with reference to something else like friendships, proximities, subordinations, likenesses, equalities," as well as "positions, possessions, places, times, doings, and undergoings."[27] Hence, the Trinitarian relations implied by the names "Father" and "Son" do "not have the same sort of reference to each other as friends or neighbors."[28] Although he strains to say exactly what sort of relation applies to the divine persons, he is clear that the relations produced by "communion or fellowship" do not.

Further, Augustine often shies away from applying the words "communion" or "fellowship" unequivocally to the love of the Trinity in either its economic or immanent form, for he considers the love of friendship a peculiarly human love. Augustine's understanding of friendship follows that of classical thought: Friendship (*philia*) is a love of equals united in a common pursuit, purpose, end, or good.[29] Such a love, however, is not the same as the love of God that Augustine calls charity (*caritas*), a love of complete devotion to God, out of which one loves all others as neighbors rather than friends.[30] "You only love your friend truly, after all," Augustine writes in a sermon, "when you love God in your friend, either because he is in him, or in order that he may be in him."[31] Accordingly, the shape of our loves in this world should resemble a pilgrimage that keeps the enjoyment of the final destination of God in mind and is not distracted by the pleasant sights along the way.[32] Only those who love their neighbors through the love of charity love rightly; all other loves are at best distorted images of *caritas*. This reservation regarding the love of friendship recurs in *The Trinity*, where Augustine insists that friendship not be strictly attributed to the Trinity, for the love of God is not a love of friendship. The "Holy Spirit is something common to the Father and the Son, whatever it is, or is their very commonness or communion, consubstantial and coeternal. Call this friendship, if it helps, but a better word is charity."[33]

With little modification, Augustine's preference for the psychological analogy and ambivalence toward the social analogy resonates throughout Western Trinitarian theology. One notable departure is an interpretation developed by Richard of St. Victor (d. 1173) and refined by Bonaventure (1217–1274). In book 3 of *The Trinity*, Richard offers an account of the Trinity based on the diffusive nature of goodness and love, which he draws from an axiom of Pseudo-Dionysius the Areopagite (c. 500) that goodness is self-diffusive (*bonum est diffusivum sui*).[34] If God is perfectly good and loving, there must be "another" to whom these attributes are directed and shared, for the "perfection of one person requires fellowship with another."[35] Furthermore, through the communion between Father and Son, the organic unity of the relation of divine goodness and love represented by the Holy Spirit also has ontic status. For goodness and love are diffusive and social, and it is the nature of both to transcend and overflow. Hence, Richard's understanding of the social analogy is not binary, but ternary, and the "consummation of true and supreme goodness cannot subsist without completion of the Trinity."[36] All the same, the social analogy does not hold a central position in Richard's theology. Richard does not use it to cast light on his understanding of human persons and society, and he retains the Augustinian understanding of unity in terms of simplicity of substance.[37]

In three works, Bonaventure converts Richard's argument into an overarching metaphysics that is based on the diffusive nature of goodness.[38] For Bonaventure, the communicative nature of goodness does not undermine divine simplicity; in fact, it is precisely because of God's simplicity that the divine "essence is communicable and able to be in several." Hence, God's triune plurality "is not repugnant to simplicity but rather to solitude." In his depiction of the processions within the immanent Trinity, it is the Father's self-diffusive goodness which stands as primary—"there is in the Father a fontal plenitude for all emanations." The Son and Spirit are the expressions of the Father's perfect nature and will. The Son represents the Father's perfect contemplation of the Father's nature; as the Logos, the Son is "conceived by the force of intelligence contemplating itself." The Spirit represents the perfect procession of the Father's will—love is the "perfection of delight and union and rectitude from mutuality." Hence, "the person proceeding by way of love must proceed by way of mutual love."[39] Nonetheless, despite his vision of the diffusive goodness of God, Bonaventure observes the boundaries of the psychological analogy and avoids applying the social analogy per se to the economic Trinity or to the interpersonal relations of the church. One finds vestiges of the Trinity throughout creation, Bonaventure allows, but the focus of Trinitarian reflection is personal contemplation rather than the church. All knowledge ultimately is concerned with, and bears some trace of, the Trinity. Consequently there are three stages of spiritual perfection, he writes in *The Triple Way*: purgation, illumination, and perfective union. These three stages represent different points at which the soul sloughs off its natural, sensual desires and ecstatically cleaves to God.[40]

However intriguing, Thomas Aquinas in the *Summa Theologiae* dismisses even the modest proposals of Richard and Bonaventure. Thomas rejects the argument that the Trinity is a plurality of persons because "there can be no joyful possession of any good without a companion." Such an argument, Thomas believes, overlooks the difference between the goodness that pertains to God's perfection and the interpersonal goodness that pertains to humans. The latter sense of goodness only "applies when we do not find perfect goodness in one person, and so need for perfect enjoyment the good of having a companion."[41] Therefore, one cannot use the latter to describe the goodness of God without threatening the principles of divine perfection and sufficiency. Accordingly, though he continues to speak of the Spirit as "Love" and "Gift," Thomas does not employ the social analogy in his explication of the immanent Trinity, preferring instead the psychological analogy.[42] Thomas also circumscribes the extent to which the meaning of the term "person" (*persona*) can be "used in exactly the same sense of God as of creatures." Within the context of God's triune relations, Thomas is careful to note that he uses the term "person" in a strictly analogical sense, as a way to identify that there are three "subsisting beings in the divine nature," whose relations are "incommunicable" with regard to human nature.[43]

Thomas does, however, use the love of friendship to describe how the missions of the Son and the Spirit shape the Christian life. Thomas describes sin as "lost grace and other gifts of God's friendship,"[44] and it is in the interest of restoring friendship that Christ redeems humanity: "By suffering in order to save us, Christ conferred benefits on us over and above the mere escaping from sin. First, because now we realize how much God loves us, and now we can be roused to love him in return; this friendship is the heart of spiritual health."[45] Therefore, the nature of the Christian life is one of friendship with God through the indwelling of the Spirit.

Where Augustine sees the love of friendship and *caritas* as contradictory, Thomas describes "charity" as "our friendship for God arising from our sharing in eternal happiness."[46] Returning to the classical definition of friendship as "mutual loving" that is "based on something in common," Thomas states that through charity "there is a sharing of man with God" through God "sharing his happiness with us, and it is on this that friendship is based."[47]

Among Edwards's immediate theological predecessors, the social analogy recurs in *Blessed Unions* (1694), a series of sermons preached by Cotton Mather (1663–1728) celebrating an ecumenical agreement between Congregationalists and Presbyterians. When he speaks of the immanent Trinity, Mather follows the psychological analogy construed within its traditional context of substance metaphysics. "God cannot be infinitely and absolutely perfect without the perception of himself," Mather writes. This self-perception of God as "the Alsufficient Good" expresses "an immense Joy and Love." Hence, "God has a *substantial* representation of Himself within Himself, and a *substantial* satisfaction thereupon." The "Father is the Fountain of the Deity, the Son is the Express Image," and the "Holy Ghost is the wonderful Joy and Love, which God has within himself by the grateful perception which the Father and the Son eternally have of one another." Compared to this "essential union," the union creatures have to God is "modal," a mere "resemblance to this."[48]

When Mather turns to the economic Trinity, his reserve partially evaporates, and he offers an ecclesiology that sees the relations between the persons of the Trinity as the source and pattern of the unity that should govern the church. The "whole undivided, adorable Trinity is concerned in the union which believers have with Jesus Christ." For through their union with Christ, believers "become temples for the whole Trinity; there is an ineffable concurrence of all Three persons of the Godhead, therein to take possession of us."[49] Mather emphasizes the "intimate union" believers have with Christ as members of his "mystical body," and he bids his listeners to prepare their hearts as if they were disciples who have been asked to prepare a room "for the entertainment of the Blessed Jesus."[50] But more importantly, the same "blessed union" believers have in Christ is to be the source of the union that "through Him" they "have with one another." It is "not enough that we have an invisible union with all the saints of God," Mather argues, "but we must have a visible union too."[51] Among believers, there must be union in profession, affection, and sympathy. For "our union with one another must carry a resemblance to the union between the Father and the Son in the Eternal Godhead: This is the pattern for our union given here, 'As thou, Father, art in me, and I in thee'" (John 17:21).[52] Therefore, the union of the church "must be a *spiritual* union, and not founded on civil or natural matters only. Again it must be an *orderly* union; there must be the distinction of all persons preserved entire." Finally, "our unity must give us a near perception of one another's cares, and our unity must fill us with joy in, and love to, one another. We must after a sort find in one another our very selves, and call and count each other another self. We must be concerned with one another, as if our very self were bound up in one another."[53]

These representative theologians illustrate the ambivalence of the Western Christian tradition's engagement with the social analogy. On one hand, the social analogy provides a way to articulate how the interpersonal relations of the Godhead form a community in which the diffusive nature of goodness and love find perfect expression both within the Godhead and throughout existence. In addition, the social analogy provides a context for seeing how the interpersonal relations we experience in this world, specifically those we encounter in the church, reflect the goodness and love that exists between the persons of the Godhead. But on the other hand, each of the theologians we have examined is aware of certain tensions surrounding the social analogy, and is reluctant to place it at the center of his Trinitarian reflection. Much of this reluctance stems from the conviction that the psychological analogy better safeguards God's unity. In addition, when aspects of the social analogy are used to explore the economic Trinity, each of the theologians we have examined seeks to reinforce the ways in which the interpersonal relations of the Trinity *in se* are fundamentally different from their expression in human relations *ad extra*. Even Bonaventure, who offers the most unambiguous embrace of the social analogy of the theologians we have examined, emphasizes this difference. Although Bonaventure argues that the social analogy provides an important way to apprehend the processions of the immanent Trinity, in his exposition of the economic Trinity his focus is on the reflective soul rather than on interpersonal love.[54]

In contrast, Edwards views the social analogy with appreciation rather than ambivalence. The primary reason he does so is on account of his distinctive understanding of the psychological analogy. As we observed in chapter 1, Edwards conceives of the unity of God in terms of mutual participation in an identical idea rather than as an undifferentiated substance. As a result, the complexity of self-communication in social relations poses no inherent threat to the principle of divine simplicity, as it does for most of the theologians we have examined. Indeed, because Edwards's psychological analogy views communion in the form of dialogical self-consciousness as integral to personhood, Edwards has a more open stance regarding the social analogy's interpersonal view of communion. In the psychological analogy, personhood is not an individualistic concept, for we are realized as persons to the extent we live in relations of identity, mutuality, contemplation, and affection. Thus, implicit in Edwards's psychological analogy is the belief that the love and goodness of God is essentially communal and interpersonal. In the psychological analogy, love is depicted as the governing disposition of an entity, such that to be is to be in love.

Consequently, Edwards's social analogy provides his psychological analogy with needed amplification of this theme of love. In the social analogy, God's love is not viewed through the lens of self-reflection, but in social relations of mutual self-communication, self-donation, and benevolence. For in the final analysis, love is a reality that exists primarily through the complete donation of one's self to another. Goodness is relational rather than static, and requires community and communication to be realized. One alone cannot be excellent.

2. THE SOCIAL ANALOGY AND MORAL REFLECTION

Edwards's social analogy also plays a distinctive role in his moral reflection. Generally, the representative theologians we have examined hold that a moral relationship exists between the mutuality and love of the persons of the Trinity and the relations of love that should predominate in the church. Nonetheless, the theologians we have examined argue that there is an essential difference between the relations among the divine persons and the relations that exist among human persons. As a result, the distinctive moral teaching of the social analogy is that the tripersonal love of God provides an immutable template of divine unity from which to trace the proper social relations of the church. Thus, the social analogy discloses a pattern of love and harmony that exists in a kind of parallel universe, which human social relations should try to imitate as best as possible.

Edwards agrees that the perfect love expressed between the divine persons serves as an exemplar for the love that should be operative in human relations. Edwards also sees, however, a more profound interaction between the divine love disclosed through the social analogy and the moral life. Edwards argues that the church is a community constituted by God's triune love, a position that expresses, in his opinion, the New Testament promises regarding the communion that the saints experience through the Son and the Spirit. In "Miscellanies" entry 376, he writes:

> It can no other way be accounted for, that in I John 1:3, our fellowship is said to be "with the Father and with his Son, Jesus Christ," and not that is it said also, "with the Holy Ghost," but because our communion with them *consists* in our communion of the Holy Ghost with them. 'Tis in our partaking of the Holy Ghost that we have communion with the Father and the Son and with Christians; this is the common excellency and

delight in which they are all united; this is the bond of perfectness, by which they are one in the Father and the Son, as the Father is in the Son and the Son is in the Father. (Y13:448)

Accordingly, Edwards writes in the "Essay" that the "communion of saints is twofold: 'tis their communion with God and communion with one another" (H:116). There is the *vertical* dimension of communion, where the saints interpersonally participate in the Godhead through the indwelling of the Holy Spirit. This dimension is vital and irreplaceable. In the "Treatise," Edwards writes that there is "no communion without union," that is to say, "those that are not in Christ, and are not united in him, can have no degree of communion with him" (H:31). At the same time, communion also has a *horizontal* dimension, where the saints experience friendship and communion with each other on the basis of this shared goodness and love. Edwards writes in "Miscellanies" entry 211 that the word *koinonia* in the New Testament connotes not only one's individual incorporation in the life of the Godhead, but the "common partaking of the Holy Ghost with other saints" (Y13:342).

Edwards's social analogy therefore offers a vision of the moral life that both respects the insights of the psychological analogy while at the same time expands its focus so that it includes the interpersonal aspects of communion. In chapter 1, we observed that Edwards believes the core of Christian ethics "consists essentially and summarily in love to God and love to other creatures." The source of this love consists in "the perfect and intimate union and love there is between the Father and the Son." The "Spirit that proceeds from the Father and the Son is the bond of this union, as it is of all holy union between the Father and the Son, and between God and the creature, and between the creatures among themselves" (H:63–64). When viewed from the perspective of the psychological analogy, this passage emphasizes Edwards's belief that *theosis* through the indwelling of the Holy Spirit is decisive in his theological ethics. But when viewed from the perspective of the social analogy, the implication of this passage concerns the connection between the relations of the Trinity and human society. Through the self-diffusive goodness of God, expressed in the person of Jesus Christ and communicated to the saints by the Holy Spirit, the church is admitted into the love and life of the Trinity. Hence, equally vital in Edwards's theological ethics is the concern that our relations with one another express the love of Christ that resides in the church through the Spirit. Where the psychological analogy bids us to know ourselves as we are known in God, the social analogy bids us to love one another with the very love of the God whose triune life we share.

The social analogy also offers another perspective on personhood. As we observed in the previous chapter, the psychological analogy defines

personhood as self-consciousness. But the social analogy views personhood in terms of interpersonal communion. The desire for self-donation,
mutuality, and communion is not peculiar to human beings, for Edwards
believes that "no reasonable creature can be happy without society and
communion," because "he delights to communicate himself to another."
Given that God is a "society" of three persons, the human desire to live
in communion is not "because of our imperfection, but because we are
made in the image of God." Therefore, "the more perfect any creature is,
the more strong this inclination," for "Jehovah's happiness consists in communion, as well as the creature's" (Y13:264). In other words, the *imago dei*
is as much evident in the human inclination to live in communion as it is
in self-consciousness.

Finally, the social analogy articulates an understanding of love that better accommodates individuality. As we observed in the previous chapter,
the psychological analogy struggles to develop a positive account of individuality. This tension is particularly evident in the psychological analogy's depiction of the sanctification of the saints, a process in which they
"are all transformed into love, dissolved into joy, become activity itself,
changed into mere ecstasy" (Y13:261). Such a vision of ecstasy is at once
awe-inspiring and chilling. On one hand, it captures the psychological
analogy's depiction of personhood as perfected in *perichoresis*. But on the
other hand, it raises the troubling prospect that in Edwards's theology, one
must lose one's individuality in order to lose oneself in love.

In the social analogy, however, personal identity and individuality
receive special emphasis. Although the Son and the Spirit follow "one
design" in the work of redemption, there is a necessary mutuality and self-
differentiation in their individual missions. Thus, there is within the Godhead a sense of the individual agency of the three divine persons; indeed,
salvation is a work of concerted effort rather than undivided action. Further, the economic missions themselves reveal that God's triune love values individuals as well as relations. The incarnation represents the
accommodation of the divine nature to the limitations of human nature, a
kenotic accommodation that God makes out of love. In "Miscellanies" entry
571, Edwards writes that "Christ took on himself man's nature for this
end," to allow for "a more familiar conversation than the infinite distance
of the divine nature would allow of," a "communion and familiar conversation" that befits "the relation that Christ stands to believers as their representative, their brother, and the husband of the church" (Y18:108). As a
result of this *kenotic* love, the nature of the relationship between Christ and
the saints takes the form of a deep, intimate friendship, in which the
beloved is valued in all of his or her particularity. Edwards writes in "Miscellanies" entry 81 that the ascended Christ's "faculties" are "so enlarged
that he can, with a full view and clear apprehension of mind, at the same

time think on all the saints in the world" and express "an actual and even a passionate love (such as we experience) to all of them in particular." The nature of Christ's love for the church, then, is not a "general" or universalized love, but addresses "those particular persons that he loves." Christ "desires communion" with the saints as individuals in all their uniqueness. Thus, in his glorified state, "there is the same delight in the man Christ" in the individual experience of spiritual communion with each saint "as if he were bodily present with them, talking and conversing with them." For the "one glorious end of the union of the human to the divine nature" is "to bring God near to us," so that "his terrible majesty might not make us afraid," and "Jehovah, who is infinitely distant from us, might become familiar to us" (Y13:247–48).

Likewise, the mission of the Spirit consists of the gift of God's other-regarding love to the church, so that the church is incorporated into the triune society. From the perspective of the social analogy, the Spirit confers authentic identity and uniqueness in God, for through the indwelling of the Spirit the church becomes the recipient of God's eternal and infinite love. The Spirit therefore enacts "God's design to admit man as it were to the inmost fellowship with the Deity," a fellowship in which "no degree of intimacy will be too much" (Y18:367–68). In addition, in heaven—where the gift of the Spirit's love is complete—the saints will love each other without jealousy and will take joy in the fact that others receive Christ's love. Thus, "in the future world, the saints' love one to another will be such that it will be a very delightful consideration to them that Christ Jesus dearly loves the other saints; and it will fill them with joy to see him manifesting his love to them" (H:13:303).

2.1. Ecclesiology, Eschatology, and the Created Order

Clearly, Edwards's social analogy generates an exalted moral vision for the church. Indeed, this vision is so exalted that it raises the question, Is such a vision realistic? Although Edwards believes that the fundamental identity of the church is its heavenly destiny to live for eternity in communion with the triune God, he also clearly recognizes that the church does not yet exist in this state of perfection. One reason that the church's transformation is a "gradual process" is the sinfulness of the church (Y18:285). The "union is but begun in this world, and there is a great deal that remains in this world to separate and disunite them" (Y18:109). Until the eschaton, the "body of Christ" labors under the burden of "sin and sorrow" (Y13:443). The main reason, however, for the church's gradual progress is that each moment that the world persists in time plays a positive role in the work of redemption. In "Miscellanies" entry 547, Edwards writes that God's redemption of the world through Christ is a historical process of "revolutions from the beginning of the world to the end" that compose "various parts of one scheme." As such, each historical moment has significance or else it would not exist. The "various successive states of the world" are "connected in a scheme" and "together attain God's great design." Indeed, the very persistence of the world signifies that the particular circumstances in which the church finds itself are integral to its progress and growth. This significance is implicit in the eschatological vision of the church, for the concept of an eschaton establishes that the world has an end, not only in the sense of a limit to its temporal duration but also in the sense of a definite, God-given purpose, otherwise God would not "continue to uphold it, and dispose and govern it." No time is wasted, but all time is redeemed. The "revelation" of the church's eschatological identity therefore serves as a way for God to reveal "the principal parts of the scheme" of redemption, so that human persons and communities may participate in this scheme as "subjects and friends of God" (Y18:94–95).

In addition to being "realistic" in terms of the church's progress toward the kingdom, Edwards's eschatological vision of the church's consummation is also realistic in the sense that it affirms the value of the created order. As we have seen, Edwards argues that the church's fundamental identity is its heavenly destiny to live for eternity in communion with the triune God. Such a vision, however, directs attention not only to the nature of the church, but also to the nature of creation, which is ordered according to the church's triune identity and destiny as the "bride" and "body" of Christ. Indeed, one of the presuppositions that guides Edwards's ecclesial interpretation of the *Hexaemeron* is that throughout creation, the Father kept "an eye to the Son of God" and his "mediatorial kingdom." In addition, the work of creation was "properly the work of the Son" and "belongs to him" (Y18:284). Therefore, in order to know the full meaning of the church's identity, one needs to appreciate the created order that bears witness to the church's eschatological transformation.[55]

Further, to view the created order rightly, in light of its eschatological fulfillment in Christ, acknowledges both the form the created order takes *prior* to the transformative power and communication of the Holy Spirit's love, and the form it takes *as a result of* the Spirit's transformation. As we observed in chapter 1, Edwards sees the cosmos divided between the "typical" and "antitypical world"—"the moral, spiritual and intelligent world, or the City of God," is the "consummation" of the "material and natural world" (Y11:91). Edwards reiterates this distinction in "Miscellanies" entry 702. The "creation of the visible world was in order to the work of redemption," so that "all things in the formation and constitution and disposal" of "heaven above and in the earth," particularly "in the state and circumstances of the world of mankind, shadow forth the things that appertain to this work and point to them many ways" (Y18:284).

Within Edwards's Trinitarian writings, we see the interplay between the created order and its eschatological consummation most clearly in the social relationships of friendship and marriage that Edwards uses in his development of the social analogy. As we have seen, Edwards often speaks of the church's relation with the Trinity, and the relations among the divine persons of the Trinity, as a kind of friendship. But within the created order, friendship is ubiquitous and not particularly redemptive. In "Miscellanies" entry 473, Edwards notes that persons can have less than godly motivations in their friendships. From simple "self-love a person may come to love another person for good qualifications of mind," or if the friend might "do him good and minister to his profit or pleasure." Such a love is entirely natural and has nothing of the love of God in it (Y13:515).[56] But even when it exists in its natural state, there is a "kind of benevolence" and mutuality that is emblematic of God's triune love. Moreover, on account of the incarnation, the natural inclination of friendship is assumed and transformed. Edwards writes in entry 510 that "there is a natural inclination in the creature, not only to the adoration of a glorious being infinitely superior, but to friendship." If God "had not thus descended to us," this "inclination to friendship and love to a companion might have been subordinate to a supreme regard to God." In Jesus Christ, however, "God is come down to us, has taken our nature, and is become one of us, that he might be our companion" (Y18:54–55).

Of course, Jesus Christ is the best friend anyone could have. Christ "has those qualifications that are the most endearing and qualifying for a friend possible; and he hath done that for us which, above all things conceivable, tends to attract our hearts and unite them to him, in entire love and confidence" (Y18:55). Nonetheless, the incarnation enables the love of friendship to become a mode for living the moral life in light of the church's eschatological destiny. In entry 639, Edwards reflects that the "special affection that the saints have in this world to other saints that are their friends will in some respects remain in another world." For "God and Christ will reward" those "that have loved one another with a virtuous love, and from such a love have shown kindness one to another." Indeed, in heaven the spiritual love of friendship will only increase, for God "will reward them and favor them the more for such love, and all the fruits of it, to all eternity" (Y18:172). The love that friends "have in them by their acquaintance here, may be what they carry to heaven with them" (Y18:172). Edwards therefore concludes that "this should move us to lay religion and virtue in the foundation of all our friendships, and so to strive that the love we have to our friends be a virtuous love, duly subordinated to divine love. For so far as it is so, it will last forever; death don't put an end to such friendship, nor can it put an end to such friends' enjoyment of each other" (Y18:172–73).

Edwards develops a similar interplay between the created order and its eschatological fulfillment in the relationship of marriage. As we have seen, the intimacy of marriage is emblematic of the intimacy of the church's communion with the Father and the Son through the Spirit. But the inclination of erotic love that the institution of marriage orders is ubiquitous, and in many cases less than godly. When this is the case, the happiness in a marriage is short-lived. "How soon do earthly lovers come to an end of their discoveries of each other's beauty," Edwards writes in entry 198, "how soon do they see all that is to be seen!" (Y13:336). Nonetheless, through the incarnation the natural inclination of erotic love is assumed and transformed. "We see how great love the human nature is capable of," Edwards writes in entry 189, "not only to God but to fellow creatures." As fully human, Christ also experiences erotic love, for "Christ has an human nature as well as we," and therefore "has an inclination to love those that partake of the human nature as well as we." Of course, Christ's erotic love is "of a purer and better and more benevolent nature" than ours, and "that inclination which in us is turned to the other sex, in him is turned to the church, which is his spouse." Thus, "when we feel love to anyone of the other sex, 'tis a good way to think of the love of Christ to a holy and beautiful soul" (Y13:332).

As with friendship, the erotic relationship within marriage can provide a mode for living the moral life in light of the church's eschatological destiny. An "exalted and fervent love to God" does not "hinder" erotic love, "but only refines and purifies it." For God "has created the human nature to love fellow creatures, which he has principally turned to the other sex" (Y13:332). And if founded in God's love, erotic love will take the form of "an eternal progress" in which "new beauties are continually discovered, and more and more loveliness, and in which we shall forever increase in beauty ourselves." For in such a relationship, "we shall be made capable of finding out and giving, and shall receive, more and more endearing expressions of love forever"; "our union will become more and more close, and communion more intimate" (Y13:336–37).

Finally, the interplay between the created order and its eschatological fulfillment is apparent in Edwards's aesthetics. As we have seen, Edwards argues that there must be a plurality of persons within the Godhead on the basis of the beauty and excellency we encounter in the created universe. Taken on its own terms, however, this argument is suggestive rather than conclusive. While the experience of beauty is universal, it is also unintelligible; viewed in isolation, nothing is more "without definition than excellency" (Y6:332). Only when we view beauty and excellency as a "shadow of love" do we see beauty rightly (and ultimately) from a Trinitarian perspective (Y6:380). Indeed, beauty is properly a category of divine revelation before it is a category of human experience. The paradigm of all beauty is the triune God, who has become incarnate in Jesus Christ. Thus, Edwards writes in "Miscellanies" entry 108 that "when we are delighted with flowery meadows and gentle breezes of wind, we may consider that we only see the emanations of the sweet benevolence of Jesus Christ; when we behold the fragrant rose and lily, we see his love and purity." For "there really is" an "analogy, or consent, between the beauty of the skies, trees, fields, flowers, etc. and spiritual excellencies: though the agreement be more hid and requires a more discerning and feeling mind to perceive it" (Y13:278–230).

Short of the eschaton, the perception of visible beauty and excellency is merely analogous to the direct communication that results from the indwelling of the Spirit, for "Christ communicates himself properly only to spirits." While Christ "communicates a sort of shadow or glimpse of his excellencies to bodies," these communications are indirect, and "are but the shadows of being, and not real being" (Y13:279). The experience of beauty in this life, however, points toward a more integrated experience of beauty that will exist when the church's consummation in Christ is complete. "In this world we behold" even "spiritual beauties" through the "intervention of our senses." But in heaven, the saints will "behold the beauties of minds more immediately than now we do the colors of the rainbow." For in the "resurrection," the saints will be better able to perceive the spiritual beauties that exist not only between the saints but between the persons of the Trinity. Indeed, in heaven there will be the same "exquisite spiritual proportions" between "one mind and another," between "all" the "minds" of the saints and "Jesus Christ," and "among the persons of the Trinity, the supreme harmony of all" (Y13:328–29).

Therefore, in heaven all sensible beauty will be transformed so that it is identical to the highest beauty of perfect love and mutual consent. Natural and visible beauty is not abolished as a result of this transformation, but becomes integrated with the moral and spiritual beauty of the triune God. We see an image of this integration in the body of the resurrected Christ, who presents a visible promise of the "harmony" of body and mind that will exist in the "bodies of the saints after the resurrection" (Y13:263). In several "Miscellanies" entries, however, Edwards argues that the most immediate foreshadowing of the harmonious integration of material and spiritual beauty that will reign in heaven is the "singing in divine worship" (Y13:303). Edwards writes in entry 188 that on this side of the eschaton, "the best, most beautiful and most perfect way that we have of expressing a sweet concord of mind to each other is by music." For nothing so much represents in sensible terms the "inward concord and harmony and spiritual beauty" of a "society" as souls "sweetly singing to each other." Thus, in heaven there will be singing and music that is beautiful in ways "we cannot conceive" (Y13:331).[57]

2.2. Eschatology, Ethics, and the Social Analogy

Appreciating the interplay between the created order and its eschatological fulfillment is essential for understanding the implications the social analogy has for Edwards's theological ethics. On the one hand, Edwards uses the created order to emphasize the uniqueness of the church's communion with the triune God. Indeed, Edwards believes that the created order generates its own moral obligations that represent God's providential government of creation. Thus, in "Miscellanies" entry 864, Edwards writes that God "maintains a moral government over the world of mankind," specifically by making it "natural and necessary" that human beings "should be concerned with one another, and linked in society" either in "nations, provinces, towns or families." From this inclination toward society, it is possible and necessary to develop "universal" principles or "rules" of "distributive justice" that help maintain order and peace. Without this sense of a transcendent moral order, "the preservation of the species is but very imperfectly provided for." For "if men have nothing but human government to be a restraint upon their consciences," they are "left in a most woeful condition."[58] Nonetheless, the obligations that derive from the created order *do not* identify what is decisive for living the Christian moral life. As we have seen, friendship and marriage are not redemptive until they are founded on God's triune Spirit and thereby provide a context through which to realize the church's eschatological destiny. "Communion, we know, is nothing else than the common partaking of others of good," Edwards writes in "Miscellanies" entry 330. In contrast, "communion with God is nothing else but a partaking with him of his excellency, his holiness and happiness" (Y13:409). Therefore, the ultimate question in the moral life is whether or not our social relations are founded in the Spirit's happiness and joy that comes to those who are members of God's triune society. For in Edwards's theological vision, the indwelling of the Spirit marks the beginning of our participation in the eschatological reality that the triune God establishes.

On the other hand, Edwards uses the created order to expand the social analogy's conception of love. As we have seen, the social analogy emphasizes the self-giving aspect of God's love, which is initiated between the Father and the Son and is manifested in Christ's death on the cross. But if benevolence has an irreplaceable role in Edwards's understanding of the moral life, it does not represent the sum total of love. Not only does

Edwards equally emphasize the love of complacence revealed in the psychological analogy, but friendship and marriage reveal other aspects of love that figure in the moral life. The love and intimacy of friendship and marriage provide emblems of the mutual love of the triune persons, into which humanity is invited through the indwelling of the Spirit. Moreover, through the incarnation, the human loves of friendship and marriage are assumed and transformed. Consequently, all the different aspects of love in the created order enrich the sense of intimacy between Christ and his church. Thus, in "Miscellanies" entry 741, Edwards writes that while nothing expresses the love of God as much as the "death and sufferings of Christ," the saints have an uncommon "intimacy" with Christ as a result of the assumption by the Logos of human nature. In heaven "there will be no restraint to his love, no restraint to their enjoyment of himself; nothing will be too full, too inward and intimate for them to be admitted to, but Christ will say to his saints, as in Cant. 5:1, 'Eat, O friends; drink, yea, be drunken, O beloved'" (Y18:370, 372). Not only does the incarnation elevate other forms of love in the created order, but the love expressed through Christ's "last sufferings" is the principle cause for the "intimacy" between Christ and the saints. For "Christ's condescension in taking on him our nature, invites us to ascend high in our intimacy with him," even to "the kisses of his mouth." For on the cross Christ "gave himself" to the saints "from eternity." Thus, "he is theirs to eternity" (Y18:369–70).

As we proceed to trace Edwards's Trinitarian ethics in the following chapters, the interplay between the created order and its eschatological fulfillment continues as an underlying theme in Edwards's ethical writings. In subsequent writings, the particular point Edwards pursues, or conversation partners he engages determine how he defines the interplay and what facet of it comes to the forefront. Nonetheless, the interplay is evident in all of his ethical writings, and it is impossible to fathom Edwards's theological ethics without recognizing its presence. To give three examples from writings we will examine in detail: In the *Religious Affections*, which we will explore in the next chapter, Edwards opposes the natural affections to the spiritual affections in order to argue that the source of the latter is the direct communication of the Holy Spirit. Such a task is imperative, given Edwards's thesis is to establish that natural religious affections alone cannot sustain the moral and spiritual life. Edwards depicts, however, the natural affections and their role in the faculties in such a way that they are analogous to the spiritual affections. Indeed, for all intents and purposes, Edwards's depiction of the natural affections derives from the role he assigns to the will in the psychological analogy. Thus, even when he depicts the created order and its eschatological fulfillment as polar opposites, there are significant points of continuity between the two.

The interplay between the created order and its eschatological fulfillment is also evident in the *Freedom of the Will*, which we explore in chapter 4. Here Edwards's task is to argue that the will is determined by the greatest apparent good and does not choose indifferently. Edwards holds this thesis, however, not merely because he believes that his understanding of the will reflects the created order, but because he believes that the incarnate Christ, whose will perfectly coincides with the will of God, provides the model of fully realized human freedom. Therefore, even when Edwards's primary concern is the created order, his position is informed by his vision of its eschatological fulfillment. Indeed, as we will see, recognizing the extent to which his understanding of the eschatological fulfillment of the created order determines Edwards's thesis regarding the will is essential to the continued credibility of his argument.

Finally, the interplay between the created order and its eschatological fulfillment is evident in *The Nature of True Virtue*, which we examine in chapter 5. Here Edwards opposes the natural expressions of benevolence, which are part of the created order, with an absolute benevolence that encompasses all being, which is the only true virtue and nothing less than the soul's eschatological participation in the love of God. Nonetheless, even though these two forms of benevolence are completely different, there is a great deal of similarity between the two, for "it pleases God to observe analogy in his works" and "to establish inferior things in an analogy to superior" (Y8:564).

3. DIFFICULTIES AND POINTS FOR FURTHER DEVELOPMENT

Edwards portrays the social analogy, then, as the center of God's overflowing love, which pours out on all creation so that the church may join the "society of the three." As a result, in addition to serving as an exemplar for the church's interpersonal relations, the social analogy's vision of the moral life is one in which all our interpersonal relationships participate in the church's eschatological fulfillment in Christ. The social analogy teaches us that goodness, excellence, benevolence, and happiness can only be realized in interpersonal relationships. Therefore, we must look upon every personal relationship as a mediation of God's triune love and holiness. Further, by defining love in terms of mutuality and benevolence, the social analogy compensates for the shortcomings in the psychological analogy that we noted in the previous chapter, particularly regarding individuality and personal distinctiveness. All the same, there are difficulties and tensions inherent in social analogy itself, specifically concerning freedom, personhood, hierarchy, and the Holy Spirit, which recur in Edwards's later writings. In this section, I will discuss each in turn.

3.1 The Social Analogy, Freedom, and Necessity

As we have seen, one objection that Thomas raises concerning the social analogy is that it threatens the principles of divine perfection and sufficiency. For Thomas, to apply the principle that "there can be no joyful possession of any good without a companion" to God implies a state of deficiency in God. But the root of the problem Thomas identifies has less to do with the fact that God "needs" a companion as it does with the social analogy's definition of God's goodness as necessarily diffusive. Traditionally, Christian theology holds that God creates *ex nihilo*, that is, God created the universe "out of nothing," with an absolute act of will, in order to protect the divine freedom regarding the creation. For if it were necessary for God to create, then God would not be sovereign over the creation. Therefore, God's motivation to create could not originate in the divine nature, but in the divine will. Accordingly, Thomas argues that "one must hold, without any doubt, that God produced creatures in existence by a free choice of the will, without any natural necessity."[59] But if God's goodness is necessarily diffusive and social, as the social analogy holds, does this not imply a state of metaphysical necessity in God regarding the creation of the universe?

Edwards agrees that there is no need or deficiency in the Godhead. In "Miscellanies" entry 679, he writes that "God stands in no need of creatures, and is not profited by them." At the same time, he argues that God "hath a real delight in the excellency and loveliness of the creature," for this excellency and love is nothing other than the "shining forth" of God's "own goodness." Further, there is a sense in which God has "more delight" beholding the "loveliness and happiness of the creature" than if God had not created, for "God would be less happy if he were less good" (Y18:238). In other words, he maintains that God's motivation for creating the universe flows from God's supremely good nature, and does not originate in God's will.

Edwards's justification for this position is implicit in the social analogy itself.[60] As we have seen, the first object of God's communicative disposition is toward a being "equal" to the Father, for God cannot "communicate all his goodness to a finite being." The "Father's begetting of the Son is a complete communication of his happiness, and so an eternal, adequate and infinite exercise of perfect goodness, that is equal to such an inclination in perfection" (Y13:272). Therefore, within the Godhead there is already a relation of perfectly diffusive goodness that cannot be affected by the creatures' response. While the diffusive goodness of God serves as God's motivation for creating the world, God was under no necessity to create, for the Father's goodness was already perfectly communicated to the Son. Nonetheless, it was an appropriate "exercise" of God's "own perfection" to will that finite beings share in God's love according to their capacities. For this reason, Edwards writes in entry 662, "it was the will of God" that God's goodness and love "should be expressed and shine forth" (Y18:200). Indeed, Edwards defines God's freedom as the liberty to express the divine goodness toward creation on account of the infinite goodness that is already expressed within the Godhead. Edwards writes elsewhere that God's "propensity to communicate goodness" to the creature is a perfectly "free" expression of God's "loving and good nature" (Y13:395).

The genius of Edwards's position is that it holds together the thesis that God's creation of the world is an exercise of the will and the social analogy's thesis that creation is an expression of the inherent goodness of God's nature. But Edwards himself would have to admit that in his proposal the expression of God's communicative nature still falls under the category of necessity. For though he establishes that it is not necessary for God to create in order to be perfect, on account of God's goodness God is necessarily a creative being. "God's goodness is not an inclination to communicate himself as occasion shall offer, or a disposition conditionally to communicate himself, but absolutely," Edwards writes in "Miscellanies" entry 445. Therefore, God must make "creatures to communicate himself to," otherwise God "can't do what he is himself disposed" to do (Y13:484). In "Miscellanies" entry 104, Edwards articulates this thesis in explicitly Trinitarian grammar. While the "Father's begetting of the Son" is an "infinite exercise of perfect goodness," the Son also has "an inclination to communicate himself, in an image of his person that may partake of his happiness" (Y13:272). The Father cannot be the recipient of this communication of goodness, "for the Father is not a communication of the Son, and therefore not the object of the Son's goodness" (Y13:282). Therefore, humanity "is the immediate subject" of the Son's communicative nature, and the church "is said to be the completeness of Christ (Eph. 1:23)." Indeed, there is even a sense in which Christ is not perfect without the church, notwithstanding the principle of divine perfection. For just as "we are incomplete without that which we have an inclination to," so "Christ is not complete without his spouse" (Y13:273).

Further, Edwards's proposal operates with a different understanding of the divine freedom than is usually associated with the principle of *creatio ex nihilo*. Where Thomas understands freedom primarily as the freedom to choose, Edwards defines freedom primarily as the liberty to express one's nature. As we have noted, Edwards's motivation for holding his understanding of freedom is so that he can give pride of place to the diffusive goodness of God's nature. One could argue, however, that Edwards's necessitarian interpretation of freedom diminishes, rather than increases, the sense of God's extravagant goodness implicit in the traditional interpretation of *creatio ex nihilo*. As Irenaeus writes, to say that all creation rests on God's free and arbitrary decision, and not on God's nature, is to underscore the fact that creation is a work of utter grace and manifestation of God's sovereign goodness.[61] Moreover, if freedom is not primarily defined in terms of the freedom to choose, how are we to understand the moral life? For if God does not have the freedom to choose, one can scarcely assign such a freedom to human beings.

Although significant, this difficulty is far from irrefutable. If Edwards's necessitarian interpretation leaves too little to the theological imagination, the traditional libertarian interpretation of *creatio ex nihilo* leaves too much. That is to say, the traditional interpretation cannot explain why an absolutely perfect being would choose to create anything in the first place. Nonetheless, in his Trinitarian writings Edwards does not offer an extended justification of his necessitarian interpretation of the will, and his fullest answer to these issues does not come until *Freedom of the Will*, which we will discuss in detail in chapter 4. There Edwards argues that the freedom that matters most is not the freedom that surrounds an individual's choices, which he believes does not exist, but the freedom to love. Consequently, he believes that the essence of virtue lies not in the will's actions or deliberations, but in the will's inherent "nature" and "beauty," which the will receives through participating in God's triune love through the transforming power of the Holy Spirit (Y1:339–40).

3.2. The Social Analogy, Personhood, and Tritheism

A second point of tension in the social analogy concerns personhood. As we have seen, Edwards assigns a tremendous amount of individuality and agency to the divine persons in his development of the social analogy. The individuality and agency of the divine persons is implicit in Edwards's initial articulation of the social analogy, and becomes explicit in his depiction of the covenant of redemption, in which all three divine persons come to agreement concerning the creation and redemption of humanity. Finally, the individuality and agency of the three divine persons is evident in Edwards's descriptions of the specific missions of the Son and Spirit. Where traditional theology holds that the works of the Trinity in the economy of salvation are indivisible, Edwards views the work of redemption as a concerted effort by distinct persons who "help one another and mutually forward each other's ends" (Y18:191).

Certainly, the individuality and agency Edwards assigns to the divine persons has benefits over the sense of personhood that the psychological analogy generates. As we observed in chapter 1, one of the implications of the psychological analogy is that it attenuates the sense of personhood as it applies individually to the Father, Son, and Spirit. Thus, Augustine writes that the term "person" when applied to the divine persons is simply a way to answer the question "Three what?" and does not apply it in the same sense to human persons.[62] Similarly, in this chapter we observed that Thomas argues that the term "person" applies to God in only an analogous sense, as a way of identifying the "three subsisting beings in the divine nature," and not in its "original" sense of an individual substance with a rational nature.[63] Both Augustine and Thomas establish this distinction because they believe that the psychological analogy provides the best safeguard to God's unity. More importantly, both also want to avoid the heresy of *tritheism*. In their opinion, to apply the human sense of personhood unequivocally to the "three subsisting beings" of the Trinity would be to imply that there were three rational natures and centers of agency in the Godhead. Thus, one of the underlying reasons for Augustine's and Thomas's suspicion of the social analogy is that it generates a view of the divine persons that is inherently vulnerable on this account.[64]

Edwards does not explicitly respond to this objection. At one point, he writes that it is wrong to view the "Father, Son, and Holy Ghost as three distinct gods, friends to one another," but he does not explain why such a view would not follow from his depiction of the Godhead as a "mutual friendship" (Y18:84; H:129). It is clear, however, that Edwards's social analogy does not degenerate into tritheism for two reasons.[65] The first is that Edwards does not accept the presupposition that gives rise to the charge of tritheism, which is that individuality is identical to rationality and personhood. For Augustine and Thomas, rationality is connected to one's substantive nature and is the distinguishing mark of personhood. Therefore, one cannot ascribe to the Godhead different centers of rationality without undermining God's unity. In contrast, for Edwards the psychological analogy's conception of personhood is relational rather than individualistic. He holds that there is a kind of discourse within each act of self-reflection, and therefore his understanding of self-consciousness is not threatened by the plurality suggested through the social analogy. Indeed, Edwards defines personhood in such a way that there must be some sort dialogical relation within the consciousness, or else identity is impossible. God is not free to be a "stone" but is necessarily a reflective, and therefore Trinitarian, being (Y13:262). The second reason that Edwards's social analogy does not degenerate into tritheism is that he believes that the psychological and social analogies provide complementary, rather than alternative, accounts of the Trinity. Therefore, the emphasis that the social analogy places on the individuality and agency of the divine persons is balanced by the emphasis that the psychological analogy places on the perichoretic unity and identity of the divine nature. To argue then that Edwards's social analogy degenerates into tritheism is to forget that the social analogy reveals only one aspect of Edwards's Trinitarian thought.

Nonetheless, though Edwards's proposal is not guilty of tritheism, it is also clear that he cannot directly translate the sense of personhood generated by both his Trinitarian analogies into a comprehensive theological anthropology. As we have seen, while the psychological analogy provides Edwards with his fundamental vision of the relation between knowledge of God and the knowledge of the self, he needs to develop another way to articulate his belief that "the Spirit of God" immediately "communicates and exerts itself" to the "soul," one that better distinguishes the moral experience and capacities of the regenerate and the unregenerate (Y13:513). A similar project is also required for the social analogy. As we have seen, the social analogy provides Edwards with his fundamental vision of the relations that should exist between persons, a vision that is as definitive of personhood as that provided by the psychological analogy. Where the psychological analogy locates the *imago dei* in self-consciousness, the social analogy locates the *imago dei* in our interpersonal relations. Not every interpersonal relationship, however, is redemptive, and the relationships that reflect the created order are importantly different from those that participate in the church's eschatological communion in Christ. As a result, Edwards needs to develop a more comprehensive account of human nature that can distinguish those relations that participate in the Holy Spirit and those that do not. As we will see, Edwards redraws the *imago dei* in the *Religious Affections* so that the central interpersonal relationship is between the soul and the triune God. And in *The Nature of True Virtue*, Edwards redefines the difference between social relations built upon natural inclinations of benevolence, and those that derive from our communion with God.

3.3. The Social Analogy, Equality, and Hierarchy

A third point of tension concerns equality and hierarchy. As we have seen, in the "Observations" Edwards is careful to establish that the divine persons are ontologically equal to each other, and the Father and the Son enter into a "mutual, free agreement" concerning the covenant of redemption. At the same time, he also argues that there is an economic hierarchy within the Trinity, wherein the "Father" acts "as head of the Trinity, and the Son under Him, and the Holy Spirit under them both" (H:77–78).

Both of these aspects of the "economy of the Trinity" originate in the social analogy. The egalitarian aspect is evident in the diffusive goodness of God, as well as in the relations of mutuality and self-donation between the Father, Son, and Spirit. All the same, the social analogy is also responsible for the economic relations of subordination between the divine persons. For the social analogy emphasizes the Father's role as the initiator of the relations of self-donation and love between the divine persons. Accordingly, the economic hierarchy is not established "arbitrarily," but reflects the "order of subsisting" within the Godhead, and is "prior to," and "diverse" from, "all that is established in the covenant of redemption" (H:78, 82). As the Father is the "fountain of the Deity," so the Father "should be the fountain of all the acts of the Deity." Finally, the economic hierarchy of the Trinity is "in itself fit, suitable, and beautiful" (H:79). Although the "three persons of the Trinity may be looked upon as a kind of family," no family exists without an "economic order," Edwards writes in a sermon on John 15:10. "Thus the Father, though he be no greater than the Son or the Holy Ghost, yet he is the first in order, and the Son next, and the Holy Ghost last."[66]

The tension between egalitarian and hierarchical aspects of order and harmony are not only evident in Edwards's conception of God's triune relations, but recur in his writings on human social arrangements. As we have seen, in "Miscellanies" entry 864 Edwards notes that God has constituted humanity so that throughout the created order it is "natural and necessary" that human beings "should be concerned with one another, and linked in society." God's providential government of the world, however, is not only expressed in relations of mutuality, but also in relations of hierarchy. In "constituting human moral governments," God institutes special "rights and obligations" for "those that he has appointed to be rulers." Thus, in civil government God "hath set those to be moral rulers that are the wiser and stronger" to provide for and govern those who are "less knowing and weaker." Likewise, there is an inherent and appropriate hierarchy in "the government of parents over their children," which is "most evidently founded in nature."[67] There is also an inherent hierarchy in the relations between men and women, Edwards writes in entry 37. God has made man with "more wisdom, strength, and courage" in order "to protect and defend," but God "has made woman weaker, more soft and tender, more fearful, and more affectionate, as a fit object of generous protection and defense" (Y13:220).

Finally, relations of hierarchical authority also exist in the church. In "Miscellanies" entry 403, Edwards writes that while each member of the church "equally partakes" of "the benefit and the reward" of salvation, ministers have received a "different degree" and "greater share" of the Spirit, and therefore occupy a more exalted place within the body, closer to the head. Returning to the somatic metaphor of the church as Christ's body, Edwards explains:

> As it is in a natural body that enjoys perfect health, the head and heart and lungs have a greater share of it, they have it more seated in them, than the hands and feet, because they are parts of greater capacity; so in

the mystical body of Christ, all the members are partakers of the benefit, of the righteousness of the head, but 'tis according to their different capacity and place they have in the body. . . . God efficaciously determines the place and capacity of every member here in this world, by giving different degrees of his Spirit; them that he intends the highest place in the body, he gives them, while in this world, most of his Spirit, the greatest share of the divine nature of the Spirit, and the nature of Jesus Christ the Head, whereby they perform the most excellent works. (Y13:468)

Commentators on Edwards have long noticed and criticized his defense of hierarchy. Some attribute Edwards's preference for hierarchical social arrangements to his personal oddities. Thus, Ola Winslow writes that "all his life" Edwards thought himself "to be one standing before many; never one of a group sitting side by side in friendly equality and comradeship."[68] Some attribute it to his political preferences. Thus, Patricia Tracy argues that "Edwards' views on government were those of a Tory" who "never escaped the anachronistic grip of the Patriarchal model."[69] Still others find that the theological tension between hierarchy and equality in Edwards's thought express his preferences concerning proper domestic relations as much as his beliefs about the nature of the Christian life. Thus, Ava Chamberlain writes that by stressing the "hierarchical and affectionate" aspects of Christ's marriage to the church, "Edwards was encouraging his congregation to emulate his idealized portrait of the marriage bond in their own lives, both as Christians and family members."[70] In any event, all agree that Edwards's affirmation of hierarchy is problematic. Thus, Amy Pauw argues that the "anthropomorphism" Edwards employs in the "covenant of redemption" perpetuates a scenario in which "subordinationist language and narratives within the Godhead tend to shore up subordinationist schemes within human communities."[71]

No doubt, elements of these criticisms are valid. Particularly those raised by Chamberlain and Pauw point to tendencies in Edwards's theology that are without defense and must be resisted in any retrieval of his theological ethics. Edwards's acceptance of gender hierarchies as part of the created order indicates the vulnerability in his theological scheme to the unwitting perpetuation of systemic injustice. In addition, the frequent occurrence of abuse by persons invested with hierarchical authority in even the most grace-filled of human societies raises the question as to whether the "economy of the Trinity," such as it is, can provide a viable social model for fallen human beings.[72]

Nonetheless, it is important to connect the tension between hierarchy and equality in Edwards's thought directly to his Trinitarian theology. The theological point of origin for Edwards's affirmation of hierarchy is not his anthropomorphic depiction of the divine society per se, or the patriarchy that pervades his milieu, but his understanding of the Father's communicative nature as the "Fountain of the Deity." At the same time, in Edwards's social analogy we also find the sense of equality and mutuality that can form the basis for a retrieval of Edwards's Trinitarian ethic that is more resolutely egalitarian. As Catherine LaCugna notes, the depiction of the fatherhood of God in the social analogy challenges "all biological, cultural, political, and commonsense notions of fatherhood." For in the social analogy, the Father's goodness and love is realized in the Father's living "as relation-to-another-who-is-equal."[73] Further, as Margaret Farley argues, "if the ultimate normative model for relationships between persons is the very life of the Trinitarian God, then a strong eschatological ethics suggests itself" that takes the form of a loving commitment to "interpersonal communion characterized by equality, mutuality, and reciprocity." In this ethic, "any pattern of relationship, in home, church, or civil society" that does not exhibit the mutuality evident in God's own triune love "is thereby an unjust pattern of relationship."[74]

Indeed, there are moments in Edwards's thought where he views equality not merely as one aspect of the divine economy but as its fulfillment. Notwithstanding his comment in the "Observations" that the "economic order" will become even "more visible and conspicuous" at the eschaton (H:90), in "Miscellanies" entry 609 Edwards suggests that "in heaven" the Father and the Son will share authority over the new creation. Christ the "God-man shall reign" even "after he has delivered up the kingdom to the Father." For now, however, "he reigns by a delegated authority, as a king's son may reign in some part of his dominions as his viceroy or over the whole, by having the whole government and management committed to him and left with him for a time." But in heaven Christ will "reign by virtue of his union with the Father," for while "the Father will take the government upon himself," through their perichoretic unity the "Son shall reign in and with the Father" (Y18:143–44). As we will see in chapter 5, this sense of eternal progress toward equality represents for Edwards not only the destiny of the Son but the destiny of the church.

3.4. The Social Analogy and the Holy Spirit

A final point of tension concerns the Holy Spirit. In chapter 1, we observed that one of the shortcomings in Edwards's psychological analogy is its attenuated sense of the Spirit's personhood. To a certain extent, Edwards compensates for this shortcoming through developing a fuller depiction of the Spirit's equality and individuality in the social analogy, particularly his depiction of the triune missions. All the same, in the social analogy

Edwards does not assign to the Spirit a discrete locus in the communion of the triune persons, and it remains the case that the Holy Spirit is the divine person who is best described as a "divine principle" (H:72). Moreover, as we just noted, the Spirit is subordinate to both the Father and the Son in the work of redemption.

At several points, Edwards argues that his understanding of the Spirit reflects the relations among the divine persons that he finds in the New Testament, specifically the Pauline and Johannine literature concerning the triadic affirmations of salvation through Jesus Christ, in the power of the Holy Spirit.[75] "Though we often read in Scripture," Edwards writes in the "Treatise," "of the Father loving the Son, and the Son loving the Father, yet we never read either of the Father or the Son loving the Holy Spirit, and the Spirit loving either of them." This is so, Edwards argues, "because the Holy Spirit is the divine love itself, the love of the Father and the Son" (H:63). In "Miscellanies" entry 341 Edwards confesses, "I can think of no other good account that can be given of the apostle Paul's wishing grace and peace, or grace, mercy and peace, from God the Father and the Lord Jesus Christ in the beginning of his epistles without ever mentioning the Holy Ghost," other than that "the Holy Ghost *is* the grace, the love and peace of God the Father and the Lord Jesus Christ." Conducting his own survey, he writes, "We find it so fourteen times in all his salutations in the beginnings of his epistles; and in his blessing at the end of his second epistle to the Corinthians, where all three persons are mentioned, he wishes grace and love from the Son and the Father, but the *communion* of the Holy Ghost, that is, the partaking of him" (Y13:415). This depiction of God's triadic relations is not only evident in the Pauline letters but is also evident in passages such as 1 John 1:3.[76] There "our fellowship is said to be 'with the Father, and with his Son Jesus Christ,'" but "it is not said also, 'with the Holy Ghost,'" for "our communion with them *consists* in our communion of the Holy Ghost with them" (Y13:448).

Nonetheless, the source of Edwards's understanding of the Holy Spirit seems clearly to be the social analogy itself. In the social relations of the Godhead, the "third person may be said to be beloved of God, but not so properly, for he is the infinite love of God itself." The Spirit, then, is "the delight that the Father and the Son have in each other," and does not represent a discrete object of love. For "a person may be said to love the delight he has in a person that he loves, but not so properly as he loves that person, because this would make love to that love, and delight in that delight, and again delight in that delight that he has in that delight, and so on *ad infinitum*" (Y18:364). Accordingly, Edwards views the Holy Spirit as the principle through which the church participates in the mutual love of the Father and the Son:

In this family or household, God is the Father, Jesus Christ is his own natural and eternally begotten Son. The saints, they are also the children in
the family; the church is the daughter of God, being the spouse of his Son.
They all have communion in the same spirit, the Holy Ghost. (Y18:110)

Edwards is not alone in his describing the Spirit in such a fashion. For
all intents and purposes, his position reaffirms the *filioque* clause, or the
doctrine expressed in a later addendum (589) to the Niceno-Constanti-
nopolitan Creed (381) that the Spirit proceeds from the Father and the Son
as from one principle. As John Kelly notes, this doctrine receives special
emphasis by Augustine, who argues that, "since the Father has given all
he has to the Son, he has given him the power to bestow the Spirit."[77] While
the authoritative nature of the *filioque* was unquestioned for centuries
within Western Christianity, within recent Trinitarian theology many
argue that the *filioque* provides an inadequate account of the "specific
hypostatic uniqueness of the Holy Spirit."[78]

As we have seen, this assessment has some merit with regard to
Edwards's understanding of the Holy Spirit, and this tension persists
throughout his other writings. Nonetheless, it is also important to note that
Edwards's adherence to the *filioque* doctrine stems from his belief that
through the Holy Spirit, the diffusive goodness and love of God overflows
so that humanity can join in the mutual love of the Father and the Son for
eternity. The Holy Spirit does not represent an inconsequential moment in
Edwards's theology, but represents its most dynamic moment, for the
indwelling of the Spirit enables the church to participate in its eschatological destiny. The indwelling of the Spirit is also decisive in the moral life. The
"Holy Spirit dwelling" in the saints "is their principle of life and action"
(Y18:146). Therefore, "walking in the Spirit and walking in love" are "the
same thing" (Y13:455). The Holy Spirit, then, is the *telos* and principle of the
koinonia of the church, for the Spirit is the "necessary bond of union" that
holds together the "whole family" of God's triune society (Y18:363).

4. EDWARDS'S SOCIAL ANALOGY AND
RECENT TRINITARIAN THEOLOGY

Unlike the psychological analogy, the social analogy is often viewed favorably in recent Trinitarian theology. Indeed, many propose eliminating the
psychological analogy altogether in preference for the social analogy, particularly if articulated in a way that reflects the current emphasis on the
economic Trinity. Thus, Jürgen Moltmann argues that "the three divine
persons exist in their particular, unique natures as Father, Son, and Spirit
in their relationships to one another, and are determined through these
relationships." Accordingly, God's triune love to the world is expressed

through the divine persons' individual involvement in human suffering and redemption. For "it is the nature of the person to give himself entirely to a counterpart, and to find himself in the other most of all. The person only comes to himself by expressing and expending himself in others."[79]

At the same time, the social analogy's popularity is not universal. Some are concerned with tritheism. Thus, Barth argues that when the "attribute of individuality" is "related to the Father, Son, and Spirit as such instead of the one essence of God, the idea of a threefold individuality is scarcely possible without tritheism."[80] Others argue that the social analogy tends to obscure important features, such as sin and finitude, which make human relations importantly distinct. Thus, Kathryn Tanner argues that "one should avoid modeling human relations directly on Trinitarian ones," for to do so either downplays "the difference between social relations and Trinitarian ones," or loses "a realistic sense of human relationships."[81] Finally, others argue that a theological vision based in the "social harmony of the Trinity" generates a sense of Christ's mission that is inherently conservative and inappropriately focuses on shoring up social arrangements rather than transcending them. Thus, Rowan Williams argues that the social analogy "gives us very little *theological* ground for asking awkward questions about the social realities of belonging, let alone for suggesting that there is a rather fundamental Christian vocation of not belonging, in families, nations," and "patriarchal 'organic' states." Therefore, instead of making concrete the economy of salvation, the social analogy encourages "a marked degree of *abstraction* from the story of God incarnate" and tends to forget that "*the world we inhabit* is the potential scope of the community that is created by relation to Jesus."[82]

These criticisms echo some of the tensions noted in the previous section regarding Edwards's social analogy. Nonetheless, Edwards generates a theological vision that in many ways accommodates these criticisms and avoids their hard edges. As we have seen, by viewing the social analogy and the psychological analogy as complementary visions of the Trinity, Edwards's proposal does not collapse into tritheism. Further, while the sense of personhood generated by Edwards's psychological and social analogies does not offer a sufficient account of sin and finitude, Edwards uses this understanding of personhood to develop a Trinitarian anthropology in his major writings, which we will review over the next three chapters. Finally, while Edwards does not recognize the inherent difficulties within patriarchal and hierarchical relationships, there are resources within his social analogy that can offer ways in which one can retrieve its insights regarding mutuality and equality. Despite its affirmation of the created order, Edwards's social analogy maintains contact with the eschatological transformation of the church and creation through the missions of the incarnation of Jesus Christ and the indwelling of the Spirit. Indeed, Edwards believes the moral life hinges not on the former but on the latter.

At the end of the "Essay," Edwards acknowledges that nothing he has written on the Trinity provides an adequate "explication of this mystery." If "some difficulties are lessened" in his development of the psychological and social analogies, "others that are new appear." In retrospect of the different tensions and difficulties noted in the first two chapters, this resignation comes as no surprise. But Edwards recognizes that the term "mystery" has two senses: It can refer to that which is obscured from view and never fully revealed, or it can refer to the unfolding knowledge of that which is never fully comprehended. Therefore, "he that looks on a plant, or the parts of the bodies of animals, or any other works of nature, at a great distance" may see things "wonderful and beyond his comprehension." But "if he views them with a microscope, the number of wonders will be increased still" (H:127–29). As this study turns from Edwards's Trinitarian writings to offer a Trinitarian interpretation of his major works, it will be clear that Edwards not only continues to find the Trinity a mystery in the first sense, but in the second sense as well. For as deep as the mysteries of the microscope may be, deeper still is the mystery of the triune God's infinite love.

3

"A LIGHT THAT SHINES IN THE SOUL":
THE TRINITARIAN ETHICS OF EDWARDS'S
RELIGIOUS AFFECTIONS

> The Spirit of God so dwells in the hearts of the saints, that he there, as a seed or spring of life, exerts and communicates himself, in this his sweet and divine nature, making the soul a partaker of God's beauty and Christ's joy, so that the saint has truly fellowship with the Father, and with his Son Jesus Christ, in thus having the communion or participation of the Holy Ghost.
>
> Edwards, *Religious Affections* (Y2:201)

The first two chapters sketched Edwards's Trinitarian thought, in particular his understanding of the psychological and social analogies. In the following chapters, the task now turns to provide a Trinitarian interpretation of Edwards's major writings, specifically *A Treatise concerning Religious Affections* (1746), *Freedom of the Will* (1754), *Original Sin* (1758), *Two Dissertations* (1765), and *Charity and Its Fruits* (1738; 1851). Admittedly, the doctrine of the Trinity is not explicit as a governing logic in Edwards's major writings. That is to say, Edwards does not organize his theological ethics in a way that corresponds to God's activity as the "Command of God the Creator," the "Command of God the Reconciler," and the "Command of God the Redeemer," as Barth does.[1] Nor does Edwards see the dramatic narrative of the paschal mystery as the fundamental revelation of God's triune being, after which all descriptions of God and narratives of faith must conform, as von Balthasar does.[2] Rather, for Edwards the doctrine of the Trinity reveals the distinct nature and character of God, which radiates through the missions of the Son and the Spirit. Accordingly, the central task of ethics is to define those virtues and dispositions that express the nature and character of the triune God, through whom and in whom Christians find their life and identity.

Edwards's doctrine of the Trinity therefore functions as the conceptual horizon for his theological ethics, and Edwards's major writings proceed from within his Trinitarian perspective. As a surveyor uses the different points on a landscape to map the countryside, Edwards uses his doctrine of the Trinity as his point of reference to plot the Christian moral life. Edwards's starting point changes depending on the specific aspect he explores—for example, the nature of the affections, or the nature of will, or the nature of true virtue. But no matter his starting point, Edwards's orientation for the moral life is humanity's communion with the Father and Son through the Spirit. In this sense, Edwards's ethical writings are grounded in and continue to reveal the mystery of the Trinity.

In this chapter, I will examine Edwards's *Religious Affections*. Interpretations of the *Religious Affections* typically fall under two general headings. Under the first heading are those who consider the *Religious Affections* as a study of religious psychology that initiates a line of inquiry, which includes F. D. E. Schleiermacher, Ralph Waldo Emerson and William James. On this reading, the most significant passages in the *Religious Affections* are those where Edwards argues that the affections are an indispensable aspect of religious experience.[3] Under the second heading are those who see the *Religious Affections* as Edwards's attempt as a pastor to grapple with his experience of the excesses and false promise of the Great Awakening. On this reading, the most important passages are those where Edwards demonstrates a more complex portrait of the capacities and limitations of human nature, and a diminished confidence in religious revival as a vehicle for authentic moral and spiritual transformation.[4]

Without denying the legitimacy of these interpretations, this chapter will offer a Trinitarian interpretation of the *Religious Affections*. Despite their differences, the previous interpretations consider Edwards's category of affections as a distinct "sense of the heart" that stands equidistant from the extremes of rationalism and emotional fanaticism.[5] A fuller depiction of the affections follows, however, when we view Edwards's project in the *Religious Affections* from the perspective of his psychological and social analogies. Though Edwards defines the affections as distinct from "speculative knowledge," the psychological analogy operates as Edwards's paradigm for authentic personhood (Y2:255). As the divine mind is constituted so that God's perfect "idea" is never without God's perfect "love," so too in human minds, the knowledge of God begets a supernatural love that orients the soul toward God. Edwards explores the nature of the affections, then, not so much to discover a new sphere of religious experience or inquiry, but to refine and restate his contention that what is decisive in the Christian life is the saints' communion and participation in God through *theosis*. In addition, though Edwards's focus is on the inner person, his understanding of the saints' participation in God and of the diffusive goodness, excellency, and beauty of God follows the social analogy. The intra-Trinitarian society provides the paradigm of the beauty and goodness that the spiritual affections perceive, after which the moral life is ordered.

Consequently, the *Religious Affections* represents Edwards's attempt to articulate his Trinitarian vision of the human person transformed by the knowledge and love of God. Edwards's development of the affections is not, then, the most original moment in his theology. Rather, a Trinitarian interpretation of the affections locates the originality of the *Religious Affections* in Edwards's attempt to flesh out the implications of his Trinitarian reflection into a fuller moral and theological anthropology.

In the second part of this chapter, I describe the way in which a Trinitarian interpretation of the *Religious Affections* brings into bold relief the fact that this treatise is as much an exercise in theological ethics as it is in religious psychology. Edwards conceives of the moral life in terms of virtue, duty, and practice, all of which emanate from the triune love of God. For Edwards, "there is no other true virtue, but real holiness" (Y2:255). He conceives of virtue in general, and the particular virtues of humility, meekness, and forgiveness, as flowing from the saints' participation in the triune love of God. As such, Christian virtue proceeds from the character of God, and follows the pattern of Jesus Christ, who is the perfect temporal manifestation of God's triune love. This understanding of virtue differs from Aristotle's conception of virtue as an acquired habit of practical reasoning and action, and Edwards is careful to distinguish these two accounts. In terms of duty, the love of God is the "measure" against "which the rule of our duty extends" (Y2:325). This understanding of duty differs from the more familiar Reformed understanding of divine commands, which express God's will in a way that transcends human experience or analysis. And in terms of "practice," Edwards sees practice as the "*principle* sign by which Christians are to judge, both of their own and other's sincerity of godliness" (Y2:406–7). Where others shy away from emphasizing Christian practice to avoid the charge of works righteousness, for Edwards practice represents a necessary and natural part of the soul's experience of new being.

In the third part of this chapter, I compare Edwards's Trinitarian understanding of virtue with recent retrievals of Aristotelian virtue in contemporary ethics. While several writers see Edwards offering a corrective to these retrievals of Aristotelian virtue, a Trinitarian interpretation of the *Religious Affections* suggests that Edwards offers an entirely different account of virtue and the moral life.

1. FROM ANALOGY TO ANTHROPOLOGY

"There is no question," Edwards writes, of "greater importance" than that which asks, "wherein do lie the distinguishing notes of that virtue and holiness that is acceptable in the sight of God?" (Y2:84–85). Accordingly, the task Edwards takes on in the *Religious Affections* is to distinguish the "gracious operations of God's Spirit" from all that which is "not of a saving nature" in the "minds of men" (Y2:89). Edwards organizes his inquiry into three parts. He opens his treatise with a brief discussion of the affections and their importance in the moral and spiritual life, followed by two sections that examine respectively those phenomena that are *not* reliable signs of genuine religious affections, and those that *are*. By organizing his treatise in such a manner, Edwards hopes to present his arguments on a potentially volatile topic in an objective, almost scientific, manner. Particularly on the topic of the affections, Edwards notes that it is "difficult to write impartially" as well as to "read impartially" (Y2:84). While understandable, however, this organization tends to obscure the theological anthropology Edwards articulates over the course of his study. Therefore, rather than trying to retrace the specific steps Edwards takes in developing his anthropology, what follows is a presentation of its basic contours.

1.1. The Affections

The first aspect of Edwards's theological anthropology concerns the faculties in the mind or soul. There are two faculties: One is "that by which it is capable of perception and speculation," whereby the mind "discerns and views and judges." The other is the power whereby the mind "is in some way inclined with respect to the things it views and considers, or is disinclined, and avers" to them. In the second faculty, the mind is never an "indifferent, unaffected spectator," but is either "liking or disliking," "pleased or displeased." Further, the second faculty goes by different names depending on what it apprehends. With respect to the "actions" it governs, it is called the "will." And with respect to affections it instills, it is called the "heart." The "exercises" of the will and heart therefore "are not two faculties," for the "affections are not essentially distinct" from "the mere actings of the will and inclination of the soul." Only the "degree" of "inclination or disinclination" differs. Some exercises of the will and heart carry the soul only a "little beyond a state of perfect indifference." Other exercises cause the soul to act "vigorously and sensibly," in such a way that the "blood and animal spirits" are altered, which explains why "in all nations and ages" the affections are often called the "heart" (Y2:96–97).

In arguing that the "will" and "affections" derive from the same faculty, Edwards allows that his "language" is "somewhat imperfect," his meaning "loose and unfixed," and that he flies in the face of "custom, which governs the use of language." In one sense, the will never acts without being first "affected one way or another." In every action where "we act voluntarily, there is an exercise of the will or inclination," for "'tis our inclination that governs our actions." Nonetheless the "common actions of life" directed by the will are not properly affections. Affections are those inclinations where the soul is moved "in a high degree" to love or hate, to joy or sorrow (Y2:97).

Edwards draws a further distinction between "affections" and "passions." Due to the "laws of union of soul and body," there is never a time in which the affections do not effect a corresponding alteration in the "body" or the "animal spirits." There are even moments where, by virtue of the body-soul union, different forces at work in the body "may promote the exercise of the affections." Nonetheless, the affections have their "seat" in the "mind" and not the "body," to the extent that the body itself is in "no way essential to them." Indeed, an "unbodied spirit" is equally "capable" of affections as a spirit that is joined with a body. Passions, on the other hand, are "sudden" and "violent" emotions that short-circuit the body-soul union in such a way that mind is "overpowered" by animalistic desires and "less in its own command" (Y2:98).

Although he uses the term "faculties," Edwards does not adhere to the traditional model of faculty psychology, that is, the belief that the mind or soul is composed of discrete components, most often the intellect, will, and desire.[6] Faculty psychology in this form originated in Plato's *Republic*. Plato sees the soul as a kind of society, made up of parts (*meros*) that vie for supremacy. In the virtuous soul, the part that prevails is the rational part (*to logistichon*), which knows and desires the good and regulates the other parts, namely, the aspirational (*to thumoeides*) and the appetitive (*to epithumetichon*).[7] As it evolved, faculty psychology came to represent one of the givens of human nature. Central teachings of the Enlightenment, however, undermined its metaphysical foundations, specifically the belief that individual entities have innate ideas and substances. For this reason, both Locke and Malebranche developed alternative accounts of the faculties. In *An Essay concerning Human Understanding* (1689), Locke conceives of the faculties as inherent powers of "understanding" and "will" that have the functions of "perceiving" and "preferring." Locke continues to call these "faculties," so long as one understands that they do not "stand for some real beings"—that is, actual parts of the mind—or that they are not "distinct agents in us." Therefore, in the "mind, the intellectual faculty, or the understanding" and the "elective faculty, or the will," are simply designations of certain abilities the mind has, for "faculty, ability, and power" are "different names of the same things."[8] Similarly, in *The Search for Truth*, Malebranche writes that there are two faculties in the mind, "the understanding," or that "of perceiving various things," and the "will," or that of "receiving inclinations." These faculties are not "entities different from the soul itself," but are modifications in the soul as an integrated whole. Hence, it is the soul, not just the intellect, that "perceives," and the will is the "soul itself insofar as it loves its perfection and happiness" or "wills to be happy" through the "impulse God constantly impresses in it" to love "everything that appears to be good."[9]

Edwards follows Locke's and Malebranche's definition of "faculties," and sees the "perception" and "will" as distinct functions of the whole soul. Edwards takes this understanding of the faculties further, however, than either Locke or Malebranche. Despite their differences concerning the nature of knowledge, both Malebranche and Locke believe the virtue of the mind or soul depends on the extent to which the will is subordinated to the understanding—such is the means through which persons become reasonable and responsible. In contrast, for Edwards the affections are the locus of virtue: "True religion consists in great measure in vigorous and lively actings in the inclination and the will of the soul, or the fervent exercises of the heart" (Y2:99).

Human nature is therefore a dynamic state of action and affection: "We see the world of mankind to be exceedingly busy and active; and the affections of men are the springs of the motion." Take away "all love and hatred, all hope and fear, all anger, zeal and affectionate desire, and the world would be, in great measure, motionless and dead; there would be no such thing as activity amongst mankind, or any pursuit whatsoever." And just as in "worldly things," where "worldly affections are very much the spring of men's motion and action," so "in religious matters, the spring of their actions are very much religious affections" (Y2:101). Edwards therefore argues, "I am bold to assert that there never was any considerable change wrought in the mind or conversion of any one person, by anything of a religious nature," that "had not his affections moved," or "his heart deeply affected by those things" (Y2:102).

Because they are a basic constituent of human persons—the affections not only "necessarily belong to the human nature," Edwards writes, "but are a very great part of it"—the affections determine the ontological status of *both* regenerate and unregenerate persons (Y2:101). "As from true divine love flow all Christian affections, so from a counterfeit love in like manner, naturally flow other false affections," Edwards writes. For both regenerate and unregenerate, "love is the fountain," and the "various faculties, principles and affections of the human nature are as it were many channels from one fountain." Consequently, the fundamental question concerns the quality of the water, or love, that flows in the fountain of one's soul: "If there be sweet water in the fountain, sweet water will from thence flow out into those various channels," but "if the water in the fountain be poisonous, then poisonous streams will also flow out into all those channels" (Y2:151). Love therefore is not merely "the chief of the affections," but it is also the "fountain of all other affections" (Y2:106).

The affections, accordingly, determine the ontological orientation of a person. At the same time, they do not transcend the understanding, for true religious affections hinge upon the understanding's grasp of the knowledge of God. There "must be light in the understanding," as well as the heat of "an affected fervent heart." Those for whom there is "heat without light" feel their emotions stirred greatly in a way that circumvents the understanding and do not experience religious affections, but merely natural passions. And those for whom there is "light without heat" have a "head stored with notions and speculations" but "no true knowledge of divine things" (Y2:120).

Although implicit, the influence of the psychological analogy is evident in Edwards's depiction of the interdependent relation between the understanding and the affections. As we observed in chapter 1, a perichoretic unity exists between God's knowledge of God's "perfect idea" as the Son and the love of God's "perfect act" as the Spirit. Correlatively, the saint's knowledge of God culminates in the love of God; in other words, the saint's epistemological experience of having a true idea of God coincides with the dispositional experience of the love of God. For this reason, Edwards writes in "Miscellanies" entry 397 that the "prime alteration that is made in conversion, that which is the first and the foundation of all, is the alteration of the temper and the disposition of the Spirit of the mind," or the "spiritual understanding," from which follows "immediately" the "sense" of God's "excellency, glory, and delightfulness" (Y13:462–63). Likewise, in the *Religious Affections* Edwards writes that "knowledge is the key that first opens the hard heart and enlarges the affections, and so opens the way" into "the kingdom of heaven" (Y2:266). Hence, while Edwards places more emphasis on the affections in the *Religious Affections* than he does in his Trinitarian writings, the interaction between the knowledge and love of God nonetheless follows the paradigm of the psychological analogy.

Edwards's reliance on the psychological analogy is also evident when he speaks of the *nature* of religious affections. As we have seen, the mere experience of affections does not make one a spiritual person. Affections are both "natural" and "spiritual." In drawing this distinction, Edwards cautions that he does not mean merely the "immaterial" desires that emanate from the "spiritual part" of the person "in opposition to the body" and its "corporeal" desires (Y2:198). Rather, he refers to the *origin* of the affections and their transformative effect on the soul. Natural affections, in addition to referring to an inclination for sensate objects, represent any desire persons have apart from the direct communication and indwelling of the Holy Spirit. Hence, persons may have a *natural* affection for *religious* truth. Persons may have "a strong persuasion that the Christian religion is true," either from "evidence" or "arguments" (Y2:295). They may cultivate a "sweet natural temper," possess a "good doctrinal knowledge of religion," and have a "long acquaintance with the saints' way of talking and expressing their affections and experiences" (Y2:183). They may experience fervent affections born of images in the mind as vivid as that of a Christ-like "person with a beautiful countenance, smiling on him, and with arms wide open, and with blood dripping down" (Y2:149). The "natural springs of affections are so various and so secret," working through "the imagination," "education," and the "common influences of the Spirit of God," that no "philosophy or experience" will ever "be sufficient to guide us safely through" the "labyrinth and maze" of the human soul (Y2:460).

On the other hand, spiritual affections are the result of the "indwelling and holy influences of the Spirit of God," who is the "third person of the Trinity" (Y2:198). In the souls of the saints, there is the "Spirit of God dwelling as a vital principle," wherein "he communicates himself in his own proper nature." Hence, the spiritual affections themselves proceed from the "beauty and holiness of the divine nature," much like "heat" proceeds from "fire," or an odor of "sweetness" proceeds from "oil." To explain how it is that the saints experience the Holy Ghost as an indwelling principle, Edwards all but lifts a passage from his Trinitarian writings. "The Spirit of God so dwells in the hearts of the saints," he writes, "that he there, as a seed or spring of life, exerts and communicates himself, in this his sweet and divine nature, making the soul a partaker of God's beauty and Christ's joy, so that the saint has truly fellowship with the Father, and with his Son Jesus Christ, in thus having communion or participation of the Holy Ghost" (Y2:201).

A final point where the influence of the psychological analogy is evident in the *Religious Affections* is Edwards's use of the sun as an image for true spiritual affections. As we observed in chapter 1, Edwards sees the sun as a "lively image" of how the "light" of the Son and the "heat" of the Spirit proceed from the Father, who is the source of light and heat. Additionally, the sun presents an image of how the knowledge and love of God emanates from God to the saints: God "communicates" God's self through the "emitted beams of the sun" that "enlightens, warms, enlivens, and comforts the world" (H:126). Similarly, in the *Religious Affections* Edwards describes the nature of the Christian life as that of becoming "little images of the Sun." Through "Christ living" in the saints and having the "Spirit united to them," the "Sun of Righteousness" is "so communicated to them that they shine also, and become little images of the Sun which shines on them" (Y2:200–201). The "soul of a saint receives light from the Sun of Righteousness, in such a manner that its nature is changed, and it becomes properly a luminous thing; not only does the sun shine in the saints, but they also become little suns, partaking of the nature of the fountain of their light" (Y2:343).

1.2. The New Sense and Knowledge of God

Although the psychological analogy guides his thought in the *Religious Affections*, Edwards moves beyond his previous understanding of the "new sense" or "new knowledge" the saints have of God. Where Edwards in his Trinitarian writings defines the knowledge of God in terms of self-consciousness, in the *Religious Affections* he stresses the discontinuity between the "knowledge" or "sense" of God and self-consciousness. The "effects of God's Spirit" in the soul are "supernatural," that is, they "are entirely above nature, altogether of a different kind from anything that men find in themselves by nature, or only in the exercise of natural principles." At the same time, the indwelling of the Spirit does not elevate or improve the faculties of the mind, for the "new spiritual sense is not a new faculty of understanding, but it is a new foundation laid in the nature of the soul, for a new kind of exercises of the same faculty of understanding" (Y2:205–6).

Just what is this "new sense"? Edwards first draws an analogy between the mind's apprehension of the Spirit and the knowledge one acquires through the senses, primarily the "sweet taste of honey." Like the sensations of color or taste, the "sensation" the saint has in his or her mind of God is simple and immediate. To those who have this sense, the beauty and attractiveness of the object is irreducible, irreplaceable, and incommunicable; and to those who lack this sense, no image, argument, or description can serve as a substitute. "Natural" persons "may have conceptions of many things about spiritual affections; but there is something in them which is as it were the nucleus, or kernel of them, that they have no more conceptions of, than one born blind has of colors" (Y2:208). The taste and desire for honey to one born without the "sense of tasting" is an unattainable experience. But for one "who knows the taste of honey," its "excellency and sweetness" is "the foundation of his love," and his or her experience of it "is entirely different from anything the other has or can have." In the same way, spiritual persons alone can perceive "spiritual objects" and their "excellency" (Y2:209). Natural persons "not only cannot experience" the spiritual sense, but they inhabit a world that is "exceeding diverse" and comparatively impoverished (Y2:210). Only "those that are regenerated" receive the "divine spiritual taste," which is "in its whole nature diverse from any of the other five senses," and "entirely different from anything that is perceived" by "natural persons" (Y2:259–60).

When he compares the knowledge and love of God to the sense of taste, Edwards uses terminology that has a venerable pedigree in Calvinism, as well as critical purchase with the empiricism popular in his day. Following Calvin, central figures in the Puritan tradition that precede Edwards refer to the saving knowledge of God's election and redemption manifested to the saint as a kind of inner sense of God's sweetness, or *suavitatem*.[10] And Edwards's likening spiritual knowledge to a kind of sense resembles Locke's belief that all knowledge is the product of sense experience.

Edwards uses the metaphor of taste, however, neither to reaffirm Puritan soteriology nor to extend Locke's empiricism. For in Edwards's understanding, the new sense differs radically from knowledge of God's election, and resembles the physical senses only in that both are simple and irreducible experiences. Rather, his point is that, like the perception of colors, the perception of God is a sense over which the saint has no claim or control. Edwards therefore uses it to emphasize the difference, rather than similarity, between those who can and cannot taste the beauty and goodness of God. Moreover, as Edwards himself notes, metaphors like that of "taste" potentially obscure as well as illuminate. Because "spiritual things" are "invisible, and not things that can be pointed forth with the finger, we are forced to use figurative expressions in speaking of them, and to borrow names from external and sensible objects to signify them" (Y2:212). Ignorant persons are therefore liable to confuse the sensibilities conveyed by the "spiritual sense" with "lively and strong and imaginary ideas," and "look and wait for some such external discoveries." But these "external ideas" in the mind "have nothing in them which is spiritual and divine." Indeed, rather than a sign of "the advancing or perfecting" of "human nature," an abundance of "lively and strong imaginary ideas" is a symptom of "weakness of body and mind" (Y2:213).

Ultimately, Edwards uses the metaphor of taste to expand the idealism that frames his psychological analogy. The "new sense" of God reiterates his belief that a true apprehension of God is a repetition, rather than a representation, of God's idea in the mind. Edwards begins the process of reiteration in "Miscellanies" entry 782.[11] Edwards at first read appears to restate the two modes of apprehension he uses in his development of the psychological analogy—the apprehension of external objects, and the apprehension born of self-consciousness. There are "two ways" that one can cognitively engage in "spiritual" or "mental things" in one's "reflection or consciousness." The first way apprehends an entity only "indirectly" through their "signs." In this mode, there is "a *mere cognition* without any proper apprehension of the things thought of." The second way "is more properly called *apprehension*, wherein the mind has a *direct view* or *contemplation* of the thing thought of" (Y18:458). In this mode, one sees things as God sees them; a true idea of an entity repeats "perfectly" how it exists in God's own self-understanding, for God "understands himself, and all other things, by the actual and immediate presence of an idea of the things understood" (Y18:457–58).

A closer examination of the entry, however, reveals that Edwards's understanding of the "two ways" of apprehension in entry 782 has changed slightly from what it was in his Trinitarian writings. Within the first mode, Edwards places not only the apprehension of external objects but any kind of signification or representation in the category of external knowledge. For example, a person reading a page of theology comes across several images and symbols, such as "'God,' 'man,' 'angel,' 'people,' 'misery,' 'happiness,'" and so forth, but these are not "actual ideas of all those things." They are only "representatives of things," or the "names" we give to "some external sensible thing that in some way belongs to the thing" (Y18:452–55). Within the second mode, Edwards deemphasizes the stress upon self-consciousness as the primary mode of ideal apprehension. Although he continues to hold that the ultimate pattern of knowledge as repetition remains that of God's own self-understanding, he no longer sees human participation in this knowledge occurring in exactly the same manner. In the human mind, "ideal apprehension" either concerns "the faculty of understanding," or "mere SPECULATION," which consists in "the modes of mere discerning" and "judging"; or it concerns the "faculty of the will" and "consists in the SENSE OF THE HEART," that is, "all the affections of the mind." And of these two faculties, Edwards places the greater emphasis on the heart's discernment of God's "beauty," "excellency," and "value" (Y18:459).

Edwards uses this expanded understanding of the two modes of apprehension when he discusses the "new sense" in the *Religious Affections*. The "imagination" is that power of the mind where "it can have a conception, or idea of things of an external and outward nature." The most straightforward definition of externality is that it pertains to those objects and relations "we perceive by our five external senses" (Y2:211). But externality includes not merely the perception of color, figure, and the like, but all representative knowledge that occurs when an "image" or idea makes an "impression" in the "mind." The impressions and suggestions gained from the "letters and words written in a book," or excited by the "words of Scripture" and points of doctrine, are also "external ideas" (Y2:211–16). While these ideas ordinarily "attend" true "spiritual experience," they are not "spiritual," "supernatural," and "divine." Moreover, "when persons' affections are founded on imaginations, which is often the case, those affections are merely natural and common, because they are built on a foundation that is not spiritual" (Y2:217).

In contrast, the new sense of God is a direct apprehension of the excellency and goodness of God that occurs through the "communication of the Spirit of God" (Y2:236). Instead of working via the imagination, the Spirit infuses and sheds "abroad the love of God, the spirit of a child, in the heart" (Y2:239). This privileging of the affections does not mean, Edwards cautions, that one should make "a clear distinction" between "the two faculties of understanding and will," as if "they acted distinctly and separately in this matter" (Y2:272). Rather, he means that the "spiritual understanding primarily consists in this sense, or taste of the moral beauty of divine things; so that no knowledge can be called spiritual, any further than it arises from this, and has this in it." With this knowledge, the affections provide the foundation for the imagination: The "imagination is only the accidental effect, or consequent of the affection" that the Spirit infuses (Y2:291).

Hence, the terms "taste" or "sense" convey Edwards's mature belief that what serves as the foundation for all true knowledge of God is the apprehension of the value and beauty of God. This apprehension precedes all other categories of knowledge. It is, as Edwards writes at one point, "a kind of intuitive knowledge" of the intrinsic goodness and excellence of God (Y2:298). Unless "the beauty of the Godhead" be first "understood, nothing is understood that is worthy of the exercise of the noble faculty of understanding." And lacking this new sense, "we ourselves had better never to have been." One "knows nothing, that knows not this: his knowledge is but the shadow of knowledge, or the form of knowledge" (Y2:274).

1.3. The Natural and Moral Image of God

With this expanded understanding of the new "sense," Edwards can provide a more complete theological anthropology than he could through the psychological and social analogies. As we have seen, one of the problems Edwards fails to resolve in his articulation of the psychological and social analogies is how to distinguish those relations of love that truly participate in the Holy Spirit from those that do not. Edwards's expanded understanding of the "new sense" and of the "affections," however, offers a unique way to view divine and human participation. As I noted earlier, in the *Religious Affections* Edwards retains his Trinitarian belief that the saints have "fellowship" with God through their communion in the Spirit. There is no work so "high and excellent" as that in which "God does so much communicate himself, and wherein the mere creature hath, in so high a sense, a participation of God," as "it is expressed in the Scripture by the saints being made 'partakers of the divine nature.'" Nonetheless, this participation does not mean that the saints "are made partakers of the essence of God, and so are 'Godded' with God, and 'Christed' with Christ" (Y2:203). Rather, the saints' participation marks the decisive moment in which the saints share in "the moral excellency" of God, which "is the first beginning and spring of all holy affections" (Y2:254).

By using the term "moral," Edwards notes that he departs from its normal understanding. Most often, persons use the term to refer to "an outward conformity to the duties of the moral law" or to those "seeming virtues" that proceed from "natural principles," such as "honesty, justice, generosity, good nature, and public spirit." Edwards uses it, however, to distinguish between the moral and metaphysical attributes of God. In God, there are metaphysical attributes or "natural" perfections, such as God's omnipotence, omniscience, omnipresence, and majesty. There are also "those attributes which God exercises as a moral agent, or where the heart and will of God are good, right, and infinitely becoming as lovely," such as God's "righteousness, truth, faithfulness, and goodness; or, in one word, his holiness." Correlatively, there is a "twofold image" of God in human nature. There is the "natural image" of God's metaphysical attributes in human "reason and understanding," and there is the "image of God's moral excellency," which is nothing other than the full participation in God's goodness and holiness (Y2:255–56).

Therefore humans, by virtue of their reason and understanding, bear the image of God's natural attributes. These attributes are present in the soul's purchase of any "natural good" God endows it with in accordance with human nature. Thus, "pleasure is a natural good; so is honor; so is strength; so is speculative knowledge, human learning, and policy." Conversely, to suffer the loss of these natural goods falls under the category of "natural evil." And "so the evil of suffering is called natural evil," along with "pain," "torment, disgrace, and the like." It is knit within the soul's nature to desire natural goods and to abhor natural evils. This striving itself is not unique, but something all created intelligent beings experience—humans, "angels," and "devils" (Y2:255).

True human fulfillment and participation in God hinges on whether or not human souls bear the "moral" image of God in addition to the "natural" image of reason or intellect. The goodness, beauty, and love of God that finds its summation in the word "holiness" is "the sweetness that is the proper object" of the "spiritual sense" (Y2:260). Consequently, "God's implanting that spiritual, supernatural sense, which has been spoken of, makes a great change" in the soul (Y2:275). There is not only "an alteration of the present exercise, sensation, and frame of the soul," but also a moral "alteration in the very nature of the soul." The "soul is deeply affected by these discoveries and so affected as to be transformed." This transformation is nothing other than a "conversion," a turning "from sin to God" through "God's communicating himself and his Holy Spirit," such that "in the soul where Christ savingly is, there he lives" (Y2:340). In this way, Edwards can better articulate how persons experience the divine nature in a way that completes their human nature. In terms of natural attributes, finite human nature never approaches the infinite perfection of God. Nor does human participation in God through sharing in God's holiness increase one's purchase of God's natural attributes. Human nature, however, can receive and participate in the moral excellency of God. For "as the beauty of the divine nature" consists in "God's holiness," so the "beauty of the saints" is "the moral image of God in them" (Y2:258).

Moreover, moral excellency is the only true excellency created intelligent beings can attain or know. Natural attributes are morally neutral. For it is "moral excellency alone, in and of itself" that is the "excellency of intelligent beings" and "gives beauty to, or rather is the beauty of their natural perfections." Hence, "strength and knowledge" in and of themselves "don't render any being lovely, without holiness." Indeed, the strength and knowledge of a being may add to its "hateful" nature. Demonic beings, for example, "are very strong and of great natural understanding," but lacking moral excellency, their strength and knowledge only render them more loathsome (Y2:257). God's moral excellency is the one thing the "devil cannot imitate" in his manifold ability to tempt and deceive (Y2:233). In addition, while all intelligent beings are able to grasp the natural attributes of God, particularly God's power and majesty, only those who share God's moral beauty recognize the beauty of God's "moral attributes" (Y2:264). "Natural" persons (i.e., the unregenerate) have "no sense of the goodness and excellency of holy things"; but the "saints" alone have "that supernatural, most noble and divine sense given them" (Y2:262).

Not only do the saints alone recognize God's moral excellency, but this recognition is the foundation for all true love of God: "A true love of God must begin with a delight in his holiness, and not with a delight in any other attribute." For "it is impossible that other attributes should appear lovely, in their true loveliness, till this is seen; and it is impossible that any perfection of the divine nature should be loved with true love, till this is loved" (Y2:257–58). Nonetheless, the true love of God for "the beauty of his moral attributes leads to, and necessarily causes, a delight in God for all his attributes; for his moral attributes can't be without his natural attributes" and "all the attributes of God imply one another" (Y2:256–57).

Although implicit, insights from Edwards's psychological and social analogies form the substratum of the distinction he draws between the natural and moral attributes of God. As we observed in chapter 1, Edwards argues that the metaphysical attributes that are often attributed to God, such as immutability, omniscience, and omnipresence, do not identify the "real attributes of God." Only the relations that derive from God's triune nature, in particular God's "*Logos*" and "*Agape*," reveal that which is truly "distinct in God" (H:119; Y13:367). Therefore, by placing God's "moral" attributes in a separate category, Edwards identifies that which identifies God's triune being and love. All other distinctions identify attributes that do not have the same ontological status.

Similarly, the social analogy is also implicit in the distinction between the natural and moral attributes. As we observed in chapter 2, Edwards sees God's diffusive goodness as God's motivation for creating the world, and it is on account of the diffusive nature of God's goodness that human beings participate in the triune society of God. Correlatively, in the *Religious Affections*, when he distinguishes between God's moral and metaphysical attributes, God's beauty, goodness, and excellency take precedence over God's other metaphysical attributes: "God is God, and distinguished from all other beings, and exalted above them, chiefly by his divine beauty," a beauty that is "infinitely diverse from all other beauty" (Y2:298). The "beauty of the Godhead" is "the good of the infinite fountain of Good; without which God himself (if that were possible to be) would be an infinite evil; without which, we ourselves had better never been; and without which there had better have been no being" (Y2:274). Likewise, "excellency" is "that goodness" which "goes forth and flows out from the fullness of God's nature, the fullness of the Fountain of Good, without any amiableness in the object to draw it" (Y2:455).

Edwards also gathers the different aspects of the *imago dei* generated by his Trinitarian analogies into a unified account in the *Religious Affections*. As we have seen, each analogy reveals a particular aspect of the *imago dei*. In the psychological analogy, the *imago dei* is defined in terms of self-consciousness. In the social analogy, the *imago dei* is defined in terms of interpersonal communion. These two aspects identify different spheres of relation—intrapersonal and interpersonal—in human nature. Yet running through both spheres is the thesis that the indwelling of the Holy Spirit represents the realization of human nature, a thesis Edwards struggles to articulate fully within the context of the psychological and social analogies themselves.

But in the *Religious Affections*, Edwards defines the *imago dei* in terms of the affections and thus identifies the common thread of divine love that runs through each analogy. For in the psychological analogy, the love that exists within the self-consciousness determines the nature of one's basic "disposition," or the overall bent of a person. As the "sum of God's temper is love," so participating in the divine love represents the fulfillment of self-reflection (H:110). And in the social analogy, the love of the Holy Spirit represents the "intimate union and love" between "the Father and the Son," between "God and the creature, and between creatures among themselves" (H:64). Through the "two-fold image" of God in human nature, then, Edwards identifies the Spirit's love as the "moral image" of God, which is communicated to the saint in the "new sense" of God's "beauty." This "moral image" represents the transformation of the soul's affectional state, so that the soul is both changed internally but also inhabits a new interpersonal reality. For "truly gracious affections" are "built elsewhere," and "have their foundation out of self, in God and Jesus Christ" (Y2:253). Therefore, to live in relation to God is to find ourselves complete as persons, participating fully in God's love. Nonetheless, the "natural" image of God, which Edwards identifies as "reason and understanding," also identifies a locus for humanity's distinctiveness in contrast to the rest of creation. The "natural" image is the source of all "natural" affections and "natural principles" that bear a faint resemblance to true love and virtue, such as "honesty, justice, generosity, good nature, and public spirit" (Y2:254).

As Robert Jenson notes, though derived from a mistaken interpretation of the Hebrew parallelism in Genesis 1:26 ("Let us make humankind in our *image*, according to our *likeness*"), the *imago dei* represents a "comprehensive rubric" under which to discuss two aspects of human uniqueness in relation to God and other creatures. In the first aspect, which is traditionally attributed to the term "image" (*eikon*), the *imago dei* refers to those "essential faculties" of "soul," "mind," or "will." In the second, which is traditionally attributed to the term "likeness" (*homoisis*), the *imago dei* refers to those moral virtues such as "justice" and "sanctity." Although theologians have tended to argue the merits of one aspect over the other, the "issue is certainly undecidable." For if one holds to the first aspect alone, even "the very devils must be in God's image," but if one holds to the second, then fallen humanity "must now be at best partially human." Ultimately, a complete theology must hold both aspects of the *imago dei* in tension.[12] For all intents and purposes, such a tension is precisely what Edwards establishes with his "two-fold" account of the *imago dei*. On one hand, the "natural" image of God identifies "man's reason and understanding, his natural ability, and dominion over the creatures." But on the other hand, the "moral" image of God enables human beings to participate in God's own holiness in such a way that human holiness is "but the image of God's holiness," which is "its fountain" so that there "is grace in the image answerable to grace in the original" (Y2:256).

1.4. The Beauty and Excellency of Jesus Christ

As we have seen, in Edwards's Trinitarian writings, the paradigm for God's beauty is the triune God, who has become incarnate in Jesus Christ. In the *Religious Affections*, Edwards continues to follow this paradigm. God's beauty is evident in all God's works of "creation and providence," but in Jesus Christ performing his work as "mediator" the "moral perfections of God . . . wonderfully shine forth in every step of this method of salvation" (Y2:273–74). Beauty and excellency are also manifest in the person of Jesus Christ, who is "altogether lovely" and "chief among ten thousands." All the "spiritual beauty of his human nature, consisting in his meekness, lowliness, patience, heavenliness, love to God, love to men, condescension to the mean and vile, and compassion to the miserable, etc. all is summed up in his holiness." Likewise, the "beauty of his divine nature, of which the beauty of his human nature is the image and reflection, does also primarily consist in his holiness" (Y2:258–59).

In the *Religious Affections*, however, Edwards now considers beauty and excellency from the standpoint of the individual person's affections. That is to say, in his Trinitarian writings, the proper correlate of God's beauty and excellency are the interpersonal relations of the social analogy. But in the *Religious Affections*, he maintains an almost exclusive focus on the soul's affectionate love of God as the intrinsic good that organizes all secondary goods. "Although it be true," Edwards writes, that Christian love of God and neighbor is often defined as "a sincerely benevolent propensity of the soul," this "propensity or inclination of the soul, when in sufficient and vigorous exercise" is an "*affection*" and "no other than affectionate love." Certainly it is in terms of the affections that "Christ speaks of" the "vigorous and fervent love" that is "the sum of all religion" and the fulfillment of the command to love God "with all our hearts, with all our souls, and with all our minds, and our neighbor as ourselves" (Y2:107).

Love of God's goodness, then, is the foundation of the saints' personal distinctiveness and fulfillment. "Various kinds of creatures show the difference of their natures" in "the different things they relish as their proper good," and thus one person delights in "that which another abhors." The "true saints" are those for whom the "moral and spiritual excellency of the divine nature" is not merely a "*bonum utile*, a profitable good to me," or a good considered solely on the basis of one's "interest," but a "*bonum formosum*, a beautiful good in itself" and the pattern and source of all goodness. The saints are those who "have had their hearts affected, and love captivated by the free grace of God" (Y2:262–63).

In other words, God's self-diffusive love is inherently attractive to the saint and the source and end of true spiritual affections. Such an articulation of the diffusive goodness of God as an end in itself is evident in Edwards's Trinitarian writings. In chapter 2, we observed that in his presentation of the social analogy Edwards at times speaks of the expression of God's self-diffusive goodness as the satisfaction of a "natural inclination" that flows from God's nature as a communicative being. Hence, "God takes complacence in communicating felicity" (Y13:256). Similarly, Edwards also emphasizes that the benevolence "the Father and Son have in each other is not to be distinguished from their love of complacence one in another, wherein love does most essentially consist" (H:64). It does represent, however, a different rendering of the complacence in the Godhead than what we observed in the psychological analogy. In the psychological analogy, the basic pattern for complacence is the conscience's sense of the soul's worthiness, loveliness, and value. Hence, the Father's delight in the Son, which forms their "bond of union," is God's "infinite delight" in God's own perfect idea—a love of like for like (H:61). But in the *Religious Affections*, the complacence of the saint for God is first and foremost a love of God's self-diffusive goodness; this is the "moral excellency" that the saint first perceives, and that forms the basis of the soul's transformation.

Nonetheless, in a way reminiscent of the mutuality inherent in benevolence and in the saints' inclusion in the "society of the three," the new sense the individual saint receives of God's goodness generates within the soul a desire to be like God. Returning to the metaphor of taste, Edwards compares the desire for God's goodness to an appetite that increases the more it experiences its favorite food. The "more a true saint loves God with a gracious love, the more he desires to love him, and the more uneasy is he at his want of love to him." Likewise, the "more he mourns for sin," the more "his heart is broke," and the "more he thirsts and longs after God and holiness" (Y2:377). Hence, it is "the nature of spiritual affections, that the greater they be, the greater the appetite and longing is after grace and holiness" (Y2:379).

1.5. Conscience and Self-love

With his expanded moral anthropology, Edwards can better accommodate the difficulties he encounters in the psychological analogy, namely, its depiction of conscience and self-love. As we have seen, in Edwards's Trinitarian writings the conscience occupies two roles in the self-consciousness, depending on one's spiritual state. In the regenerate, Edwards considers the conscience a faculty that experiences a "participation of the divine essence" and craves the life of the Trinity; in the unregenerate, the conscience is merely a natural understanding of right and wrong that grasps the connection between action and retribution (Y13:342, 514–15). Such ambiguity, I noted, leaves unresolved what place the conscience holds in the moral and spiritual life: as a unique means of God's revelation, or as a naturally acquired sense of desert based on experience? But with his understanding of the "new sense" and "moral image" of God in the saints, in the *Religious Affections* Edwards argues that what first differentiates the regenerate from the unregenerate are the affections the conscience examines rather than the conscience itself. That is to say, the role of the conscience becomes secondary to God's instilling of spiritual affections through the indwelling of the Spirit. Hence, the conscience no longer provides the primary mode of revelation, but the means through which the soul discerns the new sense and moral image of God. When "God sets his seal" on a person's "heart by his Spirit, there is some holy stamp, some image impressed and left upon the heart by the Spirit, as by the seal upon the wax." This "impressed image" exhibits "clear evidence to the conscience that the subject of it is a child of God" who has received a "spirit of adoption" (Y2:232). In this way the "Spirit of God" testifies to "our spirit, or our conscience" that we have received the communication of God (Y2:239).

Although the conscience becomes subordinate to the spiritual affections and moral image of God, it continues to play an important role in the moral life, particularly from the perspective of Christian "duty." In both the regenerate and the unregenerate, the conscience is a power of self-reflection. Following his distinction between natural and moral attributes, the Holy Spirit "naturally assists" the conscience in its "apprehension of right and wrong" and in the knowledge of the "natural good" there is "in divine things," in particular the "awful greatness and natural perfections of God," and the "strictness" of God's "law" (Y2:207, 277, 311). Deviating from these dictates of conscience fills both regenerate and unregenerate souls with a sense of sin and guilt, which Edwards calls "legal humiliation" (Y2:311).

Further, in the regenerate, the conscience possesses "a sense of the transcendent beauty" of "God's holiness and moral perfection" (Y2:311). This sense of God's goodness awakens in the conscience a "conviction" or inner testimony and evidence of the saint's election (Y2:232). The nature of this revelation does not "stupefy" the conscience or bring an end "to convictions of sin," but on the contrary makes the conscience "more sensible, more easily and thoroughly discerning the sinfulness of that which is sinful" and the saint "more convinced of his own sinfulness and wickedness" (Y2:363). Such "evangelical humiliation" fills the saint with "tenderness of heart" and "godly sorrow" (Y2:360). At the same time, it also instills an intuitive sense of God's will and a positive desire to live according to God's moral perfection. The "holy disposition and spiritual taste, where grace is strong and lively, will enable a soul to determine what actions are right and becoming for Christians, not only more speedily, but far more exactly, than the greatest abilities without it" (Y2:283). For example, "an eminently humble, or meek, or charitable disposition, will direct a person" to "such behavior, as is agreeable to Christian rules of humility, meekness and charity, far more readily and precisely, than the most diligent study and elaborate reasonings, of a man of the strongest faculties who has not a Christian spirit within him" (Y2:284). Hence, the "gracious leading of the Spirit" in the conscience consists "partly in *instructing* a person in his duty by the Spirit, and partly in powerfully *inducing* him to comply with that instruction." The content of this instruction, Edwards emphasizes, is an immediate and true "relish" for the "holy beauty and sweetness in words and actions," in a way similar to how one knows what good food is, "without the reasoning of a physician" (Y2:281).

Edwards therefore sees the conscience at work in both contemplation and action. There are "two kinds of exercises of grace." First, there are "immanent acts" and "contemplation," that is, "those exercises of grace that remain within the soul," without a direct "relation to anything to be done outwardly, or to be brought to pass in practice." Equally important, however, are the "acts of grace that are more strictly called practical, or effective exercises, because they immediately respect something to be done" and are "the exertions of grace in the commanding acts of the will, directing the outward actions" (Y2:422–23).

Besides the conscience, another topic that Edwards revisits in the *Religious Affections* is self-love. As I noted in the previous chapters, the question of self-love presents an enduring problem to Edwards. Edwards sees self-love in different lights, depending on whether it is a love that takes delight in the goodness of another (i.e., "compounded" self-love), or in a narrow focus on one's private good (i.e., "simple" self-love) (Y18:74). But he also realizes that self-love exists across the continuum of existence. Although Edwards sees compounded self-love as most godlike, he also admits that compounded self-love exists in the souls and relations of the unregenerate as well as the regenerate. From "self-love a person may come to love another person" if that person "would enable him to do good and to minister to his profit or pleasure," yielding a desire for "union" and "friendship" (Y13:515). Consequently, one persistent question that Edwards has not yet fully answered concerns what special place, if any, self-love occupies in the souls of the redeemed.

Edwards reaches a similar point of resolution with self-love. The difference between the self-love of the regenerate and unregenerate is not a difference in self-love per se, but the place self-love occupies in the soul's framework of affections. In the regenerate, self-love is not the first "spring" in the affections, for "they first rejoice in God as glorious and excellent in himself," and only "secondarily" rejoice that "so glorious a God is theirs." In one passage, Edwards phrases this distinction in terms of excellency. The redeemed "first have their hearts filled" from the "view of Christ's excellency" and his "grace," before they consider that "so excellent a Savior, and such excellent grace is theirs" (Y2:250). In another, he phrases it in terms of goodness. The "concern our interest has in God's goodness, is not the first foundation" of true spiritual affections, but "God's goodness," set "before our eyes," serves "to fix the attention and heighten the affection" (Y2:248). From the standpoint of either goodness or excellency, the phenomenology remains constant: The regenerate soul "must first love God" before it recognizes God as the source of "highest happiness" (Y2:241).

What helps Edwards gain perspective on self-love is his expanded understanding of how the new sense is distinct from all discursive thought and ideal representations. Besides the mere desire for happiness or that which makes one happy—the most universal and tautologous definition of self-love—in either simple or compounded form, self-love is the result of reflection, and thus excluded from true spiritual affections. Hence, while self-love may have general utility as a natural affection and good, it is distinct from the true taste for the beauty of God.

Approaching the question of self-love from this perspective provides Edwards with two further points regarding the place of self-love in the moral life. First, self-love may provide the foundation for a doctrinally correct love of God in Christ that is at the same time devoid of any true spiritual affections. There "are many things exhibited in the gospel concerning God and Christ, and the way of salvation, that have a natural good in them, which suits the natural principle of self-love" (Y2:277). Even unregenerate persons may "be much affected with the wonderful goodness of God to mankind, his great goodness in giving his Son to die for fallen man, and the marvelous love of Christ in suffering such great things for us" (Y2:246). The form of this natural self-love of Christ may be either simple or compounded. That is to say, persons may love God solely for the benefits they believe God gives them either as individuals or "as parts of a community." Their "consideration or conception of their interest" may extend to a "nation," to "the world of mankind," and even beyond to "the inhabitants of other planets," but it falls short of the love that "primarily consists" in the "view or contemplation of the divine and holy beauty of these things, as they are in themselves" (Y2:247, 249). Second, the optimal place of self-love in the saint is one in which it is a vestigial concern that threatens to distract the saint from his or her main focus on the "glory of God in Christ." A "true saint," Edwards writes, is "too much captivated and engaged by what he views without himself, to stand at that time to view himself, and his own attainments." To focus on one's own private interest "would be a diversion and loss" from the "ravishing object" of "contemplation" which the saint "could not bear." This self-forgetfulness derives from the fact that true "gracious affections" have "their foundation out of self, in God and Jesus Christ." It also stems from the saint's recognition of his or her own relative "deformity" in comparison with the beauty of God (Y2:252–53).

2. THE SHAPE OF THE MORAL LIFE

The greatest benefit Edwards reaps from the anthropology he develops in the *Religious Affections* is that it offers a more complete portrait of the complexity of the moral life. As we observed in chapter 2, although Edwards includes the soul in his depiction of the spousal and somatic images of the church, the main focus of the social analogy is ecclesial. In the *Religious Affections*, however, the focus of Edwards's attention is the individual soul. Like the church, the shape of the moral and spiritual life in the soul is as much one of gradual progress as one of instant communion with God. Though he likens conversion to the acquisition of a new taste or sense, Edwards also admits the "very imperfect degree" in which "this sense is commonly given at first" when the "light" of God "first dawns on the soul" (Y2:275). In addition to being gradually given, the light of God also illuminates the "infinite distance" between the saint's love and the love of

God. Though they are "covered" with the "righteousness of Christ" and have their "deformities swallowed up and hid" in the "beams of his glory and love," the saints "see God as he is" and see themselves as they truly are (Y2:328). As the "soul in a spiritual view is convinced of infinitely more in the object, yet beyond sight; so it is convinced of the capacity of the soul, of knowing vastly more, if the clouds and darkness were but removed." The "enjoyment of a spiritual view" causes the soul to complain "greatly of spiritual ignorance, and want of love, and long and reach after more knowledge, and more love" (Y2:324–25). Hence, it is "the nature of grace, and of true spiritual light," that spiritual affections "dispose the saints" to "look upon their grace and goodness little, and their deformity great." As one progresses in the spiritual life, the sense of one's own sinfulness only increases: Those "that have the most grace and spiritual light, of any in this world, have the most of this disposition," or sense of spiritual inadequacy (Y2:323).

Edwards offers two representative figures that capture this double dynamic of true spiritual affections. The premier figure is Jesus Christ, particularly in his role as spiritual head of the church and exemplar of the triune love of God. Christ is "he whom God sent into the world, to be the light of the world, and head of the whole church, and the perfect example of true religion and virtue, for the imitation of all" (Y2:111). The beginning of the spiritual life is not the saint's orderly affirmation of the doctrines of justification and atonement, however vividly told or fervently grasped. Rather, the "new birth" of conversion is a moment of "confused chaos" like one's "first birth," and conforms to the pattern of Christ's incarnation. The "conception of Christ in the womb of the blessed Virgin, by the power of the Holy Ghost, seems to be a designed resemblance of the conception of Christ in the soul of a believer, by the power of the Holy Ghost" (Y2:161). By having Christ born in the soul, believers receive from Christ the fullness of his grace, so that there is "grace for grace," that is, "there is grace in Christians answering to grace in Christ" (Y2:347). Moreover, just as the incarnation is the temporal manifestation in a historical person, Jesus Christ, of the triune love of God, so the indwelling of the Spirit of Christ in the soul of the believer marks another temporal manifestation of the eternal love of God.

Within the figure of Christ, Edwards weaves a number of metaphors to emphasize the affections that flow from the soul's membership in the mystical body of Christ through the Spirit. One metaphor follows straightforwardly from the christological claims found in the New Testament. Edwards introduces the metaphor of the vine and the branches (John 15:1ff.) and writes that "the branch is of the same nature with the stock and root, has the same sap, and bears the same sort of fruit" (Y2:347). In addition, Edwards uses the metaphors of oil and the dove, which he uses in his Trinitarian writings to explain the mission of the Spirit. As "Christ was anointed with the Holy Ghost, descending on him like a dove, so Christians also have an anointing from the Holy One." The "dove is a noted emblem of meekness, harmlessness, peace and love," and the Spirit communicates to the saints a "dovelike temper and disposition." Likewise, the "oil of Aaron's garments" symbolize "the savor of Christ's sweet ointments," which flow out in "Christian affections" and "Christian behavior" (Y2:348).

In sum, for Edwards the figure of Christ represents not only a concrete, historical person that Christians must faithfully imitate, but also the new, generative identity and relationship that believers experience through the coordinated work of the Son and the Spirit. Christ's example to believers is therefore as one who has received in full the Spirit's self-gift in the form of holiness and godly affections, for the "same Spirit that descended on the Head of the Church, descends to the members" so there is "but one Spirit to the whole mystical body, head, and members of Christ" (Y2:348).

Besides the figure of Christ, another secondary figure represents the saints' recognition of their spiritual poverty when confronted with this abundance—the woman of ill repute who anointed Jesus in the house of Simon the Pharisee (Luke 7:36–50), whom Edwards identifies as Mary Magdalene (Y2:339). The woman, Edwards writes, "that we read of in the 7th chapter of Luke" was "an eminent saint, and had much of that true love that casts out fear." She "approached Christ in an amiable, and acceptable manner, when she came with that humble modesty, reverence, and shame, when she stood at his feet, weeping behind him, as not being fit to appear before his face, and washed his feet with her tears" (Y2:363). Hence, "Christian affections are like Mary's precious ointment, that she poured on Christ's head." Just as the ointment pours from a broken "alabaster box," so "all Christian affections, that are a sweet odor to Christ, and that fill the soul of a Christian with the heavenly sweetness and fragrancy, are brokenhearted affections." A "truly Christian love, either to God or men, is a humble brokenhearted love" (Y2:339).

2.1. Virtue

For Edwards, Christian ethics proceeds from the character of God. As we have seen, holiness in "the more extensive sense of the word" refers to God's "moral excellency," or God's "beauty as a moral agent." Likewise in humans, "holiness comprehends all the true virtue" of a "good" person, particularly his or her "love to God," "gracious love" to neighbors, "charity," "gracious meekness and gentleness, and all other true Christian virtues." Human holiness is "but the image of God's holiness: there are not more virtues belonging to the image than are in the original: derived holiness has not more in it, than is in that underived holiness, which is its fountain: there is no more than grace for grace, or grace in the image answerable to grace in the original" (Y2:255–56).

Hence, Edwards sees no strict distinction between authentic piety and the dispositions that govern the Christian moral life. There "is no other true virtue, but real holiness" (Y2:255). All other supposed virtues, such as "honesty, justice, generosity, good nature, and public spirit" are illusory, merely "seeming virtues," evident "in many of the heathen" (Y2:254). Moreover, the holiness of Christian virtue is a specific love of God's goodness and moral excellency that differs from the natural devotion to God on the basis of God's "natural perfections." While the "sense of God's greatness and natural attributes" is "exceeding useful and necessary," it is the product of natural, rather than spiritual, affections (Y2:266). No true virtue is "enkindled" in those whose love is based entirely on a sense of "God's greatness" (Y2:264–65).

In addition to the overarching correspondence between virtue and "everything that pertains to holiness of heart," there are also "particular graces" that "may more especially be called the Christian spirit or temper." These are the virtues of "humility, meekness, love, forgiveness, and mercy." Like the "special agreeableness" between the moral excellency of God and "the work of redemption by Jesus Christ," these virtues are "peculiarly agreeable to the special drift and design of the work of redemption" and the "relation that it brings us into, to God and one another" (Y2:346).

Of these special virtues, foremost is humility. Edwards distinguishes, we observed earlier, between "legal" and "evangelical" humiliation. The former humiliation comes as a response to one's deviation from God's law, but has no spiritual value in itself. The latter is an "answerable frame of heart, consisting in a disposition" in the saints "to abase themselves, and exalt God alone" (Y2:312). The former is a response to one's shortcomings regarding the Golden Rule; the latter is a response to one's shortcomings regarding the New Commandment. Evangelical humility, therefore, is the "great and most essential thing in true religion," for the "whole frame of the gospel," including "everything appertaining to the New Covenant and all God's dispensations," are "calculated to bring to pass this effect in the hearts" of the saints (Y2:312).

True humility follows the dynamic of the woman of ill repute. Following the woman's "manner," humility stems from the realization of one's own sinfulness when confronted with God's "dispensation of grace" (Y2:312). The end of humility, however, lies beyond a posture of penitence toward God. Indeed, if humility rests merely on one's recognition of personal sinfulness, it can quickly degenerate into a "counterfeit humility" where persons "glory of their own humility" and have a "high opinion of their abasement" (Y2:319). True humility inspires the "Christian duty of self-denial," which consists in the twofold mortification, first, of "worldly inclinations" and "enjoyments" and, second, of "natural self-exaltation" (Y2:315). A "truly humble person" is therefore "emptied of himself" and "modest in his speech and behavior." He or she "is not only disposed to honor the saints in his behavior; but others also, in all those ways that don't imply a visible approbation of their sins" (Y2:339).

The virtues of forgiveness, mercy, and meekness follow the dynamic of Christ, who provides a "blessed example" of Christian virtue (Y2:346). "Truly gracious affections" clothe the saint with "the lamblike, dovelike spirit and temper of Jesus Christ," and they beget "such a spirit of love, meekness, quietness, forgiveness, and mercy, as appeared in Christ" (Y2:344–45). Forgiveness is, first and foremost, "a disposition to overlook and forgive injuries," and is a sign that "we are in a state of forgiveness and favor ourselves" (Y2:353). Mercy is a "disposition" the "true saints" have "to pity and relieve their fellow creatures, that are poor, indigent and afflicted" (Y2:355).

Meekness is a disposition of "gentleness" and "quietness" (Y2:351). In the saints it is a willingness to be childlike, that is, "not guileful and deceitful, but plain and simple," "yieldable and flexible, and not willful and obstinate" (Y2:349). Although typically contrasted with fortitude, Edwards argues that the disposition of meekness actually requires fortitude. The Christian life, he notes, is often "fitly" compared to "warfare," so long as one understands that "Christian fortitude" is the antithesis of "brutal fierceness." Christian fortitude "consists in strength of mind, through grace, exerted in two things: in ruling and suppressing the evil, and unruly passions and affections of the mind; and in steadfastly and freely exerting and following good affections and dispositions, without being hindered by sinful fear, or the opposition of enemies." Though Christian fortitude at times necessitates resisting "enemies that are without us," it "more appears in resisting and suppressing the enemies that are within us," for the inner enemies "are our worst and strongest" and "have greatest advantage against us." In this sense, the "good soldier of Christ" follows the example set by Christ "in the time of his last sufferings" and maintains "the holy calm, meekness, sweetness, and benevolence of his mind, amidst all the storms, injuries, strange behavior, and surprising acts and events of this evil and unreasonable world" (Y2:350–51).

When he frames the Christian life in terms of virtue, Edwards follows a long-standing practice in Christian theology of appropriating non-Christian understandings of virtue to inform its own vision of the moral life. Although Edwards engages the virtue ethics of his contemporaries in the *Two Dissertations*, in the *Religious Affections* his conversation partners are those from pre-Enlightenment classical and Christian thought. Briefly stated, in classical thought virtue, or *arete*, refers to the general excellence of a person in fulfilling his or her potential. Within this general under-standing of virtue, two schools of thought formed.[13] For Plato, human nature is fulfilled according to the degree to which the mind rationally grasps the Form of the Good and proportionately subordinates all other desires and affections in the parts of the soul. Virtue, then, for Plato is a kind of insight—one must know the Good in order to be good, and the standard of goodness against which to measure all other instances of goodness is absolute and eternal.[14] For Aristotle, human nature is fulfilled to the extent the practical intellect, or *phronesis*, is sufficiently educated to make the right choices regarding those actions and goods that are particu-lar to human nature. Virtue, then, for Aristotle is a cultivated state of char-acter, or *hexis*, that an individual learns like a craft, or *techne*, for living well. Where Plato measures goodness against a standard that is absolute and eternal, Aristotle sees virtue in terms of the more proximate end, or *telos*, of human flourishing and the preservation of the good city-state, or *polis*. Against these more proximate standards, specific virtues represent the rea-sonable mean between acting excessively or deficiently.[15]

Within Christian theology, two dominant approaches to virtue arose that reflected the differences between the Platonic and Aristotelian schools of thought.[16] Augustine follows Plato's definition of virtue as a kind of insight. But unlike Plato, Augustine emphasizes that illumination is com-plete only if the love of the triune God in the form of charity, or *caritas*, dwells in the soul and instills the desire for union with God and compas-sion for one's neighbor. Accordingly, specific virtues are denominations of *caritas*; the theological virtues of faith, hope, and love (love for Augustine is both a particular virtue and the foundation for all virtue), and the cardi-nal virtues of prudence, justice, fortitude and temperance are properly forms and exercises of love. Virtue, then, for Augustine culminates in the life of beatitude; virtue expresses the soul's ontological movement toward God through participating in the divine *caritas*. All so-called virtues that do not directly express the divine *caritas* are counterfeits—pagan "virtues" are merely "splendid vices."[17] Without seeking to undermine the insights of Augustine, Thomas Aquinas develops an understanding of virtue that incorporates central aspects of Aristotle's approach. With Aristotle, Thomas understands a virtue as a "habit," or *habitus*, that perfects human nature through the education of the intellect. Thomas therefore sees the cardinal virtues as the actualization of natural human dispositions within the soul that persons can acquire to a certain extent through their own resources. The theological virtues, however, complete human nature's supernatural end of participation in God through the infusion of *caritas* in the soul. And considered from the perspective of human nature's super-natural end, the cardinal virtues themselves cannot fully exist without *car-itas*. Accordingly, Thomas sees the theological virtues as "infused," as something that "God works in us without us," while the cardinal virtues are "acquired," as something that "God works in us with us."[18]

Some of the terms and concepts Edwards uses are similar to those found in the Aristotelian and Thomistic accounts of virtue. Edwards seems to allude to the Aristotelian definition of virtue as a dispositional state of character when he writes that the moral image of God in the saints is one of "character." That is to say, the saints experience the same "disposition wherein Christ's character does in a special manner consist," so that "the same things that belong to Christ's character" belong "to theirs" (Y2:347). Edwards also speaks of the spiritual affections the saint experiences of God as a new "habit or principle of action" (Y2:398). And in a way that is reminiscent of Thomas's treatment of the cardinal virtues, Edwards admits that through participating in the "natural" image of God, humans are capable of expressing "honesty, justice, generosity, good nature, and public spirit" (Y2:254).

Nonetheless, despite these points of contact with the Aristotelian and Thomistic accounts, Aristotelian habituation runs counter to the basic tenets of Edwards's moral anthropology. Though he speaks of virtue as a settled state of "character" or "habit" in the soul, Edwards rejects habituation as a means for moral development, in either the "natural" or "moral" image of God in human nature. In Edwards's understanding, a "habit" is a principle that is internal to an entity, and not, as Aristotle understands it, an acquired state or condition of a given entity.[19] For as we have seen, the affections and dispositions within the soul determine the moral content of a person's character, regardless of the specific choices or actions that a person takes. In both the regenerate and the unregenerate, human nature is defined in terms of the affections. Consequently, the moral orientation of a person is the direct result of that person's greatest love, rather than a state of being acquired through thoughtful practice. Thus, in the *Religious Affections,* Edwards explicitly rejects the role of moral "education" in producing virtuous action (Y2:295). For "nature is a more powerful principle of action than anything that opposes it." When a "natural" person "denies" his or her "lusts, and lives a strict, religious life" it is "all a force against nature." Edwards believes it makes as much sense to try to learn virtue through thoughtful cultivation of the practical intellect as it does to throw a stone repeatedly upward in the hope of teaching it to fly (Y2:296).[20] As a result, though Edwards does not directly address the topic of acquired and infused virtues in the *Religious Affections*, he argues in "Miscellanies" entries *l* and *p* that "the notion of acquired habits is wrong" when applied to the Holy Spirit's operation in the soul (Y13:169). To "say that the Holy

Spirit" merely "assists" the soul "in acquiring the habit" of grace directly undermines the sense in which the Holy Spirit "infuses" grace in the soul. For "grace consists very much in a principle that causes vigorousness and activity in action," and this is the meaning of the word "infusion" (Y13:171).

More importantly, Edwards believes that to accommodate Aristotelian virtue in the way that Thomas does obscures the fact that virtue represents human nature's participation in God's moral excellency through the indwelling of the Holy Spirit. Accordingly, Edwards rejects any other account of the development of virtue that would ascribe to human effort the role of moral transformation that is properly reserved for the triune God alone. Edwards's disavowal of the role of habituation in true virtue and spiritual affections does not mean that he sees these other aspects of human experience and development as God-forsaken, for as we observed in chapter 1, Edwards believes that the Holy Spirit does provide "assistance" to natural persons through the conscience (Y13:513). But it does mean that Edwards paints a sharper contrast between human effort, the Spirit's assistance, and the Spirit's indwelling than Thomas does.

Further, though Edwards ascribes limited moral capabilities to the unregenerate, and does not portray these capabilities in an entirely negative light, he believes these capabilities have no redeeming value. Where Thomas appropriates the cardinal virtues to develop an account of virtue that can accommodate the general capabilities of human nature, Edwards introduces the distinction between the natural and moral *imago dei* to dichotomize true virtue and all other "seeming virtues." As we have seen, Edwards does not ascribe value to the natural attributes a person has—the moral attributes alone are the sole source of value and excellence. Thus, Edwards writes that the word "moral" is commonly applied to the "justice, generosity, good nature, and public spirit" that proceed from "natural principles," but these are only "seeming virtues" that must be viewed "in opposition" to those virtues that are "spiritual and divine," such as "holy faith, love, humility, and heavenly-mindedness" (Y2:254).[21] Consequently, Edwards reasserts Augustine's belief that the moral achievements of non-Christians are actually splendid vices. One might "be tempted to think that many of the heathen philosophers were truly gracious" and possessed "many virtues, and also great illuminations" (Y2:315). But the "heathen philosophers," as well as "Jews," "Mahometans," "Papists," "heretics," and "enthusiasts," are unaware that the transforming love of the triune God is the basis of all true virtue, and therefore their understanding of virtue is fatally flawed.[22]

With Augustine, Edwards sees virtue directly and irreducibly flowing from God's triune love, and all specific virtues as denominations of this love. Edwards's depiction of the soul's dynamic progress toward God through illumination and love recalls Augustine's well-known metaphor in the *Confessions* that the love of God is a kind of weight (*pondus*) in the soul that draws it to God, who is the center of gravity. As a "body gravitates to its proper place by its own weight," Augustine writes, "love is the weight by which I act." Likewise, Edwards's account also retrieves the Trinitarian context in which Augustine presents his metaphor of weight; for Augustine, the weight of God's love in the soul is the "Gift" of the Spirit given by the "one God, Father, Son and Holy Spirit."[23]

Yet Edwards does not owe the debt Augustine does to Plato for his understanding of virtue. Though Edwards places a similar emphasis on illumination, he understands illumination not in terms of the Platonic replication of universal ideas and values, but in terms of an immediate sense and actual participation in the triune God through partaking in the Spirit. This more immediate sense of participation affords an account of virtue that brings to the fore the personal relation of intimacy and imitation that believers have with God through their spiritual membership in the body of Christ. Within the soul, this relation of intimacy and trust manifests itself both in a general affection and orientation toward God and, following the figures of Christ and the woman of ill repute, in the specific virtues of humility, meekness, mercy, and forgiveness.[24]

2.2. Duty

Although Edwards articulates the central features of the moral life in terms of virtue, he also speaks of it in terms of duty and divine commands. Living the moral life fulfills Christ's "new" commandment that "ye love one another as I have loved you" (Y2:354). Edwards's scriptural touchstones for the New Commandment are the Johannine commandments of love present in the Gospel of John and 1 John. In these passages divine commands derive from the nature of God. That is to say, these passages consider the command to love one another as a necessary outcome of having received the Spirit of love from the triune God, who is love. "Christ calls the law of love, by way of eminency, *his* commandment, 'A new commandment I give to you, that ye love one another'" (John 13:34). And the "Beloved Disciple, who had so much of this sweet temper himself, abundantly insists on it, in his Epistles," writing "'Beloved, let us love one another; for love is of God; and everyone that loveth is born of God, and knoweth God: he that loveth not, knoweth not God; for God is love'" (1 John 4:7–8; Y2:354–55).

Hence, the content of Christian duty is no less than receiving and returning the love of God. Our obligations are manifest in the "joint consideration" of two things: first, the "manifestations" of God's "glory," particularly in the "gospel of his Son, and what he has done" for "sinful" persons; second, "the capacity there is in the soul" and its "intellectual faculties" for "seeing and understanding the reasons, which God has given us to love him." Accordingly, "we must take our measure from that height to which the rule of our duty extends." To fail in this "duty" to love God wholly is an act of disobedience and sin. For "the whole of the distance we are at from that height, is sin," and the "failing of duty is sin, otherwise our duty is not our duty" (Y2:325).

Edwards's understanding of the command of God differs from that typically found in Reformed theology, where divine commands have a heteronomous aspect that entails that they transcend human experience or analysis.[25] In this account, divine commands are based in God's metaphysical attributes, specifically God's sovereignty and omniscience, and serve the purpose of indicating or justifying the nature of moral obligation. In contrast, Edwards generates the requirements of Christian duty from the saint's sense of God's moral attributes of goodness and excellency. The "holy disposition and spiritual taste" enables the saint "to determine what actions are right" and "agreeable" to the "Christian rules of humility, meekness and charity" (Y2:283–84). Not only do God's moral attributes indicate and ground God's commands, but the fundamental "rules" of Christian obligation are to cultivate the virtues that reflect a Christian spirit, that is, the "rules" of "meekness and forgiveness," "mercy and charity" (Y2:419).

Thus, Edwards comprehends under the category of obligation both negative and positive duties, and inward and outward acts. That is to say, Christians must be "universally obedient" to "Christ's commands" and make the "business of religion, and the service of God" the "main business of their lives." It is not enough to avoid "wicked practices, consisting in sins of commission," for "sins of omission are as much breaches of God's commands" (Y2:386–87, 419). "Merely that a professor of Christianity is what is commonly called an honest man, and a moral man"—that is, there is "no special transgression" or "blot on his character"—offers "no great evidence of the sincerity of his profession." Such behavior is not a "light" that shines before others. But there must be "positive evidence" of a "life in the service of God." The saints must "follow the example of Jesus Christ" and "those excellent rules in the 5th, 6th, and 7th chapters of Matthew, and 12th of Romans, and many other parts of the New Testament." They must be "universal in the performance of the duties of the first table" of the Ten Commandments, "manifesting the fear and love of God," as well as the second table's rules of "love to saints and love to enemies." The saints must "walk as Christians in all places, and at all seasons, in the house of God, and in their families, and among their neighbors, on Sabbath days and every day, in business and conversation, towards friends and enemies, towards superiors, inferiors, and equals" (Y2:419).

Acts of obedience, Edwards stresses, are acts of the whole "soul." The "good works" and "keeping of Christ's commandments" do not only regard "what is external, or the motion and action of the body, without including anything else, having no respect to any aim or intention." Considered externally, human "actions" are no more acts of obedience than "the regular motions of a clock," and as such are "neither acts of obedience nor disobedience." Rather, "the whole exercise of the spirit of the mind, in the action, must be taken in, with the end acted for, and the respect the soul then has to God, etc.; otherwise they are no acts of denial of ourselves, or obedience to God, or service done to him, but something else" (Y2:423).

Similarly, one cannot love one's neighbor only in spirit; the love of neighbor is a love of body and soul. "Some" show a "love to others as to their outward" person, and "give to the poor, but have no love to, or concern for, the souls" of their neighbors. "Others pretend a great love" for their neighbor's souls, but "are not compassionate and charitable towards their bodies," making "a great show of love, pity, and distress" that "costs them nothing." True Christian love of one's neighbors "extends to both their souls and bodies," and therefore is "like the love and compassion of Jesus Christ," who healed the sick and fed the poor while he preached the gospel (Y2:369).

A final aspect of obligation concerns "trials." Mention of trials, or moments of suffering, persecution, and temptation, appears at different points in the *Religious Affections*.[26] Early on in the treatise, for example, Edwards writes that "true virtue never appears so lovely, as when it is most oppressed, and the divine excellency of real Christianity is never exhibited with such advantage, as when under the greatest trials." In circumstances such as these, "true faith" is "more precious than gold" (Y2:93). "If persons, after they have made a profession of religion, live any considerable time in this world so full of evil," Edwards writes at another point, "it can't be otherwise than that they should meet many trials of their sincerity and steadfastness" (Y2:389).

Edwards takes up the question of trials directly when he speaks of obligation. Trials "render" the Christian's "continuance" in "duty and faithfulness to God, difficult." It is God's "manner, in his providence, to bring trials on his professing friends and servant designedly," to manifest to "their own consciences" and often "to the world" the "state they are in" (Y2:389). God makes use of trials not to learn any new "information" God does not otherwise know, but so that the saints themselves can learn "whether they will keep his commandments or no." For example, "when God tempted or tried Abraham with that difficult command of offering up his son," it was not for God's own "satisfaction, but for Abraham's own greater satisfaction and comfort, and the more clear manifestation of the favor of God to him." Trials accordingly serve a twofold purpose. On one hand, trials provide the occasion in which the saints can test the mettle of their faith. The "surest way to know our gold is to look upon it and examine it in God's furnace, where he tries it for that end that we may see what it is." For "if we would weigh ourselves justly, we must weigh ourselves in God's scales, that he makes use of to weigh us" (Y2:432–33). On the other, God uses them to complete the gifts of faith and love. God brings the trial on Abraham to give greater "evidence to Abraham's conscience" that he was "upright in the sight of his Judge." Hence, the trial ends in "comfort and rejoicing" (Y2:431–32).

Edwards does not explore the tensions often associated with divine commands. He does not dwell, as Kierkegaard does in *Fear and Trembling* (1843), on the conflicts and paradoxes surrounding Abraham's binding of Isaac. Edwards offers no "teleological suspension of the ethical," and no defense of "radical interiority" or "infinite resignation" (Y2:389). Nor does Edwards use the binding of Isaac, with its complex layers of meaning, to justify the individual's "absolute," particular relation to God over and against the "universal" social requirements of ethics and commonplace judgments of right and wrong.[27] No doubt, Edwards would commend Kierkegaard's insistence that God be the subject of unique veneration and his conviction that an ethics not sufficiently grounded in this veneration is inadequate. But unlike Kierkegaard, Edwards does not consider divine commands, even those given in trials, as contrary to the saints' experience of God through the spiritual affections. Both the "new sense" and the commands of God express the same moral excellency and goodness of God. Although God retains the initiative in revealing God's goodness and excellency, once the "new sense" is given, the saints intuitively know the "reality and certainty of divine things," which grounds their understanding of God's commands (Y2:291).

In sum, Edwards sees divine commands as essentially pedagogical and diagnostic. Commands teach the way of virtue, and the saint can use them to discern and test his or her affections, in order to renounce those desires that are sinful and to cleave to the triune love of God. This purpose becomes clearest during trials and temptations, when the saint is "brought to the dividing of paths, the one which leads to Christ," the other to Christ's "competitors," such as "the world" and the "objects" of his or her "lusts." In these moments, God's commands help the saint see "which preponderates" as the "superior inclination" of his or her "heart" (Y2:434).

2.3. Practice

The final dimension in Edwards's depiction of the moral life in the *Religious Affections* concerns the connection between piety and practice. Edwards considers "practice," or those actions that embody the Christian

life, as "the *principle* sign by which Christians are to judge, both of their
own and others' sincerity of godliness" (Y2:406–7). In retrospect of what
we have examined so far in the *Religious Affections*, it is clear why he thinks
so. Edwards's understanding of the affections, and the place affections
occupy in the soul, necessitate that actions manifest inner dispositions.
Affections are the "spring" of "actions" (Y2:101). Human beings are
dynamic entities, constantly pursuing those things that they love most.

Further, the saints are those whose affections are "spiritual." They have
received "a communication of God, a participation of the divine nature,
Christ living in the heart, the Holy Spirit dwelling there, in union with the
faculties of the soul, as an internal principle, exerting his own proper
nature, in the exercise of those faculties." Correlatively, true grace has an
inherent "activity, power and efficacy"(Y2:392). "Godliness" has a "direct
relation to practice, as a fountain to a stream, or as the luminous nature of
the sun has to the beams sent forth, or as life to breathing, or the beating
of the pulse, or any other vital act." Like the relation a "habit or principle
of action has to action," the "very nature and notion of grace" is a "principle of holy action or practice" (Y2:398).

Finally, it is only through action or practice that the virtues and duties
of the Christian life find completion. "Practice is the proper proof of the
true and saving knowledge of God" and "all the virtues of the mind"
(Y2:444). All "the duties of the second table of the law" are things "wherein
Christian practice does very much consist" (Y2:396). "Practice is the proper
evidence of a gracious love, both to God and men" (Y2:447).

The relation, then, between "the tendency of grace in the heart" and
"holy practice" is direct, a "connection most natural, close, and necessary"
(Y2:398). To illustrate this connection further, Edwards speaks in terms
of regeneration. "Regeneration" is "that work of God in which grace is
infused" and "has a direct relation to practice," for Christian practice is
"the very end" of "this mighty and manifold change wrought in the soul"
(Y2:398). But Edwards moves beyond regeneration's normal confines
when he argues that "to speak of Christian experience and practice as if
they were two things, properly and entirely distinct, is to make a distinction without consideration or reason" (Y2:450). Traditionally, the Puritan
doctrine of regeneration holds that the connection between faith and
works is an orderly, sequential relationship subordinate to the experience
of justification: One is justified before God by faith alone, but faith without works is dead; works testify that the experience of faith is authentic.
As we have seen, however, for Edwards the beginning of the spiritual life
is a "chaotic" moment of new birth rather than an orderly acceptance and
affirmation of the central doctrines of the faith (Y2:161). Edwards thus
believes that Christian piety and practice flow from the same experience of
new being.[28]

Edwards is aware that it is possible to misconstrue his position as one of works righteousness. "Some may object" that the emphasis he places on practice "magnifies works," diminishes "the glory of free grace," and runs counter to "that great gospel doctrine of justification by faith alone." To this, Edwards responds that he nowhere suggests that Christian works can earn "God's favor," or that the grace God bestows on the saints is in any way dependent on the "worthiness or loveliness of any qualification or action of ours" (Y2:457). On the contrary, misplaced vigilance concerning the purity of the doctrine of justification by faith has "hurt" the cause of "religion" by neglecting the "effectual operations of grace in practice" and overemphasizing the "discoveries, and method and manner of the immanent exercises" of "grace in contemplation" (Y2:459). Certainly, Edwards believes that contemplation plays an important role in the religious life. He is careful, as I noted earlier, to include contemplation as one of the "exercises of grace" in the conscience that has an indirect relation to action (Y2:423), and in both the *Religious Affections* and his Trinitarian writings, it is evident that Edwards appreciates deeply the importance of self-reflection.

Nonetheless, Edwards is aware that it is easy to confuse natural affections in the form of heightened experiences with spiritual affections, and that such confusion tends to produce a prideful hypocrisy that is the antithesis of the Christian self. Though hypocrisy is often defined as a state of affairs in which persons are deceived by someone's "outward morality and external religion," more threatening and insidious is the hypocrisy that cries "down works" and "righteousness," and talks "much of free grace" in order to deceive persons by "false discoveries and elevations" (Y2:173). This "evangelical" hypocrisy conceals a self-aggrandizing will-to-power under the guise of Christian humility. Such hypocrites "abundantly cry down works, and cry up faith in opposition to works, and set up themselves very much as evangelical persons, in opposition to those that are of a legal spirit." While they "make a fair show of advancing Christ and the gospel, and the way of free grace," they are in actuality "some of the greatest enemies to the gospel way of free grace" and "pure, humble Christianity." For their supposed "humility is a swelling, self-conceited, confident, showy, noisy, assuming humility" (Y2:318–19). To counter this tendency, Edwards reworks the metaphor of the tree and its fruits (Matt. 7:16), one of the definitive statements in the New Testament of the relation between piety and practice: "Christ nowhere says, ye shall know the tree by its leaves or flowers," but by its fruit. Likewise one cannot know the spiritual authenticity of others "by the good story they tell of their experiences," by the "manner and air of their speaking," or by their "emphasis and pathos of expression," but by their "good works" (Y2:407).

Edwards anticipates Dietrich Bonhoeffer's polemic against "cheap grace" in *The Cost of Discipleship* (1937). Both Edwards and Bonhoeffer rec-

ognize that the unconditional love preached through the doctrine of justification can undermine the authenticity and struggle that is clearly man-
dated in the New Testament. With Bonhoeffer, Edwards argues that
"words are cheap" and that "Christian practice is a costly, laborious thing"
(Y2:411). Yet somewhat different motivations drive Edwards and Bonhoeffer. Bonhoeffer's main concern is secularism, that the Christian life
has become indistinguishable from the "world," so that "the antithesis
between the Christian life and the life of bourgeois respectability" comes
to an end.[29] But Edwards's main concern is that the church would no
longer be a temple of the triune God. That is to say, through receiving the
spiritual affections, the saints' "hearts are united to the people of Jesus
Christ as their people, to cleave to them and love them as their bretheren,
and worship and serve God and follow Christ in union and fellowship
with them, being willing and resolved to perform all those duties that
belong to them, as members of the same family of God and mystical Body
of Christ" (Y2:417). In short, spiritual affections are the basis of true fellowship and communion in the church with the triune God. Thus, from
Edwards's perspective, the church could persist for generations as a distinct institution with a unique ethos, peopled by fervent adherents confident of their own spirituality, and yet be full of persons who had no true
experience of or desire for the love of God and neighbor.

3. INSIGHTS FOR CONTEMPORARY VIRTUE THEORY IN THEOLOGICAL ETHICS

Within contemporary theological ethics, Aristotelian virtue theory has
experienced a renaissance that is comparable to the renewed interest in the
Trinity in recent theology.[30] Tracing the reasons behind this renewed interest in Aristotelian virtue theory is beyond the scope of this book.[31] But one
general explanation is that Aristotelian virtue offers an alternative way to
transcend the central Enlightenment problem concerning the unreliability
of external beliefs. Where Immanuel Kant, for example, believes the categorical imperatives generated by autonomous reason can enable the self to
transcend its immediate knowledge, desires, and self-interest, retrievals of
Aristotelian virtue seek to integrate these aspects of the self into a comprehensive account of human nature and the human good.[32]

The different retrievals of Aristotle's virtue theory in current ethics are
neither unanimous nor straightforward. But the most influential is that of
Alasdair MacIntyre.[33] MacIntyre turns to Aristotelian virtue not merely to
place questions of character above those of duty (deontology) or outcomes
(consequentialism). Rather, his argument concerns as much the intelligibility of moral accounts and the extent to which ethical reasoning derives

from a particular historical-ethical community. Drawing from Aristotle's understanding of virtue as ordered by the *telos* of human flourishing and the good society, MacIntyre argues that any given account of virtue stems from a particular society's formative narratives and social practices, which form an overarching tradition that shapes one's understanding of the moral life. Every moral account therefore must recognize its tradition dependency—that its view of human nature and the human good is shaped by a specific history, narrative, and set of practices that not only determine its answers to moral questions but which moral questions it asks in the first place. MacIntyre's influence, then, on Christian ethics is not only in terms of the general point of departure (i.e., virtue) but also in terms of the recent priority given to canonical texts, paradigmatic theologians, and communal practices in ethical reflection.

In recent theological ethics, three authors explore what insights Edwards's account of virtue offers in light of MacIntyre's retrieval. Paul Lewis argues that Edwards offers a corrective to the "excessively intellectualized conception of moral agency" of "Neo-Aristotelian virtue ethics."[34] Where current studies of character ethics reinforce a "rationalist bias" pervasive in "Western thought," Edwards's understanding of the affections recognizes the importance of the "emotions" for the unified self, without negating the possibility for some limited moral transformation through social practices.[35] Similarly, James Gilman argues that Edwards augments MacIntyre's account of virtue by "reenfranchising" the "emotions or passions" to their "proper status" in the moral life.[36] By prioritizing love as the chief virtue, Edwards makes the emotions central to his account of virtue, and his articulation of specific virtues such as humility express the solidarity, mutuality, and sympathy that structures authentic Christian community. Hence, an Edwardsian account of moral development would attend to the education of the emotions that occurs through the Christian narratives, practices, and covenantal communities.[37] Finally, Stephen Wilson argues that Edwards presents the possibility of a "second wave" in virtue ethics.[38] Approaching Edwards's moral anthropology from the perspective of Edwards's *Freedom of the Will*, Wilson argues that Edwards's "metaphysics of freedom" can sufficiently accommodate the retrieval in "first wave" virtue ethics of Aristotelian habituation as a source for moral development. Though Edwards believes it impossible for human agents to experience regeneration by their own efforts, and that the will is not free in terms of its *present* inclinations and dispositions, Wilson argues that Edwards does acknowledge the ability to desire different *future* inclinations and dispositions. Given that Aristotle's understanding of habituation itself does not require a high degree of autonomy, Wilson concludes that a "place for a habituation model of moral development can be found" in Edwards's moral anthropology.[39] Therefore, Edwards's theory of virtue serves the dual purpose of setting forth, in a way similar to Thomas, points of continuity (habituation) and discontinuity (charity) with Aristotle, as well as providing a critique of the "uncircumscribed self-fashioning" that modern theories of moral agency presuppose.[40]

While these assessments recognize some of the differences between Edwards and MacIntyre, all three of these interpretations fail to take account of the dichotomy Edwards draws between his theological anthropology and the Aristotelian account of habituation in the *Religious Affections*. As we have seen, Edwards explicitly dismisses Aristotelian habituation as a means for moral development, particularly as it pertains to the spiritual affections that compose the heart of the virtue. In addition, Edwards explicitly dismisses those affections that arise from a person's socialization in a particular community. For a person with a "wicked and deceitful heart" can possess "a good doctrinal knowledge of religion," and exhibit a "decency of expression and behavior, formed by a good education" (Y2:183). Thus, "those affections" learned through "long acquaintance" with the church's practices "are merely natural and common" and "are built on a foundation that is not spiritual" (Y2:217; 183). Finally, while Edwards emphasizes "practice" in the moral life, he is careful to note that practices derive from the heart's inclinations. If the opposite holds—that is, if one's inclinations derive from one's practices, the affections developed are natural, not spiritual.

Granted, the above writers do not seek to present Edwards's definitive thought on habituation or social practices so much as to establish the possibility for a rapprochement between Edwards and Aristotle. But such efforts at rapprochement need to recognize *why* Edwards considers these mediums problematic. As we have seen, Edwards's immediate reasons for rejecting habituation and socialization as mediums for moral transformation are theological and anthropological. In Edwards's eyes, Aristotelian accounts of moral development run counter to his belief that true virtue is none other than an affective participation in the moral excellency and love of God, conferred to the soul through the direct indwelling of the Holy Spirit. Accordingly, the Aristotelian emphases on habituation and social practices privilege a part of human nature that Edwards considers, at the most, extraneous and trivial, as we will see in the next chapter.

Further, though Edwards emphasizes the role of the affections, it is clear that his main concern lies elsewhere. Unlike, say, Friedrich Schleiermacher, Edwards does not define the religious life merely in terms of an affection or feeling of absolute dependence, nor does he see the experience of God as having a determinate consciousness but no determinate content.[41] Though Edwards believes the affections constitute the very nature of a person, they do so because God has created us so that we may participate in the life of the Trinity. For Edwards, the affections apprehend a wider reality that transcends the soul and draws the soul into deeper knowledge of God's goodness and love, which form the basis for the life of virtue. Thus, the affections are validated not on the basis of their fervency or centrality per se, but by virtue of their being true apprehensions of the excellency and beauty of the triune God. Recalling Edwards's comparison between the soul's affections and the water in a fountain, what is decisive is the *nature of the water* that runs in the fountain of the soul, not merely the fact that the soul's affections are like a fountain.

Edwards, then, does not offer a corrective of MacIntyre's retrieval of Aristotelian virtue, but a genuinely alternative account. Like MacIntyre, Edwards is no stranger to the unreliability of external beliefs. But unlike MacIntyre, Edwards writes out of a context one can characterize as tradition-dependent. Indeed, it is hard to conceive of a culture more imbued with a thick sense of the centrality of narrative, practices, and the community than the New England of Edwards's time. Yet Edwards is well aware of the inability of his tradition to instill true virtue in the soul. Particularly in the *Religious Affections*, he argues that these supposed mediums of moral development actually prove counterproductive to the realization of the moral life, particularly when they obscure the extent to which true virtue and holiness proceed directly from the souls' participation in the triune love of God.

Accordingly, Edwards constructs a theological anthropology whose ultimate source is his doctrine of the Trinity. As we have seen, this anthropology presents a unified account of the *imago dei* that draws from both the psychological analogy's insight on self-reflection and social analogy's insight on communion. In this account, the triune love of God represents the restoration of the soul's "moral" image of God, as well as the soul's *theotic* transformation through the indwelling of the Holy Spirit. As such, the generative experience in the soul of the new "sense" and apprehension of God's moral excellency is at once the soul's experience of true identity and communion. Edwards places this experience in a class by itself and distinguishes it from all other kinds of human knowledge and love. The Trinity in Edwards's thought, then, has both ontological and epistemic primacy. That is, it guides Edwards's moral inquiry and provides the basis for all other beliefs concerning the nature of the moral life.[42] Likewise, the virtue that flows from God's triune love is *sui generis* in comparison to all other forms of morality, which exhibit but the "shadow" or "form" of the true goodness and beauty of the "Godhead" (Y2:274). Those schemes of morality that do not proceed directly from the character of God at best reflect the "natural image" of God in human nature. But they do not represent the "moral image" of God in human nature, which is the source of the beauty and value in the moral life. Only those virtues, commands, and practices that express, and are consistent with, the transformation of the soul through the indwelling of the love of Christ and the Spirit provide an adequate description of the Christian moral life.

Though he distinguishes his own proposal from those that would incorporate aspects of unregenerate human nature into their positive conception of the moral and spiritual life, Edwards does not take refuge in theological esotericism or fideism. Throughout his development of both his Trinitarian analogies and moral anthropology, Edwards works to make his arguments for a Trinitarian vision of the moral life reasonable to a wide audience and draws from those who do not share his particular commitments. As we have seen, Edwards turns to Locke and Malebranche to form his basic understanding of self-consciousness and the faculties. And despite his emphasis on the discontinuities between true virtue and so-called virtues, Edwards carefully articulates where his perspective on virtue departs from other accounts.

Nonetheless, Edwards does appear to subscribe to a version of what MacIntyre calls the state of "incommensurability" between moral accounts.[43] That is to say, despite their different orientations toward the moral life, both Edwards and MacIntyre believe there are limits to what the adherents of one belief system or moral tradition can understand of another. For MacIntyre, incommensurability primarily concerns intelligibility. Following an extended analogy concerning the difficulties of translation from one language into another, and from one language's particular cultural and historical context into another, MacIntyre argues that there are limits to what persons in a given belief system can reasonably translate into another language. Consequently, in order to acquire a sufficient knowledge of another tradition, persons must first recognize the extent to which they already operate in a specific tradition, and then immerse themselves as much as possible in the conceptual language and culture of another tradition. To do so authentically necessitates a degree of openness and vulnerability, for persons must be prepared to discover that another tradition of moral inquiry provides a more compelling account of those issues that their own tradition struggles to resolve, such as the nature of virtue or justice. Nonetheless, engagement with rival belief systems is crucial if persons are to extend and develop their own tradition.

In contrast, Edwards views the incommensurability between moral accounts as anthropological. Where MacIntyre compares the knowledge of a belief system to translation, Edwards uses the analogy of sense and taste. To know what honey tastes like, persons must taste honey. The purpose of this analogy, we have observed, is not merely to illustrate the immediacy of the experience of God, but to show that the Christian moral life consists in the apprehension of God's triune goodness, love, and beauty, through which each person becomes a new creation. Although one remains open to better ways to articulate the mystery of becoming a new creation, this moral anthropology, grounded in the epistemologically prior doctrine of the Trinity, remains an enduring check upon any new formulation, and guides one's encounter with other belief systems or moral traditions. While it is possible to provide intelligible definitions of words such as "goodness," "love," and "beauty" to a person who does not know and love God, in the end full knowledge of the meaning of these words requires that he or she become a new creation also.

4

THE "SOUL OF VIRTUE": A TRINITARIAN INTERPRETATION OF *FREEDOM OF THE WILL* AND *ORIGINAL SIN*

> If the *Logos*, who was with the Father before the world, thus engaged in covenant to do the will of the Father in the human nature, and the promise, was as it were recorded, that it might be made sure, doubtless it was impossible that it should fail; and so it was impossible that Christ should fail of doing the will of the Father in the human nature.
>
> Edwards, *Freedom of the Will*, Y1:287

In this chapter we turn to *Freedom of the Will* (1754) and *Original Sin* (1758), where Edwards addresses the topics of the will, sin, and evil. Commentators on Edwards often view these works from a respectful distance, admiring the virtuosity of Edwards's arguments but distancing themselves from his conclusions. Indeed, in his recent appraisal of Edwards's theology, Michael McClymond omits these works from his investigation and suggests that they are not "central to Edwards' lifelong intellectual concerns."[1] In this chapter, however, I offer an interpretation of these writings from the perspective of Edwards's Trinitarian thought that views these works as both central to Edwards's concerns and directly related to concepts from his Trinitarian writings.

Viewing these works through the lens of his Trinitarian reflection also provides a way to retrieve the positions Edwards defends in these writings. Using terms his adversaries might find acceptable, Edwards frames his arguments in accord with classical theism—that is, he speaks of God under a separate doctrine of the divine attributes, principally omnipotence, omniscience, benevolence, and immutability, instead of speaking of God in explicitly dogmatic terms.[2] Edwards devotes a great deal of space, for example, to arguing how God's omniscience and omnipotence necessarily entail God's absolute foreknowledge, and how an omnipotent and benevolent God is not responsible for sin and evil (Y1:375–419; Y3:380–88). When taken on this level, however, Edwards's arguments fail to refute the opposing views of his contemporaries, and have little to offer current theology and ethics.[3] But when viewed in light of his Trinitarian thought, the positions Edwards takes on the will, sin, and evil acquire an explanatory power they do not have otherwise.

Why Edwards constructed his apologetics within the terms of classical theism rather than in more explicit Trinitarian terms is no mystery given his milieu. As Paul Ramsey and Clyde Holbrook note, many of the persons Edwards engaged harbored doubts concerning the orthodox doctrine of the Trinity, rendering any "constructive Trinitarianism" difficult.[4] For example, John Taylor (1694–1761), who serves as an antagonist in both *Freedom of the Will* and *Original Sin*, held heterodox views concerning the Trinity.[5] Therefore, any defense Edwards offered concerning the will or sin that explicitly drew from Taylor's Trinitarian thought would have raised more questions than it answered. In addition, most of Edwards's adversaries saw classical theism as an appealing alternative to a theological project that would proceed by way of explicit doctrines such as the Trinity. For example, in *A Demonstration of the Being and Attributes of God* (1705), Samuel Clarke (1675–1729) argued that "the being and attributes of God are not only possible or barely probable in themselves, but also strictly demonstrable to any unprejudiced mind from the most incontestable principles of right reason."[6] Accordingly, Clarke defended theism not in terms of Christian doctrines— indeed, Clarke harbored heterodox opinions of the Trinity—but in terms of a God who is a necessarily omnipotent, omniscient, eternal, omnipresent, intelligent, and supremely benevolent being.[7] Similarly, in *An Essay concerning Human Understanding* (1690) John Locke, an empiricist who defined reason quite differently as the ideas the mind gains through experience, nonetheless argued that all human knowledge is dependent on a God "who is eternal, omnipotent, perfectly wise and good."[8] Hence, the "foundations of our duty and rules of action" are the "ideas of a supreme Being, infinite in Power, Goodness, and Wisdom, whose workmanship we are, and on whom we depend; and the Idea of ourselves, as understanding, rational Beings."[9] By framing his arguments accordingly, then, Edwards's aim was not so much to defend classical theism as it was to argue his positions in terms and concepts his adversaries accepted.

Admittedly, in his apologetical writings Edwards exhibits no crises in confidence regarding classical theism. And it is counterproductive to divest theology entirely from any mention of the divine attributes, for at issue is whether the divine attributes constitute an independent starting point for theology, rather than whether God transcends human limitations. Nonetheless, as we will see in this chapter, throughout his apologetical writings Edwards refers to fundamental relationships from his Trinitarian thought to justify the positions he defends. This recourse to Trinitarian concepts is indicative of how deeply Edwards's apologetical stance is indebted to his Trinitarian reflection, and points the way to a reading of Edwards's apologetics that places his Trinitarian thought in the foreground.

Though the interpretation I pursue is revisionary, it does not run counter to the direction of Edwards's thought we have observed so far. As we have seen, in his Trinitarian writings Edwards argues that God's triune relations condition our understanding of the divine attributes. In the "Essay" and "Miscellanies" entry 259, Edwards argues that the "attributes of infinity, eternity and immortality," as well as God's "power," are merely "modes" of God's existence (Y13:367). Apart from God's triune relations, all language concerning the divine attributes is vacuous, lacking "any rational meaning." Therefore, "we find no other attributes of which it is said that they are God in Scripture or that God is they, but *Logos* and *Agape*, the reason and love of God" (H:119). As we will see, the priority Edwards places on the triune relations in his Trinitarian writings provides a crucial hermeneutic for retrieving the constructive points of his apologetical writings.

1. FREEDOM OF THE WILL[10]

Edwards's aim in *Freedom of the Will* is to defend the Calvinist anthropology dictated by the Synod of Dort (1618–1619).[11] In this sense, he defends a long-established doctrine on the will that begins with Augustine.[12] In his later writings, Augustine emphasized *libertas*, or the freedom to will rightly, rather than *liberum arbitrium*, or the will's freedom to choose. *Libertas* was lost through the fall, and can only be restored through grace. Lacking *libertas*, sinful humanity without exception uses the will's freedom to choose wrongly. Lacking regeneration, humanity therefore labors under a "cruel necessity of sinning."[13] This necessity is not of the metaphysical kind (i.e., a determinism that "destroys liberty") but of a moral kind (i.e., we necessarily choose what our sinful hearts desire).[14] Hence, the freedom that truly matters is the freedom from servitude to sin and material lusts that we receive only as a gift from God.

In addition to this theological context, however, Edwards also writes within a philosophical context. Questions concerning the will—its relation to the faculty of understanding, to the passions and emotions, to inclinations and choice, and to the will of God—preoccupied moral philosophy in the seventeenth and eighteenth centuries. At one end of this spectrum were those who believed that the will was determined by the greatest apparent good, such as Thomas Hobbes (1588–1679), John Locke (1632–1704), and Francis Hutcheson (1694–1746). At the other end were those who believed that the will's freedom to choose between goods and to initiate action was essential to the moral life, such as Herbert of Cherbury (1582–1648), Samuel Clarke (1675–1729), and Thomas Reid (1710–1796).[15]

Edwards's recognition of the philosophical as well as theological stakes in the debate over the will is evident in his definition of the term "Arminianism," the position he refutes in his treatise. Theologically, Arminians held that while humans were unable to exercise saving faith or do any good apart from regeneration, God's grace nonetheless hinges upon the will's free decision. As a result, Arminians rejected the Calvinist doctrines of irresistible grace, predestination, divine foreknowledge, total depravity, limited atonement, and the perseverance of the saints.[16] But Edwards defines Arminianism as holding that the will's freedom is a "liberty of indifference, or that equilibrium whereby the will is without all antecedent determination or bias, and left hitherto free from any prepossessing inclination to one side or the other" (Y1:203). By defining Arminianism in this way, Edwards stakes out two positions. First, he can argue that Arminianism falls short not merely in terms of the doctrines it espouses, but on the basis of empirical observation—that is, he can argue that there is no such thing as "liberty of indifference." In this way, he can refute not only thoroughgoing Arminians but also those who held an Arminian understanding of the will yet hesitated to affirm every one of the Arminian doctrines. Second, by defining Arminianism in terms of the "liberty of indifference," Edwards can represent the free will position in its most extreme form, at the far end of the spectrum in his philosophical milieu. In this way, he can reject it as beyond the pale. For many others along the spectrum of ideas in Edwards's philosophical context were willing to say that the will was in some way determined by the goods or desires it apprehends, and that this determination did not compromise the integrity of the moral life.[17]

Though intricate, careful, and exhaustive, Edwards's argument against Arminianism can be summarized as follows. "Every act of the will has a cause, or it has not" (Y1:270). If the will is determined by a cause—here Edwards defines cause in the widest possible sense as the intellect's apprehension of any end, good, motive, or desire—then the will is not free in the way the Arminians argue. But if the will does *not* have a cause, then the will's actions "are connected with nothing whatsoever that goes before them and determines them," and there is a state of "absolute contingence." Such a state of contingency does not represent freedom, but the opposite. "For if the volition comes to pass by perfect contingence, and without any cause at all," then the will is a "purely passive subject," necessarily "subjected to what falls upon it" (Y1:271). Rather than privileging the "noble principle of human liberty," the Arminian scheme promotes freedom in the form of a "liableness to act altogether at random, without the least connection with, or restraint and government by, any dictate of reason, or anything whatsoever apprehended." Edwards asks, "what dignity or privilege is there, in being given up to such a wild contingence as this, to be perfectly and constantly liable to act unintelligibly and unreasonably, as much without the guidance of understanding, as if we had none, or were as destitute of perception as the smoke that is driven by the wind?" (Y1:273).

Edwards also points out logical problems in the Arminian position. Arminians claim that the will itself is its own cause. But such a claim is inconsistent, for it assigns the will a role both "active" (i.e., the cause of its action) and "passive" (i.e., that which is acted upon). In addition, to claim that the will is in some sense determined by a prior act of will raises the question of what determines that prior act of will, "which carries us back from one design to a foregoing design determining that, and to another determining that; and so on *in infinitum*" (Y1:272).

Edwards's argument against Arminianism does the most damage to those who locate freedom exclusively in the will rather than the intellect. Such a position ascribes to the will its own discrete power of agency, distinct from the agency that "applies to persons as a whole." But "to be free," Edwards counters, "is the property of an agent, who is possessed of powers and faculties," and not of the faculties themselves. The "will itself is not an agent that has a will; the power of choosing, itself, has not a power of choosing" (Y1:163). The proper question is not whether or not the will is free, but whether or not one wills freely. The will is the power that the whole soul exerts in relation to action.

Edwards notes that his understanding of the will and its liberty in relation to the integrated person essentially follows Locke (Y1:164).[18] But the deeper rationale that informs his understanding is the anthropology he develops in the *Religious Affections*. As we observed in the previous chapter, human nature is a fountain of affections; the mind is never an "indifferent, unaffected spectator," but is either "liking or disliking," "pleased or displeased" (Y2:96).The intellect and will are interrelated aspects of the dynamic self, enabling it to sense and pursue that which it loves. Consequently, the will is merely a power to act on what the soul desires and the intellect discerns, and freedom is defined entirely in terms of one's ability to act in accord with one's affections. For this reason, Edwards writes in *Freedom of the Will* that "the soul always wills or chooses that which, in the present view of the mind, considered in the whole of that view, and all that belongs to it, appears most agreeable" (Y1:217). The "will is as the greatest apparent good is," that is, the "volition has always for its object the thing which appears most agreeable" (Y1:143). "Liberty," in turn, is "that power and opportunity for one to do and conduct as he will, or according to his choice," following the "motives exhibited to the view of understanding and reason" (Y1:164–65).

Therefore, Edwards holds that "moral necessity" attends the will. This necessity is not a condition of overwhelming force that smothers all opposition, nor a "mathematical" certainty such as "that two and two should be four" (Y1:150–54). Rather, it is a condition of certainty regarding the consequential connection between the moral "cause" that arises from "some previous habitual disposition or some motive exhibited to the understanding," and the "effect" of "volition of the soul, or voluntary action" (Y1:158).

1.1. Edwards and Clarke

Though effective against those who believe that the will's freedom is distinct from the intellect, Edwards's arguments encounter difficulty with Samuel Clarke, who also considers the will and intellect an integrated whole yet defends the freedom of self-determination. Clarke agrees that the true question is "not where the *seat* of liberty is," but "*whether* there be at all in man any such power as a liberty of choice and of determining his own actions."[19] Clarke accepts that the universe exists according to a causal nexus. But he disagrees that freedom can only be defined in terms of the liberty to do as one pleases. It is a mistake, Clarke argues, to assert that liberty understood in terms of self-determination is impossible, because every event, including volitions, must have a cause. First, as the "supreme cause of all things," God necessarily has the liberty of self-determination, and therefore it is probable that, being made in the image of God, human beings have the same liberty. Certainly, "it is possible to infinite power to endow a creature with freedom or liberty of will," because "liberty must of necessity be in the supreme cause." Therefore it "implies no contradiction to suppose it communicated" to humanity.[20]

Second, it is a mistake to confuse causality as it applies to minds with causality as it applies to external matter, for to do so confounds "moral motives with physical efficients, between which two things there is no manner of relation."[21] Materialists such as Hobbes hold that consciousness and will are wholly due to the operation of material agencies, and therefore reduce all causal relations to those discernable through sensory experience. But liberty is inherent in the nature of consciousness and agency, for "intelligence without liberty" is "no intelligence at all."[22] This freedom inherent in intelligence exists not only in God but also in humanity. Returning to the principle of divine omnipotence, Clarke argues that it is possible for a being with "infinite power to create an immaterial cognitive substance" that is "endowed with consciousness and thought." This possibility is necessitated by the principle of consistency, that is, we cannot assert both that God is omnipotent and that God cannot create an immaterial consciousness at the same time. But it also appears necessary because each person's "own experience convinces him that he himself is such a substance."[23] Indeed, our own experience of the liberty of self-determination is "so strong, that nothing less than a strict demonstration that the thing is absolutely impossible" can "make us in the least doubt that we have it not."[24]

Though Clarke rejects "absolute necessity," freedom—divine and human—is properly constrained by a special kind of necessity. There is a "necessity indeed of *fitness*, that is, that things could not have been otherwise than they are without diminishing the beauty, order, and well-being of the whole."[25] This necessity is "consistent with the greatest freedom and

most perfect choice," for it is founded in God's infinite wisdom and goodness, which makes it impossible for God to "resolve to act foolishly" or "to
do that which is evil."[26] Analogously, although humans can abuse the gift
of freedom, the fitness that determines the will of God *"ought* also constantly to determine the will of all subordinate intelligent beings."[27] In this
way persons freely choose the "moral motives" they follow.

Edwards responds that Clarke proves not the existence of liberty, but of
necessity. First, by accepting that the will and intellect act interdepen-
dently, Clarke shows that the will necessarily follows the "last dictate of
the understanding." But if "the dictate of the understanding be the very
same with the determination of the will or choice, as Dr. Clarke supposes,"
then no "liberty of choice has any hand in it" (Y1:222). Second, Clarke's
necessity of fitness negates the liberty of self-determination. Particularly
from the perspective of God's foreknowledge and government of the
world, the necessity of fitness eliminates the contingency that makes possible the liberty of self-determination. "If God's will is steadily and surely
determined in everything by supreme wisdom, then it is in everything necessarily determined to that which is *most* wise." But God could not follow
through on what is most wise if the "divine will" is "liable to be carried
hither and thither at random, by the uncertain wind of blind contingence,"
a condition of "imperfection and meanness infinitely unworthy of the
deity" (Y1:380).

Both of these criticisms, however, fall short. Concerning the first objection, there are salient differences between Clarke's "necessity of fitness"
and Edwards's "moral necessity."[28] Clarke locates his necessity in the reasons that should guide and motivate all intelligent action. From his perspective, to be a rational agent is not only to be able to be moved by reasons;
it is also to be unable to escape being moved by reasons. In this way,
Clarke's necessity leaves room for rational choice.[29] Edwards, on the other
hand, locates his necessity in the will's desire for the greatest apparent
good. He holds that the "choice of the mind" coincides with the "objects of
the will" that appear "most agreeable and pleasing, all things considered"
(Y1:147). Even Edwards, however, acknowledges a difference between
"what reason declares to be best" and the will's pursuit of the greatest
apparent good. While he believes "reason" alone insufficient to move the
will, it is "one thing that is put into the scales, and is to be considered as a
thing that has concern in the compound influence which moves and
induces the will" (Y1:148).

Concerning Edwards's second objection, Clarke would reply that
Edwards's position shortchanges God's omnipotence. While he admits
that he is unable to "explain distinctly" how it is that God "can foresee
future things without a chain of necessary causes," Clarke believes that this
kind of foreknowledge is common in human experience. It often happens

that one "who has no influence over another person's actions can yet often perceive beforehand what another will do." Analogously, it is "reasonable" that "God, without influencing men's wills by his power, yet by his foresight cannot but have as much more certain knowledge of future free events, than either men or angels can possibly have, as the perfection of his nature is greater than that of theirs."[30]

1.2. A Trinitarian Understanding of Freedom

Edwards's most effective argument in *Freedom of the Will* is not that the freedom of choice does not exist, but that it is inadequate. That is to say, Clarke's (and the Arminian) elevation of rational choice threatens to eliminate the distinctive features of the Christian moral life. Edwards makes this argument most often from the perspective of God's own moral virtue. There "needs no other confutation of this notion of God's not being virtuous or praiseworthy, to Christians acquainted with the Bible, but only stating and particularly representing of it" (Y1:278). If the moral life depends on choice as opposed to nature, then it is impossible for God to possess virtue, because all allow that God's goodness is a matter of God's nature rather than God's will. For if choice becomes primary, God's acts of virtue "are no more virtuous" than the goodness of a "being that is not a moral agent," such as the "brightness of the sun, and the fertility of the earth are good, but not virtuous, because these properties are necessary to these bodies, and not the fruit of self-determining power" (Y1:278).

Further, if choice becomes primary, the sense in which God's own moral agency serves as the pattern and source for human moral agency becomes obscured. From Edwards's perspective, God is "in the most proper sense, a moral agent, the source of all moral ability and agency, the fountain and rule of all virtue and moral good." All the "essential qualities of a moral agent are in God, in the greatest possible perfection," such as "understanding, to perceive the difference between moral good and evil," as well as the "capacity for choice" that is "guided by understanding," and the "power of acting according to his choice or pleasure." In these qualities of moral agency "consists the *natural* image of God" in humanity, as well as God's "*spiritual* and *moral* image," that is, the "moral excellency" that humanity is "endowed with" by grace (Y1:166). But from the Arminian perspective, God is not to the same extent the "fountain or pattern" of the moral life, for by choosing to be good, the virtuous person "may claim a peculiar esteem, commendation and glory, that God can have no pretension to." Indeed, "God has no right, by virtue of his necessary holiness, to intermeddle with that grateful respect and praise, due to the virtuous man, who chooses virtue, in the exercise of a freedom *ad utrumque* [i.e., 'to will otherwise'] any more than a precious stone, which can't avoid being hard and beautiful" (Y1:279).

Edwards makes a similar argument in terms of the economic Trinity, specifically the mission of the Son agreed upon in the covenant of redemption. If the "*Logos*, who was with the Father, before the world, and who made the world, thus engaged in covenant to do the will of the Father in the human nature, and the promise, was as it were recorded, that it might be made sure, doubtless it was impossible that it should fail; and so it was impossible that Christ should fail of doing the will of the Father in the human nature." In the covenant of redemption, "God did as it were trust to what his Son had engaged and promised to do in future time; and depended so much upon it, that he proceeded actually to save men on account of it, as though it had already been done" (Y1:287). For this reason, "it was impossible that the acts of the will of the human soul of Christ should be otherwise than holy, and conformed to the will of the Father; or in other words they were necessarily so conformed" (Y1:289).

At issue, of course, in Edwards's discussion of the human soul of Jesus is his earlier point concerning the praiseworthiness of necessarily good beings.[31] As the Son of God, Jesus also possesses God's necessary goodness—the nature of goodness itself—and no account of the moral life is adequate from a Christian perspective that cannot recognize this goodness. The more crucial issue at stake, however, is the logic and integrity of the incarnation as the means of God's redemption of humanity. Following John of Damascus (655–750), orthodox Christianity maintained that, through the incarnation, the Logos assumed human nature in all its distinctiveness, for "that which is not assumed" is "not transformed" by grace. One of the outcomes of this doctrine was the declaration at Constantinople III (680) that Christ had a human will distinct from his divine will, but that the two coincide "without separation, without change, without partition," and "without confusion."[32]

Accordingly, Edwards argues that if freedom of choice was not essential to the human soul of Christ, then it is not essential for the moral transformation of human souls in general. Christ took on "our nature, and dwelt with us in this world, in a suffering state, not only to satisfy for our sins," but that "being in our nature and circumstances, and under our trials," he could be "our most fit and proper example, leader and captain, in the exercise of glorious and victorious virtue." But if the freedom of choice is essential to virtue, then "there was nothing of any virtue or merit, or worthiness of any reward, glory, praise, or commendation at all, in all he did, because it was all necessary." Indeed, if freedom of choice is central to the moral life, Christ is not the "highest of all creatures," but "less worthy of reward or praise, than the very least of the saints; yea, no more worthy than a clock or mere machine, that is purely passive, and moved by natural necessity" (Y1:291).

Had he put this recourse to his Trinitarian thought at the forefront of *Freedom of the Will*, Edwards's argument concerning the nature of the will would have taken on more force and clarity. Indeed, the psychological and social analogies provide a view of freedom that approximates Clarke's positions on rational choice and the individual "experience" of freedom, as well as accommodates the freedom that is essential to God's triune economy of salvation. Central to the psychological analogy is the dialogical act of self-consciousness, where the mind reflects upon itself. Self-reflection is a free act that is essential to personhood; what separates human beings from animals is that animals only act from "direct consciousness," but humans are "capable of viewing what is in themselves contemplatively." Therefore, human minds are "not only passive, but abundantly active" (Y6:374). Unlike the apprehension of external objects and relations, self-reflection is not entirely determined by the external world. In his discussion of the psychological analogy, Edwards emphasizes conscience and self-love as the primary acts of self-reflection. But inherent in both is the capacity for rational judgment and "speculation," which Edwards includes in the "faculty of understanding" (Y18:459).

Of course, three forms of necessity accompany self-reflection. First, one cannot choose to engage in self-reflection. Even God is constrained by this necessity, for it is essential to God's own personhood as a triune being that God engage in reflection on God's "perfect idea" of God's self. God is not free to be a "stone" (Y13:262). Second, a relation of necessity exists between the mind of God and human minds. All human ideas of self-reflection, both regenerate and unregenerate, are the immediate communication of the perfect idea of God (Y13:513). Third, as we will explore in more detail shortly, on account of original sin human minds can only see and will rightly once they have experienced the indwelling of the Spirit.

Nonetheless, the idealism that frames the psychological analogy offers an account of freedom that is not defined solely in terms of the apprehension of the greatest apparent good. Indeed, in some passages of his "Miscellanies" notebooks that precede *Freedom of the Will*, Edwards leaves room for the capacity to act on reason alone, which he terms the "rational will" (Y13:484). For example, in an entry on the Spirit's "preparatory work"—that is, the bestowal of prevenient grace that leads persons to seek redemption—Edwards writes that often the "Spirit makes more use of rational deductions, to convince" the unregenerate "that 'tis worth their while to seek earnestly for salvation" (Y13:283). Perhaps for this reason, Edwards leaves a small amount of room in *Freedom of the Will* for what Stephen Wilson calls an "indirect desire" for a different volition in the future than one experiences in the present.[33] These desires do not issue in intentional action, and are ineffective, sentimental, and trivial, but they persist as a kind of wish that one could will otherwise (Y1:313).

More crucial than the freedom of self-reflection, however, is the social analogy's characterization of freedom. From the perspective of the social analogy, freedom is defined in terms of the freedom of self-donation, the freedom to give oneself to another. Within the Trinity, there is the free and perfect act of mutual self-donation between the Father and the Son in the person of the Holy Spirit, from whom proceeds God's free and diffusive love for the saints, who are admitted "into that society of the three persons of the Godhead" (Y18:108–9). God's benevolence toward creation, then, flows "freely" and "absolutely" to humanity from God's own "loving and good nature," independently of human "perfections, natural or moral" (Y13:395).

God's free, diffusive love is evident not only in the general shape of the covenant of redemption, but also in the specific missions of the Son and the Spirit. As the incarnate Son, Jesus Christ is the perfect revelation of the Trinity, for "in a sense" the whole Godhead was "communicated to him" (Y18:287). Through his suffering on the cross, Jesus Christ perfectly reveals in temporal terms the love of God freely given to humanity, for the "passionate love of Christ, by virtue of the union with the divine nature, is in a sort infinite" (Y13:176–77). Jesus Christ also represents in his person the perfect freedom of humanity's fulfillment of its *theotic* "union with God," in which the saints "partake of the beauty, life, honor and joy of the eternal Son of God; and so are made gods by communion of his Spirit, whereby they are partakers of the divine nature" (Y18:288). As we have seen, the social analogy depicts goodness, excellence, beauty, love, and happiness as relational entities; to experience any of these, there must be the presence of another with whom one can live in relation. Total achievement of personhood, then, is a state of being where one can freely give oneself for others, as Jesus gave himself for us.

Consequently, although Edwards refers to the moral necessity of Christ's human soul in *Freedom of the Will*, his social analogy shows how Christ provides the model of fully realized human freedom. True freedom is only available to those who, through the indwelling of the Holy Spirit, live as Christ lived in communion with the Godhead, in solidarity with humanity. The ultimate locus of freedom in the moral life, then, is not in terms of the conditions surrounding an individual's choices or ends, but, as Edwards argues in the *Religious Affections*, in terms of those virtues of character communicated to the soul that embodies the love of Christ. True freedom is a correlate of true virtue, which is nothing other than the soul's participation in God's own moral excellency.

Though it is undeniable that Edwards does not assign a high place to freedom of choice even from the perspective in his Trinitarian thought, this is because in his Trinitarian theology love, rather than freedom of choice, holds the ontological center. Consequently, he writes in *Freedom of the Will* that "God himself has the highest possible freedom according to the true and proper meaning of the term," for God is "in the highest possible respect an agent, and active in the exercise of his infinite holiness" (Y1:364). Correlatively, human freedom takes the form of the free "expression of benevolence," which we show to God and to those God appoints "to stand in his stead as the objects of our beneficence," particularly "our indigent brethren" (Y1:280). The essence of virtue lies not in the will's actions or decisions, but in the will's inherent "nature" and "beauty" (Y1:339–40). Any conception of freedom that fails to recognize the centrality of this love is inadequate, if not misleading.

1.3. Edwards and Swinburne

In the terminology of current moral philosophy and ethics, Edwards's position is that of *compatibilism*—he holds that agents are free and morally responsible for their actions even though these actions are causally necessitated.[34] Though technically correct, this term fails to recognize the distinctiveness of Edwards's Trinitarian understanding of God and humanity, which differentiates his account of the will from other compatibilists such as Hobbes or Hume. Nonetheless, the term accurately portrays Edwards's conception of the will per se. That the will is activated by the mind's apprehension of the greatest good is, for Edwards, a law of nature that, like self-love, exists across the continuum of existence. In the unregenerate, the greatest apparent good is most often determined by the basest sort of self-love. In the regenerate, the greatest apparent good is nothing other than the goodness of God. In either case, the operation of the will is the same, and agents are free and responsible for their actions if they do them intentionally and voluntarily.

The most prevalent position contrary to compatibilism is *incompatibilism* or *libertarianism*—the belief that agents are capable of acting freely and responsibly only when their actions are not in any way caused or determined. As we have seen, Clarke anticipates this position when he argues that moral action and responsibility depend upon the capacity to act freely and consistently in accord with rational principles. In recent work in Christian ethics, Richard Swinburne's *Responsibility and Atonement* offers an account of freedom that restates some central features of Clarke's argument.[35] Like Clarke, Swinburne works to provide an account of freedom that both refutes compatibilism and affirms central doctrines of Christian theology.[36]

Swinburne locates moral responsibility foremost in an agent's "intentional actions"—those actions that an agent reasonably chooses on the basis of "moral beliefs" regarding what is good and evil.[37] Swinburne grants that moral beliefs are to a certain extent "involuntary." He argues that "we cannot choose immediately what to believe about some matter"; that intentional acts are often thwarted by irresistible "desires," themselves both good and evil; and that reasons for acting are often not "overriding" or even moral.[38] Nonetheless, Swinburne argues that reasons are an inescapable part of human actions, both guiding and justifying them, and that persons deserve praise or blame on the basis of the reasons they choose to structure their actions.

The problem Swinburne sees with compatibilism is that it cannot account for the freedom inherent in intentional action. If actions are "causally necessitated," then they do not convey moral responsibility, for the locus of responsibility lies in the agent's choice regarding intentional actions. Actions themselves, he allows, have moral status independent of their causal origin. For example, "whether or not our actions are caused, it is still good to feed the starving on our doorstep, and bad not to do so." But actions only convey moral responsibility if, given "all the causes operating on the agent," the agent "had uncaused freedom to act one way or to act the other way." Though inherent in intentional action, this "uncaused freedom" is not reducible to "rationality," for "the free agent is one who *chooses* whether to be rational and is not necessitated to be determined by reason." In this way, "an agent is morally responsible if, and only if, he has free will and moral beliefs."[39]

One option in bringing Edwards's project in *Freedom of the Will* to bear on Swinburne's incompatibilism is to reiterate Edwards's specific arguments against liberty defined either as indifference or self-determination. In making this retrieval, one could draw on the work of Harry Frankfurt, who argues that necessary volitions are far less remote to human experience than Swinburne's freedom to will otherwise, and that the freedom Swinburne articulates is either irrelevant or nonexistent.[40] Or one could argue that, after Freud, there is greater appreciation of how unconscious desires and motivations affect supposedly free decisions and actions, and that it is difficult to reconcile the formative influence of social and developmental experiences on the psyche with a straightforward argument for autonomy and responsibility.[41] In this manner, one could argue in an Edwardsian fashion that incompatibilism fails to satisfy significant empirical observations concerning the act of willing.

A better approach, however, is to explore the theological differences that underlie the positions Edwards and Swinburne take on the freedom of the will. As we have observed, what is unique and finally compelling about Edwards's understanding of the freedom of the will is not his specific arguments against Arminianism, but the Trinitarian account of God and humanity on which this understanding hangs. Likewise, as we will see, what is unique about Swinburne's account of the will in *Responsibility* is not his incompatibilism per se, but the role that it plays in his theology. In addition to identifying what is unique in each proposal, this approach also offers an alternative to the interminability that has characterized debates over the will's freedom. For every account of freedom presupposes a philosophical and theological framework, and any discussion of freedom that proceeds in isolation of these presuppositional frameworks misses the true differences between rival accounts. Therefore, instead of trying to "win" the debate over the will's freedom, a more constructive approach examines the framework of each particular account and evaluates its benefits and liabilities.

Swinburne takes up incompatibilism in order to provide a "more liberal" depiction of the Christian faith. Consistent with Christian orthodoxy, he maintains that the world was created by "a God," who "became incarnate in Christ," lived "a saintly human life, allowed himself to be crucified," rose "from the dead, founded a Church to carry on his work, and seeks man's eternal well-being in friendship with himself." At the same time, against the "hardline" position that insists humans can do nothing without God, he argues that "God does not act outside the web of natural causes in order to overrule human free will" and that humans "have the power to act independently." In this way, God "generously allows creatures to determine their own destiny." If a person chooses to act well, and continually repents from her sins, she will receive eternal life and friendship with God. But if a person consistently chooses to act wickedly, and repeatedly engages in sinful acts, she will gradually lose "sensitivity" to what is good and pass out of existence.[42]

To his credit, Swinburne avoids some of the theological problems usually associated with his position. Although he defines the moral life in terms of solitary decisions, he recognizes the importance of interpersonal relations, particularly friendship. The "greatest human well-being is to be found in friendship with good and interesting people in the pursuit of worthy aims," and this well-being is best achieved when we see God as our friend, for God is "an infinitely better friend" and brings more to a friendship than any human being.[43] Further, Swinburne accepts that, although persons can avoid sinning, they inevitably do, and therefore need atonement that only God can provide. He maintains that Christ's sacrifice on the cross provides a means to God that exceeds the capacities of human willing, and that by virtue of Christ's atoning death, "God's action in redemption leads" persons "to use that act to become forgiven and to become holy." In this way, God's "cooperating" grace leads a person toward God, but leaves intact the "free will to choose whether or not to co-operate with this grace." Swinburne is unclear whether God's grace is internal or external to the soul, but the emphasis he places on the cross and God's cooperating grace avoids many of the difficulties associated with Pelagianism.[44]

Without question, Swinburne's project appeals to those who prioritize the role of the undetermined will in their theology. But when viewed in light of the theological framework from which Edwards develops his understanding of the will, it is hard not to be struck by the high theological price Swinburne pays to accommodate incompatibilism. First, while both Swinburne and Edwards recognize the importance of interpersonal relations to the development of the moral self, Edwards defines the will in terms of these relations rather than its solitary decisions. Though he often describes the will in *Freedom of the Will* in terms that are objective—the will "always is as the greatest apparent good is" (Y1:142)—within the context of his Trinitarian theology, the greatest apparent good is interpersonal and relational; the triune God is the source and organizing principle of the goodness that emanates throughout creation and indwells the saints. For this reason, Edwards writes in the preface of *Freedom of the Will* that "our greatest happiness" consists "in an intercourse between ourselves and our Maker" (Y1:133). Edwards's depiction of the will, then, better accommodates the importance of relations that both he and Swinburne acknowledge as essential to the moral life.

Second, while both Swinburne and Edwards consider the culmination of the moral life to be communion with God, Swinburne's understanding of responsibility is unable to show how God and humanity belong to a single moral community through the economy of salvation. Because he locates responsibility in the will's ability to choose apart from any cause, Swinburne privileges good actions done in the presence of a "contrary desire" over "spontaneous" actions that express a good desire. Hence, a person "who gives generously because of irresistible desire is no more to praise for his act than the habitual criminal subject to irresistible desire to steal is to blame."[45] But, as we have seen, to describe responsibility in this way renders the moral goodness of God and the role of the human soul of Christ incomprehensible. Perhaps for this reason, Swinburne in a later writing struggles to articulate how Christ's human and divine natures coincide, both in terms of Christ's experience of human desires, and in terms of Christ's possession of a discrete human soul.[46] Edwards, then, provides a better description of how humanity participates in the moral excellency of God by ensuring that his understanding of the will accords with the triune missions of the Son and the Spirit.

Finally, by viewing the crucifixion mainly through the prism of humanity's moral failures, Swinburne minimizes the role of the divine in the moral life. Though God "could have forgiven our sins without there being any need for a crucifixion," the crucifixion testifies to the fact that "our actions and consequences matter" by providing the "costly gift" of God's Son to atone for our sins. Accordingly, the crucifixion provides a reconciliation that exceeds human capacities, yet still requires individual human initiative. Through the cross, Swinburne argues, God removes the "obstacles" that stand in the way of our progress to heaven, a path each person proceeds along by his or her "good deeds."[47] For Edwards, however, Christ did not become incarnate merely "to satisfy for our sins," but to manifest the free and diffusive love of the Trinity (Y1:291). Hence, the will's freedom is fully realized when, like Christ, it freely loves another, and not merely when it is free from sin. More importantly, the moral life is not an individual achievement, but the attainment of mystic communion between persons united in the free and infinite love of the Trinity.

Edwards's Trinitarian account of freedom would represent a minority view in the discussions on the will in current moral philosophy and ethics, but it would concur with many appraisals of freedom in recent Trinitarian theology, particularly those from a liberation or feminist perspective. Thus, Jürgen Moltmann argues that the emphasis on autonomy in current moral philosophy and ethics derives from the bourgeois concern for control over property. But freedom defined in this manner entails relationships of lordship and oppression of rich over poor, ruler over subject, and men over women. In contrast, freedom defined in terms of the diffusive love of the Trinity breaks down these barriers, and "leads to unhindered, open communities in solidarity." Only "this freedom as community" can "heal the wounds which freedom as lordship has inflicted, and still inflicts today."[48] In a similar vein, Catherine LaCugna writes that on account of the Trinitarian relations, "the exercise of freedom requires a plurality of persons" living in equality and communion with each other. As a result, rather than the "patriarchal theology of male dominance and control," a Trinitarian vision of community makes "mutuality rooted in communion" the "nonnegotiable truth about our existence, the highest value and ideal of the Christian life."[49]

2. ORIGINAL SIN[50]

One topic that Edwards does not explore in detail in *Freedom of the Will* is original sin. The topic of sin arises logically, for although Edwards examines the dispositions that causally determine the will in *Freedom of the Will*, he does not explain why the greatest apparent good of the will consistently pursues things short of the goodness of God. For this reason, Edwards's next apological work engages in a "general defense" of original sin (Y3:102).

The understanding of original sin Edwards defends arises in the thought of Augustine and has three aspects: (1) The innate depravity of heart and proneness to sin that vitiates human nature; (2) the moral and physical devastation wreaked on human nature—that is, original sin is the root cause of human ignorance, weakness, lust, and death; and (3) the transmission of this state of guilt and devastation to us by the first sinner, Adam, through physical generation. Humanity's inheritance of Adam's original guilt is both generic, that is, human nature participates in and embodies the devastation Adam incurred, and individual, that is, each possesses the personal guilt of original sin at birth.[51]

Though regnant in Western theology, original sin encountered opposition from the beginning. Julian of Eclanum (386–454) argued that Augustine held an implausible view of the transmission of sin, specifically that sin passed seminally from parent to child, and that his pessimism toward human nature undermined individual freedom.[52] In Edwards's time, these objections took a different form. John Locke objected not to the fact that biological transmission is implausible, but that Adam could stand as humanity's representative, which violated his sense of fairness. Why should anyone suffer for the sins of another? It is inconsistent, Locke argued in the *Reasonableness of Christianity* (1695), "with the justice or goodness of the great and infinite God" that "all Adam's posterity" is "doomed to eternal infinite punishment, for the transgression of Adam, whom millions had never heard of."[53] Locke's objection was incorporated into John Taylor's systematic rejection of original sin in *The Scripture-Doctrine of Original Sin* (1740), the text Edwards aims to refute in *Original Sin*. Along with Locke's objection to representative guilt, Taylor argued that original sin's depiction of the necessity of sinning undermined moral responsibility. Drawing from Clarke's libertarian account of the will, Taylor argued that "what proceedeth necessarily can be no sin," for no one should be blamed for an event he or she "could no ways hinder its coming to pass." Consequently, rather than defining regeneration as the Holy Spirit imparting a new nature that humanity lost as a result of sin, Taylor defined it as "gaining those habits of virtue and religion, which give us the real character of the children of God."[54]

Further, Taylor argued that there is little scriptural support for original sin. For example, the creation narratives in Genesis (2:16–17; 3:1–19) concerning the disobedience of Adam and Eve are a description of humanity's natural, rather than moral, condition. The death described in these narratives is not spiritual but physical, and is a benefit rather than a burden. Death has the "tendency to excite sober reflections, to induce us to be moderate in gratifying the appetites of a corruptible body, to mortify pride and ambition, and to give us a sense of our dependence on God." Thus, physical death is what is at stake in the parallel Paul draws in Romans 5:12–21 and 1 Corinthians 15:21–22 between Adam and Christ. While humanity suffers death after Adam's sinning, and death symbolizes the destructive tendencies of sin, each person is guiltless regarding Adam's sin. In contrast, Christ's own obedience demonstrates "that obedience to God, and conformity to the rules of truth and righteousness, are the only foundation of the divine favor, and the only source of life and enjoyment."[55]

One of Edwards's strategies in *Original Sin* is to refute Taylor's account following the method of empirical observation. In order to argue that there is an "innate depravity of the heart," one only has to observe "what is constant or general" in "a great variety of circumstances." And in order to identify the "true tendency of the natural or innate disposition" of human nature, one must "consider things as they are in themselves, or in their own nature, without the interposition of divine grace" (Y3:107–9). Unsurprisingly, the conclusion Edwards arrives at as a result of this survey is that "all are sinners" regardless of "constitutions, capacities, conditions, manners, opinions and educations." Sin is pervasive in "all countries, climates, nations, and ages; and through all the mighty changes and revolutions, which have come to pass in the habitable world" (Y3:124). Where Taylor portrays sin as an avoidable, if commonplace, misuse of free will, Edwards holds that the "general continued wickedness" of humanity proves that the cause of sin "is fixed . . . *internal*" and "very *powerful*." Indeed, the universality of sin renders Taylor's argument implausible, for how can something so unfixed as the freedom of the will account for the "permanent, fixed, and constant" presence of evil? (Y3:195).

This strategy fails, however, for Edwards's examination of human nature is far from scientific.[56] Not only does Edwards use examples from the Bible to prove sinful behavior, a less than objective source, but his depiction of human nature "without the interposition of divine grace" enables him to credit whatever good qualities he finds to divine assistance rather than to humanity. Further, on account of his belief in the necessity of the will, Edwards disqualifies any contrary tendencies in the will that occasionally issue in virtuous action as instinctual acts that have no connection to the will's prevailing disposition. For this reason, he argues it is "absurd" to "talk of the innocent and kind actions" that even "criminals" do, just as it is absurd to call a spouse "faithful" if he or she is adulterous only on occasion, or a ship "good" if it manages to make it halfway across the ocean before sinking (Y3:128–29). As in *Freedom of the Will*, then, Edwards's argument for the necessity of sin depends on a theological framework that his empirical observations presuppose.

Edwards's empirical strategy also fails because it does not theologically vindicate those aspects of the doctrine of original sin that Taylor rejects. As Edwards himself notes, he and Taylor basically agree that sin pervades human existence (Y3:115–19); their disagreement concerns primarily sin's definition and role in their respective theologies. For Taylor, the doctrine of original sin was an affront to "the God of our nature," for it describes humanity—the work of God's hands—as "originally corrupted" and unfairly magnifies the imperfections of our being. It also encouraged pessimism and evasiveness regarding the spiritual life, teaching that the cause of sin belongs to Adam, "whereas in truth you ought to blame or condemn yourself alone for any evil habits you have contracted, any sinful actions you commit."[57] The only adequate response to such a challenge is to construct a more adequate theological justification for the different aspects of original sin, which is the second strategy Edwards employs. Throughout this justification, Edwards employs concepts from his Trinitarian thought.

2.1. The Nature and Definition of Sin

Certainly, in spite of the weaknesses noted, Edwards is not alone when he tries to prove the reality of sin on empirical grounds. Perhaps the longest-running axiom of Christian theology is that one can argue for the doctrine of original sin on empirical grounds alone. The doctrine of original sin, however, is also fundamentally an exercise in theological anthropology. In order to describe the nature of sin adequately one must describe the nature of personhood, for any description of alienation from God identifies (either explicitly or implicitly) that which is central to communion with God.

As we have seen, in his Trinitarian writings, Edwards sees personhood as complete in *theosis*, in our participation in the triune community of the Godhead through the indwelling of the Holy Spirit. As such, personhood is defined primarily in terms of relation. Relationality is Edwards's supreme ontological predicate; the relationality between the Father, Son, and Spirit emanates throughout the universe, and is communicated to human nature, such that to be is to be in God's love. In the *Religious Affections*, Edwards converts this understanding of personhood into a full-fledged anthropology. Human nature is a dynamic state of being, in which the intellect and will are ordered according to the affections. The nature of these affections determines the status and orientation of the self's relation to God, and is decisive in the moral life. If one's affections are spiritual, rather than merely natural, the self's affections are a direct communication of God's moral excellency. Edwards therefore plots the moral life according to the soul's enlarged capacity to know and love God. We "must take our measure from that height to which the rule of duty extends" (i.e., the complete knowledge and love of God); the "whole of the distance we are at from that height, is sin," for the "failing of duty is sin" (Y2:325).

In *Original Sin*, when Edwards turns to define exactly what sin is, as opposed to speaking about its existence in general terms, he draws from this Trinitarian anthropology. Returning to the correlation he draws between sin, love, and duty, Edwards writes that the "grace set before us" in the "extreme sufferings of the Son of God" was a "love whose length and breadth and depth and height passes knowledge" (Y3:143). Therefore, the "chief and most fundamental of all the commands of the moral law requires us" to love God "to the utmost extent of the faculties of our nature." To the extent that the love of God has "the most absolute possession of all the soul, and the perfect government of all the principles and springs of action that are in our nature," we are "excused." But whoever withholds that "love or respect of heart from God which his law requires" has "more sin than righteousness" (Y3:140–41). Once we view the moral life from this perspective, it is easy to see "how vastly the generality" of humanity "fall below their duty, with respect to love of God." Indeed, "how far, how exceeding far, are the generality of the world" from "coming half-way to that height of love"? (Y3:142).

Edwards acknowledges that "it is not easy precisely to fix the limits of man's capacity" concerning "love to God." Following the perichoretic relation between intellect and will that he establishes in his Trinitarian writings and the *Religious Affections*, Edwards believes that "in general we may determine" that humanity's "capacity of love is coextended" with its "capacity for knowledge," for the "exercise of the understanding opens the way for the exercise of the other faculty," that is, the will (Y3:141). While a "proper positive understanding of God's infinite excellency" is impossible, the "human faculties are capable of a real and clear understanding of the greatness, glory and goodness of God, and of our dependence on him, from the manifestations which God has made of himself," specifically "that eternal salvation which is procured by God's giving his only begotten Son to die for sinners" (Y3:141–42).

Edwards offers a more definitive description of human capacities in his description of Adam before and after the fall.[58] Alluding to the distinction he draws in the *Religious Affections* between the *natural* and *moral* image of God, Edwards writes that when God first made humanity, God "implanted" two "kinds of principles." The first are "inferior" principles, which "the Scriptures sometimes call *flesh*," and are those "natural" principles of human nature, such as "self-love" or the personal love of "liberty, honor and pleasure." The second are "superior" and "supernatural" principles, which the Scriptures call the "divine nature," and are those "summarily comprehended in divine love" and that comprise the "spiritual image of God." While the supernatural principles are "concreated" in human nature, they are "divine communications and influences of God's spirit" and "immediately depend on man's union and communion with God." In a footnote, Edwards explains that supernatural principles were present "in Adam, as soon as humanity began, and are necessary to the perfection and well being of the human nature." Nonetheless, they are not "necessary" to humanity's "being," insomuch "as one may have everything needful to his being *man* exclusively of them" (Y3:381–82).

Before the fall, humanity's supernatural principles were intact, provided order and harmony to the natural principles, and were the "dignity, life, happiness, and glory" of humanity. But after the fall, "that communion with God, on which these principles depended, entirely ceased; the Holy Spirit, that divine inhabitant, forsook the house." As a result, "self-love" and the "natural appetite" became "reigning principles," and "having no superior principles to regulate or control them, they became absolute masters of the heart." In this way, God did not implant any "bad principle" or "corrupt taint" in human nature. God only withdrew God's Spirit, leaving humanity's natural principles "to themselves" (Y3:382–83).

Edwards offers two images to describe the spiritual devastation wrought when the inferior principles alone possess the heart. The first is that of an uncontrollable house fire. The "inferior principles are like fire in a house," which "is very useful when kept in its place, but if left to take possession of the whole house, soon brings all to destruction" (Y3:382–83). The second is that of a person destroyed by alcoholism, an image that speaks to the insidious nature of sin and its effect on humanity's plight as a result of the first sin. Imagine a person, who "through the deceitful persuasions of a pretended friend," drinks "a liquor which he had no inclination to before," but "after he has once taken of it," has "an insatiable, incurable thirst after more of the same" (Y3:190). In the same way, though "there was no natural sinful inclination in Adam," an inclination to the sin of "eating the forbidden fruit was begotten in him by the delusion and error he was led into" (Y3:229). Once Adam gave in to this deceitful inclination, he died not only physically but "spiritually," that is, a "dismal alteration was made in the soul by the loss of that holy divine principle" (Y3:238). As a result, human nature is now "exceeding corrupt, utterly depraved, and ruined," and knows nothing of the supernatural principles Adam once had except through the indwelling of the Holy Spirit (Y3:279).

Distinctive in Edwards's position on fallen human capacities is his optimism concerning the powers of the fallen intellect and fallen humanity in general. The Reformed tradition typically follows Calvin's view that the intellect was damaged by the fall, making it necessary for God to accommodate the weakness of the human mind by revealing the message of salvation through the Word. Therefore, the major teaching of original sin is that of epistemological humility, that in order to know God we must submit ourselves to the special revelation God has made known through the Word incarnate in Christ and declared in Scripture.[59] More recently, Reinhold Niebuhr argues that this attitude of *epistemological* humility entails a *performative* humility regarding the ambitions of social institutions, including religious communities. According to Niebuhr, original sin teaches that "no matter how wide the perspectives which the human mind may reach, how broad the loyalties which the human imagination may conceive, how universal the community which human statecraft may organize, or how pure the aspirations of the saintliest idealists may be, there is no level of human moral or social achievement in which there is not some corruption of inordinate self-love."[60] Therefore, in addition to instilling a sense of humanity's personal limitations, original sin instills a sense of humanity's corporate limitations; no social ethic or political theory is acceptable unless it recognizes humanity's tendency to advance self-interested causes under the cover of universal ideals and utopian visions.

In contrast, Edwards holds that the seat of sin lies not as much in the intellect's failure to have a "clear and real understanding" of God as it does in the whole soul's inability to "savor the things that be of God, and to receive the things of the Spirit of God" (Y3:141, 278). Reminiscent of the position Thomas Aquinas defends in the *Summa Theologiae*, Edwards argues that the doctrine of original sin teaches that human perfection lies in a transformation that only God can effect.[61] While in their "natural state," persons are unable to "do any good thing" (Y3:280). Only after being "created anew, or made new creatures" through having the Holy Spirit indwell the heart, can we attain full personhood (Y3:369). Further, the attainment of personhood does not merely entail the subduing of natural principles such as self-love, but the advent of new principles that make possible new relations of love. "Holiness in the Christian" derives its "strength and efficacy from the divine fountain, and by this means overcomes" (Y3:146). Original sin therefore reaffirms Edwards's belief that the moral life is one of gracious participation in the triune love of God. This is, to reiterate, the underlying bone of contention between Edwards and Taylor, for in some ways their debate is as much over the nature of regeneration and its place in the moral life as it is over original sin.

From Niebuhr's perspective, Edwards's relatively high estimation of the intellect runs the risk of generating a theology unconscious of its own "ideological taint" and "corruption of self-interest." Nonetheless, as we observed in the previous chapter, Edwards recognizes the danger of those who feign true religious affections. And in *Original Sin*, he demonstrates keen awareness of the performative failures of social institutions and religious communities, particularly in his own New England. "How careful and eagle-eyed is the merchant to observe and improve his opportunities and advantages," he observes, and "how greatly have we forsaken the pious examples of our fathers!" (Y3:154; 198). Consequently, Edwards would refuse Niebuhr's "realism" regarding human nature and human communities for two reasons. First, from Edwards's perspective Niebuhr's understanding of sin is incomplete, for Niebuhr's understanding of human nature does not adequately depict the divine principles of love that are essential to human nature's fulfillment through *theosis*. Thus, one advantage Edwards has over Niebuhr concerns the feminist criticism that Niebuhr's account of sin as inordinate self-love and pride overlooks sin in the form of "sloth" and "hiding," or the failure to develop one's own God-given individuality.[62] For Edwards, sin in any form is fundamentally a diminishment of one's personhood, the essence of which occurs in relation with God. Pride and sloth therefore are manifestations of the more basic state of being out of relation with God, which is the meaning of depravity.

Second, from Edwards's perspective, Niebuhr's account of communal unity is unduly narrow. While Niebuhr believes that communities are essential for human flourishing, he acknowledges that communities invariably represent the basest drives of individuals, and that coercion is therefore "an inevitable part of the process of social cohesion."[63] As a result, the best way to avoid absolute evil is to achieve a balance of power, between the community and the individual, and between different communities and nations themselves. As I show in more detail in the next section, however, Edwards would argue that Niebuhr's "realism" neglects the positive point that all communities reflect the paradigm of community established by the triune God, whose victorious love brings the church into a communion of perfect unity, individuality, and friendship. Where Niebuhr's doctrine of original sin provides a vision for how pluralistic and fragmented societies can maintain a fragile sense of equilibrium, Edwards's doctrine of original sin provides a vision for the church's unique confidence and hope in Christ.

2.2. Solidarity with Adam and Christ

The most original contribution Edwards's Trinitarian anthropology makes to his defense of original sin concerns the nature of humanity's solidarity with Adam in the first sin. To reiterate, the question of humanity's participation in Adam's sin appeared to many implausible, specifically Augustine's teaching that humanity was seminally present in Adam when he sinned, and that sin was transmitted biologically thereafter. But to Arminians like Taylor, it also violated commonplace understandings of justice, for it seemed unfair that humanity should suffer on account of Adam's sin, or that "Adam and his posterity are dealt with as one" by God (Y3:397). Not only did this punish persons for something they did not do, but it also implied that the first parents inhabited a moral universe different from ours. For if human nature has been wounded through the first parents' sin, our current moral state is compromised by an action to which we could give no "consent," thus lessening our moral responsibility (Y3:408).

Edwards's response is to propose a novel way of viewing humanity's unity with Adam.[64] Drawing on the idealism that frames his psychological analogy, or the "late improvements in philosophy," Edwards argues that there are two kinds of "unity" or "identity" operating in the universe, one appropriate to the Creator, the other to the creation (Y3:385, 398). The first is the "absolute identity of the first being," whereby God "is the same yesterday, today, and forever." The second is the "dependent identity" of created existence, whereby "God does, by his immediate power, uphold every created substance in being" (Y3:400). As such, the "existence of created substances, in each successive moment" is a result of the "immediate" communication of God's wisdom and will. Hence, God's "preserving created things in being is perfectly equivalent to a continued creation, or to his creating things out of nothing at each moment of their existence" (Y3:403; 401).

Dependent identity itself has two aspects: the unity something has in itself and the unity it has through time. These aspects of unity are distinct from any physical properties that exist in something. For example, in a tree that is "an hundred years old," there is "perhaps not one atom the very same," yet God "has in a constant succession communicated to it many of the same qualities, and most important properties, as if it were one." With regard to the *personal identity* of created intelligent beings," these two aspects of dependent identity take the form of having the "same consciousness," that is, one's particular sense of self, and the "communication" of that "same consciousness and memory" through time (Y3:397–98).

Working from this understanding of unity and identity, Edwards turns to the Arminian "difficulties" leveled against original sin. Both Arminian objections operate from the premise that one's personal identity is entirely "derived down from past existence, distinct from, and prior to any oneness that can be supposed to be founded on divine constitution" (Y3:404). Edwards's metaphysics of identity, however, shows that this premise is "demonstrably false." For if all things exist through the immediate communication of God, then "all oneness" in terms of an individual person's "consciousness of acts that are past" and the "continuance of all habits, either good or bad" depends "entirely on a divine establishment" and not on past existence per se. Further, it is God alone who maintains the "guilt" or "evil taint on any individual soul in consequence of a crime committed twenty or forty years ago," and "even to the end of the world and forever" if God so chooses (Y3:405). In other words, like any other property that comprises personal identity, the persistence of sin and guilt in each person depends entirely on God.

Therefore, it is far from an "absurd and impossible" thing for the defenders of original sin to argue that humanity participates in Adam's sin and guilt, or that "Adam's posterity should be without that original righteousness, which Adam had lost" (Y3:406). In fact, the unity asserted by original sin between humanity and Adam is analogous to the way God structures the rest of the universe, human nature in particular. Just as all humanity is united with God through the communication of consciousness, so there is a similar kind of "oneness or identity of Adam and his posterity" (Y3:390). The unity between humanity and Adam is that of "*communion* and *coexistence* in acts and affections; all jointly participating and all concurring" as "*one* complex person, or *one* moral whole." Although infinite time and circumstances separate Adam and the rest of humanity, God maintains this relation as if "Adam and all his posterity had *coexisted*" (Y3:391).

Edwards's conception of humanity's solidarity with Adam has distinct advantages over the Augustinian account as well the Arminian alternative. First, Edwards offers a more compelling explanation of humanity's real participation in Adam's sin. In place of Augustine's biological account of sin, Edwards asserts that by virtue of its communion with Adam, humanity acted in concert with Adam's act of disobedience. While Edwards believes it possible for humanity to have "somehow grown out" of Adam biologically, in his account humanity "approved" of the "first act of sin" and experienced "an evil disposition of heart" as a result (Y3:405; 390). Therefore, the "first depravity of heart, and the imputation of that sin" are merely the consequence of humanity's "established union" with Adam. The "established principle" of sin in humanity is not a burden unearned, for through its union with Adam, humanity participated in Adam's act of sin as if each had committed it and had "perfect consent of heart to it" (Y3:391). In this way, Adam and the rest of humanity are not "distinct agents," but do indeed occupy the same moral universe. Likewise, Edwards rejects the view of some of his contemporaries, who believed that humanity inherits original sin "merely because God imputes it to them," rather than because it is "truly and properly theirs" (Y4:408–11).[65] In Edwards's scheme, each of us bears equal responsibility for original sin, and the Arminian objection concerning fairness is refuted.

Second, Edwards's account of humanity's solidarity with Adam provides a better description of the relational and communal state of estrangement incurred by humanity through original sin. For both the traditional Augustinian account and the Arminian alternative, the focus of the debate over original sin remains the individual's state of culpability. But Edwards's account of humanity's solidarity with Adam reinforces the teaching that God "naturally" unites persons in society, leading them to desire relations of "close union . . . manifold intercourse, and mutual dependence" so that all "partake together in the natural and common goods and evils of this lower world." Such a vision of human society provides a better sense of humanity's collective guilt before God. Where the Arminian position holds that sin is necessarily an individual act, Edwards argues that sin necessarily has a communal component. Hence, it is not "unheard of," nor "unscriptural," that persons "should be ashamed of things done by others, whom they are nearly concerned in," particularly since "they are justly looked upon in the sight of God, who sees the disposition of their hearts as fully consenting and concurring" (Y3:407).

Correlatively, for Edwards the practical point that original sin teaches is social as well as personal. The "doctrine teaches us to think no worse of others, than ourselves," for it teaches "that we are all" by "nature *companions* in a miserable condition, which, under a revelation of divine mercy, tends to promote mutual *compassion*" (Y3:424).

Finally, Edwards's account of humanity's solidarity better reflects the theology expressed by Paul in Romans 5:12–21.[66] As many note, this passage represents the *locus classicus* of the doctrine of original sin, specifically the parallel Paul draws between the life we have in Adam and in Christ:[67]

> Therefore, just as sin entered into the world through one man, and death came through sin, and thus death passed to all, so that [*eph' ho*[*i*]] all have sinned . . . as through one man's disobedience many were sinners, so through one man's obedience many were made righteous. (Rom. 5:12, 18b)[68]

Working with an inadequate Latin translation, Augustine understands the term "so that all have sinned" as "in whom all sinned" (*in quo omnes peccaverunt*), which justifies his argument that humanity was seminally present in Adam. Indeed, to offer any other interpretation of the phrase "in whom all sinned" is "to twist a perfectly clear statement into some other meaning."[69] Taylor, on the other hand, argues that the connection between the words "sin" and "death" is merely a metonymy, a rhetorical device, to refer to the physical death all suffer as a result of Adam's sin. Accordingly, what Paul is really saying is not that humanity sins with Adam, for Taylor believes it obvious that one is guiltless regarding the sins of another, but only that humanity suffers physical death as a result of Adam's sin. And it is in this sense alone we "are made *Sinners* by the Disobedience of *another*."[70]

Edwards avoids Augustine's implausible theory of seminal unity as well as Taylor's clear act of exegetical "violence" against the text (Y3:326). Consistent with his understanding of solidarity, Edwards argues that Paul's meaning is that humanity shares in Adam's personal identity, and therefore in the effects of Adam's sin. In this way, Paul can "magnify" the "greatness and absoluteness of the dependence of all mankind on the redemption and righteousness of Christ, for justification and life" (Y3:336). Further, while humanity's solidarity with Adam in the first sin is clearly implied in the passage, "this is not the main thing the Apostle designs to prove" (Y3:338). For Paul's main point is to set in opposition "the *first* and *second* Adam, in the *death* that comes by *one*, and the *life* and happiness by the *other*" in order to give "proper instruction for the Jews, who looked on themselves a holy people" (Y3:313, 338). More than either Moses or Abraham, Adam represents the highest ancestor of the "Jewish nation." At the same time, on account of Adam, "sin, guilt, and desert of ruin became universal in the world long before" the establishment of the covenant with

Abraham and the "law given by Moses had any being" (Y3:338). Consequently, it is "our natural relation to Adam, and not to Abraham, which determines our native moral state." Therefore, our "being natural children of Abraham will not make us by nature holy in the sight of God, since we are the natural seed of sinful Adam" (Y3:341). Only a "second Adam" can fulfill what God intended for Israel and by extension humanity. As the "antitype of Adam," Christ both restores what the first Adam lost and represents the eschatological fulfillment of all the promises God made to Israel through the patriarchs, for in relation to Christ, Adam is merely "the figure of him that was to come." The "great benefit" of Christ "goes beyond the damage sustained by Adam" and brings into being eternal life, happiness, and communion with God (Y3:317–18).

From Edwards's perspective, then, the doctrine of original sin appears throughout the passage (Y3:345). Edwards also recognizes that Paul's intent is to compare the difference between the solidarity that we have with Adam through sin and the solidarity that we have with Christ through "the free grace of God" (Y3:318). The former solidarity is one of "universal" sin, "death, and final destruction" (Y3:346). The latter solidarity is one of "righteousness, justification, and a title to eternal life come by Christ" (Y3:338). Although the two relations of solidarity are utterly different in terms of their respective rewards and punishments, there is a distinct "resemblance" between the two—each derives its nature from its representative figure (Y3:346). Given the inescapability of our solidarity with Adam, our only hope is to receive solidarity with Christ.

Philip Quinn concludes that Edwards's interpretation of Romans 5:12–19 is "defensible," and offers "the best available interpretation of that chapter."[71] Indeed, Edwards's interpretation of humanity's twofold solidarity with Adam and Christ overlaps with some recent appraisals of this passage in New Testament studies. Thus, Christopher Bryan argues that a "communal understanding of personality" operates in the parallel Paul draws between Adam and Christ. Where Adam's "disobedience places Adam's community in alienation from and opposition to God," Christ's "obedience places Christ's community in a proper relationship to God." Such an understanding of "human existence as having little meaning except in relationship to others" was common in the ancient world, Bryan writes, and therefore Paul's argument "perhaps appeared less dramatic" to his audience "than to us."[72] And Edwards's understanding of Christ's role as the second Adam anticipates recent developments of a distinct "Pauline theology" from the perspective of ancient Jewish literature. Thus, N. T. Wright notes that a consistent theme in the "intertestamental and rabbinic literature" is that "God's purposes for the human race in general have devolved onto, and will be fulfilled in, Israel in particular." Within this context, Adam represents "the whole eschatological people of God." The parallel that Paul draws between Christ and Adam, then, is a veritable "Adam-christology." As the second Adam, Christ not only replaces the first Adam, but signifies the eschatological fulfillment of God's abundant and merciful love for Israel, as well as for humanity.[73]

In recent philosophy and theology, however, Edwards's efforts have not found widespread acceptance. Although William J. Wainwright grants that Edwards's defense of original sin is "one of the most plausible," he argues that Edwards operates with a moral psychology that mistakenly conflates "inclination and choice." As a result, Edwards's doctrine of original sin overlooks the difference between "corruption" and "guilt," for "once one assimilates inclination and choice, it is easy to assimilate sinful (corrupt) inclinations and sinful (guilty) choices."[74] That a difference exists between corruption and guilt appears obvious to Wainwright. Consider a situation in which everyone drives home from a party drunk, but only one person kills a pedestrian. Everyone's actions are heinous, but only one person is guilty, even if the others are in some way liable for that person's actions.[75] This is so, Wainwright argues, because "one must have committed an act to be guilty of it, and one cannot commit another's act." Therefore, "even though liability can be transferred from one person to another, guilt cannot."[76] By analogy, "Adam's posterity cannot be guilty of Adam's fault unless Adam's act is somehow *literally* their own." Though Edwards's theory of solidarity establishes that "Adam's fault can in some sense be regarded as the fault of the 'species,' i.e. of humanity as a whole," Edwards fails to prove that God can "reasonably impute Adam's guilt to his descendents."[77] Consequently, Wainwright accepts Edwards's retrieval of the Augustinian account to the extent that it emphasizes that God redeems "a humanity which is unable to extricate itself from its own egoism and blindness," but not to the extent that persons are guilty for actions that do not spring directly from their individual wills.

As with the previous comparison between Edwards and Swinburne, it is impossible to resolve the disagreement between Edwards and Wainwright by viewing human nature in isolation. All the same, it is worth noting that Wainwright's argument is far from airtight. First, Wainwright's example of the drunk drivers does not prove a difference between inclination and choice. For the inclinations and choices of the drivers are all the same; the only difference is that one person's bad choice caused another's death. Second, though it is undeniable that we hold persons more accountable (at least legally) for their objective acts than for their subjective inclinations, this difference seems at least as much due to our limitations as finite creatures—we ascertain each other's objective acts easier than each other's subjective inclinations. Hence, Wainwright's distinction between inclination and choice may not rest on an ontological separation of the two, and this separation may have little relevance within the theological context of sin. For as an infinite being God knows our hearts well and judges them as justly as our actions, as several passages of Scripture attest.[78]

Nonetheless, the more important difference between Wainwright and Edwards concerns the role solidarity plays in their respective theologies. In addition to limiting the extent of humanity's solidarity with Adam, Wainwright also limits the extent to which social relations constitute personal identity. Though he grants that communities shape our identity significantly, "our metaphysical identity is not a social product."[79] As a result, Wainwright does not see relationality as constitutive of authentic personhood as Edwards does.

Had Edwards made explicit his reliance on his Trinitarian thought in *Original Sin*, he could have written more concerning this connection between Adam, Christ, and personhood. For as we observed in chapter 2, in "Miscellanies" entry 702, Edwards writes that Christ, the second Adam, completes what is missing in the first Adam's fallen nature—thus representing the true *imago dei* in human nature—and also communicates the fullness of the love of the Godhead to humanity. Christ represents "transcendent advancement of men in their union with God" through the "communion of his Spirit, whereby they are partakers of the divine nature" (Y18:288). This relational transformation is social as well as personal. For just as Eve came from Adam's rib, so Christ is "he out of whom the church is, as it were taken, from his transcendent love and by the deep sleep of death." Hence, in an ultimate sense the church is both the body and the bride of Christ, and the solidarity that we have in Christ is a solidarity we have with other saints that increases for eternity. From Edwards's perspective, to deny our collective guilt in original sin is to deny the fact that our communion with others is integral to our eternal participation in the triune society of God. Like the previous discussion of Swinburne's accommodation of incompatibilism, then, it is hard not to be struck by the high theological price Wainwright pays to privilege the individual sense of personal guilt.

While Edwards's account of original sin is at odds with philosophers and theologians who hold views similar to Wainwright's, it anticipates a recent attempt by Alistair McFadyen to present the Augustinian account of original sin in Trinitarian terms. McFadyen argues that we live in a "culture of practical atheism," which sees sin only in terms of "acts for which one is personally responsible." Such a view, however, fails to recognize the dynamic relationality that is equally constitutive of persons and ignores the power the Augustinian account of original sin offers to explain the devastation wrought in instances where our sin participates in grave moral evil. For the Augustinian account operates within a Trinitarian understanding of God. "To say that God is trinity is to say that there is no divine being without relationship," writes McFadyen, and that "God is Godself in the dynamic of God's life, and that the character of that dynamic is love." Consequently, "sin is failure in orientation in the world to God as God" and "disruption of the proper conditions and practices of right worship." For it is "through worship of the living God in the spirit of faith that people are incorporated into the joyful dynamic of life in abundance."[80]

3. EDWARDS AND EVIL

As the previous remarks suggest, another topic that is important to address is theodicy, or the study of why an omnipotent and omnibenevolent God permits evil to occur in the world. Though a distinct area of study, most explorations in theodicy involve ethical concepts in their attempt to accuse or excuse God for the presence of evil. Hume presents the fundamental problem of theodicy in parts 10 and 11 of his *Dialogues concerning Natural Religion* (1779).[81] Hume believes it impossible to reconcile the "miseries of life, the unhappiness of man, the general corruptions of our nature" as well as the "cursed and polluted" state of the "whole earth" with commonly held notions of the "moral attributes of the Deity," that is, "justice, benevolence, mercy, and rectitude." The statements that "God exists" and "evil exists" are logically incompatible. Hume argues, "Is he willing to prevent evil, but not able? then he is impotent. Is he able but not willing? then he is malevolent. Is he both able and willing? whence then is evil?" Given this incompatibility, as well as the ample empirical evidence for the existence of evil, one may justifiably conclude that God does not exist. Although framed in terms of a test of logical consistency, Hume conceives of God's goodness in terms of a "benevolence that resembles the human," rather than in terms of aseity or self-sufficiency. Therefore, even if his argument of logical inconsistency fails, as some contend, the moral difficulty that Hume identifies remains: Why would a good God treat his creatures in this way? If capable, would not a good God prevent suffering? Hume believes he at least establishes that God lacks "moral sentiments" such as we have.[82]

In response, Christian theists have developed moral justifications for the presence of evil, often from the perspective of human freedom. Some appeal to created freedom as a necessary prerequisite for attaining an optimal state of affairs. Thus, Alvin Plantinga, drawing from Gottfried Leibniz (1646–1716), argues that in the interest of creating an optimal world, it is possible that God created beings that have free will, and that evil is an unavoidable result of this bestowal of freedom. Hence, all the moral evil that exists in the world is due to the choices of free moral agents whom God created, and God could not have created a world that would have had a better balance of good over evil than the actual world has.[83] Others argue that created freedom itself is integral to human agency and dignity, and therefore represents an intrinsic good that compensates for the evils we experience in this world. Thus, Richard Swinburne argues that God not only grants the freedom to choose, but always honors this freedom. Though human happiness centers on God, each of us must learn to recognize and pursue God as the source of our happiness. While God has the power to keep us from experiencing the evil that results from the misuse of our freedom, God's goodness precludes this action, for to do so would interfere with our maturation as moral beings.[84]

Though Plantinga and Swinburne offer differing justifications and assessments of the value of freedom, they both adhere broadly to the Augustinian account of original sin and evil.[85] In contrast, John Hick seeks to replace the Augustinian account of original sin as part of his own presentation of the "person-making" freedom mentioned above.[86] According to Hick, the Augustinian account suffers from two fatal flaws. First, its focus on the biblical story of Adam and Eve and its thesis that human action "brought about the almost universal carnage of nature" lacks plausibility for most "educated inhabitants of the modern world." Hence, we need an understanding of sin and evil that reflects the modern theory of evolution and is not dependent on a prescientific worldview. Second, it does not provide an adequate characterization of human freedom, for it holds that humans once had in their "immediate consciousness" the knowledge of God. But in order for there to be "genuine freedom, the creature must be brought into existence, not in the immediate divine presence, but at a 'distance' from God." Hence, we need an account of freedom that establishes freedom in its fullest possible sense, in an "autonomous system" in which the presence of God is not "overwhelmingly evident" and belief in God itself is a real alternative.[87]

Accordingly, Hick offers his own "Irenaean approach" to sin.[88] Where the Augustinian account "hinges upon the fall as the origin of moral evil," the "Irenaean" account "hinges upon the creation of humankind through the evolutionary process as an immature creature living in a challenging and therefore person-making world." Drawing from Irenaeus's distinction between the "image" (*eikon*) and "likeness" (*homoiosis*) of God in the *imago dei*, Hick develops a two-stage conception of the creation of humankind. The first stage covers the "gradual production of *homo sapiens*" as "intelligent and ethical animals," so that they are capable of the "complex demands of social life" as well as "of an awareness of the divine." The second stage describes the point at which human beings, as "intelligent, ethical, and religious animals," freely choose "to know and love their Maker." God creates this two-stage process to provide humanity epistemic "space" to exist as finite beings in a "religiously ambiguous" world in order to protect the authenticity of their decision for God. Further, the transition from the first to the second stage happens as a result of each person's autonomous development into virtuous persons. Virtue, for Hick, is directly "formed within the agent as a hard-won deposit of right decisions in situations of challenge and temptation" rather than as a "given nature" created within the agent "without any effort on her part."[89]

Thus, the world is a classroom of "person-making" activity. The world provides a context in which humans can transcend the selfishness that is part of their natural instinct for survival and gradually become "capable of love, of self-giving in a common cause, of a conscience that responds to others in needs and dangers." Humanity's "self-regarding animality" has been the cause of "moral evil" in the world "expressed over the centuries both in sins of individual selfishness and in the much more massive sins of corporate selfishness, institutionalized in slavery, exploitation, and all the many and complex forms of social injustice."[90] We therefore live in an "ethically demanding world" in which there is the presence of both *moral* evil (i.e., selfishness) and the *natural* evil that comes from living in a "challenging and even dangerous environment." Like moral evil, natural evil serves a "person-making purpose." But whereas each person must transcend moral evil, natural evil continues to perform a pedagogical function in the moral life. For "the very mystery of natural evil, the very fact that disasters afflict human beings in contingent, undirected, and haphazard ways, is itself a necessary feature of a world that calls forth mutual aid and builds up mutual caring and love." In this way, both natural and moral evil "are necessary aspects of the present stage of the process through which God is gradually creating perfected finite persons" so that they can live "in filial relationship with their Maker."[91]

Hick realizes that the account of sin and evil that he offers in his Irenaean account would "collapse" without a corresponding eschatology, or belief in the eventual realization of "perfected personal community in the divine kingdom." This is so, for the "perfect all-embracing humanity" he envisions "has evidently not been realized in this world." Thus, the Irenaean account "presupposes each person's survival, in some form, of bodily death, and further living and growing towards that end-state." In addition to eternal life, the Irenaean account elicits an eschatology that embraces universal salvation. For only if salvation includes "the entire human race can it justify the sins and sufferings of the entire human race through history."[92]

Of course, there are relevant differences between the defenses of freedom offered by Plantinga, Swinburne, and Hick. Nonetheless, all three hold that human freedom makes possible the integration of the seemingly incompatible theses that God is omnipotent and benevolent and that evil exists in the world. Further, all three appeal to human freedom because of its connection with goods that God could not achieve without the presence of evil. Hick's proposal differs to the extent that he systematically works out the theological implications of the valorization of freedom offered by all three. For if human freedom is integral to God's fulfillment of God's purposes for the world, then we need a theological construal of sin and evil that respects this freedom. And, as we have observed, the Augustinian account fails to do this sufficiently, for it views human freedom in a much more restricted sense, as limited by our solidarity with Adam, and in possession of a nature that has already been vitiated by sin.

3.1. Hick and Edwards

It is clear from what we have observed in the previous chapters that Edwards views the whole process of "person-making" differently than Hick. In addition to seeing personhood as a relational state of being, Edwards paints a radically different picture of what constitutes virtue, how virtue is attained, and what role it plays in the moral life. Further, it is clear from what we have discussed in this chapter that Edwards views freedom quite differently than Hick. These differences concerning personhood and freedom partly explain Edwards's comfort with the Augustinian account of original sin.

In regard to the specific question of theodicy, Edwards would object that Hick's Irenaean account of evil fails to accommodate the abject suffering and death that exists throughout the world. For all intents and purposes, Hick's view of evil is that of Edwards's opponent, John Taylor.[93] Like Hick, Taylor believes that evil exists to provide a context so one can develop a character that withstands temptation and freely chooses God. In *The Scripture-Doctrine of Original Sin*, he writes that the "reason why we are now in a state of trial and temptation" is "to prove and discipline our minds, to season our virtue, and to fit us for the kingdom of God."[94] Accordingly, natural evil, specifically "affliction and death," represents merely the "limiting of existence" that is in actuality "a great benefit," for it teaches us "to be moderate in gratifying the appetites of a corruptible body, to mortify pride and ambition, and to give a sense of our dependence on God."[95] Edwards argues, however, that the depiction of the pedagogical role of suffering loses its explanatory power in the face of "terrible afflictions." For "if death be brought on mankind" to "wean" us "from the world," is "it not strange that it should fall so heavy on infants, who are not capable of making any such improvement of it?" Taylor at times suggests that "the death of infants may be for the good of parents," but this is unacceptable. "Are there not ways enough," Edwards asks, that God "might increase their trouble, without destroying the lives of such multitudes of those that are perfectly innocent," and "not capable of any reflection or making any improvement of it?" (Y3:211–12).

For Edwards, the tragic death of infants is indicative of the general afflictions of humanity. Although often overlooked, death itself is the greatest calamity to befall humanity, given the original blessing of immortality. Nothing compares to the "universal havoc which death makes of the whole race of mankind, from generation to generation, without distinction of sex, age, quality or condition, with all the infinitely various dismal circumstances, torments and agonies which attend the death of old and young, adult persons and little infants" (Y3:208). To describe the suffering of death as "the chastisements of our heavenly Father" is therefore absurd. For "those would be strange chastisements from the hand of a wise and good Father which are wholly for nothing, especially such severe chastisements as to break the child's bones" (Y3:212).

In sum, Edwards would argue that Hick's Irenaean account fails to answer the central problem posed in theodicy. While Hick's Irenaean account maintains God as both omnipotent and benevolent, he cannot accommodate those evils that can in no way serve a pedagogical purpose. Hick hopes to provide a more plausible explanation for why we live in "a world in which sadistic cruelty often has its way, in which selfish love-lessness is so rife, in which there are debilitating diseases, crippling accidents, bodily and mental decay, insanity, and all manner of natural disasters."[96] But, in the end, he can account only for those evils that contribute to one's development as an autonomous and virtuous agent, and ignores those abject evils that threaten to disintegrate us as persons.[97]

Moreover, from Edwards's perspective it is hard to see how, even within the context of person-making, evil contributes to the development of virtue. Hick sees virtues as "a hard-won deposit of right decisions in situations of challenge and temptation" that "are intrinsically more valuable than ready-made virtues" created within the agent "without any effort on her own part." As we observed in the previous chapter, Edwards agrees with this thought to the extent that he appreciates the purgative role of "trials" in the soul's development (Y2:431–33). But for Edwards every virtue is a gift from God; indeed, true virtue is the self-gift of God. Accordingly, from Edwards's perspective Hick's calculus of evil and virtue seems warped. Just because God redeems the evil that occurs in our lives does not mean evil rightly exists in the first place. Further, the consistent lesson among those who have maintained their faith and hope in the midst of suffering is not one of autonomy, but dependence. If suffering teaches a lesson, it seems to be that God bears us through our suffering. Paul's expression "I can do all things through him who strengthens me" (Phil. 4:13) describes not the victory of the autonomous self but the realization that God holds us in being as we are conformed to the image of Christ.

3.2. Evil and Beauty

But what is Edwards's theodicy? Though he wrote at the cusp of the development of theodicy as an independent topic of study, Edwards did not write a discrete work of theodicy. We can gather, however, the general outlines of his thought on evil from several texts, notebook entries, and a sermon. As we have seen, in *Original Sin* Edwards most often describes evil in terms of the punishment received as a result of sin. Primarily, Edwards describes this punishment in terms of privation, that is, the diminished existence we have when our souls are not in communion with God. This privation, however, includes *positive* evil—states of being and events that have real ontological status. Humanity suffers real evil as a result of Adam's sin, and the moral devastation we experience and perpetuate constitutes our identity as fallen persons. Fundamentally, then, evil threatens personhood.

In other writings, Edwards transposes this description of evil into aesthetic terms. Edwards writes in "The Mind" that the triune beauty and excellence of God—God's "infinite mutual love"—is the ultimate measure of good and evil (Y6:363). If all goodness and beauty is defined in terms of relations of consent, then all evil and deformity is defined in terms of dissent. Dissent is a state of "deformity," a withdrawal from relation that is especially hideous in the presence of a being who already expresses "consent." Dissent therefore is a breach of love and an act of injustice, for dissent is fundamentally a refusal "to exert ourselves towards any being as it deserves" (Y6:364). Like the sense we have of God's goodness, evil is an objective state of relation that we can subjectively apprehend both naturally and spiritually. While true moral and spiritual goodness can be perceived only when we experience the communication of God's Spirit, even "natural" persons have an apprehension of evil, Edwards writes in "Miscellanies" entry 782. "Natural" good and evil is that "which is agreeable or disagreeable to human nature as such, without regard to the moral disposition." Like the perception of "beauty and deformity" in sensible objects, we have a sense in our heart of pleasure or displeasure when we encounter natural good and evil (Y18:462).

Consistent with the Augustinian tradition, Edwards uses his aesthetics as a justification for the presence of evil in certain entries.[98] God's beauty is infinitely comprehensive and envelops all relations that are of a "contrary" nature (Y6:336–38). And though God's victory over evil is complete, the presence of evil in the form of divine retribution persists in eternity to "double the ardor" of the love and joy of those in heaven. The "sight of the wonderful power, the great and dreadful majesty and authority, and the awful justice and holiness of God" manifested in the punishment of the wicked will make the elect "prize his favor and love exceedingly the more" (Y13:379). Hence, the "terribleness of God is part of his glory, in that a sense of it should be kept up in the minds of creatures" so that we have "the more complete happiness in a sense of his love" (Y13:469). In other words, like shading in a painting, evil highlights our appreciation of the brightness and beauty of the whole more than would be the case were it absent.

In other writings, however, Edwards views God's aesthetic transformation of the world as fundamentally christological. In "Miscellanies" entry 479, Edwards returns to the typological relation between the old creation and the new: "God's causing light to shine out of darkness is a type of his causing such spiritual light and glory by Jesus Christ to succeed, and to arise out of, the dreadful darkness of sin and misery." And God's "bringing the world into such a beautiful form out of a chaos without form or void, typifies his bringing the spiritual world to such divine excellency and beauty after the confusion, deformity and ruin of sin" (Y13:523). Through the believer's union with Christ, Edwards continues elsewhere, "the justice of God is not only appeased to those who have an interest in him, but stands up for them." For on account of their union with Christ, "justice demands adoption and glorification" with greater necessity that it had "been for Adam." God's justice to Adam was based on a "promise," but "it is obliged to believers on the account of the absolute merit of the Son of God, and upon the account of an eternal agreement between God and his Son" (Y13:221).

Within this christological aesthetic, beauty is not *unitive*, but *bivalent*, that is, both negative and positive aesthetic values are present in Christ's creation and redemption of the world.[99] Edwards's most extensive exploration of this aspect of his aesthetics is his early sermon "The Excellency of Christ" (1738). Within Christ, there are "incompatible" and "diverse excellencies" to match the union of divine and human natures in the same person. In Christ, there is both "infinite worthiness of good, and the greatest patience under the sufferings of evil," such as "is not properly predicable of God the Father, and of the Holy Ghost." Christ as the "mediator" and "God-man" represents the perfect "conjunction of innocence, worthiness, and patience under suffering." In Christ, there is both "majesty" and "meekness," "holiness" and "humility," "self-sufficiency" and "an entire trust and reliance on God."[100]

Particularly in the crucifixion, these incongruous attributes make manifest the "dying love" and saving power of Christ for humanity. Christ "was never so in his enemies' hands, as in the time of his last sufferings" when he no longer felt the "comforts" of God's presence. Yet at the same time, "it was principally by means of those sufferings that he conquered and overthrew his enemies." For "the devil had as it were swallowed up Christ, as the whale did Jonah," but "it was deadly poison to him," gave him "a mortal wound, and forced him to vomit him up again."[101] The crucifixion also represents the perfect conjunction of God's infinite justice and mercy toward sinners. Christ has "grace sufficient for every sinner, and even the chief of sinners." Finally, the crucifixion makes it possible for Christ "to bestow the greatest good" of admitting sinners into "friendship" and "union" with him, through which they experience the spiritual union of "the Father and the Son."[102]

Had Edwards explored the topic of theodicy directly, his best response to the problem of evil would proceed from the christological aesthetic he proposes in "The Excellency of Christ." For the traditional Augustinian aesthetic fails to grant God total victory over evil. Even in the form of retribution directed toward those who rightfully deserve it, the persistence of vindication in heaven allows evil a victory that is hard to reconcile with a God who is perfectly good and powerful. That God would construct a world in which the suffering of others furthers the saints' appreciation of God's goodness and love calls into question the very existence of these attributes. Moreover, given that evil destroys the personhood of individuals, as Edwards himself holds, the belief that the universal good of divine harmony compensates for particular evils underestimates God's resourcefulness in responding to, and ultimately defeating, evil. As Dostoevsky argues through the character of Ivan in *The Brothers Karamazov*, the unitive and universal "harmony" promised in the traditional Augustinian aesthetic cannot accommodate the "unrequited suffering" of children.[103] To respond adequately to the problem of evil, one must show how God's goodness extends to particular persons and redeems the devastation of evil in particular lives.[104]

But Edwards's christological aesthetic maintains that God at once assumes evil's effects and overthrows evil's power. The christological aesthetic sees evil fully vanquished, and God's omnipotence and benevolence ultimately victorious, through Christ's full involvement and participation in humanity's suffering. Christ is "great enough" to "become one *of* them, that he might be one *with* them," even "to expose himself to shame and spitting" and "to yield up himself to an ignominious death for them." Christ's participation in suffering does not lessen the abject nature of suffering, nor does it contribute to his own development as a person, as Hick holds. That Christ experiences suffering raises our awareness of the horrendous nature of suffering in any form. While the paradigm of Christ's suffering is the crucifixion, Christ suffered throughout the time of his incarnation. Christ's "humiliation was great, in being born in such low condition," in "living in poverty," and "in suffering such manifold and bitter reproaches as he suffered while he went about preaching and working miracles."[105] Further, that Christ is God incarnate shows the extent to which God identifies and redeems particular human suffering. The particularity of Christ's suffering and death ensures that Christ knows suffering from the viewpoint of a specific person. In this way, Christ knows in a representative way the depth of individual suffering and fully appreciates the threat it poses to personhood.

Accordingly, in "The Excellency of Christ" Edwards addresses the "poor distressed soul." Christ "has had experience" of "the afflictions you now suffer." For Christ has "come down to us, and has taken our nature, and is become one of us, and calls himself our friend, brother, and companion." Hence, "if Christ accepts of you, you need not fear but that you will be safe; for he is a strong lion for your defense; and if you come, you need not fear but that you will be accepted; for he is like a lamb to all that come to him, and receives them with grace and tenderness." Christ "will give himself to you, with all those various excellencies that meet in him, to your full and lasting enjoyment." And Christ "will ever after treat you as his dear friend; and you shall ere long be where he is, and shall behold his glory, and shall dwell with him, in most free and intimate communion and enjoyment."[106]

As we have seen, Edwards does mention the suffering and the two natures of Christ in *Freedom of the Will* and *Original Sin* (Y1:289, 291; Y3:143). And had he made recourse to this christological aesthetic in these works he could have offered a more complete theodicy in both works. First, it would have helped him further unpack his protest concerning the abject suffering of infants in *Original Sin*. Edwards rejects the argument that all evil serves a pedagogical purpose, because evil affects those who could in no way benefit from its lessons. Following the logic of solidarity, however, Edwards would have to admit that he uses the phrase "perfectly innocent" regarding infants in a restricted sense (Y3:211). For given that he believes "infants become sinners by that one act and offense of Adam," they are "by nature children of wrath," even if they are to "a lesser degree guilty of sin" (Y3:343; 215; 114).[107] But Edwards could have argued on the basis of this same logic of solidarity that Christ fully participates in and redeems the suffering of infants. Indeed, to limit the scope of the solidarity we have through Christ in comparison to the solidarity we have with Adam contradicts the typological relationship Edwards establishes between the first and second Adam. For as the second Adam, Christ reverses the damage caused by the first Adam and restores the personhood of all humanity, which presumably includes those infants whose only sin is the original sin they share in solidarity with Adam. Perhaps for this reason, Edwards writes in his "Book of Controversies" that an infant who would have believed in Christ if given the opportunity is "accepted as if he actually believed in Christ and so is entitled to eternal life through Christ."[108]

Second, Edwards's christological aesthetic would have provided an alternative to the constructive role of suffering developed by Taylor and Hick. For as we observed in chapter 2, Christ's suffering is the temporal expression of the triune God's benevolence. Christ's love for humanity originates in the love between the Father and the Son: The "divine excellency of Christ and the love of the Father to him is the life and soul of all that Christ did and suffered in the work of redemption" (Y13:524). Further, by virtue of the union of his human nature with the Logos, Christ's self-sacrificial love for humanity was "derived from the love of the *Logos*, or else they would not be one person" (Y13:327). Hence, the "passionate love of Christ, by virtue of the union with the divine nature, is in a sort infinite," and the desire for union expressed in the "love of the Son of God for human nature" is "something like the union in the persons of the Trinity, nearer than there can be between any two human beings" (Y13:177, 329). Cast within his christological aesthetic, Christ's identification and participation in human suffering manifests not only the triune God's compassion and empathy but also God's own suffering love. Accordingly, those who suffer become capable of viewing their personal suffering as a participation in Christ's infinite love for humanity. In other words, suffering itself has redemptive and revelatory value, but of a different kind than that identified by Taylor and Hick. Instead of contributing to one's individual project of "person-making," suffering construed within Edwards's christological aesthetic provides a way to enter the heart of God.

Finally, had Edwards made recourse to his christological aesthetic in *Freedom of the Will* and *Original Sin*, he would have been able to provide a more satisfying account of the advent of evil—why Adam sinned in the first place, or how God is not the "author of depravity" (Y3:380). Given his conception of the "spiritual" principles inherent in human nature before the fall, neither of Edwards's answers to these propositions is straightforward. In reference to the first sin, how could a being with perfect inclinations develop an inclination to sin? Edwards argues that Adam was led by "ignorance" to believe that the act of disobedience somehow represented a "great increase and advancement of dignity and happiness" (Y3:193). But this response runs counter to his whole anthropology, for it rests on a compartmentalization of knowledge and will. It also runs counter to his understanding of the condition of humanity before the fall, which he holds was a state of perfect communion with God rather than one of ignorant simplicity. And in reference to God's role in the advent of evil, Edwards recognizes that such an event could only occur if God withheld sufficient grace from Adam. Nonetheless, he insists that God's act was only one of "permission" rather than one of a "*positive* cause" (Y3:394; 381). That is to say, no "evil quality" was directly "infused, implanted, or wrought" in humanity by God (Y3:380). God only allowed evil to occur and take its course. But this explanation assigns to God an oblique role in the advent of evil, and it is hard to see—particularly given Edwards's broad understanding of causality—how construing God's action under the species of omission rather than commission makes God less responsible. Further, it fails to explain why God withheld grace in the first place. Edwards eventually admits it is a "mystery" why God did, but nonetheless insists we can rest assured that the act conforms to God's ultimate will for humanity (Y3:394; Y1:409).

In contrast, from the perspective of Edwards's christological aesthetic, all things have come into being so that humanity might know the love of the triune God. As we have seen, in the covenant of redemption all three persons of the Trinity agreed that the Son would manifest and communicate the "fullness" of the Trinity to humanity (H:78). God therefore allows "evil" and "sin" to "come to pass" primarily so that we might behold Jesus Christ as the perfect revelation of the Godhead. In this way, sin and evil are necessary because they reveal the gracious character of the Trinity to humanity. While this thought may be hard to accept given the abject suffering brought on by sin and evil, it is balanced by the thought that Christ himself fully participates in suffering and fully redeems the suffering of all persons. Hence, as Edwards writes at one point in *Freedom of the Will*, "Christ's crucifixion, though a most horrid fact," was of such a "glorious tendency" that it was "permitted and ordered of God" (Y1:409, 412).

Admittedly, the priority I assign to Edwards's christological aesthetic directly challenges his stated position against universal salvation. In both *Freedom of Will* and *Original Sin*, Edwards maintains his belief that "however Christ in some sense may be said to die for all," through his death God only redeemed "a certain number only." Edwards offers two reasons why this is so. First, it is the witness of Scripture that not all will be saved, and therefore it is impossible that "God should prosecute a design or aim at a thing, which he at the same time most perfectly knows will not be accomplished" (Y1:435).[109] Second, given the pervasiveness of sin it is clear that few "have actually been partakers of this new fund of light" offered through Christ (Y3:322–23). Nonetheless, despite the scriptural evidence Edwards cites and in light of all that he writes concerning human inability and the victorious love of Christ, these reasons seem unacceptable. For if we are unable to will what is right without God, why would a God who is omnipotent and perfectly good hold us accountable for acts and affections over which we are powerless? Edwards, of course, argues in *Freedom of the Will* that we incur moral responsibility when we do as we please (Y1:357–64). But if our perception of what pleases us depends entirely on God, would it not be more in accord with God's perfect goodness and benevolence to ensure that ultimately all receive their hearts' true desire?

Perhaps a better way to understand Edwards's stance against universal salvation is that God's redemption of humanity is never of humanity as an undifferentiated collective, but always of particular persons. As we observed in chapter 2, Edwards writes in "Miscellanies" entry 81 that the "faculties" of the ascended Christ are now "so enlarged" that he can think on all the "saints in the world" and behold them with "a passionate love." Jesus Christ "loves the church in general, because it is made up of those particular persons he loves." Further, the ascended Christ's "communion" with his saints is "as much as if his human soul were present" and "talking and conversing with them." Hence, "one glorious end of the union of the human to the divine nature" is "to bring God near to us; that even our God, the infinite Being, might be made as one of us" (Y13:248). But if an omnipotent God has determined to redeem all persons through the incarnation of the Son, who is the perfect revelation of God, would anyone knowingly refuse this act of goodness?

Like his understanding of the topics of the will and sin, Edwards's christological aesthetic would represent a minority opinion among current studies of theodicy. Nonetheless, his christological aesthetic resonates with a recent work in theodicy by Marilyn Adams. Adams challenges the terms of the debate that have attended theodicy from its inception. Typically, theodicy discusses the "compossibility" of God and evil in the terms of a "restricted standard theism" that defines God generally as "omnipotent, omniscient, and perfectly good." This approach, however, obscures the heteronomy of beliefs underlying each theological tradition's definition of these attributes. And it tends to ignore "horrendous evils"—evils of personal degradation that resist assimilation into a defense of theism on the basis of global goods such as freedom or the "best of all possible worlds." Consequently, the only adequate response to evil is one that does not attempt to solve the logical problem of evil such as it is, but draws directly from the resources available in Christian theology. Like Edwards, Adams argues that a christological aesthetic comforts those who suffer by giving witness to Christ's own participation in, and victory over, horrendous evil. For it is "God's becoming a human being, experiencing the human condition from the inside, from the viewpoint of a finite consciousness, that integrates the experience" of evil "into an incommensurately valuable relationship." In this way, the "individual is ushered into a relation of beatific intimacy with God and comes to realize how past participation in horrors is thus defeated."[110]

In a similar vein, Moltmann writes that the only adequate response to suffering is one that tries to describe how the triune God "actively suffers" with us: "For we can only talk about God's suffering in trinitarian terms." That is to say, each person of the Trinity experiences a unique suffering that expresses the depth of the divine compassion for humanity's suffering: The Father suffers in sending the Son, the Son suffers in feeling the abandonment of the Father on the cross, and the Spirit suffers in pouring out the suffering love of God to humanity in solidarity with the poor and oppressed. Such a view, Moltmann recognizes, does not settle the question posed by theodicy, but "no one can answer the theodicy question in this world." The only answer is one that lives with it as an open question, an "open wound," that awaits "the new world in which 'God will wipe away every tear from their eyes.'" Short of the eschaton, "does Job have any real theological friend except the crucified Jesus on Golgotha?"[111]

4. CONCLUSION

Typically, those who view *Freedom of the Will* and *Original Sin* in a sympathetic light direct Edwards's polemical fire towards the individualism and optimism that defines the sense of self in American culture. Thus, Perry Miller argues that Edwards offers "penetrating analysis of modern culture, and specifically of the American variant." He stands "against the cult of progress" espoused by "an emerging, competitive America" that holds "a high estimate of human nature" vindicated "by a geometrical increase of wealth and comfort." Therefore, in *Freedom of the Will* and *Original Sin* he calls upon America to "surrender its pretensions to exceptionalism, to acknowledge its share in the propensity of the race, and to confess from evidence 'that wickedness is agreeable to the nature of mankind in its present state.'"[112] In a similar vein, Robert Jenson asserts that these works highlight that "America's communal entity has been undone by the practical supposition that we can be free only by treating one another and regarding ourselves as inertial masses, bouncing merely causally against each other in public space." Though the Arminian position ends in "absurdity, American society has adopted it," because it has enabled the "new bourgeoisie" to defend the "transcendent value of social differences, differences produced not by organic place in the whole but by the individual's ability to free himself from the organic whole, by individual initiative."[113] Allen Guelzo opines that both Edwardsian and Arminian accounts shed light on how "thinned out and vapid the modern sense of self has become." For the "post-modern industrial state" grants us "the unheard of power to make ourselves over into our desire; but at the same moment, it also demands levels of planning and personal regulation at every stage beyond anything even the maddest Calvinist could have dreamed of." Further, "the luxury of power has rendered us incapable, to a point no eighteenth-century Arminian could have anticipated, of either setting or recognizing limits on our demands for an endless vista of economic and technological progress." Hence, the real question is not whether Edwards's account holds water, but "whether we are still humane enough to believe his answers."[114]

These assessments offer pointed social criticism, but they do not do justice to the defenses of autonomy we have examined in this chapter. For while the defenders of autonomy we have examined at length—Clarke, Taylor, Swinburne, Wainwright, and Hick—differ from one another on significant theological issues, they all develop their understanding of autonomy within the context of Christian theology. And though some of their efforts might appear no more than an artless construction of modest theological edifices on the commonplace belief that a correlation exists between autonomy and the moral life, the incorporation of this belief makes these edifices appear strong and unassailable. The concept of autonomy is deeply entrenched in current theological ethics. It has moved beyond being a necessary postulate for understanding the moral life, as Kant argues, and has become a settled intuition in the minds of many that one transgresses at the peril of being marginalized.[115] And if one is tempted to ask whether this intuition bears out in reality, one must realize that intuitions are difficult to refute, for they express what is self-evident and unarguable to most people. In this sense, Clarke's early argument, that our experience of autonomy is so powerful that the burden of proof is on those who deny it rather than those who defend it, remains the most persuasive.

Even those who appreciate Edwards's theology find this intuition hard to deny. Thus, while finding Edwards's account of original sin theologically persuasive, Quinn nonetheless confesses, "I am powerfully attracted to the Arminian assumption on moral grounds independent of my theological beliefs."[116] And the current theologians with whom aspects of Edwards's thought resonates, particularly McFadyen and Adams, are careful to note that their proposals lie outside the usual parameters of ethics on account of their skepticism of autonomy.[117] Nonetheless, in this chapter the Trinitarian interpretations of *Freedom of the Will* and *Original Sin* suggest that the intuition of autonomy cannot provide a theological ethics of sufficient richness and explanatory power to address well the topics we have discussed.

On the topic of the will, Edwards argues that what is crucial to personal freedom is not the freedom of self-determination, but the freedom to live in relation and to love as God loves us. Where the defenders of autonomy understand the will as morally realized only when it guides the individual's cultivation of character, Edwards understands the will as morally realized only when it enables the self to live in relation to God and others. To privilege the role of autonomy in the moral life therefore obscures the role of the Trinity in the moral life. For as we have seen, both Clarke and Swinburne have difficulty in conceiving how the triune God and humanity live in a unified moral community, as well as how Jesus Christ serves as the perfect expression of the divine love and the exemplar for authentic personhood.

On the topic of original sin, where the defenders of autonomy define sinfulness exclusively in terms of personal behavior and action, Edwards argues that sin is fundamentally a diminishment of the personhood that we have when we live in communion with God. On account of their fidelity to the concept of autonomy, both Taylor and Wainwright have difficulty appreciating the solidarity we have with Adam, as well as the solidarity we have with Christ. For as we have seen, Edwards sees both Adam and Christ as integral to our sense of "personal identity." The extent to which our identity is defined in relation to Adam determines the extent to which we suffer the curse and punishment of Adam. And the extent to which our identity is defined in relation to Christ determines the extent to which we experience the restoration of our nature in communion with God. Moreover, Edwards's expanded sense of the two kinds of solidarity we have with Adam and Christ enables him to provide a fuller description both of the collective and relational nature of sin, as well as of the collective and relational nature of grace.

And on the topic of evil, Edwards is better able to reconcile the existence of evil with the belief in a perfectly good and powerful God. Where the defenders of autonomy, specifically Swinburne, Taylor, and Hick, are only able to accommodate those evils that contribute to one's individual development as a person, Edwards resists any assimilation of evil that sees it as less than the calamity it is. Only the crucified Christ can reconcile the presence of evil with the goodness and power of God.

Certainly, theological richness and explanatory power alone cannot persuade those who see autonomy as the foundation of the moral life. But at the very least, Edwards's treatment of these topics should give pause to those who believe that the concept of autonomy provides a better understanding of how these topics relate to the moral life, as well as a more expansive view of human nature and capacities. In comparison, the vision provided by those who build their ethics on autonomy appears not grand, but small.

5

THE "GLORIOUS SOCIETY OF CREATED BEINGS": A TRINITARIAN INTERPRETATION OF *TWO DISSERTATIONS* AND *CHARITY AND ITS FRUITS*

> Love is the principle thing which the gospel reveals in God and Christ. The gospel brings to light the love between the Father and the Son, and declares how that love has been manifested in mercy; how that Christ is God's beloved Son in whom he is well pleased.... The gospel teaches us the doctrine of the eternal electing love of God, and reveals how God loved those who are redeemed by Christ before the foundation of the world; and how he gave them to the Son, and the Son loved them as his own.
>
> Edwards, *Charity and Its Fruits* (Y8:143–44)

In this chapter we turn to Edwards's *Two Dissertations* (1765) and *Charity and Its Fruits* (1738; 1851). As I noted in the introduction, these writings often serve as the point of entry into Edwards's theological ethics, and when they do, the Trinitarian themes present in these writings receive little attention, if any. In this chapter, however, I will offer an interpretation of these writings from the perspective of Edwards's Trinitarian thought. As Stephen Holmes has recently argued, Edwards's language in *God's End of Creation*, the first of the *Two Dissertations*, evokes a "Trinitarian interpretation," particularly regarding Edwards's emphasis in this work on God's act of self-glorification as the end God pursued in creating the world.[1] While I completely agree with this characterization, in this chapter I offer a fuller analysis of the Trinitarian themes present throughout the *Two Dissertations*, as well as *Charity and Its Fruits*.

I will argue that Edwards's Trinitarian thought is indispensable for understanding the ethics of love he articulates in the *Two Dissertations*. While many commentators on Edwards view the *Two Dissertations* as an attempt to construct a freestanding metaphysics, I argue that these writings are best viewed as an apologetical effort that engages moral sense philosophy, particularly the form it takes in the work of Francis Hutcheson (1694–1746). As such, Edwards follows the apologetical strategy that we observed in the previous chapter, that is, he places his Trinitarian thought in the background and develops concepts and arguments that work from commonplace philosophical assumptions. As with his other apologetical writings, however, these apologetical arguments fail to persuade, and we can only appreciate the compelling nature of Edwards's ethics of love once we are cognizant of the Trinitarianism from which it derives.

Likewise, Edwards's Trinitarian thought is essential for interpreting *Charity and Its Fruits* correctly. Viewed in isolation of his Trinitarian thought, *Charity and Its Fruits* can appear as no more than a preliminary version of the moral anthropology that Edwards later perfects in the *Religious Affections*. But when viewed in light of his Trinitarian thought, *Charity and Its Fruits* provides an essential articulation of Edwards's vision of the moral life set within the context of the church. Thus, a Trinitarian interpretation of this work rightly sees it as the ecclesial corollary to the personal exposition on the moral life Edwards provides in the *Religious Affections*.

As with the previous chapter, the interpretation I offer in this chapter places greater emphasis on the Trinitarian nature and implications of these writings than what Edwards himself thought necessary. Particularly in the *Two Dissertations*, Edwards indicates that he believes his arguments are persuasive without having to make his debt to his Trinitarian thought explicit. For example, during his exegesis of the word "glory" in Scripture, Edwards remarks, "[H]ere I might observe that the phrase, 'glory of God' is sometimes manifestly used to signify the second person of the Trinity. But it is not necessary at this time to consider this matter, or stand to prove it from particular passages of Scripture" (Y8:512). Nonetheless, as with the writings we have analyzed in previous chapters, Edwards's Trinitarian thought provides a crucial hermeneutic for retrieving the contributions the *Two Dissertations* and *Charity and Its Fruits* offer to current theological ethics.

1. *TWO DISSERTATIONS*

Edwards's purpose in writing the *Two Dissertations* is to continue the apologetical effort he initiated in *Freedom of the Will* and *Original Sin*. While Edwards believes he deals sufficiently with libertarian theories of the will in these earlier treatises, he now turns to those who argue that the moral life issues from an inherent "moral taste" or "moral sense." Edwards signals the continuity between these previous writings and the *Two Dissertations* toward the end of *Original Sin*:

> As to the arguments made by many late writers from the universal moral sense, and the reasons they offer from experience, and observation of the nature of mankind, to show that we are born into the world with principles of virtue; with a prevailing natural disposition to dislike, to resent and condemn what is selfish, unjust, and immoral; a native bent

in mankind to mutual benevolence, tender compassion, etc. . . . and desire to see them particularly considered, I ask leave to refer them to a *Treatise on the Nature of True Virtue*, lying by me prepared for the press, which may ere long be exhibited to public view. (Y3:433)

As Edwards's shorthand description indicates, moral sense philosophers, such as the third Earl of Shaftesbury (1671–1713), Francis Hutcheson (1694–1746), and David Hume (1711–1776), defined the moral life in terms of social affections rather than in free decisions or in discrete considerations of personal interest and self-love. These affections are an irreducible part of human nature, and they attend the mind's apprehension of relations of beauty, harmony, and proportion that exist throughout the world. Accordingly, moral sense philosophers define virtue not in Aristotelian terms as the development of the practical intellect, but as the propensity to feel and act in response to the beauty one perceives in human relations. Hutcheson, who tried to reconcile moral sense philosophy with Christianity, defines the moral sense as the approval of all that maintains sociality and the public good. Just as we have an "internal sense" of beauty in physical proportions and relations, so we have a "moral sense" of those "affections, actions, or characters of rational agents, which we call virtuous." Virtue has but "one general foundation" and "principle" in benevolence. "Benevolence," or the disinterested "desire of the happiness of another," is the "foundation of all apprehended excellence in social virtues," and has three levels of extensiveness. In its most universal scope, benevolence is a "calm, extensive affection, or good-will towards all beings capable of happiness or misery." In a more restricted scope, benevolence is the desire for the "happiness of certain smaller systems or individuals," in the form of "patriotism," "friendship," and "parental affection." Finally, benevolence issues in individual acts of goodwill that express "particular passions of love, pity, sympathy," and "congratulation." All three forms of benevolence are good, but only the most extensive kind reflects the "good of the whole." Hence, in living the moral life we should cultivate our inclination to "universal benevolence" and work for the "most extensive happiness of all the rational agents to whom our influence can reach."[2]

In *Original Sin*, Edwards speaks approvingly of moral sense philosophy, particularly as Hutcheson develops it. In his argument for humanity's "original righteousness" before the fall, Edwards appeals to Hutcheson's moral sense philosophy as being "evidently reasonable to the nature of things, and the voice of human sense and reason" (Y3:224). And, as we will see, in the *Two Dissertations* Edwards's definition of virtue as absolute benevolence resembles closely Hutcheson's most extensive understanding of benevolence. Substantive disagreements, however, exist between Edwards and Hutcheson concerning the foundation of the moral sense. First, Hutcheson believes the moral sense is entirely natural. Though Hutcheson believes that human benevolence suggests the existence of a benevolent God, and that God is the supreme object of benevolence, the expression of benevolence represents the realization of unaided human nature. In other words, in Hutcheson's account there is merely correspondence and concurrence between divine and human benevolence—divine and human love operate side by side. In contrast, for Edwards all true benevolence represents the communication and participation of God's love in human nature through the indwelling of the Spirit.

Second, unlike Edwards, Hutcheson does not see the love of God as the source and object of all other loves in the universe. Hutcheson rejects the Augustinian doctrine that we cannot love rightly unless we love all things as they are in God, and that which is of God in all things. He argues that this doctrine overlooks three kinds of particularity: (1) those particular expressions of benevolence we do without thinking; (2) the particular beauty of creatures as "distinct natures"; and (3) the particular loves we have for different beings. In and of themselves, the "instincts and natural affections" that compose the moral sense do not lead one to God. Hutcheson asks, "[D]oes the parental affection direct a man to love the Deity, or his children?" Though it is true that "we must approve the highest affections toward the Deity," particular "affections towards creatures, if they be distinct natures, must also be approved."[3]

Therefore, the apologetical project Edwards embarks on in the *Two Dissertations* is more complex and constructive than that of *Freedom of the Will* and *Original Sin*.[4] Edwards appropriates some of Hutcheson's terms and insights to develop his own proposal regarding love. Indeed, Edwards's decision to divide his project into "two dissertations" appears to be a self-conscious attempt to emulate Hutcheson's principal work of moral philosophy, which was an "inquiry" into the nature of the moral sense organized into "two treatises." But notwithstanding this appropriation, Edwards develops a very different theological vision than Hutcheson does, namely, one that sees a profound interconnection between the love of God and all other particular loves in the universe.

1.1. God's End

Edwards's project in *Concerning the End for which God Created the World* is to argue theocentrism—that God alone is the only appropriate end for God's creation of the world, and that therefore as the "center" of all things, the moral life must proceed with a view toward God as the ultimate source of beauty, order, love, and obligation (Y8:535). Edwards develops this argument over the course of two chapters. In the first chapter, Edwards proceeds on the basis of what "reason seems to dictate" regarding God's end independently of "revelation" (Y8:419). If an agent's highest "end" is determined by what that agent values absolutely and intrinsically, then there can be no other end that could serve as God's end in creation other than God's self. As the "Supreme Being" and ground of all "existence," God is also the sum of all "excellence," and therefore is more valuable, or worthy of "regard," than any other being in the universe. Simple justice dictates this to be the case. If a "third being of perfect wisdom and rectitude," who was "neither the Creator nor one of the creatures" and "perfectly indifferent and disinterested," were to determine the "proper measures and kinds of regard that every part of existence should have," he or she would "determine that the whole universe" should proceed "with a view to God as the supreme and last end of all" (Y8:423–25). Thus, as an "all-comprehending being," God's "supreme and infinite regard to himself" represents a "fit and decent" attitude that anyone with sufficient objectivity would share (Y8:455–56).

Building on this conclusion, Edwards turns in the second chapter to inquire "what is to be learned from Holy Scriptures" (Y8:417, 465). In both the Old and New Testaments, the predominate explanation given for God's motivation for acting is regard for God's own "glory." God's "glory" is the external "praise" of God's inherent "excellency," and is exhibited through God's creation and redemption of humanity. Humanity's highest end therefore consists in "beholding God's glory, in esteeming and loving it" (Y8:533). God's delight in the glory of intelligent creatures is an extension of God's own delight in God's self; nonetheless, God's delight in the manifestation of God's glory to humanity does not fulfill any interest or need in God. For "in God the love of himself, and the love of the public are not to be distinguished, as in man, because God's being as it were comprehends all" (Y8:455). God's "respect to the creature's good, and his respect to himself, is not a divided respect; but both are united in one, as the happiness of the creature aimed at is happiness in union with himself" (Y8:533).

Essentially, Edwards's argument in *God's End* is a reiteration of Neoplatonism, similar to that of so-called Cambridge Platonists, such as John Smith (1618–1652), Henry Moore (1614–1687), and Ralph Cudworth (1617–1688).[5] Consistent with Neoplatonism, Edwards places his description of the divine nature and agency within a framework of *exitus* and *reditus*. God is a unitary and all-sufficient being; at the same time, God possesses an effulgent nature that emanates throughout created existence and communicates to intelligent creatures the desire for knowledge and union with God as the ground of all being.[6] There is "an infinite fullness of all possible good in God, a fullness of every perfection," such that there is a "communication or emanation *ad extra*" flowing "out in abundant streams, as beams from the sun" (Y8:432). The communication of the glory of God to humanity therefore marks the point at which there is "both an *emanation* and *remanation*." The divine "refulgence shines upon and into the creature, and is reflected back to the luminary"; the "beams of glory come from God, and are something of God, and are refunded back to their original" (Y8:531).

Edwards describes this Neoplatonic vision, however, using terms and concepts borrowed from Hutcheson's moral sense philosophy. This reliance is at some points obvious: Edwards cites the practice of "late philosophers" to define the "essence of virtue" as "public affection or general benevolence" in order to argue that the love of God provides the point of intersection for all benevolent love. For if a person "truly loves the public, he necessarily loves Love to the public." Thus, "universal benevolence in the highest sense" is "the same thing with benevolence to the divine being, who is in effect Universal being" (Y8:456). At other points, this reliance is more subtle: Edwards's argument for the value and esteem due to God restates Hutcheson's articulation of what is known as the ideal observer theory.[7] Hutcheson believes it is obvious that "every *spectator*" approves of "the pursuit of public good more than private." The origin of this judgment is not "any *reason* or *truth*," but the "*moral sense* in the constitution of the soul," absent any prejudice or consideration of self-interest.[8] Likewise, as we have seen, Edwards believes the judgment that God alone is worthy of highest regard reflects what an impartial and disinterested being would determine to be just, all things considered.[9]

The most substantive point at which Edwards appropriates Hutcheson's moral sense philosophy occurs early in *God's End*, when Edwards develops a teleological framework for his Neoplatonic vision of divine emanation. Though Hutcheson believes that affections, passions, and desires are primary in human nature, he also believes that reason has a role to play. Reason for Hutcheson is simply the power to determine the truth of a "proposition." Nonetheless, any intentional action conforms either to *justifying* or *exciting* reasons. Justifying reasons identify what it is about an action that leads to its approval or disapproval, such as that *robbery* disturbs *society*. Exciting reasons identify those ends that lend coherence and rationality to human action. These ends in turn are either "ultimate," that is, "desired without a view to anything else," or "subordinate," that is, "desired with a view to something else." Hutcheson does not take this teleology very far. In the final analysis what excites us to act is a desire, even if it is possible to describe that desire as an intelligible end.[10] Further, Hutcheson believes it is a mistake to extrapolate from ultimate ends an overarching conception of the "infinite good, or greatest possible aggregate, or sum of happiness, under which all particular pleasures may be included." Unlike the moral sense, "the reasons which excite one nature may not excite another." Included in this heteronomy of exciting reasons are those of "the Deity." Even if we could know the exciting reasons of God's desire "to promote the public good," Hutcheson argues, it is impossible to know whether or not these exciting reasons are applicable, or even analogous, to ours.[11]

Edwards draws from Hutcheson's teleology in the introduction to *God's End*, when he outlines the terms and general positions he defends. With Hutcheson, Edwards places the ends that structure intentional action into the categories of "ultimate" and "subordinate." Edwards establishes, however, three additional categories of ultimate ends. The first category is between a "chief" end, that is, "an end that is most valued; and therefore most sought after by an agent," and an "inferior" end, that is, an end that may be ultimate—in that unlike a subordinate end it does not "depend on another" for its desirability—but plays a secondary role in the organization of an agent's action (Y8:407). The second category is between a "chief" end that organizes a given act, such as eating a piece of fruit, and the "supreme" end, that is, that "one ultimate end" that influences all that an agent does in a "great variety of operations," such that "no other end can be superior to it" (Y8:410). The third is between an "original" end, that is, one that an agent loves "*independent* of all conditions" or "circumstances," and a "consequential" end, that is, an end that the agent loves only "*hypothetically* and consequentially" in a "particular case" (Y8:411).

With this expanded teleological framework, Edwards offers an extended analogy for God's "original" and "supreme" end in creation, along with the other "consequential" and "ultimate" ends that are agreeable to the divine nature but not central to the creation of the world. Out of a simple love for "society," a person desires to have a family. But once he or she has a family, there are other desirable values, such as "peace, good order and mutual justice and friendship." All of these desires are ultimate desires, and yet the "justice and peace of a family" are consequential ends in comparison to the original end of desiring a family. "In like manner," Edwards reasons,

> we must suppose that God before he created the world had some good in view . . . that was originally agreeable to him in itself considered, that inclined him to create the world, or bring the universe with various intelligent creatures into existence in such a manner as he created it. But after the world was created, and such and such intelligent creatures actually had existence, in such and such circumstances, then a wise, just regulation of them was agreeable to God, in itself considered. (Y8:412)

This original end, we have observed, is God's glory. Edwards's appropriation of Hutcheson's teleology, however, enables him to offer a more precise description of God's glory, specifically the divine attributes that serve as God's original end in creation. While all of the divine attributes are manifested through the creation and redemption of humanity, the attributes that served as God's original end in the creation of the world derive from God's diffusive goodness. Following the analogy of seeking society in a family, the manifestation of God's attributes of infinite wisdom and justice are essential aspects of God's glory, just as the "wise and just regulation" of a family is essential to its well-being. But in the same way that no one starts a family simply in order to be wise and just, God's wisdom and justice did not serve as God's original end in creation. Rather, there is in God an inherent desire to express benevolence and communicate goodness to others. God's original end was "to communicate of his own infinite fullness of good," so "that there might be a glorious and abundant emanation of his infinite fullness of good *ad extra*" (Y8:433).

This "good disposition" in God's nature "to communicate of his own fullness," Edwards continues, is also "benevolence or love, because it is the same disposition that is exercised in love: 'tis the very fountain from whence love originally proceeds, when taken in the most proper sense." Although "love or benevolence strictly taken presupposes an existing object, as much as pity, a miserable object," God's love reflects God's "communicative disposition in general, or a disposition in the fullness of the divinity to flow out and diffuse itself" (Y8:439; 435). Thus, God's original and absolute end in creating the world is not merely "to communicate himself *to the creature*" as such, but to create beings who are capable of participating in the divine fullness (Y8:434). For "a disposition in God, as an original property of his nature, to an emanation of his own infinite fullness, was what excited him to create the world; and so that the emanation itself was aimed at by him as a last end of creation" (Y8:435). Hence, " 'tis a thing infinitely good in itself that God's glory should be known by a glorious society of created beings" (Y8:431).

By appropriating Hutcheson's teleology, Edwards can appeal to a common starting point in order to argue the merits of his theocentrism. Both Edwards and Hutcheson see human nature as essentially social and understand intentional action as determined by an agent's fundamental affections or desires. But where Hutcheson limits his teleology to account for intentional action on the level of human nature, Edwards argues that the same teleology can accommodate the divine nature as well.

Nonetheless, as an exercise in apologetics, Edwards's synthesis of Neoplatonism and moral sense philosophy falls short. Hutcheson would object that Edwards's teleology assumes more unanimity than actually exists on the ends that structure intelligible action. As we have seen, Hutcheson believes that exciting reasons are particular to each person and cannot reliably be predicated of another. To assign a greater role to exciting reasons than this would undermine the priority he places on benevolence and the moral sense. Further, Hutcheson would object to Edwards's use of Neoplatonism to construct a unitary account of love in the universe. Edwards's Neoplatonism depicts God's love as the diffusion of a singular being who is the source and end of all love in the world; consequently, all particular instances of benevolence are valued to the extent they reflect the love of God as a solitary being. In contrast, Hutcheson argues that unitary approaches to love overlook the particularity that attends different kinds of love. While this criticism especially applies to human love, as I will later discuss in detail, it also applies to divine love. For the different kinds of human love suggest that God has created a plurality of loves in the universe.

In addition to its failure to accommodate the particularity of love, Edwards's synthesis does not attend to the central issue that distinguishes his theocentrism from Hutcheson's moral sense philosophy. For what is at stake is not merely the scale of value Edwards establishes between partic-ular instances of love and the love of God, but the extent to which human love itself can embody and express the divine love. That is to say, Edwards hopes to articulate a conception of divine and human benevolence that is not merely concurrent, as Hutcheson holds, but communicative. Because God's original end in the creation of the world was to express the divine fullness, humanity's recognition and reception of this fullness becomes integral to the realization of God's end of creation. Human benevolence therefore is a "participation of what is in God," for "what is communicated is divine, something of God, and each communication is of that nature that the creature to whom it is made is thereby conformed to God and united to him" (Y8:442).

Although Trinitarian grammar does not lie at the forefront of his argu-ment, Edwards's theocentrism in *God's End* appears indebted to his Trini-tarian thought, particularly in regard to his understanding of glory.[12] As we have observed, Edwards describes glory as the manifestation of God's infi-nite fullness or goodness to humanity. This understanding of God's good-ness, however, presupposes both the psychological analogy's view that persons are realized through *theosis*, as well as the social analogy's view that God's goodness and love is expressed through community. Indeed, in his "Miscellanies" notebooks, Edwards develops a similar line of reasoning concerning glory as that found in *God's End*, the only difference being that in the "Miscellanies" entries, Trinitarian terms and concepts are explicit. Thus, in entry 448 Edwards writes that the primary meaning of glory is Trinitarian: "God is glorified within himself . . . by appearing and or being manifested to himself in his own perfect idea, or in his Son," and in the "flowing forth in infinite love and delight towards himself, or in his Holy Spirit." From the "glory" that exists in God *in se*, there is glory "in the more extensive sense of the word, viz. his shining forth, or the going forth of his excellency, beauty and essential glory *ad extra*" to the regenerate, so that God's glory "is then received by the whole soul, both by the understanding and the will" (Y13:495). Similarly, in entry 1218 Edwards argues that "there are two parallel, coordinate ends of God's creating the world . . . one, to exercise His perfections *ad extra*, another to make his creatures happy." But it "can't properly be said that the end of God's creating the world is twofold." For "both of these dispositions of exerting Himself and communicating Himself may be reduced" to one total "communication of Himself *ad extra*," which is "agreeable to the twofold subsistencies which proceed from Him *ad intra*, which is the Son and the Holy Spirit."[13]

Though largely muted, Edwards's Trinitarian grammar surfaces in *God's End* when no other terms for his theocentric vision will suffice. Thus, in order to describe his conviction that the saints' love for God in this world is a spiritual, interpersonal relationship of deepening intimacy that enables them to participate in the life of God for eternity, Edwards explicitly refers to the perichoretic union between the persons of the Godhead. The culmination of the spiritual life is one where we "will forever come nearer and nearer to that strictness and perfection of union which there is between the Father and the Son" (Y8:443). Consequently, our loves and joys in this world must draw us in an "infinity of progress" toward the love "between God the Father and the Son" (Y8:533). As there is no end to the infinite nature of God's triune communion, so "there will never come a moment, when it can be said, that now this infinitely valuable good has actually been bestowed" (Y8:536).

Had Edwards placed his Trinitarian reflection at the forefront of his argument in *God's End*, he could have better articulated his theocentrism, as well as offered an account of God's love that could accommodate Hutcheson's concerns. For both the psychological and the social analogies offer a distinctive view of the relation between divine and human love that recognizes both unity and particularity. In the psychological analogy, participation in God's love is decisive for the realization of one's personhood. Although God's self-love is the fundamental love in the universe, this self-love does not derive from the inherent simplicity and value of the divine essence, as in Neoplatonism, but from the dialogical communion between the Father and the Son. As such, the psychological analogy considers God's self-love as generative, relational, and comprehensive, as well as unitive. Further, the psychological analogy sees participation in the relationality that exists through God's self-love as fundamental to human personhood. Humanity's participation in the love of God is not merely a replication of God's eternal and perfect love, but the actual repetition in the soul of God's knowledge and love through the indwelling of the Holy Spirit. The *perichoresis* that exists between the persons of the Trinity therefore models the saint's participation in God through *theosis*.

In terms of the social analogy, the concern for particularity is even more integral to the mutuality and love that provide the foundation for the communion of the Trinity. God's love is expressed through the Father's communication of goodness to the Son, which in turn is expressed to humanity through the love of Christ and the Holy Spirit. God's triune decision to create and redeem humanity therefore expresses the love and mutuality that already exist between the persons of the Trinity so that we are incorporated into the triune society. On the cross, Christ manifested God's particular love for the church, and the love that indwells humanity through the Spirit is a self-differentiating love which both recognizes the importance of the beloved as well as the beloved's incorporation into a community of perfect self-donation and mutuality. Therefore, God's end in creation—to use words Edwards writes in "Miscellanies" entry 571—is to bring the saints "into the household of God," so that with the Father and Son "they should be" admitted "into that society of the three persons of the Godhead." For this reason, the "glory" and exaltation of Christ is "not as a private person for himself only," but consists in "the greatest nearness, intimacy, and communion of good" the saints have with Christ, who is "their representative, their brother, and the husband of the church" (Y18:108–9).

1.2. True Virtue

In *The Nature of True Virtue*, Edwards develops an alternative account of theocentrism that proceeds by examining what in human benevolence represents the source of authentic virtue, rather than merely the force of natural affection, instinct, or self-love. Edwards argues that the only source of true virtue is the benevolence which expresses "consent to," or love for, "being in general," that is, God and all that is of God. Edwards interweaves two arguments to demonstrate why this is the case.

The first is aesthetic. While many disagree about the nature of virtue, all accept the commonplace definition of virtue as a moral "*beauty* or excellency" that has its seat in the "*disposition* and *will*," or the "heart" (Y8:539). The question, however, arises as to what comprises the beauty of virtue that all recognize. Like all beauty, virtue is considered beautiful not from a limited perspective but from the most comprehensive standpoint possible. In other words, virtue is not a "particular beauty," or something that appears beautiful within a limited "private sphere," but a "general beauty," or something that appears beautiful "when viewed most perfectly, comprehensively and universally, with regard to all its tendencies, and its connections" (Y8:540). Further, the beauty of virtue is not merely the recognition of harmony, order, or proportion in objects and relations, which Edwards calls "secondary beauty," but a relation of "consent, agreement, or union of being" that attends "spiritual and moral beings," which Edwards calls "primary beauty" (Y8:561). Given these premises, Edwards concludes that true virtue must consist in "benevolence" to God, understood as "being in general." For if virtue is a general beauty, and general beauty refers to that which is beautiful in all its relations and connections, then true virtue must be a "union of heart" and "consent with the great whole," which is "immediately exercised in a general good will" (Y8:540). And if virtue is a primary beauty, and primary beauty is exercised only in spiritual or moral relations, then God as the source and sum of all moral and spiritual relations is the proper object of true virtue.

Edwards's second argument concerns love, and is related to his previous argument concerning beauty. If virtue is an *instance* of beauty, as the aesthetic argument suggests, then something *other than beauty* must be its source or object. To maintain otherwise would fall into circular reasoning—"that the beauty of intelligent beings primarily consists in love to beauty, or that their virtue first of all consists in their love to virtue." But if beauty is not the object of the love of true virtue, then the love of true virtue is not one of complacence, or a love that "presupposes beauty" in the "beloved." Nor can it be a love of benevolence motivated by gratitude, or by the "beauty of its object." For in either case, the cause of benevolence is external to the agent, and therefore does not originate in the agent's nature. The only love, then, that can be the source of the beauty of virtue is, ironically, a love that does not recognize in "particular beings" any special "virtue or beauty." This love is one of "absolute benevolence," or a "propensity and union of heart to Being simply considered" (Y8:543–44). Consequently, the love of true virtue embodies the diffusive love of God. The "benevolence or goodness in the divine Being" is the "ground" of creaturely "existence" and "beauty." Indeed, God's benevolence precedes all consideration of an individual being's particular beauty, for it precedes the existence of all individual beings. Likewise, the benevolence of true virtue is a "disposition to the welfare of those that are not considered as beautiful; unless mere existence be accounted a beauty" (Y8:542). Any love that rests on a "private circle or system of beings" represents only "part of the whole," and is not "of the nature of true virtue" (Y8:540–41).

Essentially, the apologetical argument Edwards mounts in *The Nature of True Virtue* is that Hutcheson makes a category mistake when he places the most extensive sense of benevolence he identifies—"good-will towards all beings capable of happiness or misery"—alongside the benevolence expressed toward particular social spheres and entities. As we have seen, though Hutcheson sees universal benevolence as optimal, he considers the benevolence expressed toward "smaller systems" as legitimate and important aspects of virtue. In contrast, Edwards argues that virtuous benevolence irreducibly exists in love for God. Not only must benevolence express "supreme love to God," but all other particular loves in the universe have validity to the extent one realizes that they are at best reflections of the love of God. No "affection whatsoever to any creature, or any system of created beings, which is not dependent on, or subordinate to a propensity or union of heart to God, the Supreme and Infinite Being, can be of the nature of true virtue" (Y8:556–57). For "that consent, union, or propensity of mind to Being in general" is "virtue, truly so called," and "no other disposition or affection but this is of the nature of true virtue." Hence, "all schemes of religion or moral philosophy that treat benevolence in any other way are defective, if they ignore the essential subordination of virtue to God" (Y8:559–60). Referring no doubt to Hutcheson, Edwards writes that "there seems to be an inconsistence in some writers on morality." While "they don't wholly exclude a regard for the Deity out of their systems," they "esteem it a less important and subordinate part of true morality and insist on benevolence to the *created system*." But "if true virtue consists partly in respect to God, then doubtless it consists chiefly in it" (Y8:553).

As with *God's End*, the position Edwards holds in *True Virtue* is that participation in the love of God is the fundamental norm of the moral life. "They are good moral agents whose temper or mind or propensity of heart" seeks "union with God" (Y8:559). By developing his account of virtue in conversation with Hutcheson, Edwards offers a more subtle integration of the love of God and the love of neighbor, which accepts the moral sense argument that sociality and benevolence are fundamental aspects of the moral life. Defining true virtue as the love for "being in general" enables Edwards to argue that absolute benevolence not only entails an exclusive love for God as the ground of being but also a love for all that God holds in being. Consequently, the love of true virtue "will seek the good of every *individual* being unless it be conceived as not consistent with the highest good of Being in general" (Y8:545). The love of God thus includes the love for those "created understandings" who are capable of receiving the communication of God's "fullness." For insofar "as a virtuous mind exercises true virtue in benevolence to created things, it chiefly seeks the good of the creature, consisting in its knowledge or view of God's glory and beauty, its union with God, and conformity to him, love to him, and joy in him" (Y8:559).

Further, though Edwards considers true virtue properly defined as "absolute benevolence" to "Being in general," he also emphasizes that he is "far from asserting that there is not true virtue in any other love than this absolute benevolence" (Y8:544–45). For the love of true virtue includes other loves that arise in human relations if they are subordinated to the love of absolute benevolence. Ideally, our love for individual beings concerns those who also express absolute benevolence, and it is on this basis that other forms of love develop. Thus, perceiving absolute benevolence in others elicits a virtuous "complacence," "benevolence," and "gratitude" for them. Of course, these persons "are beautiful" only "on this account"—

that is, love of absolute benevolence—for these other forms of love "imply *consent* and *union* with Being in general" (Y8:547–48).

Finally, Edwards also allows that social relations motivated entirely by natural affections are reminiscent of true virtue and "tend to the good of the world" (Y8:616). These are instances of secondary beauty; their "mutual consent and agreement" are analogous to the primary beauty of true virtue (Y8:562–63). Within the category of natural affections, Edwards includes "immaterial" perceptions of the "beauty of order in society" that take the form of not only natural instincts such as parental affection, but also natural principles such as "justice," natural powers such as the "conscience," and natural loves such as "self-love" (Y8:567). The principle of justice is a secondary beauty that dictates those "relative duties," such as "duties of children to parents, and of parents to children; duties of husbands and wives; duties of rulers and subjects; duties of friendship and good neighborhood" (Y8:569). Similarly, "self-love," the "natural conscience," and social "instincts" also evoke expressions of particular benevolence. Our "natural affections and principles" have "something of the general nature of virtue," and may even provide a context for the expression of absolute benevolence (Y8:609). Hence, there "may be a virtuous love of parents to children," of "our town, or country, or nation," and "between the sexes" (Y8:617).

Edwards's view of natural affections remains less positive than that of Hutcheson. In and of themselves, natural affections have "negative moral goodness," that is, they are without "true moral evil" and can have the salutary effect of restraining "vice" and other "acts of wickedness" (Y8:614, 616). Inherent in this characterization, however, is the recognition that natural affections often have the same "effect" of true virtue in terms of their social utility (Y8:616). Moreover, Edwards believes that if properly enlightened, these deliverances of the moral sense coincide with the dictates of true virtue (Y8:617, 623).

All the same, it is hard to imagine Hutcheson persuaded by Edwards's project in *True Virtue*. The first objection Hutcheson would raise concerns Edwards's accommodation of natural affections. While Hutcheson might find the language of being in *True Virtue* more amenable than the Neoplatonism in *God's End*, he would still find Edwards's accommodation of the particularity that attends expressions of benevolence inadequate. As we have seen, standing behind this insistence on particularity is Hutcheson's belief that expressions of benevolence are incommensurable, even though we should on the whole act in a way "which procures the greatest happiness for the greatest numbers."[14] But Hutcheson also believes that natural affections provide an important counterbalance to the desire for universal benevolence. Drawing from classical sources, Hutcheson argues that *storge*—the traditional Greek term that describes parental affection—refers not merely to the natural affections that pertain to the special relations between parent and child, but to other natural affections for smaller communities. Certainly, God could have created "orders of rational beings" who possessed only a "universal good-will to all" without "any other bonds of affection." Therefore, it must be the case that natural affections are constitutive of human flourishing and essential for the well-being of society. Particularly regarding parental affection for "offspring," the "perpetual labor and care" necessary for raising children simply exceeds the "more general ties of benevolence."[15] Our "natural affections" and "friendships," then, suggest that often "the good of the whole requires a stricter attachment to a part." Indeed, given the necessity of these relations, "even universal benevolence" directs us to "study their interests" with "special care and affection."[16]

Edwards does not respond directly to this objection, for it concerns the nature of anthropology rather than the nature of benevolence. Indeed, Edwards develops his argument in *True Virtue* with the barest anthropology possible. Early on, he describes the moral beauty of virtue "as belonging to beings that have *perception* and *will*," and adds little to this description of human nature as he proceeds (Y8:539). Apparently, his strategy is to sidestep debates over anthropology and employ his arguments on beauty and love, which demonstrate that "benevolence to a *particular person* or *private system*" is "not of the nature of true virtue" (Y8:554).[17] This strategy falls short, however, precisely because Edwards does not make explicit the anthropology that operates behind, and would justify, these arguments.

Another objection Hutcheson would raise concerns Edwards's insistence that the beauty of true virtue has its foundation "in the nature of things." Consistent with the moral sense philosophy, Edwards notes that though describable, the beauty of virtue is not definable; like the sweetness of honey, the beauty of true virtue cannot be discovered by "argumentation on its connections and consequences" (Y8:619).[18] But if this is the case, is it not possible that God acted "arbitrarily" in making virtue appear beautiful? Could not God "have given a contrary sense and determination of mind"? (Y8:620). For Hutcheson, the viability of the moral sense philosophy depends on leaving these questions unanswered; to attribute a definitive connection between the moral sense and the nature of God would undermine the moral sense's authority by making speculation on the nature of God crucial to living the moral life.[19] In contrast, the intelligibility of Edwards's theocentrism depends on a clear connection existing between the nature of God and the nature of virtue. For if God is "in effect being in general," it would be absurd for God not to be a benevolent being and yet to create beings for whom absolute benevolence to being in general is central to their fulfillment. In such a scenario, the "greatest possible discord" would exist in the nature of being (Y8:621). Nonetheless, Edwards would have to admit that he cannot disprove Hutcheson's position on the basis of what both accept regarding virtue's beauty.

Ultimately, Edwards turns to the Trinitarian anthropology he develops in the *Religious Affections* to make his case regarding the beauty of virtue more compelling. The "sense" of beauty we experience through true virtue is a "certain spiritual sense" given "of God" (Y8:620). As such, it differs profoundly from the moral sense, for the beauty of true virtue is "the representation and image of the moral perfection and excellency of the divine Being" through which "persons" have "true knowledge of God." Edwards puts off discussion of just what he means by "this spiritual sense," explaining that the topic lies outside "the main purpose of this discourse" (Y8:622–23). But given his problems here and those concerning natural affections, it is clear that *True Virtue* succeeds only if one establishes that spiritual participation in the triune life of God is essential for human fulfillment—a position he does not fully articulate in the second dissertation.

If Edwards had placed his Trinitarian thought at the forefront of *True Virtue*, he would have been able to base his arguments on an anthropology that better recognizes the legitimacy of natural affections, as well as the unique nature and excellence of human fulfillment through *theosis*. For as we have seen, the social analogy offers a vision of how special relations and even erotic love can be emblematic of God's triune love. And in the *Religious Affections* and *Original Sin*, Edwards does not disparage the natural affections, but considers them problematic only if they operate in a moral vacuum, apart from the "spiritual sense" given through the indwelling of the Holy Spirit. No doubt, both the emblematic nature of erotic love Edwards develops in the the social analogy and the two-tiered understanding of the *imago dei* Edwards develops in the *Religious Affections* and defends in *Original Sin* stand behind the category of "secondary beauty" he creates in *True Virtue*. And had Edwards placed these concepts at the forefront of *True Virtue*, he could have interpreted the natural affections as vestiges of the Trinity, which inform our understanding of the created order as well as its eschatological fulfillment. Viewed from this perspective, the natural affections have their own legitimacy as mediations of God's triune self-expression. But as it stands, the only explanation Edwards provides for the correlation he notes between primary and secondary beauty is that "it pleases God to observe analogy in his works," the rationale of which "'tis not needful now to inquire" (Y8:564).

Edwards's Trinitarian thought also provides a better account of the different aspects of love that comprise true virtue. As we have seen, in *True Virtue* Edwards admits complacence and other forms of love motivated by beauty so long as they are subordinate to absolute benevolence. In this way, Edwards protects the priority of absolute benevolence as the "*primary* ground" of true virtue over loves founded in the "spiritual beauty," which are the "*secondary* ground" of true virtue (Y8:548). Nonetheless, however well this logic of subordination differentiates love predicated on the beauty of particular beings from love predicated on consent to being in general, it does not adequately characterize the mutuality that permeates authentic love for God through the indwelling of the Spirit. Indeed, at one point in *True Virtue*, Edwards appropriates Trinitarian grammar to describe how the mutuality evident in human relations images the love of absolute benevolence to being in general. All human love, he explains, derives from the "love and friendship which subsist eternally and necessarily between the several persons of the Godhead, or that infinite propensity there is in these divine persons one to another," which renders love of "created beings, *one to another*," virtuous "if it arise from" the "disposition to love God supremely" (Y8:557).

This recourse to the social analogy's depiction of mutuality or "friendship" points in the direction of a more profound integration of absolute benevolence and other forms of virtuous love than what Edwards articulates in *True Virtue*. For in the context of Edwards's Trinitarian thought, absolute benevolence operates alongside other forms of the love of God. As we have seen, in the "Treatise on Grace" Edwards writes that the benevolence "the Father and the Son have in each other is not to be distinguished from their love of complacence one in another, wherein love does most essentially consist" (H:64). The coinherence of benevolence and complacence expressed in the inner life of the Trinity is also manifested in God's triune redemption of humanity. The love of God flows "from the Father and the Son first towards each other" in the person of the Spirit, and "secondarily" to "the creature" (H:63). Hence, while God's love for creation is initially that of absolute benevolence, God also "takes complacence in communicating felicity" to the creature, and finds "complacence" in the saints' "holiness," for this holiness represents the indwelling of the Spirit that is God's self-gift (Y13:256, 395). Moreover, the "incarnation and death of the Son of God" manifests the "infinite love which is from everlasting between the Father and the Son" (Y13:406). Christ loves all humanity with absolute benevolence—Christ "sets a value upon the beloved's welfare or life" that is equal to the value he places on himself (Y13:525). Nonetheless, Christ also loves the church with total complacence, such that "Christ is not complete without his spouse," the church (Y13:272). Not only is complacence a legitimate expression of God's love, but Edwards also places complacence alongside benevolence at the phenomenological center of the human experience of love. In both the "Treatise on Grace" and the *Religious Affections* Edwards writes that the saints' first experience of God's love is one of complacence in the beauty and excellency of God, which provides the foundation for benevolence toward God and neighbor (H:49–50; Y2:107).

Although primarily interested in developing the theme of benevolence, complacence and mutuality continue to figure in *God's End*. As we have seen, Edwards argues that God's end in creation is motivated by God's inherent beauty and excellency, and at one point he describes Christ's love for the church in terms of the love of complacence and the desire for mutuality. The "church of Christ" is "called the fullness of Christ," for "as Adam was in a defective state without Eve," so Christ is "not in a complete state" without the church (Y8:439). In addition, the manifestation of God's glory in human experience primarily takes the form of "complacence and joy in God" (Y8:527). For "creatures, even the most gracious of them," are "not so self-moved in their goodness, but that in all the exercises of it, they are excited by some object" that appears "good, or in some respect worthy of regard," and that "moves their kindness" (Y8:462).

Viewed from the perspective of Edwards's Trinitarian thought, then, the relationship between absolute benevolence and other forms of virtuous love follows the logic of complementarity rather than that of subordination. Absolute benevolence is a critical *moment* in the *continuous* revelation of God's triune love to the world—a moment crucial and irreplaceable, yet one which necessarily involves other aspects of love so that the temporal expression of God's love is complete. Absolute benevolence describes the infinite love God manifests in the creation and redemption of humanity, as well as the individual person's consent to being in general. As such, it retains its priority as the *presenting* love in the virtuous person's encounter with others and represents the quintessence of neighbor-love. Nonetheless, while absolute benevolence looks beyond the beauty and value inherent in "particular beings," this does not mean that it is unmotivated by general complacence in God's infinite value and beauty, even when manifested in particular beings (Y8:544). For finding and receiving this complacence is equally essential to the saints' communion with God through being incorporated into the friendship and mutual love of the Trinity.

1.3. The *Two Dissertations* in Edwards's Theological Ethics

Typically, studies of Edwards treat the *Two Dissertations* as Edwards's paradigmatic work of theological ethics—a "summa" in "miniature," in the words of Perry Miller—after which one must fit Edwards's other moral writings.[20] Even those who accept this interpretation, however, admit its difficulties. Regarding *God's End*, Clyde Holbrook finds that Edwards's "Neoplatonic perspective" presents an "aesthetic vision of reality" that consumes "ethical insight and discrimination" until "nothing is left but the poetic or mystical outpourings of a mind which has lost all contact with the hard business of ethical decision wrought out in daily life."[21] And regarding *True Virtue*, Fiering notes that "Edwards' dissertation" is "about God, to be sure, but it is an extraordinary fact that Scripture is never cited in the work, nor does Edwards draw on the theological tradition for support." While Fiering holds that *True Virtue* provides Edwards's "most comprehensive statement of ethics," it is "impossible to speak very precisely about Edwards' ontological theories" due to the generality of its "metaphysics." Consequentially, Edwards's effort to reorient the secular moral philosophy of his day "through force of metaphysical reasoning alone" to the love of God leaves unanswered the question of whether Edwards's "ontological foundation for virtue is philosophically or even theologically tenable."[22]

In contrast, I have argued that the *Two Dissertations* are best viewed as an apologetical effort in the vein of *Freedom of the Will* and *Original Sin* rather than as a comprehensive account of Edwards's theological ethics. Not only does the apologetical interpretation better account for the peculiarities noted above, but it also explains the weaknesses we have observed. For Edwards follows the same strategy in the *Two Dissertations* as he does in his other apologetical writings—that is, in order to engage his contemporaries, Edwards underplays his Trinitarian commitments and develops arguments that operate from common philosophical assumptions. Nonetheless, as we observed in the last chapter, the common assumptions Edwards uses to build his apologetics have not stood the test of time, and therefore retrieving the Trinitarianism that underlies these writings is essential for identifying what these works offer to current theology and ethics.

A Trinitarian interpretation appears even more imperative for the theocentrism Edwards articulates in the *Two Dissertations* than it does for his other apologetical writings. For the necessity to recover the theological framework underlying the *Two Dissertations* differs from that observed in the previous chapter. In the previous chapter, Edwards's Trinitarian framework provided a way to avoid the interminable nature of debates over the will that proceed on the basis of our conflicting intuitions regarding freedom. Here the points of contention concern not merely whether a given account of the moral life is justifiable on the basis of empirical perceptions of beauty, order, or benevolence, but also whether developing such a freestanding ontology is appropriate for theological ethics. If Edwards operated in a context in which consensus existed on these points, we do not. Given the present skepticism toward foundationalism, few would accept either the empirical or ontological features of Edwards's theocentrism without the explicit qualification that its intelligibility rests on a particular theological framework rather than on a universal realm of moral knowledge or religious experience.[23]

In addition, a Trinitarian interpretation of Edwards's *Two Dissertations* suggests that it is misleading to consider these works paradigmatic expressions of Edwards's theological ethics. Certainly, the *Two Dissertations* rightly depict Edwards's ethics as theocentric, and Edwards develops his ethics in these treatises in important ways. Particularly in *True Virtue*, Edwards offers an important addendum to the Trinitarian anthropology he develops in the *Religious Affections* regarding humanity's natural moral capacities, specifically a more expansive depiction of natural affections and principles. The theocentrism Edwards articulates in the *Two Dissertations*, however, is conditioned by his engagement with Hutcheson's moral sense philosophy. As such, these writings do not represent Edwards's summary views on either metaphysics or love, but a specific attempt to accommodate and respond to the insights of moral sense philosophy. For as we have seen, neither the metaphysics Edwards articulates nor his arguments for benevolence adequately represent the richness of Edwards's Trinitarian account of love. It therefore appears best to consider the *Two Dissertations* as partial, if important, developments of Edwards's Trinitarian ethics.

2. EDWARDS AND CONTEMPORARY LOVE ETHICS

The preceding discussion regarding the proper interpretation of the *Two Dissertations* also guides our consideration of what the *Two Dissertations* offer to current theological ethics. If one holds that the *Two Dissertations* represent Edwards's paradigmatic work of theological ethics, then the most logical point of comparison is between Edwards and James Gustafson's two-volume *Ethics from a Theocentric Perspective* (1981, 1984).[24] Gustafson articulates his theocentrism in conversation with Edwards, drawing in particular from Edwards's insight that "the Deity" is the "center of gravity" for "construing the world."[25] Such a comparison, however, would be of limited value from the perspective of the Trinitarian interpretation I provide for two related reasons. First, Gustafson neglects the Trinitarian moments in the *Two Dissertations* that differentiate Edwards's theocentrism from his—indeed, at numerous points Gustafson and Edwards part company precisely because Edwards's theocentrism derives from his Trinitarian thought.[26] Second, Gustafson's emphasis on religious experience leads him to believe that he can articulate his theocentrism independently of particular doctrines such as the Trinity. Therefore, to engage in an extended comparison between Edwards and Gustafson from the perspective of the interpretation I offer would require that I first show why Gustafson's confidence in a freestanding theocentrism is misplaced. Such a task lies beyond the scope of this study.[27]

A more fruitful comparison, which has received little attention in studies of Edwards, is between Edwards's account of benevolence developed in the preceding discussion and contemporary reflection on love in Christian ethics. As Timothy Jackson notes, it is "standard practice" in Christian ethics to distinguish types of love, the most prominent being *agape* (disinterested love of neighbor), *eros* (preferential desire), and *philia* (mutuality and friendship). To this list, some include one or more of the following: *amor sui* (self-love), *storge* (parental instinct and affection), and *caritas* (the desire for communion with God that is the proper *telos* of the soul).[28] On the basis of this lexicon, ethicists explore how these loves are defined, their relation to each other, and their place in the moral life. In an early work that set the terms of the debate, Anders Nygren argues for the uniqueness and sufficiency of *agape* by defining it over and against *eros*. Where *agape* is "spontaneous" and "unmotivated" by the beloved's attractiveness or value, *eros* is "acquisitive" and motivated by the beloved's attractiveness or value. Where *agape* is "unselfish," "free," "overflowing," "creative," and "sovereign," *eros* is "egocentric," "evoked," "possessive" and "depends on want and need." Where *agape* is characterized by the cross and grace, which proceeds from God "down" to humanity and bestows value on the beloved, *eros* is characterized by humanity's desire for God, which proceeds "upward" and merely appraises value in the beloved. Given this fundamental opposition, Nygren concludes that *agape* has priority not only over *eros* but over the other forms of love, which all exhibit erotic tendencies.[29]

Many challenge Nygren's definitions and analysis. To give a representative selection: John M. Rist and Catherine Osborne argue that Nygren overlooks a nonappetitive *eros* that patristic writers, particularly Origen, appropriate from Classical thought.[30] John Burnaby and Oliver O'Donovan argue that Nygren misunderstands Augustine's *caritas*, specifically the positive role it plays both in ordering the self's pursuit of happiness, or *eudaimonia*, and in representing the mutuality that is the perfection of love.[31] Stephen Post and Edward Vacek argue that the dichotomy Nygren draws between *agape* and *eros* marginalizes the place of the emotions in the moral life, as well as the role *philia* plays in protecting the integrity of *agape*.[32] And John Reeder offers a counterproposal to *agape* in the form of a retrieved account of the moral sense philosophy's doctrine of "extended benevolence."[33]

2.1. Edwards and *Agape*

While not unsympathetic toward some of the criticisms mentioned above, Gene Outka and Timothy Jackson maintain that Nygren's position regarding the uniqueness of *agape* remains valid in certain important respects.[34] Outka offers a significant restatement of *agape* in *Agape: An Ethical Analysis* (1972) and "Universal Love and Impartiality" (1992).[35] He defines *agape* as "unqualified" or "equal regard"—that is, "a regard for every person *qua* human existent" that is "independent and unalterable" and distinct from "those special traits, actions, etc., which distinguish particular personalities from each other." As such, *agape* establishes that "one neighbor's wellbeing is as valuable as another's."[36] Outka avoids Nygren's absolutist claims regarding *agape*, particularly Nygren's definition of *agape* as identical to self-sacrifice and antithetical to self-regard. Although the "temporal manifestation" of *agape* can take the form of self-sacrifice, defining *agape* as "unqualified regard" recognizes that self-sacrifice "must always be purposive in promoting the welfare of others." Thus, there are relevant differences between "attention to another's need and submission to his exploitation." Similarly, commitment to the well-being of the neighbor includes a commitment to one's own well-being, and thus *agape* admits reasonable self-regard. *Agape* commands responsible service to the neighbor and does not require that one issue the neighbor a "blank check."[37]

Outka also offers a more integrated account of the love of God, the love of self, and the love of neighbor than Nygren does. For Nygren, *agape* becomes so definitive of authentic love that he suggests substituting the word "faith" for "love for God." Nygren's intent is not to deny the religious basis for *agape*, but to recognize that God is the initiator of *agape* and that the "keynote" of love for God is "receptivity, not spontaneity."[38] Outka argues, however, that this conflation neglects the centrality of the first commandment. Drawing from Barth, Outka argues that properly understood, "the first commandment is *the* commandment" and establishes the context of the second commandment, such that our "response to God is embodied necessarily if not exhaustively" in our unqualified "regard for the neighbor."[39] For "nothing is higher than God," and "at its highest reaches, love is about communion, between God and ourselves, and between each other." Consequently, "love for God includes fidelity to God in loving whom God loves." The "universal love" demanded by *agape* "enjoins us to honor anyone, neighbor and self, who bears the human countenance."[40] In addition to context, love for God establishes the content of *agape*. Although the material focus of *agape* is on "meeting the mundane needs" of the neighbor, such as "food, drink, shelter, clothing, health, and liberty," the spiritual focus of *agape* is on giving "witness" to "conscious life in relation to God."[41]

Correlatively, to love God supremely includes the recognition that our particular identity is a gift from God, and that we should view our individual "projects and goals" as our unique way "to honor God," even those projects and goals that are "non-moral." Hence, love for God has the tendency to "heighten rather evacuate particular identity; one's self awareness becomes focused rather than distracted." Further, there are aspects of the moral life that are irreducibly connected to each person's relation with God that *agape* can only commend. "Witnessing, mutual support and care, admonition, counsel, etc. are certainly integral to the life of the Christian community," but "another person cannot transmit to me" the "faith he or she has," for if "religious faith is to be genuine" it "must be uncoerced."[42]

In addition to recognizing the interconnection between the loves of God, neighbor, and self, Outka assigns an important role to mutuality, or *philia*. Where Nygren views mutuality as tainted by the concerns of *eros*, Outka argues that points of overlap exist between *agape* and *philia*. Though the supreme test of *agape* is the love of enemies, because *agape* involves true concern for the well-being of others, it is also manifested in "personal relations marked by closeness and social relations marked by concord." In the latter context, *agape* "remains unilateral in that one does not await, anticipate, or demand a response in kind as a requirement for one's attention and care," but it also appropriately "desires and hopes for a response," and in this sense "mutuality" represents the "internal ideal fruition of *agape*."[43] Nonetheless, though *philia* provides an occasion for the realization of *agape*, *agape* promotes the realization of authentic *philia*. The elements of "personal preference" and reciprocity that form the basis of *philia* are distinct from *agape*, and *philia* does not have the "permanent stability of *agape*." For this reason, in the "deepest friendships both parties always display an ingredient of unqualified regard."[44]

Finally, Outka acknowledges the legitimacy of special relations in the form of "covenants and particular commitments" between "friends, lovers, spouses, parents and children," which involve "*eros* and *philia* as well as *agape*." Commitment to *agape* does not mean that one "tries to dissolve all tensions with particular roles or practices or to resolve them in only one way," for "permanent tensions" exist between special relations and *agape*. "Our special bonds and affections—ecclesial, familial, societal, etc.—shape by necessity rather than accident our religious and moral identities." *Agape* "sensitizes us to needs, rights, and preferences" persons have categorically, but "particular roles and practices sensitize us to the importance of role-related demands" and "dispose us to recognize how pervasively our religious and moral lives are tied to certain traditions, communities, and institutional arrangements."[45]

Clearly, Edwards and Outka employ different terminology and follow different paths in their discussion of love. In the *Two Dissertations*, Edwards does not follow the current practice of using Greek and Latin terms; in fact, he rarely uses the word *agape* in any of his writings (Y8:129). Further, where Outka offers an alternative to Nygren's absolutist depiction of *agape* that incorporates the other forms of love, Edwards offers an account of benevolence that transcends those loves generated by natural instincts and affections. Finally, Edwards and Outka develop their proposals in dialogue with very different conversation partners. Outka submits theological reflection on *agape* to the analytical rigor of modern moral philosophy in order to offer an account that is "formally similar to the one philosophers have pursued in discussing, e.g. utilitarianism as an ultimate normative standard, criterion, or principle for judgements of value and obligation."[46]

Edwards, on the other hand, seeks to create space for a theological account of benevolence by demonstrating that even in its own terms, the insights of moral sense philosophy are inadequate.

Yet despite these differences, Outka's and Edwards's proposals are basically congruent regarding the nature and demands of neighbor-love. Both Edwards and Outka define neighbor-love as a love that seeks the well-being of the neighbor regardless of the neighbor's particular value or attractiveness. Edwards and Outka also articulate their account of neighbor-love from a theocentric perspective; for both, love for the neighbor derives from the love of God. Further, both Edwards and Outka appreciate other forms of love—Edwards's "natural affections," Outka's "special relations"—while at the same time insisting on the "unilateral feature" of neighbor-love. Finally, while Edwards and Outka have different motivations in their engagement with secularized approaches to the moral life, both take seriously the insights these approaches offer regarding the distinctive claims of neighbor-love.

Outka's proposal also suffers from a shortcoming similar to the one we observed in the *Two Dissertations*. Like Edwards's apologetical effort in the *Two Dissertations*, Outka's account of *agape* is conditioned by his engagement with modern moral philosophy, to the extent that the terms and concepts he uses do not adequately reflect *agape*'s theological basis. As a result, critics argue that Outka's account of *agape* is constrained by "Enlightenment assumptions," particularly his emphasis on "the individual agent's attitude in the midst of competitive self-other dichotomies" and on the Kantian doctrine of respect for persons, which commit him to "modern ethical requirements of impartiality."[47] To be sure, this criticism shortchanges the characteristics of *agape* that we observed, as well as those points where Outka sets his theocentric *agape* within a "particularist . . . Christian web of belief and practice," summarized in Hans Frei's claim that "humanity at large is the neighbor given to the church."[48] In addition, this criticism fails to appreciate the extent to which Outka's engagement with modern moral philosophy represents a continuation of the Christian tradition's long-standing practice of identifying those points of general revelation, such as the Golden Rule, which are emblematic of the demands of *agape*. Nonetheless, it seems fair to say that Outka does not describe in detail the theological framework that informs his account. In the interest of providing an account of *agape* that is formally similar to utilitarianism, Outka at times treats unqualified regard as *the* fundamental principle from which one can evaluate actions and generate more specific norms, along the lines of utilitarianism's "act in such a way that maximizes happiness."

As we have seen, Edwards's account of absolute benevolence is strengthened once we view it from the perspective of his Trinitarian thought, and a similar exercise would serve Outka's account of *agape*.

Indeed, Trinitarian themes are implicit in Outka's account of *agape*. Outka's argument that communion with God is integral to neighbor-love evokes an anthropology that sees the self as fully realized only through spiritual participation in the triune life of God. Further, as we have just seen, Outka's belief that *agape* represents the church's embodiment of neighbor-love presupposes an ecclesiology that is essentially Trinitarian. The latter is evident in the essay by Hans Frei from which Outka quotes to summarize the "particularist" roots of his account of *agape*. As Frei notes, the "church is founded on and sets forth" the "identity and presence" of Jesus Christ. Yet Christ is not present to the church directly, but only through the Spirit. Thus, the mission of the church is Trinitarian; the church is the "localized presence of Jesus Christ in and for the world," which it appropriates through emulating the story of Jesus and encountering his identity through the Spirit. The fundamental paradigm of *agape*, in turn, is the story of Jesus; indeed, the immediate focus of the church is not on *agape* itself, but Christ. Frei explains:

> As the governing motif of Jesus' life, love is far more nearly an indirect than a direct focus of his behavior. His love is a function of his mission, but his mission is to enact the salvation of men [*sic*] in obedience to God. Love is subsidiary to that mission, though it is one way of expressing the manner in which the mission is carried out in his action toward all men [*sic*].[49]

Had Outka made these Trinitarian themes explicit and placed them in the foreground of his thought, his account of *agape* would have a theological framework that could balance his engagement with modern moral philosophy as well as counter the criticisms noted above. Indeed, not only would a Trinitarian interpretation of *agape* provide an anthropology and ecclesiology to support the claims Outka makes concerning unqualified regard, but it would also justify the basic orientation of Outka's project, namely, to articulate a more inclusive alternative to Nygren's original formulation of *agape*. For as we have seen, viewed from a Trinitarian perspective, *agape* does not function in isolation from other loves, nor do other loves have their legitimacy to the extent that they are subordinated to *agape*. Rather, *agape* represents the presenting love in the temporal expression of God's triune love. As such, the relationship between *agape* and the other forms of love is complementary. *Agape* is definitively expressed in God's creation and redemption of humanity through Jesus Christ, and is embodied in unqualified regard for the neighbor, but *agape* is only one aspect of the temporal expression of God's triune love. In a way analogous to the inseparable unity of God's triune redemption of the world, just as Christ and the Spirit cooperate while remaining distinct, so the other forms of love figure in the moral life. Hence, the church's faithful imitation of

Christ's *agape* does not take the form only of self-sacrifice, where the church shares in the suffering of Christ, but also of the self-realization that comes from the consolation, confidence, and joy in Christ's resurrection and ascension. Ultimately, the locus for *agape* is eschatological communion in the mutual love of the persons of the Trinity, out of which *agape* proceeds and into which the saints are incorporated through the Spirit.

Aspects of a Trinitarian account of *agape* are present in Timothy Jackson's attempt in *Love Disconsoled* (1999) to defend the position of "strong *agape*," or the thesis that *agape* possesses "unique authority" as the "singular source of religious and moral motivation." In comparison, "erotic love and friendship" are "dependent on *agape* for their genesis and ordered continuance," such that without *agape* they "will either never emerge or degenerate once they do." Further, where *eros* and *philia* represent merely human aspirations, *agape* is "not causally possible without the grace of God mediated by the Son and the Spirit."[50]

Jackson's Trinitarian approach to *agape* does not explore the inner relations of the Trinity. In his opinion, exploring the mutuality that existed between "the persons of the Trinity" before the creation of the world "is like cosmological speculation on the moment of or 'before' the Big Bang: dicey." Instead, his focus is on the economic Trinity, specifically "God's originating *agape* in the creation of the world" and "God's saving *agape* in the Incarnation of Christ." These acts depict *agape* as a *kenotic* love definitively manifested in "an openness to the sacrifice of life itself based on faithful imitation of Christ." Humanity therefore encounters *kenotic* love as a divine reality, a supernatural gift where we are "lifted by the Holy Spirit to a new self," while at the same time accepting the radically contingent nature of human existence. For as "God interacts with and is influenced by the world" through the incarnation, "so *agape* is not detached from other human emotions and enterprises." Thus, *agape* makes possible the achievement of authentic personhood and "nothing less than full human life"; "human persons, made in God's Image and redeemed by God's Son" will "not develop without an unearned care extended to them by others similarly made and redeemed."[51]

As a result, Jackson's account of *agape* is distinctive in three ways. First, Jackson's definition of *agape* is sensitive to the particular circumstances within which neighbor-love is expressed. He incorporates Outka's definition of *agape* in his list of *agape*'s features, which are: (1) unconditional commitment to the good of others, (2) equal regard for the well-being of others, and (3) passionate service open to self-sacrifice. Instead of offering normative content, however, these characteristics guide each person's realization of *agape* in his or her own character, actions, and social context, as he or she uniquely assumes the figure of Christ's incarnation and atoning death.[52]

Second, Jackson's account of *agape* rests on an explicit anthropology that views *agape* as the source of authentic self-realization as well as self-abnegation. "Christian love is premised on truth claims about divine agency and human nature." Because it is founded in the cross and grace, the primary experience in each individual's life of *agape* is "of being loved uncritically" with the *"kenotic* love of God." Yet, in the same gesture, *agape* reveals the extent to which we are self-absorbed and "do not know who we 'ourselves' are and what we 'ourselves' need." Hence, "Christianity preaches patient self-abnegation," but "this is paradoxically Good News for both individuals and groups." For if "the life, death, and resurrection of Jesus Christ set the pattern for human self-realization, then self-preservation is not the supreme good," but "rather obedience to God and love of neighbor."[53]

Third, Jackson depicts *agape* as an "unconditional standard" that operates in a "conditioned and flawed world." Acknowledging postmodernity's—particularly Richard Rorty's—skepticism regarding beliefs that purport to transcend the contingency that pervades human existence, *agape* recognizes the "fallible" nature of our "judgements about God, humanity and the universe." Primarily, this deep sense of fallibility means that those who live by *agape* may hope for immortality, but must recognize that no necessary connection exists between *agape* and immortality. One must find in the giving and receiving of *agape* "Immanuel enough," and realize that "God might not bestow endless life on any creatures at the end of time." In this sense, *agape* is properly "disconsoled" of any superficial, or even supernatural, resolution to the inevitable conflicts that come through imitating Christ's atoning love. Ironically, we become fully aware of the inestimable value of *agape* only to the extent we are willing to view it against a background of "metaphysical uncertainty." Hence, the "greater the love," the "more it will be disconsoled and disconsoling, yet without despairing of the works of love in caring for others." The fundamental expression of *agape*, then, remains the cross; while we believe that Christ is raised from the dead, any appropriation of the resurrection that entails our own "endlessness" is presumptuous and fails to take our own participation in the passion of Christ seriously.[54]

Jackson's Trinitarian *agape* resonates with aspects of the Trinitarian interpretation I offer of Edwards's account of benevolence. Jackson's "incarnational" definition of *agape* offers important insights for how each person can show authentic neighbor-love in his or her immediate context in a way that distinctively participates in God's *agape* manifested in the creation of the world and the incarnation of the Son. All the same, because he restricts the scope of his Trinitarian reflection to God's love for humanity, Jackson's account of *agape* is one-dimensional, and lacks the multifaceted view of love evident in Edwards's Trinitarian thought. Jackson's identification of *agape* as *the* love of God eliminates the possibility of other forms of love that equally emanate from God, and he fails to see the ways in which the Trinity provides a model for integrating the different forms of love that compose the moral life. Indeed, at one point Jackson admits that while "*agape* persists in spite of alienation," its "ideal" is the "unity within diversity" manifested between the persons of the Trinity.[55] But specifying what this perichoretic love entails would require a fuller lexicon of divine love than he allows.

More importantly, when Jackson denies the necessary connection between *agape* and immortality, he emphasizes Christ's atoning love on the cross to the extent that his proposal breaks free of a coherent Trinitarianism. As we have seen, in Edwards's Trinitarian thought the communication of God's triune goodness and love to humanity is the fundamental end that motivates God to create the world. If this communication takes the form of authentic *theosis*, then what is communicated is spiritual—that is, eternal and immaterial—which allows the saints to participate in the triune life of God. Likewise, the church's embodiment of Christ's *agape* is never without the consolation of the resurrection and the eschatological hope of communion with Christ in eternity. Jackson's separation of *agape* and immortality, however, makes such an explanation of the divine agency and human existence incomprehensible. What would motivate a triune God to create beings who could express the cost of love but not experience the joy of communion? Why would a triune God create beings who can participate in Christ's death but not his resurrection? Instead of capturing the inestimable value of *agape*, Jackson's separation of *agape* from immortality renders it absurd. Here Jackson's proposal, despite its explicit Trinitarian grammar, is conditioned by the concepts of postmodernity, particularly Rorty's skepticism regarding transcendent truths such as the resurrection.

2.2. Edwards and *Philia*

Another approach to love is that of Edward Vacek in *Love, Human and Divine* (1993). Vacek offers an account of love that involves the emotions and centers on *philia*. Central to Vacek's account is the following schema: "(1) God loves us; (2) we love God; (3) we and God form a community; (4) we and God cooperate."[56]

This fourfold schema guides Vacek's analysis of the role of the emotions in moral development. Our emotions are not "merely bodily resonances" but "cognitive acts through which we apprehend values" in mutual relationships of participatory love. In authentic love, our participation takes the form of a "unity-in-difference" modeled on the perichoretic relations of the Trinity. Just as the persons of the Trinity are completely united and yet maintain their distinctiveness and identity, so love is properly an existential relation of mutuality in which one recognizes value in, and bestows value on, another. Consequently, the task of our lives is integration, both within ourselves *intrapersonally*, where we integrate the different "parts" of our emotional "self" into a coherent unity, and between others *interpersonally*, where we integrate the different relationships and communities in which we live. The foundation and cornerstone of this integration is our "relation with God," through which God grants us a "share in God's life." Although God is not metaphysically dependent on humanity, God is existentially and personally involved in our lives to the extent that God depends on our cooperation as mediators of God's love. The guiding theological vision is therefore "theanthropy"—that "God, human beings, and their covenantal relation are central." As we emotionally grow closer to God, we learn to love as God loves, until "our love for God" becomes "our central love" and "all our activities" are "integrated into our covenant with God." Correlatively, the "union of our minds and hearts with God's mind and heart helps us to see our neighbors' precious value and to align ourselves with them in the direction of their own growth and fulfillment."[57]

Vacek's fourfold schema also guides his "pluralist" thesis concerning the definition and relation of *agape, eros,* and *philia.* Vacek argues that each term describes a particular orientation in a loving relationship. *Agape* describes love expressed "for the sake of the beloved," that is, a love "moved and attracted to affirm the beloved's (real and ideal) goodness." *Eros* describes love expressed "for our own sake," that is, a love that "springs from and is directed to fulfilling the interests of the development of the self." *Philia* describes love expressed "for the sake of the relationship we have with the beloved," that is, a love that derives from the "mutual relationship" and "reciprocity" one has with the beloved. All three loves are "necessary for human flourishing" and counteract "basic human disorders." *Agape* "enables us to appreciate the value of others in and for themselves," and "corrects for selfishness." *Eros* "increases our sense of our own goodness," and corrects self-alienation and "self-hate." *Philia* expresses our desire to be "in various mutual relationships," and corrects our feelings of "separation and loneliness." Nonetheless, though "life typically includes all three loves in rhythmically occurring ways," *philia* in the form of "friendship with God is the heart of the Christian life." As with the emotions, the fundamental paradigm of friendship with God is the *philia* that exists in the Trinity. The "friendship among the 'persons' of the Trinity or among the saints indicates that *philia* can in principle endure forever." Thus, salvation is best construed as "a personal, intimate, mutual relation with God." Given that our emotional development depends on mutual relationships of participatory love, friendship with God represents the fulfillment of human nature and activity. At the same time, cultivating friendship with God does not mean that we forsake all other special friendships and loving attachments, both erotic and agapic, but that these more particular attachments mediate our friendship with God.[58] Vacek writes:

> In brief, God loves God, the world, other persons, and me. Within our limits, what then should we love? The answer is the same: God, the world, other human beings, and myself. But whether we go to worship or to the soup kitchen, all should be done in response to and as part of our relation with God. This is not a matter of God first, after that others, and then perhaps one's self. God asks our whole heart all the time, and our love for creatures should increasingly be part of the way we cooperate with God. The Christian moral life is a love relationship with God. The mystery of our lives is that we come to share in the life of the One who loves the universe.[59]

Aspects of Vacek's account resonate with important themes in Edwards's Trinitarian thought, specifically where Edwards's focus expands from benevolence to include the loves of complacence and mutuality. Vacek's cognitive and participatory theses regarding the emotions resembles Edwards's Trinitarian anthropology, which views the affections as the source of the integrated self's order and orientation, as well as Edwards's depiction of the soul's *theotic* incorporation into the mutual love of the Trinity. As we have seen, Edwards often depicts the love expressed between Christ and the saints in intimate terms, as akin to the love expressed between parents and children, close friends, and lovers. Our spiritual incorporation into the body of Christ is akin to a "birth"—a moment chaotic and unpredictable, yet intimate, emotional and joyful, where, like Mary, we bear Christ within us. Our love for Christ is like that of the woman of ill repute described in Luke, who washed, anointed, and kissed Jesus' feet, repentant and reconciled to her Lord. The consummation of our relationship with Christ is a "spiritual marriage" and an "everlasting wedding day."[60] What moves the saint, then, is a spiritual sense of the beauty of God that is akin to our erotic attachments in these relationships. As Paula Cooey notes, these intimate and erotic images of God's love remind us that Edwards's understanding of complacence depicts the "divine love" as that which "conceives, bears, and nurtures its offspring in a most fecund, sensual, and personal manner."[61] Edwards and Vacek agree, then, that the emotions or affections play a crucial role in the moral life.

The relative priority Vacek places on *philia* resembles Edwards's stress on mutuality, which is perfectly expressed by the Spirit, who is the personification of the mutual love and "friendship" between Father and Son. As we have seen, Edwards argues that within the inner life of the Trinity, the Spirit has the "peculiar honor" of being "infinite happiness and joy itself," as the "principle" that "reigns over the Godhead" and "wholly influences both the Father and the Son in all they do" (H:122; Y21:147).

Moreover, in the economic Trinity the mutuality of the Spirit stands at the center of authentic "communion" between "the Father and the Son," between "God and the creature, and between creatures among themselves" (H:64). For this reason, the Spirit represents the completion of love that Christ bestows on the church. "The great thing purchased by Jesus Christ for us is communion with God, which is only in having the Spirit" (Y13:466). Vacek and Edwards agree, then, that while love has erotic and agapic elements, the perfection of love is incorporation into God's triune relationship of mutuality, so that "the church should be as it were admitted into the society of the blessed Trinity."[62]

Nonetheless, despite these points of agreement, Vacek's approach is lacking when compared to Edwards's Trinitarian account of love. Though he makes use of Trinitarian concepts, Vacek most often depicts God as an individual human being writ large. As a result, Vacek's depiction of the love of God does not reflect the definitive form it takes as a result of God's triune nature. Where Edwards grounds God's complacence in the psychological analogy's depiction of God's triune self-love, Vacek does not have a sense of the divine *eros* that is not the creature of need. In Vacek's scheme, "Love creates a 'need' for the beloved." Although Vacek assures us that metaphysically "God is secure no matter what we do," God's personal involvement with humanity means that "God's *eros*" is such that God "wants our fulfillment for God's relational self" and "needs us for what God will be and do in human history." Correlatively, where Edwards grounds God's benevolence in the diffusive goodness of God's nature manifested in the social analogy's depiction of communication and self-donation, Vacek is unwilling to accept a diffusive ontology, or to see how it might strengthen the appeal of *agape*. Vacek disagrees with the argument that God "creates all things" solely "to *express* his goodness" on the grounds that such "an act of pure self-expression is not really an act of love for another but only an act of *self*-love."[63] But this objection assumes that God's goodness is an individual, rather than social, reality, which is certainly not the case in Edwards's Trinitarian thought.

Vacek's neglect of the way in which Trinitarian relations define the nature and activity of God diminish his theses concerning the emotions and *philia*. In terms of the emotions, Vacek correctly emphasizes the extent to which our emotions are involved in the expression of other-regarding love, as well as the extent to which special relations mediate God's love for us and our love for God. But he leaves little room for a distinctly Trinitarian anthropology that makes the indwelling of the Spirit integral to the realization of personhood. Thus, Vacek denies the possibility for an authentic expression of disinterested neighbor-love that transcends natural human capacities. In Vacek's understanding, *agape* is spontaneous and diffusive, but the care we have for others never takes the form of unqualified regard or absolute benevolence—"*agape* essentially requires emotional affirmation of the beloved's own attractive goodness."[64] But it is one thing to say that *agape* can be mediated through our particular emotional attachments; it is another to say that *agape* cannot transcend these particular attachments. To hold the latter is to assimilate the Spirit's transformation of human nature into a process of emotional development, as well as to make all claims of the neighbor subject to our particular feelings for his or her inherent value or attractiveness. Indeed, for all intents and purposes, Vacek's account of the emotions is little different from that offered in psychotherapeutic literature concerning the development of a mature, self-differentiated, and well-adjusted individual.[65] Certainly, emotional development is an important aspect of the moral life, and every theology must include referential content in human experience in order to be compelling. But the transformation of human love through the cross of Christ and the indwelling of the Spirit must include something greater, something more universal, than merely the education of the emotions. Otherwise, the scope of Christian love collapses into solipsism.

In terms of *philia*, Vacek's lack of appreciation for the diffusive goodness generated by the mutuality of the divine persons limits his understanding of the relation between God and humanity. Vacek rightly highlights God's self-communication in creation and Christ's participation in humanity's suffering through the incarnation. Nonetheless, in his account God "has irrevocably bound Godself to humanity," and has consequently become "vulnerable" and capable of being "affected" by our "failures." Not only does God grant humanity the freedom to reject the divine initiatives, but Vacek views our "cooperation" with God as essential for the fulfillment of God's purposes, to the extent that "God's creative, salvific, and sanctifying activity cannot be complete without our cooperation." As such, Vacek implicitly follows the logic of reciprocity in his depiction of the relation between God and humanity, arguing that "God 'gets' our selves only by first 'giving' God's self." In contrast, in Edwards's Trinitarian thought God's love is depicted as a fountain that originates in the triune relations of God and flows out to creation with infinite abundance.[66] Therefore, the missions of the Son and the Holy Spirit are not bound by an economy of exchange, but, as the source of true mutuality and friendship, establish an economy of excess.[67]

2.3. Edwards's Trinitarian Account of Love

Edwards's Trinitarian account of love, then, does not agree completely with any of the representative *agape* or *philia* approaches we have examined. The reason is not that these representatives define love differently than Edwards does. While Edwards uses different terminology, he is aware of the nuance that the words *agape, eros,* and *philia* identify. And if writing today, Edwards would presumably accept the current lexicon on love, just as he accepted the standard practice in his day of speaking in terms such as "benevolence," "complacence," and "friendship." Further, aspects of the representative *agape* and *philia* approaches we have examined resonate with aspects of Edwards's account of love. Outka's and Jackson's *agape* resembles Edwards's emphasis on absolute benevolence, and Vacek's *philia* resembles Edwards's emphasis on complacence, communion, and friendship with God.

What separates Edwards's account from these representative approaches is the extent to which Edwards's Trinitarian thought is essential to his understanding of the types and relations of love he identifies. While the proponents of *agape* and *philia* we have examined at times use Trinitarian concepts and grammar, they do not generally appreciate the extent to which Trinitarian thought offers a structure of intelligibility for Christian reflection on love. Accordingly, Edwards's principal contribution to the current discussions on love in contemporary Christian ethics is not as a proponent of either *agape* or *philia,* but as an account that embraces both of these partial truths in a vision of love that is thoroughly Trinitarian.

3. *CHARITY AND ITS FRUITS*

Admittedly, the interpretation I offer regarding Edwards's contribution to the discussion on love in contemporary Christian ethics leans heavily on the Trinitarian interpretation of the *Two Dissertations* I offer earlier in this chapter. For if one adheres strictly to the arguments Edwards articulates in the *Two Dissertations,* the Trinitarian themes are as scant there as they are in the representative accounts of *agape* and *philia* we have examined. Therefore, to this point, the thesis I argue concerning the Trinitarian nature of Edwards's understanding of benevolence, complacence, and mutuality or friendship, depends on whether it is legitimate to view the *Two Dissertations* as a work constrained by apologetical strategies rather than as a work of constructive theology.

Such a Trinitarian understanding of love, however, is explicit in *Charity and Its Fruits,* a series of fifteen sermons on 1 Corinthians 13:1–3 delivered in 1738 and published posthumously in 1852.[68] Fittingly, the unifying theme of these sermons is the Augustinian love of *caritas,* or "charity"— "that disposition or affection by which one is dear to another"—which Edwards uses as a prism to refract different wavelengths of love in the Christian life (Y8:129). But in the first sermon it becomes clear that Edwards comprehends charity within a wider Trinitarian matrix. We know what love is only by knowing the Spirit of love expressed between the

Father and the Son, and subsequently through God's triune redemption of the world:

> Love is the principle thing which the gospel reveals in God and Christ. The gospel brings to light the love between the Father and the Son, and declares how that love has been manifested in mercy; how that Christ is God's beloved Son in whom he is well pleased. And there we have the effects of God's love to his Son set before us in appointing him to the honor of a mediatorial kingdom, in appointing him to be the Lord and Judge of the world, in appointing that all men should honor the Son even as they honor the Father. There is revealed the love which Christ has to the Father, and the wonderful fruits of that love, as particularly his doing such great things in obedience to the Father, and for the Father's justice, authority and law. There it is revealed how the Father and the Son are one in love, that we might be induced in like manner to be one with them, and with one another. . . . The gospel teaches us the doctrine of the eternal electing love of God, and reveals how God loved those that are redeemed by Christ before the foundation of the world; and how he gave them to the Son, and the Son loved them as his own. The gospel reveals the wonderful love of God the Father to poor sinful, miserable men, in giving Christ, not only to love them while in the world, but to love them to the end. And all this love is bestowed on us while we were wanderers, outcasts, worthless, guilty, and even enemies. The gospel reveals such love as nothing else reveals. (Y8:143–44)

Throughout the rest of the sermon series, the relations of love exhibited in both the inner life of the Trinity and in God's triune creation and redemption of humanity provide the definitive content for charity as it is expressed within the different types of love. "Benevolence is that disposition" whereby one "delights in the good of another." It represents "the most essential thing" in "Christian love," for benevolence is "an imitation of the eternal love and grace of God and the dying love of Christ" (Y8:213). "Complacence" is a delight "in viewing the beauty of another." Its paradigm is the holiness and perfection of the "Son of God," who is the Father's "infinite object of love," but it also includes the "holiness" of those "saints" who bear a spiritual "likeness to God." "Friendship" follows the paradigm of the "infinite and eternal mutual holy energy between the Father and the Son," which is personified in the Spirit, who is "nothing but an infinite and unchangeable act of love." Thus, true love "is always mutual" (Y8:373; 275; 377).

Paul Ramsey rightly argues that the *Charity* sermons present a "phenomenology of the Christian moral life" that anticipates the ground Edwards later covers in the *Religious Affections* (Y8:61). Like the *Religious Affections*, Edwards emphasizes "holy practice" and the "fruits" of the Spirit over the "gifts" of the Spirit, and he constructs an anthropology that sees communion with God as the source of human happiness and the culmination of the moral and spiritual life (Y8:161, 258). Indeed, Edwards explores similar images and virtues in the *Charity* sermons to those in the *Religious Affections*, the main difference being that in the *Charity* sermons Edwards uses these images and virtues to emphasize distinctively Christian interpersonal actions and dispositions. Thus, the figure of Christ, who is the exemplar of true spiritual affections in the *Religious Affections*, serves as the exemplar of authentic charity in the *Charity* sermons. Similarly, the virtues such as humility, long-suffering, and unselfishness all express in interpersonal terms Edwards's central contention that what is decisive in Christian virtue and love is our incorporation into God's love through the indwelling of the Spirit. For the "Spirit of God is a spirit of love," such that "when the Spirit of God enters into the soul, love enters" (Y8:132–35). Therefore, charity is the source of the soul's "truth," "freedom," "integrity," and "wholeness" (Y8:182).

What is most distinctive in the *Charity* sermons, however, is Edwards's focus on the church. This theme recurs throughout the sermon series, but is particularly evident in his last sermon, where he argues that the fulfillment of charity is realized in the church's perfect communion with the persons of the Trinity. Currently, the church struggles in a state of adolescence and "imperfection." Although in its "militant state," the church is nonetheless in "a state of childhood" in "comparison with what it will be in the heavenly state, when it comes to a state of manhood and perfection, and to the measure of the stature of the fullness of Christ" (Y8:367). What keeps the church from reaching this perfection is not that it has failed to preach the gospel to the ends of the earth, but that its people have not yet received and expressed in full the Spirit's "love and charity," particularly in their relations with one another. Therefore, the fulfillment of the moral life is not merely an individual project, even if regeneration is decisive. Redemption is a corporate affair, in which the church fully joins God's triune society. Accordingly, Edwards examines the love that exists in heaven, particularly in terms of its "cause and foundation," its "subject" and "objects," and in "itself."

The "foundation" and "cause" of love are the social relations of the triune God, which form an "infinite fountain of love" from which all creation proceeds. As "that part of creation" that "God has built" as God's special "dwelling place," heaven is a place where the love of the triune persons is perfectly present. "There dwells God the Father, and so the Son, who are united in infinitely dear and incomprehensible mutual love." There dwells the "Holy Spirit, the spirit of divine love, in whom the very essence of God . . . flows out or is breathed forth in love, and by whose immediate influence all holy love is shed abroad in the hearts of all the church." Therefore, "in heaven this fountain of love, this eternal three in one, is set open without any obstacle to hinder access to it," such that this "fountain overflows in streams and rivers of love and delight, enough for all to drink at, and swim in, yea, so as to overflow the world as it were with a deluge of love" (Y8:369–70).

The "subjects" and "objects" of the divine love are first and foremost the divine persons. God the Father is the "original seat" of all subjective expressions of love, for "love is in him not as a subject which receives it from another," but "where it is itself." The primary object of the Father's love is "his only begotten Son," who is "an object which is infinite," and therefore receives the love of the Father so perfectly that he too "is also an infinite subject of it." In return, the Father is the primary object of the Son's subjective expression of love, which entails that the Godhead is united by "an infinite and unchangeable act of love, which proceeds from the Father and the Son." Thus, "love is to God as light is in the sun, which does not shine by a reflected light as the moon and planets do; but by its own light," as "the fountain of light" (Y8:373).

God's triune subjective and objective relations of love, however, do not exist within the Godhead only, but flow out in "innumerable streams towards all the created inhabitants of heaven," specifically the "angels and saints there." If "love is to God as light is in the sun," the saints are "the planets which shine by reflecting the light of the sun." The "love of God flows out towards Christ the Head, and through him to all his members." The saints participate in the subjective and objective expression of God's love by receiving and returning the love of God, which is the source of harmony, unity, and peace in the heavenly church. Christ's "love flows out" to "every individual member" of his "whole church," and "they all with one heart and soul, without any schism in the body, love their redeemer." Moreover, in the "glorious society" of the heavenly church there is "not one heart but is full of love, nor one person who is not beloved." For having received God's love, "they are all lovely" and "see each other's loveliness with answerable delight and complacence." Thus, "everyone there loves every other inhabitant of heaven whom he sees, and he is so mutually beloved by everyone" (Y8:374).

The love "itself" that "fills the heavenly world" is patterned after the love expressed within the Trinity. Love in heaven is "perfect," both in an absolute sense in God, whose love is infinite, and in a relative sense in creatures, where perfection is "proper to their nature" and "capacities." In the love of the saints, this perfection primarily takes the form of the absence of sin—"such a sweet harmony will there be in the heavenly society, and perfect love in every heart towards everyone without control, and without alloy, or any interruption" (Y8:376). Love in heaven is also perfect in terms of the benevolence, complacence, and mutuality expressed between the saints. The "whole society" will "rejoice in each other's happiness, for the love of benevolence is perfect in them." Likewise, the "complacence" found in the beauty of each other will be perfect, for in heaven "there are no unlovely persons," that is, "no false professors, none who pretend to be saints" (Y8:370, 375). Therefore, love in heaven is always "mutual," that is, "in proportion as any person is beloved, in that proportion his love is desired and prized" (Y8:377).

In describing these different facets of the charity that the church experiences in heaven, Edwards's intent is not to provide a systematic study of the church, or even the Trinity. Rather, Edwards's aim is to reiterate his argument, noted in chapter 2, that the primary point of contact between the church's present reality and its eschatological fulfillment is located in living the life of love. Accordingly, Edwards encourages his listeners to "seek after" charity, to "turn the current" of their "thoughts and meditations towards that world of love," to be "content to pass through all difficulties in the way to heaven," and to cultivate those dispositions and relations that are of God (Y8:395–96). By "living in love" the saints partake of the "happiness," "comfort," "excellence," "peace," and "holiness" that exist in full in heaven. For "as heaven is a world of love, so the way to heaven is the way of love" (Y8:396).

In addition to developing a love-shaped character, Edwards also encourages his listeners to live in communities that are "conformed" to God's triune love and that resist the sins of "selfishness," "jealousy," "contention," "schism," "revenge," and "deceit" (Y8:386–93). Absent the love of God, human communities are nothing more than a "world of confusion," where "all are for themselves, and self-interest governs, and all are striving to set themselves up" with no regard for "what becomes of others." In such a God-forsaken world, "all" seek "worldly good, which is the bone of contention among them," and all are continually "injuring and abusing one another," so that the "world" is "full of injustice" and there is "an abundance of opposition and cruelty without any remedy" (Y8:393). In contrast, when the church lives according to its heavenly destiny, "all are highly esteemed and honored, and dearly loved by all" (Y8:394). Indeed, not only do persons within the church receive love and respect, but the ethos of the church is transformative of the surrounding society. Thus, a "Christian spirit" disposes "those who stand in a public capacity," to promote "the public good" and not to be "governed by selfish views in their administrations" in order to "enrich themselves on the spoils of others as wicked rulers very often do" (Y8:261).

In true Augustinian fashion, Edwards views the church's eschatological fulfillment in heaven as a point of decision for each individual and community. The current world we live in is like a "large wilderness" with two radically different "countries" on either side. In one country the love of God reigns supreme, but in the other "self-interest" governs. Therefore, "God gives men their choice," to the extent that they "may have their inheritance where they choose it." If "we heartily choose heaven," we will have chosen the "better country" (Y8:392–94). Most often, Edwards uses the eschatological vision of the heavenly church to reassure his listeners of the reality of the church's love—that love is eternal, and that the church's faith and hope in God rests secure. Though the church is presently in a state of pilgrimage, the "Spirit of Christ is given to his church and people forever, everlastingly to influence them and dwell in them." For the "sum of all those good things in this life, and the life to come, which are purchased for the church, is the Holy Spirit" (Y8:352–54). And when the "church of Christ shall be settled" in its "most complete and eternal state," then the "divine love" that resides in the church through the Spirit will "be brought to its most glorious perfection in every individual member of the whole elect church," until "every holy soul shall be as it were all a flame of divine love" for "all eternity" (Y8:359).

This promise of the church's eschatological fulfillment in heaven is crucial to Edwards's understanding of charity. In its present state, the members of the church are more aware of their longing for heaven than their experience of love. Even the "heart" of a "good" person does not experience the true "liberty" of loving God completely, and is aware of the fact that he or she "is not holy enough, but is very far from it" (Y8:389). In addition, in the present age the friendship and mutuality of charity is fleeting and subject to trial. The "sweetness of earthly friendship" is often diminished by "difficulties" and "afflictions," such as "distance" and "poverty," in which friends grieve "for one another." Although in such cases friends lighten one another's "burdens," nonetheless the presence of these trials "adds to persons' afflictions," because friendship "makes them sharers in other's afflictions" (Y8:380–81). Finally, like Christ, our benevolent expressions of charity often meet with resistance, rejection, and adversity. Therefore, the church in its present stage must look to Christ not only as an "example" of "patient continuance in well-doing," but also must "trust" in his "mediation" for our sins, his "intercession" before the Father, and in "his promises of heaven to those who love and follow him" (Y8:395).

3.1. Edwards and Hauerwas

The distinctiveness of the connection Edwards draws between charity and the church becomes clearer when compared with similar projects in contemporary Christian ethics. Among those who argue for a church-centered ethics, Stanley Hauerwas is the most prominent. Hauerwas's early work focused on Neo-Aristotelian virtue ethics, but in his later work he has come to see the church as integral for articulating the unique content of Christian virtue.[69] Hauerwas's emphasis on the ecclesial nature of ethics is present throughout his numerous writings, but his proposal is summarized in *The Peaceable Kingdom* (1983).

Hauerwas's point of departure is his dissatisfaction with an ethics abstracted from a particular time, place, and community. The primary examples of such an "unqualified" ethics are modern moral theories of deontology and utilitarianism, both of which represent versions of the Enlightenment "attempt to secure a foundation for the moral life unfettered by the contingencies of our histories and communities." Such theories, however, operate with a flawed anthropology, placing undue stress on "autonomy," which is a necessary postulate of a morality that transcends the "contingencies of our histories and communities." As a result, they are unable to account for those unelected relations and commitments, such as being part of a family, that are "central to the human project." In addition, their confidence in "overriding principles" fails to account for the possibility of "moral tragedy," or circumstances in which there is "irresolvable moral conflict." More dangerously, these theories perpetuate a "systemic form of self-deception" regarding our individual power to create moral worlds of our own making. This self-deception manifests itself in "unrelentingly manipulative" interpersonal relations, in which under the guise of respecting the autonomy of others, persons engage in "elaborate games of power and self-interest." It also has a propensity to underwrite "coercion," for from this perspective, "if others refuse to accept my account of 'rationality,' it seems within my bounds to force them to be true to their 'true' selves."[70]

Consequently, Hauerwas rejects those approaches in the Christian tradition that aspire to the "universality" of an unqualified ethics, specifically natural law. Not only do these attempts repeat the mistakes noted above, but they invariably distort the Christian message by ignoring the necessarily contingent and historical nature of moral existence. Rather, the proper starting point for Christian ethics is one that recognizes the centrality of the biblical narratives and the communal practices of the church for shaping the Christian character and defining Christian virtues. The biblical narratives, centered on the "life, death, and resurrection of Jesus, and the ongoing history of the church as the recapitulation of that life," envision a reality that encompasses the contingent and tragic elements of human existence into a coherent whole through which all things are redeemed through Christ. Therefore, the task of the moral life is to see oneself within this reality, as a redeemed and renewed person witnessing to Christ's reconciliation.

The church then has two roles in Hauerwas's ethics. First, the church provides a "community of virtues," in which persons recognize their sinful tendencies toward "power," "control," "self-deception," and "violence," and are transformed through acquiring the true "freedom" that comes to those who have learned "to be at peace with themselves, one another, the stranger," and "God." "Discipleship," then, is "quite simply extended training in being dispossessed," for "to become followers of Jesus means that we must, like him, be dispossessed of all that we think gives us power over our own lives and the lives of others." This process is a gradual one of learning to "lay down" one's inherent propensities for violence and sin, and become "a participant in God's community of peace and justice." Second, the church is a "servant community" in which the "peaceable kingdom" initiated by Jesus is manifested to the world. The church's responsibility is not to develop an overarching social ethics that stands apart from its communal practices, for to do so would inevitably lead to the coercion and violence that accompany "unqualified ethics." Rather, the church is called to be a nonviolent witness to the new reality made possible through Christ's peace and reconciliation. As such, the "church does not have a social ethic, but the church is a social ethic." Through its faithful imitation of the cross, the church practices nonviolence and thereby participates in the eschatological inbreaking of Christ's peaceable kingdom.[71]

Hauerwas and Edwards agree that the church is an *altera civitas* with its own peculiar anthropology and ethos centered on relations of love and reconciliation. They also agree that Christ manifests the love of God in a way that should define the church's interpersonal relations, both internal and external, and that the church's eschatological witness is indispensable to understanding the moral life. Edwards and Hauerwas, however, comprehend the connection between ethics and ecclesiology quite differently. Hauerwas's interest in the church is motivated by his concern to provide a more adequate account of the moral life than that offered by "unqualified ethics," specifically one that portrays the moral life in terms of central narratives, communal practices, and signal virtues. As a result, despite the role he assigns to witness, Hauerwas's ecclesiology is largely functional: The church is primarily a vehicle for authentic moral formation, inculcating through its story and practices Christian habits of thinking and acting. Moreover, Hauerwas's preference for Neo-Aristotelian virtue theory and his repudiation of "unqualified ethics" determine in large part his constructive account of the church's moral life. Hauerwas's identification of nonviolence as the preeminent virtue of the church is as much due to his belief that all "unqualified ethics" underwrite coercion as it is to his belief that the story of Jesus is primarily a story of peace.[72] Similarly, Hauerwas's commitment to narrative as the preferred mode of moral discourse necessitates that doctrines such as the Trinity play a secondary role in his ethics. While he affirms "that God is our creator and/or redeemer, or that God's essential nature is that of a trinitarian relationship," he holds that doctrines are "tools," sometimes "even misleading tools," that merely "help us tell the story better." Indeed, because "the Christian story is an enacted story, liturgy is probably a much more important resource than are doctrines or creeds for helping us to hear, tell, and live the story of God."[73]

In contrast, Edwards's interest in the church is as the earthly embodiment of the Spirit's love that exists in God perfectly, and in heaven eternally. Thus, what is decisive for the church is not whether its practices are able to contribute to one's moral formation, for as we observed in chapter 3, Edwards believes that the moral formation Hauerwas articulates only transforms the natural affections and leaves the spiritual affections untouched. Rather, what is decisive is whether or not God's triune love is adequately expressed in the interpersonal relations of the church, for by doing so the church bears in its interpersonal relations the *imago dei*, which is the source of its true identity and end. Moreover, defining the earthly church in terms of God's triune love allows Edwards to offer a more comprehensive depiction of the kinds of love and relations that exist both within and outside the physical boundaries of the church than Hauerwas offers. Unlike Hauerwas, Edwards does not restrict his depiction of the love and virtues of the church to those evoked by Christ's atoning death. Rather, the proper model of love is of Christ who is also risen, ascended, and drawing the saints into communion with the Father and through the Spirit. Similarly, Edwards offers a more integrated depiction of the relation between the creedal statements regarding God's triune nature and the biblical narratives than Hauerwas does. While the biblical narratives play an irreplaceable role in our knowledge of God's love, for Edwards the doctrine of the Trinity does not merely order these narratives, but also reveals God's character and purposes.

One further point of difference between Hauerwas and Edwards concerns the relation between the church and nonviolence. In the *Charity* sermons, Edwards allows that in certain circumstances self-defense is not "unreasonable," and that Christians may have "to defend and vindicate themselves, though it be to the damage of him who injures them" (Y8:191–92). In a sermon on 1 Kings 8:44 preached at the time of King George's War (1744–1748), Edwards is less circumspect: "a people of God may be called to go forth in war." For "if it be lawful for a particular person to defend himself with force, then it is lawful for a nation of people made up of persons." Not only is self-defense justified, but "God is ready in such a case to hear the prayer of his people and give them success." Granted, as Harry Stout notes, Edwards preached this sermon in dire circumstances, in which the choice was between "armed resistance" and "foreign domination."[74] Nonetheless, Edwards does not comment at length on any of the developed traditions of just war.[75] Nor does he develop a more comprehensive reconciliation of his position regarding violence with either his Trinitarian thought or with his understanding of the church's eschatological mission. Only in *The Nature of True Virtue* does Edwards explain that, out of love, one may "oppose" a "being" who is an "enemy" to "Being in general." When viewed from the perspective of the twenty-first century, however, such license seems overly broad and vulnerable to manipulation. Here Hauerwas's depiction of the church's vocation to non-violence, as well as his appreciation for humanity's penchant for self-deception, present those who would accept Edwards's views on this point with a word of caution.

3.2. Edwards and Zizioulas

Another contemporary figure who helps illuminate the distinctiveness of the connection Edwards draws between the church and the Christian life is Eastern Orthodox theologian John Zizioulas. In *Being as Communion* (1993), Zizioulas's primary interest is with issues that are more specific to ecclesiology—such as the church's identity, authority, ministry, and communion, but his thought involves moral concepts when he argues that the church plays a crucial role in the achievement of personhood.[76] For Zizioulas, personhood is defined in terms of the *perichoresis* of the Trinity. A person is not a self-existent individual or nature, but a particular *hypostasis* that exists in relation to others. Following the "ecstatic character of God" manifested in the Father's begetting of the Son and spiration of the Spirit, personhood is an "ek-stasis of being, i.e. a movement towards communion which leads to a transcendence of the boundaries of the 'self' and thus to freedom."[77]

Personhood therefore is not identified with human existence per se, which is locked within relations of "biological necessity" that culminate in death. As a "biological *hypostasis*," desires and relations that are individualistic, external, and finite confine human existence. Only as an "ecclesial *hypostasis*" can human existence become realized and fulfilled through God in Christ.[78] Baptism, which effects the transformation of humanity from biological to ecclesial personhood, represents the restoration of authentic personhood, not merely the remission of sins.[79] The "essence of baptism" consists in the "adoption of man [sic] by God, the identification of his *hypostasis* with the *hypostasis* of the Son of God."[80] In this way, Zizioulas defines personhood construed in Trinitarian and christological terms as the paradigm of humanity's *theosis*—we become realized only through our participation in the fullness and freedom of God.

Zizioulas's understanding of personhood has implications that are social as well as anthropological. Because personhood is realized in relation to others, the love of the Godhead likewise becomes "the supreme ontological predicate." Love is not a category of being or a property "of the substance of God" but is "constitutive" of God, particularly as it is disclosed in the love of "the Father, that is, to that person which 'hypostasizes'

God, which makes God to be three persons."[81] Additionally, because of the role baptism plays in the restoration of personhood, "the first and most important characteristic of the Church is that she brings man [sic] into a kind of relationship with the world which is not determined by the laws of biology." For "when man loves as a biological *hypostasis*, he inevitably excludes others: the family has priority in love over 'strangers,' the husband lays exclusive claim to the love of his wife—facts altogether understandable and 'natural' for the biological *hypostasis*." But through becoming reborn as an ecclesial *hypostasis*, human love can transcend the individuality and "exclusiveness which is present in the biological *hypostasis*." Therefore, "a characteristic of the ecclesial *hypostasis* is the capacity of the person to love without exclusiveness, and to do this not out of conformity with a moral commandment ('Love thy neighbor,' etc.) but out of his 'hypostatic constitution,' out of the fact that his new birth from the womb of the Church has made him part of a network of relationships which transcends every exclusiveness."[82] In other words, through sacramentally participating in the church, human persons embody a perichoretic unity and openness that reflects the *perichoresis* of the Trinity. If baptism represents the restoration of personhood in Christ, the Eucharist represents the "manifestation and realization" of the church's "eschatological nature" in its participation of "the very life of the Holy Trinity."[83]

Perhaps surprisingly, given that they operate within different traditions of Christianity, Edwards and Zizioulas have several points in common in their Trinitarian thought, their views of personhood, and in the connection each draws between ecclesiology and the moral life. In terms of their Trinitarian thought, Edwards and Zizioulas both view God's triune nature as ecstatic and relational. In his development of the psychological analogy, Edwards comprehends the self-reflection of the Father as a moment in which "the whole deity and glory of the Father" is "repeated, or expressed again, and that fully" (H:77). And in his development of the social analogy, Edwards articulates God's ecstatic and relational entity in terms of the diffusive and social nature of the divine goodness. The "Father's begetting of the Son is a complete communication of his happiness, and so an eternal, adequate and infinite exercise of perfect goodness" (Y13:272). Further, Edwards's depiction of the Spirit's "happiness," "consent," "communion," "love and society" that reigns in the "blessed society" of the Godhead resembles Zizioulas's depiction of the *perichoresis* that lies at the heart of God's Trinitarian existence (H:64).

Edwards and Zizioulas also have similar understandings of personhood. Both Edwards and Zizioulas view relations as constitutive of persons, and that divine personhood is the model for the personhood of human beings. Like Zizioulas, Edwards understands the realization of personhood in terms of the saint's theotic participation in God through the "communication" and "indwelling" of the Spirit, which distinguishes the Christian vision of the moral life from those that pivot on individual choice or achievement (Y13:296). And in the *Religious Affections* and *Original Sin*, Edwards draws a distinction between the "natural" and "moral" images of God that is similar to the distinction Zizioulas draws between the "biological" and "ecclesial" *hypostases*. Indeed, even in *The Nature of True Virtue*, where he operates with as minimal an anthropology as possible, the opposition Edwards draws between affection for a "private system" and absolute benevolence is similar to Zizioulas's distinction between the respective exclusiveness and inclusiveness of the biological and ecclesial *hypostases* (Y8:556).

Finally, Edwards and Zizioulas agree that the church represents the fulfillment of the divine purposes for humanity, and that the fundamental identity of the church is realized in its participation in the triune relations of God. Although it would not have occurred to Edwards to use such a word, he and Zizioulas share an "iconic" vision of the present church as the earthly embodiment of the heavenly church's communion with the triune God. Edwards and Zizioulas both emphasize the role of the sacraments in the life of the church. In the *Charity* sermons, Edwards speaks of "baptism" and the "laying on of hands" as the occasion in which Christians "receive the Holy Ghost" (Y8:163). And in other sermons Edwards preached throughout his ministry, it is evident that he viewed the Lord's Supper as an occasion in which the local congregation experiences through the Spirit "communion with the Father and with his son Jesus Christ." Thus, through the Lord's Supper, the local congregation experiences union not only with the triune God but with the "church universal throughout the whole world" and the "church triumphant in heaven."[84]

Nonetheless, Edwards and Zizioulas have different understandings of love, of personal identity, and of the Holy Spirit. Concerning love, Zizioulas sees the act of perfect "freedom" in which the Father begets the Son and brings forth the Spirit as the paradigm for all love. Thus, the Father's ecstatic act of self-donation—one may say *agape*—serves as the basis on which the other forms of love are legitimated. The mutuality of *philia* is legitimate to the extent it is implicated in the Father's love, as the end of "communion," where there is both "loving and being loved" as a result of the Father's free act. Similarly, heavenly *eros* is legitimate to the extent that in the Father's love for the other persons of the Trinity there is the desire for union with the beloved. These other loves are not characteristic of the Father's *agape*, for the Father's "being is identical with an act of communion" only because "the Father as a *person* freely wills this communion." Consequently, a logic of subordination runs through Zizioulas's understanding of the divine love, and this logic becomes particularly evident in his description of how the divine love is expressed on the human level. Zizioulas relegates the concerns of *eros* and *philia* to those of the biological *hypostasis*, which are superceded by the agapic "freedom" of the ecclesial *hypostasis* to "love without exclusiveness."[85] In contrast, as we have seen, in Edwards's Trinitarian writings the relation between the three loves follows the logic of complementarity rather than of subordination. Therefore, while both Edwards and Zizioulas locate their understanding of the divine love in the Trinitarian relations, in Edwards's proposal the different loves have equal worth and integrity. Edwards assigns a special role to benevolence, but he also believes that God's triune love consists equally in complacence and mutuality. Moreover, all three forms of love are present in the relations of the church, and each love has a particular role in the moral life.

In terms of personal identity, Zizioulas locates the source of true personal identity in the "adoption of man [*sic*] by God," specifically the "identification of his *hypostasis* with the *hypostasis* of the Son of God."[86] Defining personal identity in this way enables Zizioulas to distinguish it from attributes that exist in the biological *hypostasis*, that is, the "complex of natural, psychological or moral qualities that are in some sense 'possessed' by or 'contained' in the human *individuum*."[87] Indeed, when viewed from the perspective of the biological *hypostasis*, personal identity has an intrinsically "tragic" character, for none of these features of the person endure, and all are merely "*persona*"—the mask or role we play in our given context. Nonetheless, by assigning even our psychological and moral characteristics to the biological *hypostasis*, Zizioulas obscures what content authentic personal identity has in his proposal.[88] For what constitutes authentic personal identity, if it hinges on the "identification" of our *hypostasis* with the "*hypostasis* of the Son of God" and not on our particular consciousness as well? In contrast, as we have seen, in his appropriation of the psychological analogy Edwards locates authentic personal identity in each individual's self-consciousness. This consciousness is created through the immediate communication of God and not constituted by our historical context alone. Therefore, while the regenerate experience their true identity in Christ, even the personal identities of the unregenerate have a measure of integrity and communion with God. As a result, though both Edwards and Zizioulas see Jesus Christ as the model of authentic personhood, and define persons in terms of their relations, in Edwards's proposal personal identity plays a more important role in the love of the church. Edwards is careful to note that the subjective and objective expressions of divine love are not confined to the persons of the Trinity, but include every member of the church. Thus, God's love "flows out" to "every individual member" of the "whole church" (Y8:374).

Finally, Zizioulas's proposal presupposes the Eastern Orthodox rejection of the *filioque* principle, which holds that the Holy Spirit proceeds from the Father and the Son as from one principle. No doubt, Zizioulas agrees with the well-known Eastern Orthodox argument that the *filioque* "depersonalizes" the Holy Spirit by identifying its existence with the relation between the Father and the Son.[89] But more important to Zizioulas's proposal is that the *filioque* tends to portray love as a property of the divine essence, rather than as the expression of God's triune existence. For by portraying the Spirit as the love that transcends the relation between the Father and the Son, the *filioque* renders love an overflow of the divine essence rather than an ecstatic act of interpersonal self-donation.[90] As a result, love takes on the nature of "necessity" as "an emanation of the 'property' of the substance of God" rather than a moment of complete freedom that "constitutes" the Trinity. In addition to portraying God's love as a property of the divine nature, the *filioque* underemphasizes the transformative effect of love in human persons. For the transformation of the ecclesial *hypostasis* is not a change in the "substance or nature" of a person that conveys a new "property" that enables "him [*sic*] to become something better and more perfect than that which he is now." Rather, it is the bestowal of a new "ontological category" of being, which conveys the freedom to love as God loves, in light of an entirely different reality.[91]

In contrast, Edwards has a very different understanding of the Holy Spirit and its relation to the divine love. As we observed in chapter 2, Edwards believes the *filioque* offers the most sensible way to interpret those passages in the Pauline and Johannine literature concerning the relations between the love of the divine persons and the saints. But more importantly, the entirety of Edwards's Trinitarian thought presupposes the *filioque* principle—both the psychological and social analogies culminate in a portrayal of the Spirit as the "mutual love," "communion," or "fellowship" of the Father and the Son (H:116). This understanding of the *filioque* not only guides his depiction of the Holy Spirit's procession from the Father and Son, but it stands behind Edwards's depiction of the diffusive goodness and love of the divine nature.

Therefore, what Zizioulas views as a point of weakness in the *filioque* principle, Edwards views as a point of strength. In Edwards's thought, the *filioque* principle reveals God's nature as a loving and communicative Being, who brings all things into existence, especially the church, so that God's love may be all in all. Rather than signifying the necessity of the divine nature, then, in Edwards's thought the *filioque* principle signifies God's freedom to love, which culminates in the church's involvement through the Spirit in the triune relations of love. For "our communion" with "the Father and the Son" consists in "partaking with them of the Holy Ghost" (H:117). And in heaven, it will be by the "Spirit" that "light is continually communicated to that blessed society" (Y18:363).

4. CONCLUSION

In *Jonathan Edwards* (1889), A. V. G. Allen argues that a curious tension runs throughout Edwards's arguments in the *Two Dissertations*. Edwards's apologetical position against Hutcheson has "profound significance," particularly his thesis that the "moral sense" cannot "rise to the love of Being in general." Nonetheless, by making God "equivalent to universal existence," Edwards generates a moral vision that is finally alien to the Christian faith. Edwards's commendation of virtue in the form of absolute benevolence contradicts the teaching on love evident in the incarnation. For what else is "the significance of the Incarnation but the entrance of God into humanity, the confinement of Deity as it were to human limits, in order that he might be measured by human capacity, and known and loved as divine?" Though Edwards is certainly right that "true virtue must begin and end with loving God supremely," is "not this rather the *ultimatum*, the final good to which virtue tends, rather than its incipient motive?" Especially in light of the incarnation's valorization of human particularity, does not Edwards's vision of God neglect "the small beginnings" and "the tedious process" through which God's love seeps into our souls like "yeast"? Accordingly, Allen concludes that had Edwards placed the doctrine of the Trinity at the center of the *Two Dissertations*, he might have found resources that would have saved his project from "confusion and failure." [92]

If the *Two Dissertations* are works of constructive theology, then Allen's assessment has merit. But if the *Two Dissertations* are works of apologetics and therefore constrained by apologetical strategies, then the dichotomy Allen asserts disappears. For in light of the Trinitarian interpretation of the *Two Dissertations* provided in this chapter, the "contradiction" Allen alleges is not because Edwards's theology is insufficiently Trinitarian, but because Edwards places his Trinitarian framework in the background of the *Two Dissertations* in order to pursue his point on neutral grounds. Therefore, Edwards's "failure" stems from his misplaced confidence in the apologetical arguments he developed rather than from a flaw in his theology as a whole. Indeed, far from conflicting with the doctrine of the Trinity, the *Two Dissertations* are ultimately indebted to its vision of God's triune love. In addition, as we have seen, retrieving the Trinitarian account of love that informs Edwards's arguments in the *Two Dissertations* is essential for appreciating what Edwards offers to the discussion on love in contemporary Christian ethics.

A similar state of affairs holds for *Charity and Its Fruits*. As we have seen, the *Charity* sermons are often viewed as a phenomenology of the moral life, and when viewed from this perspective, they have often disappointed commentators on Edwards. Indeed, the same authors who find the *Two Dissertations* too abstract find the *Charity* sermons too mundane. Thus, Holbrook argues that in the *Charity* sermons Edwards exhibits a tendency for "theological utilitarianism," or the belief that holiness is a means to maximize one's personal happiness.[93] Similarly, Fiering concludes that "*Charity and Its Fruits* has peculiarities that are inconsistent with nearly all the rest of Edwards' extant writings," for "nowhere else in Edwards' writing pertaining to morals is he as prudential and 'pragmatic' as here."[94] Even Paul Ramsey, who views *Charity and Its Fruits* favorably, allows that Edwards's "characterization of virtue often sounds positively Stoic" in its commendation of "imperturbability" in the face of suffering.[95] But when viewed from the perspective of his Trinitarian thought, it becomes clear that Edwards's intent is not so much to delve into the inner life of the soul as it is to depict the relations of love that are normative in a church that bears God's triune image. Here as well, being cognizant of Edwards's Trinitarian thought is essential to understanding Edwards's proposal rightly, as well as to identifying what Edwards contributes to recent attempts to draw a connection between ethics and ecclesiology.

Nonetheless, Edwards's Trinitarian account of love cannot reconcile all the tensions we have touched upon in this chapter. As we have seen, during his engagement with Hutcheson in *True Virtue*, Edwards allows that natural benevolence and the appreciation for the "beauty of society" have "something of the general nature of virtue," even if they fall short of the universal love required in absolute benevolence (Y8:609). This "law of nature" is not to be confused with true virtue, and must be subordinated to the love of God in order to be valid (Y8:564). In contrast, the natural law tradition holds that the moral life is best defined in terms of natural human inclinations, which generate intrinsic normative principles, such as nonmaleficence and equality.[96] As Jean Porter argues, scholastic theologians developed natural law in an effort to generate an overarching theory of human nature and sociality that could transcend the diversity of beliefs and communal practices in medieval Europe. Consequently, instead of basing the moral life on specific doctrines concerning the nature of God, or on a particular social arrangement, "natural law emphasizes the immanent intelligibility and moral value of human life" in its different forms. Therefore, from the perspective of natural law, "morality is grounded in our nature as social animals and should be interpreted with its natural origins in mind."[97]

As such, natural law offers a very different depiction of the moral life than what we find in Edwards. Where Edwards's understanding of the moral life is predicated on the similarity between the divine and human nature, natural law is predicated on the relevant differences between the two. Where Edwards's account of love is not fully intelligible apart from his Trinitarian thought, natural law claims that our knowledge of moral norms is independent of any prior knowledge of revelation or doctrine. And where Edwards sees *theosis* as the central task of the moral life, in natural law "morality is desacralized"—that is, it is viewed as a "natural phenomenon, as an expression of the human person's continuity with the rest of the natural world," and not as a "medium for transcendence." Porter argues that natural law—or some theory of human nature similar to it—is essential to the "fundamental doctrinal commitments of Christianity," for without such a framework for seeing "natural goodness apart from Christian revelation or grace," the doctrine of creation remains a "bare abstraction."[98] In contrast, Russell Hittinger argues that natural law's political use is more important to retain than its theological use, for in this capacity it articulates minimal moral standards that modern liberal societies use to protect basic human goods and principles. In this context, natural law is even further removed from Edwards's proposal, in that its primary function is to establish minimal "consensus about natural principles of justice" rather than to develop a fully adequate depiction of human nature and flourishing.[99]

The task of fully resolving the tension between the natural law tradition and Edwards's Trinitarian ethics lies beyond the scope of this study. Nor would such a task be entirely desirable, given natural law's political function. As Hittinger notes, some form of a two-track scheme of "public rules and private excellencies" appears essential to the well-being of a society that is both pluralistic and democratic.[100] Nonetheless, Edwards's Trinitarian ethics helps underscore the limitations of the natural law tradition regarding its ability to generate a comprehensive ethics from universal insights concerning human nature and society. At best, the principles we identify in the created order provide fragments of a picture that we can only appreciate through knowing the creation's eschatological fulfillment in the church's heavenly communion with the Trinity. Therefore, any attempt to build an ethics that begins with natural inclinations must explicitly acknowledge from the start that the account provided is preliminary and must be completed by a wider theological framework that provides its ultimate source and standard of intelligibility. For as we have seen, when Edwards tries to develop an account of the moral life that can appeal to those who do not agree with his Trinitarian commitments, his arguments fail to persuade, and are only compelling when viewed in light of his Trinitarian thought. Therefore, in the end, Edwards's ethics depends on a vision of human nature and society that can only be fully understood in light of the triune God in whom we live and move and have our being.

CONCLUSION

The interpretation I have developed over the course of this study proposes a synthesis of Edwards's theological ethics that Edwards himself never attempted. While all the quotations woven into the preceding chapters come directly from Edwards's writings—and I have been careful to interpret them in a way that is consistent with Edwards's main themes and concerns—Edwards never put them together in exactly the way I have. As we have seen, most of Edwards's writings on the moral life followed the form of apologetical discourse. Particularly in *Freedom of the Will* and the *Two Dissertations*, Edwards places his Trinitarian thought in the background and argues his position from points of common agreement. While this strategy is understandable in exercises of apologetics, it is indicative of an internal weakness in Edwards's theological vision that paradoxically derives from his greatest strength. Edwards's confidence that one can discern the triune nature of God in the act of self-reflection and the inclination to love another is essential to the subtlety and power of his Trinitarian reflection and to the centrality of the Trinity in his theological ethics. But at the same time, Edwards's confidence that God's triune relations uphold the nature of things convinces him that he can develop arguments for the moral life that appeal to the nature of things alone.

In Edwards's major writings, this strategy tied his proposals to philosophical positions and arguments that concealed the Trinitarianism that is crucial to the final intelligibility and justification of his theological ethics. Indeed, it is remarkable how quickly the philosophical arguments Edwards developed in his apologetical writings came to be identified as the metaphysical center of his thought. In 1840, Edwards Amasa Park wrote that although Edwards's stature as a theologian was unquestioned, there was need for a more grounded, accessible theology than his:

We need and crave a theology, as sacred and spiritual as his, and moreover one that we can take with us into the flower-garden, and to the top of some goodly hill, and in a sail over a tasteful lake, and into the saloons of music, and to the galleries of the painter and the sculptor, and to the repasts of social joy, and to all those humanizing scenes where virtue holds her sway not merely as an abstract duty of a "love to being in general," but also as the more familiar grace of a love to some beings in particular.[1]

Ironically, as I noted in the introduction, Park had unique access to many of Edwards's Trinitarian writings and wrote the first study of them. Nonetheless, Park did not recognize the extent to which these Trinitarian writings offer a hermeneutic for retrieving from Edwards's thought the theology he so craved.[2]

1. RECAPITULATION

Consequently, in this study I have developed the thesis that Edwards's Trinitarian reflection is essential for understanding his theological ethics. I first explored Edwards's writings on the Trinity in order to see the ways in which the central analogies in his Trinitarian reflection serve as vehicles for his moral reflection. Through drawing comparisons with other paradigmatic Trinitarian formulations by patristic, medieval, and modern theologians, I identified the distinctive points in Edwards's Trinitarian theology. Edwards's psychological analogy discloses not only the triune processions of the Father, Son, and Holy Spirit, but also that the moral life hinges on *theosis*, or "participating in the Divine nature" through the communication of the Holy Spirit. Similarly, Edwards's social analogy discloses not only the nature of the love that exists between the divine persons, but also that the church's identity derives from its destiny to live for eternity in communion with the triune God. Therefore, the goal of the moral life is to love others in such a way that our interpersonal relationships embody the church's eschatological destiny.

In addition, both the psychological and social analogies identify specific aspects of personhood that provide important foci in the moral life. In the psychological analogy, the focus of personhood is in terms of self-consciousness; thus, we know ourselves only as we are known in God. In the social analogy, personhood is defined in terms of interpersonal relations and communion; thus, we are realized as persons to the extent we live in relations of mutuality and self-donation. Running through both of these perspectives on personhood is the common theme that participation in the divine love determines the nature and orientation of a person. Both the psychological and the social analogies portray the personhood of God in terms of love. Love is the "sum of God's temper" and the "bond of union" that unites the triune "society" (H:110; 64). Therefore, love represents the most fundamental category in Edwards's moral thought.

With this interpretation of Edwards's writings on the Trinity in place, I then turned to Edwards's major writings, specifically the *Religious Affections*, *Freedom of the Will*, *Original Sin*, the *Two Dissertations*, and *Charity and*

Its Fruits. Throughout, I argued that viewing these works through the lens of Edwards's Trinitarian thought was essential to identifying what distinctive contributions they offer to contemporary ethics. To touch upon some of the more prominent findings and comparisons: I compared Edwards's Trinitarian anthropology found in the *Religious Affections*, in particular his account of Christian virtue, duty, and practice, with contemporary retrievals of Aristotelian virtue ethics, particularly that of Alasdair MacIntyre. I developed a Trinitarian interpretation of Edwards's account of the will's freedom in *Freedom of the Will*, and compared it with Richard Swinburne's theological defense of autonomy. I developed a Trinitarian interpretation of sin in *Original Sin*, and compared Edwards's accommodation of the problem of evil with John Hick. I provided a Trinitarian interpretation of Edwards's theocentric ethics of love in the *Two Dissertations*, and compared it with discussions of love in contemporary Christian ethics, specifically Gene Outka, Timothy Jackson, and Edward Vacek. Finally, I provided a Trinitarian interpretation of *Charity and Its Fruits*, in particular Edwards's argument that the life of love connects the church's present reality to its eschatological fulfillment, which I compared to current attempts to combine ethics and ecclesiology, specifically those by Stanley Hauerwas and John Zizioulas.

Having completed this exercise, however, it is clear that in addition to identifying Edwards's distinctive perspective on selected topics and discussions within ethics, the Trinitarian interpretation I have developed offers an account of the moral life as a whole. The first feature of this account emerges in the comparison between Edwards and MacIntyre. For all of MacIntyre's insight on tradition dependency and the nature of human flourishing, Edwards's Trinitarian anthropology identifies *the* primary truth claim in Christian theology concerning the relation between divine agency and human nature—all true love for God flows from God's triune Holy Spirit. If this truth claim does not stand at the center of our theological anthropology, then it is arguable whether our anthropology is recognizably Christian. And if this truth claim stands at the center, then our description of what is essential for moral formation must conform to its understanding of the affections and love. Accordingly, Edwards develops a twofold account of human nature, in which humanity's moral excellency is located in our participation in the goodness and love of God, rather than in our natural affections and aptitudes. Further, Edwards's understanding of virtue places transformation and habituation in different categories of being.

An additional feature of this Trinitarian anthropology emerges in the comparisons between Edwards and Swinburne, and later Edwards and Hick. Where Swinburne's emphasis on autonomy yields a theological account that has the atonement as its main focus, Edwards's emphasis on the will's necessity yields a theological account that sees communion in

God's triune life through the indwelling of the Holy Spirit as the end and source of the will's freedom. Edwards defines freedom not as the freedom of choice, which he believes is essentially illusory, but as the freedom to love as God loves. To define freedom in this way maintains the sense in which God and humanity are members of the same moral community and retains the sense in which the incarnate Christ serves as the exemplar of fully realized human freedom. Edwards's understanding of the will's freedom also has implications for his understanding of original sin and evil. Hick rejects the Augustinian account of original sin and develops an account of sin and evil organized around the process of individual "person making." In contrast, Edwards reaffirms the Augustinian account of original sin, particularly the sense of solidarity in sin that is an image of the solidarity Christians have in Christ. This twofold solidarity mirrors the twofold image of God in human nature and provides an accommodation of evil that centers on Christ's transformation of evil through the cross and resurrection.

Another feature of Edwards's Trinitarian anthropology surfaces during the comparisons between Edwards and those who approach Christian ethics from the perspective of love. Although contemporary articulations of *agape* and *philia* resonate with aspects of the love Edwards defends in the *Two Dissertations* and *Charity and Its Fruits*, for Edwards no one form of love represents *the* distinctive Christian love. Rather, the different forms of love follow the paradigm of God's triune relations, which have been revealed through the missions of the Son and the Spirit. In other words, neither *agape* nor *philia* is capable of capturing the total revelation of God's love that orders the Christian life. While *agape*, or "absolute benevolence," represents the quintessence of neighbor-love, the love of *philia* also plays an essential role in our incorporation into the triune love of God. For though Christian love is "an imitation of the eternal love and grace of God and the dying love of Christ," the source and end of all love is participation in the Spirit, who is "the infinite and eternal mutual holy energy between the Father and the Son." Thus, true love "is always mutual." Finally, there is an important role for *eros* in the moral life. Not only is *eros* appropriately expressed in the sexual relations in the created order, but as "complacence" or the delight in "the beauty of another," *eros* follows the paradigm of the love that exists between the Father and the Son. Thus, we appropriately love with complacence those who bear a spiritual "likeness to God." And we appropriately love with complacence God, who is the end of all our desires (Y8:213; 377; 373; 275).

The final feature of Edwards's Trinitarian anthropology becomes evident during the comparisons between Edwards and recent attempts to connect ethics to ecclesiology. For Edwards, the church is not merely a vehicle for moral formation, as it is for Hauerwas, but establishes the *telos* for the moral life. That is to say, Edwards believes that the church's eschatological communion with the Trinity orders all our interpersonal relationships. To participate in the life of the church is to recognize that mutuality and self-giving are normative in all human relationships, for in the triune God, mutual love among persons is supreme. Thus, the church's present reality is always challenged by its future destiny, to which the moral life gives witness. Moreover, for Edwards the church is not a community in which particular relationships, and to some extent particular identities, are transcended, as it is for Zizioulas. Rather, to grow in love with God through the church is a relationship of deepening intimacy and personal discovery, for God's love "flows out" to "every individual member" of the "whole church" (Y8:374).

To be sure, the Trinitarian anthropology evident in Edwards's thought has potentially problematic implications, which can have no part in a retrieval of his theological ethics. As we have seen, Edwards sees within the created order, particularly in gender relations, hierarchies that he justifies on the basis of the economic hierarchy he believes exists in the Trinity. Edwards also does not develop a very sophisticated account for the use of force, and he appears to be unaware of the potential for self-deception and manipulation that can attend decisions to go to war. Finally, Edwards is too willing to accept that divine vindication, in the form of eternal damnation, further manifests the beauty of God. Nonetheless, as we have also seen, within Edwards's Trinitarian thought there are resources for developing more adequate accounts for each of these positions.

2. OTHERNESS AND TRAGEDY

While the Trinitarian interpretation I propose of Edwards's theological ethics offers an account of the moral life as a whole, missing from this account are two presuppositions from postmodernity that pervade a great deal of contemporary theology and ethics. The first is the recognition of "otherness," or alterity. As Colin Gunton notes, within recent Trinitarian theology, the concept of otherness has two aspects. The first reinforces the "ontological distinction or infinite qualitative difference between God and that which is not God," in particular the "contingency of the created order" and "the freedom of the human person." Thus, "because God has otherness—personal freedom and 'space'—within the dynamic of being, he is able to grant the world space to be itself." The second aspect of otherness operates within human "interpersonal relations" and reinforces "the uniqueness and particularity of each person," specifically "the finite qualitative distinction between one person and any other."[3]

The otherness that Gunton refers to is not indigenous to theology, but represents one of the basic intuitions of postmodernity. The principle of alterity was first formulated by John Stuart Mill (1806–1873), and initially turns on whether we can know the mind of another. Mill rejects all knowledge except what is gained from experience, which raises the question, "[B]y what evidence do I know, or by what considerations am I led to believe, that there exist other sentient creatures; that the walking and speaking figures which I see and hear, have sensations and thoughts, or in other words, possess minds?" Only by observation and generalization can one surmise that other minds exist.[4] As the principle of alterity develops, however, it transcends this epistemological problematic, and acquires, in the thought of Emmanuel Levinas (1906–1995), the force of an ethical mandate. For Levinas, any philosophical system that attempts to bridge the gap between the self and the other fails to maintain absolute alterity, and generates ontologies that are coercive and violent. Only by acknowledging and loving the "other *qua* other" do we avoid a similar fate.[5] Finally, for Michael Foucault (1926–1984) the principle of alterity evolves into a valorization of "juxtaposition" and "disjunction" in any form, an emphasis which is summarized in his instruction to "prefer what is positive and multiple, difference over uniformity, flows over unities, mobile arrangements over systems. Believe that what is productive is not sedentary but nomadic."[6]

At first read, Edwards's Trinitarian thought appears to be directly at odds with the concept of alterity. As we have seen, Edwards's understanding of the psychological analogy presupposes that the mind is a spiritual entity that participates in the mind of God. Indeed, Edwards sees the divine mind and human minds as so contiguous that his proposal at times seems to eliminate any sense of alterity altogether. Further, the relation of communion that the social analogy presupposes holds that individuals mutually participate in a common good or love. Although Edwards develops a more nuanced understanding of the distance that separates human minds and communities from their triune exemplars in his major writings, these visions of unity and communion represent the core of his theology, and cannot be altered without compromising its basic identity.

But if Edwards's Trinitarian thought is not able to accommodate the principle of alterity, he does offer a vision of relationality that is receptive to some of its concerns. As we have seen, despite the tendency within the psychological analogy to collapse human consciousness into the divine consciousness, the psychological analogy also stipulates that the divine mind communicates identity to each individual. Although identity is fully realized through participating in the perichoretic love of the Trinity, God maintains the identity even of those who have no inkling of God's love. Further, through the social analogy, Edwards develops an understanding of the Spirit's love as a principle both of self-differentiation as well as incorporation. To live in communion with the triune God is to possess one's individuality to the fullest extent in relation with others. For in the relations of communion, God's Spirit has been graciously bestowed upon the members of the church, so that they may experience the intimacy that exists between the Father and the Son for eternity.

Finally, there is in Edwards's Trinitarian thought an openness that in some ways acknowledges Levinas's argument concerning the coercive and violent nature of ontologies. As we have seen, at one point Edwards uses his Trinitarian reflection to justify hierarchical social arrangements, and to this extent he merits Levinas's criticism. At the same time, however, running through Edwards's Trinitarian reflection is the realization that no single ontology can do justice to the doctrine of the Trinity. This realization stands behind his decision to envision the Trinity through both the psychological and social analogies, as well as through their corresponding metaphysics of idealism and goodness. Further, there is in Edwards's Trinitarian reflection the realization that even these efforts are inadequate, and cannot capture the "mystery" of the Trinity (H:127). While Edwards's Trinitarian reflection provides the horizon against which he plots the moral life, this horizon has within it an eschatological vanishing point of communion with the triune God, which points to a relationship of "concord and harmony and spiritual beauty" that presently "we cannot conceive" (Y13:331). In this sense, Edwards's Trinitarian thought reflects the openness that is evident in many contemporary attempts to develop a Trinitarian theology that incorporates the principle of alterity. Thus, John Milbank offers an articulation of the Trinity that is reminiscent of Edwards's eschatological vision of infinite harmony, though one predicated in such a way that relationships of difference occupy the center. Within the Godhead, relations of "difference" exist between the divine persons that are at once "a response to unity that is more than unity, which unity itself cannot predict." As such, the relations of love within the Trinity cannot "be enclosed within a totality." The "harmony of the Trinity is therefore not a harmony of finished totality but a 'musical' harmony of infinity," in which God speaks "simultaneously" as "the Word incarnate, and as the indefinite spiritual response, in time, which is the Church."[7]

The second presupposition from postmodernity is that of tragedy. Within contemporary theological ethics, the nature of tragedy is not defined in literary terms as the downfall of an important or powerful person through events which expose a fatal flaw. Rather, it is defined, in one sense, as resignation in the face of the intractable contingency in which ethical decisions and actions take place. Thus, Gustafson argues that "many actions" have a "tragic character" that resides in the recognition that "the legitimate pursuit of legitimate ends" entails "severe losses to others—not only persons, but other living things."[8] In another sense, tragedy refers to the inevitable conflicts that prevent the realization of anything like the promises contained in the gospel. Thus, Reinhold Niebuhr writes that "love may qualify the social struggle of history but it will never abolish it, and those who make the attempt to bring society under the domination of perfect love will die on the cross." For those who correctly "behold the cross" recognize that it is at once the "revelation of the divine" and "of what man [sic] ought to be and cannot be" while "enmeshed in the process of history."[9]

Neither sense of tragedy, however, is present in Edwards's theological ethics. One reason for this omission is that Edwards does not place the same emphasis on choice and decision as many contemporary ethicists do, and therefore does not see the first or second sense of tragedy as problematic. If human knowledge of the world is necessarily contingent, Edwards is certain that God's knowledge is not, and therefore each event follows "the gracious design of God's sending his Son into the world" to show God's "infinite mercy and benevolence" (Y1:395). Similarly, while humanity's performative failures throughout history in living the gospel are egregious, Edwards believes that each moment the universe persists in being is evidence of the fact that God's triune redemption of the world continues. For the "various successive states of the world" are "connected in a scheme" and "together attain God's great design" of redemption, into which God invites humanity as "subjects and friends" (Y18:94–95).

Yet such a vision of the church's triune consummation does not blind Edwards to the realities of sin. If anything, it sharpens his sense of how far humanity remains from the eschaton. As we have seen, Edwards is keenly aware of the performative failures in his community to live within the triune love of God. "How careful and eagle-eyed is the merchant to observe and improve his opportunities and advantages," he observes, "how greatly have we forgotten the pious examples of our fathers!" (Y3:154, 198). Consequently, if there is a tragic moment in Edwards's thought, it does not concern the depth of sin into which humanity continually sinks. Rather, it is that we too easily forget that all things have come into being so that humanity may join in the love and joy of God's triune society. For each day is a day in which "the universe is created out of nothing every moment; and if it were not for our imaginations, which hinder us, we might see that wonderful work performed continually, which was seen by the morning stars when they sang together" (Y6:241–42).

3. FINAL REMARKS

Of course, the seriousness of Edwards's failure to incorporate otherness and tragedy depends on whether these presuppositions reflect permanent aspects of the human condition, or just its appearance in our own context.

While pervasive in postmodern thought, it would not be surprising if these intuitions exit the stage in the same way that the points of common agreement that Edwards used to construct his apologetical writings did. Perhaps Edwards provides enough of an accommodation of the concerns of postmodernity in a theological ethics that places God's triune communion at the center. Indeed, on this account, it seems important to respect Edwards's "otherness," so to speak. Now that the Trinitarianism that lies behind Edwards's theological ethics has been retrieved, Edwards's proposal exudes a vitality that is largely absent from contemporary theology and ethics. If God's triune nature was at times too obvious a truth to him, it remains too remote a truth to us. To those who struggle to proclaim the Trinitarian faith, hope, and love, he is an inspiration.

NOTES

INTRODUCTION

1. Roland Delattre, *Beauty and Sensibility in the Thought of Jonathan Edwards: An Essay in Aesthetics and Theological Ethics* (New Haven, Conn.: Yale University Press, 1968), 148–52.

2. Roland Delattre, "Religious Ethics Today: Jonathan Edwards, H. Richard Niebuhr, and Beyond," in *Edwards in Our Time: Jonathan Edwards and the Shaping of American Religion*, ed. C. Guelzo and S. H. Lee (Grand Rapids: Eerdmans, 1999), 68, 74–76. See also Delattre, "The Theological Ethics of Jonathan Edwards: An Homage to Paul Ramsey," *Journal of Religious Ethics* 19 (Fall 1991): 71–102. For an additional presentation of Edwards's ethics through his aesthetics, see Clyde A. Holbrook, *The Ethics of Jonathan Edwards: Morality and Aesthetics* (Ann Arbor, Mich.: University of Michigan Press, 1973).

3. See Y8:96–97.

4. Norman Fiering, *Jonathan Edwards's Moral Thought and Its British Context* (Chapel Hill: University of North Carolina Press, 1981), 82–84.

5. Henry Stob, "The Ethics of Jonathan Edwards," in *Faith and Philosophy: Philosophical Studies in Religion and Ethics*, ed. A. Plantinga (Grand Rapids: Eerdmans, 1964), 124–29.

6. Delattre, *Beauty and Sensibility*, 17–18.

7. See Delattre, "Theological Ethics of Jonathan Edwards," 74–75.

8. For more on the composition and major themes of Edwards's "Miscellanies" notebooks, see Thomas A. Schafer, "Editor's Introduction," Y13:1–90, and Ava Chamberlain, "Editor's Introduction," Y18:1–48.

9. For the dates that Edwards composed these essays, I have drawn from the table found in Y20:38 and in the introductory notes found in Y21:109–11 and Y21:149–52.

10. Edwards Amasa Park, "Remarks on Jonathan Edwards on the Trinity," *Bibliotheca Sacra* 38 (1881): 147–87; 333–69. For more on Park's influence, see Joseph A. Conforti, *Jonathan Edwards, American Tradition, and American Culture* (Chapel Hill: University of North Carolina Press, 1995), 108–44.

11. See, for example, Holbrook, *Ethics of Jonathan Edwards*, 38–77, 97–112, 134–60, and Delattre, *Beauty and Sensibility*, 15–26, 58–114. Although Delattre and Holbrook include in their presentations of Edwards's theological ethics other writings, both privilege the *Two Dissertations* over other writings in his corpus. This tendency is also evident in Fiering's analysis, despite his appreciation for Edwards's Trinitarianism. See Fiering, *Jonathan Edwards's Moral Thought*, 322–61.

12. For example, in his recent study of Edwards's theology, Michael J. McClymond limits his account of Edwards's ethics to the *Two Dissertations*, and dismisses *Freedom of the Will* and *Original Sin* as merely "occasional writings" that are not "central to Edwards' lifelong intellectual concerns." See McClymond, *Encounters with God: An Approach to the Theology of Jonathan Edwards* (New York: Oxford University Press, 1998), 4–5, 50–64.

13. Gene Outka, "The Particularist Turn in Theological and Philosophical Ethics," in *Christian Ethics: Problems and Prospects*, ed. L. S. Cahill and J. F. Childress (Cleveland: Pilgrim Press, 1996), 93–118.

14. Herbert Richardson, "The Glory of God in the Theology of Jonathan Edwards: A Study in the Doctrine of the Trinity" (Ph.D. diss., Harvard University, 1962); Krister Sairsingh, "Jonathan Edwards and the Idea of Divine Glory: His Foundational Trinitarianism and Its Ecclesiastical Import" (Ph.D. diss., Harvard University, 1986).

15. Robert Jenson, *America's Theologian: A Recommendation of Jonathan Edwards* (New York: Oxford University Press, 1988), 18–20, 41–43, 104–6, 121–22, 192–96; Sang Hyun Lee, *The Philosophical Theology of Jonathan Edwards*, expanded ed. (Princeton, N.J.: Princeton University Press, 2000), 173–76, 185–95, 225–27; and idem, "Jonathan Edwards' Dispositional Conception of the Trinity: A Resource for Contemporary Reformed Theology" in *Toward the Future of Reformed Theology: Tasks, Topics, Traditions*, ed. D. Willis and M. Welker (Grand Rapids: Eerdmans, 1999), 444–55; Stephen H. Daniel, *The Philosophy of Jonathan Edwards: A Study in Divine Semiotics* (Bloomington: Indiana University Press, 1994), 102–29; Stephen R. Holmes, *God of Grace and God of Glory: An Account of the Theology of Jonathan Edwards* (Grand Rapids: Eerdmans, 2001), 31–76, 96–98, 163–67, 241–47; Bruce M. Stephens, *God's Last Metaphor: The Doctrine of the Trinity in New England Theology* (Chico, Calif.: Scholars Press, 1981), 1–21; and Janice Knight, "Learning the Language of God: Jonathan Edwards and the Typology of Nature," *William and Mary Quarterly* 48 (October 1991): 531–51.

16. Amy Plantinga Pauw, *The Supreme Harmony of All: The Trinitarian Theology and Ethics of Jonathan Edwards* (Grand Rapids: Eerdmans, 2002).

17. Catherine Mowry LaCugna, *God for Us: The Trinity and the Christian Life* (San Francisco: HarperSanFrancisco, 1993), 380. See also John Thompson, *Modern Trinitarian Perspectives* (New York: Oxford University Press, 1994).

18. Perry Miller, *Jonathan Edwards* (Cleveland: World Publishing Co., 1959), vi, 305. Quoted in Lee, *Philosophical Theology*, 3.

19. Hans W. Frei, *Types of Christian Theology*, ed. G. Hunsinger and W. C. Placher (New Haven, Conn.: Yale University Press, 1992), 4, 81. For a similar typology with regard to ethics, see Gene Outka, "Particularist Turn," 114. Perhaps the closest approximation of the methodology that Frei sketches in *Types* is George A. Lindbeck, *The Nature of Doctrine: Religion and Theology in a Postliberal Age* (Philadelphia: Westminster, 1984).

20. This approach is not only evident in Delattre, *Beauty and Sensibility*, but in virtually every other attempt to present the "philosophical theology" of Edwards. It is also evident in Holbrook, *Ethics of Jonathan Edwards*.

21. Here I refer to Amy Pauw's criticism that the "ad hoc" character of Edwards's Trinitarian reflection is a weakness rather than a strength. Pauw writes that "despite their power and versatility, Edwards' Trinitarian reflections have a distinctively unsettled character. There is an experimental, *ad hoc* quality to his employment of theological traditions that stubbornly resists systematizing." Thus, Pauw later concludes that "a major challenge in drawing on Edwards for con-

structive work is that his theological writings do not reflect the same concern for coherence evident in modern 'systematic' or even 'dogmatic' theologies." See Pauw, *Supreme Harmony of All*, 50, 183–84. In contrast, following Frei, I argue that the ad hoc nature of Edwards's Trinitarian reflection ascribes to the Trinity an important priority in relation to his theological and philosophical discourse. Indeed, to ascribe this priority opens the way for a more complete synthesis of Edwards's major writings than Pauw believes possible, which is what I hope to do in this study of Edwards's Trinitarian ethics.

22. Lindbeck, *Nature of Doctrine*, 81, 87.

23. Rowan Williams, *On Christian Theology* (Oxford: Blackwell, 2000), 40, 42.

24. One particularly important argument for more gender inclusive Trinitarian formulae is Elizabeth A. Johnson, *She Who Is: The Mystery of God in Feminist Theological Discourse* (New York: Crossroad, 1992). While I retain the priority of the traditional Trinitarian formula in my study of Edwards, Johnson's sensitivity regarding the importance of the relations established by the traditional formula is admirable. Moreover, as I hope to show, many of the ethical commitments she draws from Trinitarian relations are evident in Edwards's Trinitarian reflection. See Johnson, *She Who Is*, 191–223.

25. Paula Cooey, "Eros and Intimacy in Edwards," *Journal of Religion* 68 (October 1989): 496.

26. For examples of this commitment, see Lisa Sowle Cahill, "Feminism and Christian Ethics," in *Freeing Theology: The Essentials of Theology from a Feminist Perspective*, ed. C. M. LaCugna (San Francisco: HarperSanFrancisco, 1993), 222–26. See also Cahill, *Between the Sexes: Foundations for a Christian Ethics of Sexuality* (Philadelphia: Fortress Press, 1985).

27. William Babcock, "A Changing of the Christian God: The Doctrine of the Trinity in the Seventeenth Century," *Interpretation* 45 (April 1991), 134.

28. For a sterling example of the intellectual history of Edwards's ethical thought, see Allen C. Guelzo, *Edwards on the Will: A Century of Debate* (Middletown, Conn.: Wesleyan University Press, 1989).

CHAPTER 1

1. Augustine, *The Trinity*, trans. E. Hill, ed. J. E. Rotelle (Brooklyn: New City Press, 1996), VIII.8–9, 247–48. For a concise and clear account of the psychological analogy in Augustine's thought, see Hill's notations and introductions.

2. See also "Miscellanies" entries 94 (Y13:257–58) and 383 (Y13:451–52).

3. See Thomas Schafer's notation in Y13:256.

4. This general description of the two modes draws from several entries in "The Mind," particularly 2, 7, 13, 21a, 22, 23, 24, 27, 31, 34, 40, 42, 43, 51, 53, 54, 59, 61 (Y6:332ff.). The overall content of these entries underlies the more particular quotations of specific phrases and points from "The Mind" in the body of this chapter.

5. As Wallace Anderson writes, Edwards sees "resistance" as the most basic force that attends material things and maintains order in the material universe. It is a force that "resists annihilation" or "division." "Solidity" is "that whereby we conceive a body to fill space, that is, a resistance by which it keeps all other bodies out of the space it occupies so long as it remains there." See Anderson, "Editor's Introduction," Y6:63–68.

6. The passage from the "Essay" I quote in the preceding paragraph is somewhat opaque, and Edwards conflates his thought in it in a way that he does not elsewhere. Thus, the following analysis relies not merely on this paragraph in the "Essay" but also on contemporaneous writings in "The Mind" and the "Miscellanies." In his depiction of the first mode of apprehension, Edwards apparently has in mind basically an empiricist epistemology similar to Locke's, which holds that we encounter "simple" ideas in the physical world through the senses and thereby construct complex ideas in minds that serve as approximate, corresponding reflections of existence. These "associations of ideas," returning to Edwards's terminology and his entries in "The Mind," are constantly modified by new input by the senses. The role of experience in our mental operations is not only that of a retrospective and discriminative repository of what usually pertains, but also that of an ongoing source of revision and reappraisal. But they are at their basis "mental" images that rational beings share in their parsing of experience (Y6:349, 355, 361). See Wallace E. Anderson, "Introduction" in Y6:16–17, 101–102. The formative influence of Locke, and perhaps Berkeley, on Edwards has spawned a significant, if diminishing and no longer fully persuasive, vein of interpretation in Edwards scholarship. For early articulations, see Sereno E. Dwight, *The Life of President Edwards* (New York: G. & C. & H. Carvill, 1830) and Miller, *Jonathan Edwards*, 43–68, and Richardson, "Glory of God in the Theology of Jonathan Edwards," 50–97. For examples of an alternative and opposing vein of interpretation, see Stob, "Ethics of Jonathan Edwards," 111–18; Fiering, *Jonathan Edwards's Moral Thought*, 33–40; and Anderson, "Introduction" in Y6.

7. So Edwards writes that the senses, though "not properly fallible in anything," are not "certain in anything at all, any other than by the constant experience by our senses." Indeed, "our senses are said to deceive us in some things, because our situation does not allow us to make trial, or our circumstances do not lead us to it, and so . . . we are in danger of being deceived by our senses in judging of appearances by our experience in different things, or by judging where we have had no experience of the like" (Y6:369–70). Therefore, this mode of apprehension is often the cause of "prejudice" and not perspicuity. "Those ideas which do not pertain to the prime essence of things such as all colors . . . and all sensations, exceedingly clog the mind in searching into the innermost nature of things, and cast such a mist over things that there is a need of sharp sight to see clearly through." The "world seems so differently to our eyes, to our ears and other senses, from the idea we have of it by reason, that we can hardly realize the latter" (Y6:348–49).

8. Malebranche explains: "God has within Himself the ideas of all the beings He has created." Furthermore, "through His presence God is in close union with our minds, such that He might be said to be the place of minds as space is, in a sense, the place of bodies. Given these two things, the mind surely can see what in God represents created beings, since what in God represents created beings is very spiritual, intelligible, and present to the mind." True knowledge of God therefore occurs "occasionally," in moments where God "communicates" God's idea to the mind, elevating it so that it may grasp the nature of truth (Nicholas Malebranche, *The Search for Truth*, trans. and ed. Thomas M. Lennon and Paul J. Olscamp [New York: Cambridge University Press, 1997], 230–31, 448). Edwards's and Malebranche's occasionalism is similar to that of George Berkeley, but for Berkeley not only God but any "spirit"—by which he means any thinking being—is a force of causation. See the discussion of Berkeley in part 2 of this chapter.

9. Edwards's appropriation of Malebranche's idealism takes place over the course of several essays, and reaches its culmination in "The Mind" when he asserts that "the world therefore is an ideal one" (Y6:351). But it begins in a previous essay titled "Of Being." In this essay, Edwards articulates what he believes is an incontrovertible "principle" that existence necessarily presupposes: It is an "absolute contradiction" to posit the existence of absolute nothingness or "absolute nothing." (In *Freedom of the Will*, he cites this principle as an example of "metaphysical necessity," Y1:152.) To suppose nothingness is to engage in a conceptual act of the mind, and the unavoidable nature of such a conceptual act leads Edwards to the conclusion that consciousness, or the awareness of one's existence, is a necessary part of existence itself: "How it doth grate upon the mind, to think that some thing should be from all eternity, and no thing all the while be conscious of it" (Y6:203). With this principle settled, Edwards then argues that there is no "existence anywhere but in the consciousness," either "created or uncreated" (Y6:204). This is so, Edwards reasons, because if consciousness is definitive of existence, then there can be no part of the material universe conceivable which lacks an attending consciousness. Otherwise, the whole conception of existence would "fall into contradiction," that is, to posit consciousness in one part of an otherwise cold and unthinking universe undermines the reality of the consciousness one predicates. For the purposes of clarity, it is important to note that Edwards composes this line of reasoning in "Of Being" to refute philosophical materialism, that matter is the only reality in the universe, and in this context Edwards speaks of God as identical to "space," or the distance and relations that hold matter in its state of being (Y6:203). But in "The Mind," he develops a positive statement of philosophical idealism, that reality is composed primarily of ideas in God and secondarily in the resistances of matter, and that "the existence of the whole material universe is absolutely dependent on idea" (Y6:353). For a supporting interpretation, see Anderson, "Introduction" in Y6:53–75. For more on Malebranche's influence on Edwards, see Fiering, *Jonathan Edwards's Moral Thought*, 40–45; see also Fiering, "The Rationalist Foundations of Jonathan Edwards's Metaphysics," in *Jonathan Edwards and the American Experience*, ed. N. O. Hatch and H. S. Stout (New York: Oxford University Press, 1988), 73–101; and Wallace Anderson, "Immaterialism in Jonathan Edwards's Early Philosophical Notes," *Journal of the History of Ideas* 25 (1964): 181–200.

10. While it is in some ways farfetched, Edwards holds to this conception of memory in other writings. In "The Mind" entry 57, Edwards writes that "pastness" is "nothing more than a mode of ideas" or a "certain veterascence attending our ideas." In less archaic language, Edwards holds that our memory colors the ideas generated through it with a kind of chronometric quality that puts them in a reasonable and sequential order, analogous to the "natural trigonometry of the eyes" when it judges distance. Thus, the ideas in memory are like other ideas of reflection, howbeit with this quality of "pastness." See Y6:372–73.

11. The term "objective idealism" is coined by Lee in *Philosophical Theology of Jonathan Edwards*, 65.

12. For three different accounts of the success or failure of Edwards's integration of his idealism and his belief in external objects and relations, see Lee, *Philosophical Theology of Jonathan Edwards*, 47–75; Leon Chai, *Jonathan Edwards and the Limits of Enlightenment Philosophy* (New York: Oxford University Press, 1998), 39–71; and James H. Tufts, "Edwards and Newton," *Philosophical Review* 49 (November 1940): 609–22.

13. Augustine, *Trinity*, VI.10, 213. For a recent defense of Augustine's *vestigia trinitatis*, see David Cunningham, "Toward a Rehabilitation of the *Vestigia* Tradition" in *Knowing the Triune God: The Work of the Spirit in the Practices of the Church*, ed. J. J. Buckley and D. S. Yeago (Grand Rapids: Eerdmans, 2001), 179–202.

14. Here my interpretation departs from Pauw's concerning Edwards's typology. Pauw argues that Edwards's "typological worldview" justified his use of "nonscriptural language for the Godhead," that is, the psychological and social analogies. See Pauw, *Supreme Harmony of All*, 37–43. While there is a clear connection between typology and Edwards's Trinitarian thought, it is also clear that Edwards places the divine communication that occurs in the psychological analogy in a very different category than his "types." As Edwards makes clear in "Miscellanies" entry 108, while God "communicates a sort of shadow or glimpse of his excellencies to bodies," these communications are "but the shadows of being, and not real being." Thus, "Christ communicates himself properly only to spirits" (Y13:279). This point of difference is essential for recognizing my thesis that the psychological analogy develops a vision of the moral life that centers on *theosis*.

15. For the sake of economy, I put this problematic in the predominant form it takes for Western Christianity, as opposed to Eastern Christianity, which phrased the problematic in terms of articulating a conception of the plurality of persons in the Godhead that could accommodate unity. This basic distinction follows the typology of Theodore de Regnon. While overlooking some distinctive voices and nuances, Regnon's typology appears on the whole accurate. See Theodore de Regnon, *Etudies de theologie positive sur la Sainte Trinite*, 3 vols. (Paris: Retaux, 1892–1898), quoted in LaCugna, *God for Us*, 11, 18. For more on Eastern Christianity's conception of unity and plurality in God, see Robert Jenson, *The Triune Identity: God according to the Gospel* (Philadelphia: Fortress Press, 1982), 111–14, 162–68; LaCugna, *God for Us*, 53–81; and George Leonard Prestige, *God in Patristic Thought* (London: SPCK, 1956), 242–64.

16. Augustine, *Trinity*, V.1.6, 192. Augustine's articulation of the substance-relation distinction is the main theme of books V–VII in *Trinity*, 190–232.

17. Ibid, V.3.12, 197.

18. Ibid., XV.2.11, 403.

19. Ibid., VII.3.11–4.12, 228–32.

20. Ibid., VIII.3.7, 247.

21. Edmund Hill notes that there are several "psychological trinities" for both the "outer" and "inner" person in books XI–XIV. See Edmund Hill, foreword to books IX–XIV, *The Trinity*, by Augustine, 264–65. See also Eugene Portalie, *A Guide to the Thought of Saint Augustine*, trans. Ralph J. Bastian (Chicago: H. Regnery Co., 1960), 134–35.

22. Augustine, *Trinity*, VIII.5.14, 255.

23. Ibid., VIII.13, 255.

24. Ibid., VI.7, 209.

25. Ibid., IX.4, 273.

26. Ibid., XV.1.5, 398.

27. Ibid., X.4.18, 298. My interpretation here draws from Hill's excellent notations and introductions, which accompany his translation. See, in particular, p. 202 n. 14. For a fuller treatment of these issues, see LaCugna, *God for Us*, 81–109.

28. Ibid., XV.2.11, 403.

29. Here I draw from Ellen Charry, *By the Renewing of Your Minds: The Pastoral Function of Christian Doctrine* (New York: Oxford University Press, 1997), 132–38.

See also A. N. Williams, "Knowledge of God in Augustine's *De Trinitate*" in Buckley and Yeago, eds., *Knowing the Triune God*, 121–46.

30. Here my estimation of Edwards's answer to the problem of unity and plurality in God departs from Pauw, particularly her contention that Edwards is "ambivalent" toward the "simplicity tradition," and occasionally manifests the "tendency to tailor the doctrine of the Trinity to fit with divine simplicity." See Pauw, *Supreme Harmony of All*, 69–70. As I understand Edwards's idealism, he intended it to be the means of rearticulating unity, simplicity, and identity in God in a way that can accommodate plurality better than substance metaphysics. Thus, Edwards's ambivalence is not toward simplicity per se, but toward substance metaphysics. In "The Mind," Edwards denies any of the connotations of substance from classical metaphysics that Augustine utilizes to comprehend God's unity and plurality. In classical metaphysics, substance refers primarily to the underlying stratum that is distinct from the properties, accidents, and relations it upholds, or secondarily to the genus that abstracts what is common among species. See Aristotle, *Metaphysics*, V, 8 1017b25–28. Edwards considers the distinction between genus and species as essentially "arbitrary," if "useful"—a product, in other words, of the first mode of apprehension. Writes Edwards: "What is this putting and tying things together which is done in abstraction? 'Tis not merely a tying of them under the same name; for I do believe that deaf and dumb persons abstract and distribute things into kinds. But it's so putting them together that the mind resolves hereafter to think of them together, under a common notion, as if they were a collective substance. . . . Although this ranking of things be arbitrary, yet there is much more foundation for some distribution than others. Some are much more useful and much better serve the purposes of abstraction" (Y6:340–41.) And regarding the primary sense of substance in classical metaphysics, as Wallace Anderson notes, Edwards rejects the conception of substance as "the owner of properties" in preference for a conception of substance as "the doer of deeds" (Y6:67). "Men are wont," Edwards writes in entry 61, "to suppose that there is some latent substance, or something altogether hid, that upholds the properties of bodies," but "that something is he by whom all things consist" (Y6:380). In my opinion, Edwards tables the conception of substance, considers it generally unhelpful for theological reflection, and only uses it in a broad, perhaps Cartesian, sense of an underlying and supportive rationality in the nature of things. Due to the numerous senses of the word "substance" in the seventeenth and eighteenth centuries, I believe Edwards wise to do so. For supporting arguments of this interpretation, see Lee, *Philosophical Theology of Jonathan Edwards*, 47–78. See also Louis E. Loeb, *From Descartes to Hume: Continental Metaphysics and the Development of Modern Philosophy* (Ithaca, N.Y.: Cornell University Press, 1981), 76–110, 328–35.

31. See Schafer's notations at Y13:442 (n. 4) and Y13:461 (n. 1).

32. See Jürgen Moltmann, *The Trinity and the Kingdom: The Doctrine of God* (Minneapolis: Fortress Press, 1993), 13–16, 139–48. See also Richardson, "Glory of God in the Theology of Jonathan Edwards," 239.

33. The triadic definition of self-consciousness is important to underscore, for Edwards's psychological analogy can appear to entail tritheism. Indeed, other appraisals of Edwards's doctrine of the Trinity see the repetition of the idea as the focal point of his psychological analogy, and on these grounds find Edwards wanting. For example, Paul Helm asserts that the force of Edwards's thought is "tritheistic," because in Edwards's system, "God's Idea of Himself" yields not "another person of the Godhead but another God." For "if a perfect idea of x entails

that x exists then Edwards has proved too much—not a second person of a trinity of persons, but a second *theos*" (H:21). See also Pauw, *Supreme Harmony of All*, 53. Edwards himself is aware of the possibility of this criticism, but he believes that such an objection "arises from a confusion of thought and a misunderstanding of what we say." The self-consciousness of the soul has conceptual priority in his understanding of the divine processions, and it is with this priority in mind that Edwards develops the subsidiary concepts of unity, plurality, and relation. The processions in the Godhead are the necessary outcome of God's own actualization of God's self-consciousness, rather than God's conception of "distinct understandings": "We never suppose the Father generated the Son by understanding the Son, but that God generated the Son by understanding his own essence, and that the Son is that idea itself, or understanding of the essence." Therefore in his system, "we don't suppose that the Father, the Son, and the Holy Ghost are three distinct beings that have three distinct understandings. It is the divine essence that understands, and it is the divine essence understood; 'tis the divine being that loves, and the divine being that is loved" (Y13:392). See also Edwards's reply in Y13:261–62.

34. See also "Miscellanies" entry 697 in Y18:281–82.

35. Edwards writes the same in "Miscellanies" entry 259: " 'Tis evident that there are no more than these three really distinct in God: God, and his idea, and his love or delight. We can't conceive of any further real distinctions. If you say there is the power of God, I answer, the power of a being, even in creatures, is nothing distinct from being itself, besides a mere relation to an effect. If you say there is the infiniteness, eternity, and immutability of God, they are mere modes or manners of existence. If you say there is the wisdom of God, that is the idea of God. If you say there is the holiness of God, that is not different from his love" and "is the Holy Spirit" (Y13:367).

36. Richardson, "Glory of God in the Theology of Jonathan Edwards," 275.

37. Augustine, *Trinity*, XV.5, 398.

38. Ibid., VI.7, 209.

39. Ibid., XV.37, 424. Augustine therefore gives the Spirit the name "Gift" out of respect for the Spirit's mission in the economy.

40. Ibid., XV.10, 402.

41. According to Prestige, the articulation of *perichoresis* from within the "psychological centre of God" has its roots in Athanasius. See Prestige, *God in Patristic Thought*, 284ff.

42. The analogy of the photocopy is admittedly anachronistic, but it captures Edwards's thought concerning knowledge well. The analogy of the signet ring is prevalent in the Neoplatonist thought of Edwards's time. The latter analogy is noted by Edwards in the "Essay," though he interprets it as meaning "that the Son of God is the divine idea of Himself," that is, of God the Father (H:103).

43. For more on the Platonic understanding of participation, see Julius Moravcsik, *Plato and Platonism: Plato's Conception of Appearance and Reality in Ontology, Epistemology, and Ethics, and Its Modern Echoes* (Oxford: Blackwell, 1992), 72–74, 129–67.

44. For an example of the Puritan articulation of this apology, see William Ames, *The Marrow of Theology*, trans. and ed. J. D. Eusden (Boston: Pilgrim Press, 1968), 224–32, 250–54, 300–307. In his discussion of virtue, Ames characterizes well the Puritan "hermeneutics of suspicion" toward autonomous morality with a quotation from Peter Ramus: "If I could wish for what I wanted, I had rather that philosophy were taught to children out of the gospel by a learned theologian of proved

character than out of Aristotle by a philosopher. A child will learn many impieties from Aristotle which, it is feared, he will unlearn too late. He will learn, for example, that the beginnings of blessedness arise out of a man; that the end of blessedness lies in man; that all the virtues are within man's power and obtainable by man's nature, art and industry; that God is never present in such works, either as helper or author, however great and divine they are; that divine providence is removed from the theater of human life; that not a word can be spoken about divine justice; that man's blessedness is based on this frail life" (II.ii.18, 226–27). For more of the Puritan perspective on autonomous morality, see Norman Fiering, *Moral Philosophy at Seventeenth-Century Harvard: A Discipline in Transition* (Chapel Hill: University of North Carolina Press, 1981), chapter 1; and idem, *Jonathan Edwards's Moral Thought*, 48–49.

45. For a comparision between Edwards, Thomas, and Turretin that emphasizes similarities rather than differences, see Anri Morimoto, *Jonathan Edwards and the Catholic Vision of Salvation* (University Park: Pennsylvania State University Press, 1995), 37–69. Aside from our disagreement regarding whether the similarities or differences between Edwards and the latter are more significant, I disagree with Morimoto's depiction of Edwards's alleged preference for "infusion" over "illumination" in speaking of the saints' participation in the divine nature.

46. Francis Turretin, *Institutes of Elenctic Theology*, 3 vols., trans. G. M. Giger, ed. T. Dennison Jr. (Phillipsburg, N.J.: P. & R. Publishing, 1992), 1:190.

47. Ibid., 2:182.

48. Thomas Aquinas, *Summa Theologiae: Latin Text and English Translation*, trans. R. J. Batten (New York: McGraw-Hill, 1964), 2a2ae.23, 2. I do not have the space to comment at length on Thomas's thought on grace. A fuller survey would take into account not only Thomas's remarks on charity in 2a2ae.23, which I examine here, but also his remarks on the "New Law" found in 1a2ae.106–8 and his definition of the Holy Spirit as "Gift" in 1a.38,1.

49. Ibid., 2a2ae.23, 1–2. For more on Thomas's anthropology regarding happiness, see 1a2ae.3–5.

50. Ibid., 2a2ae.23, 3.

51. As R. J. Battin notes, Thomas is more restrained here than in *De Virtutibus* (I.i), where he writes of Lombard's position that it is "ridiculous to say that the very act of love, which we experience when we love God and our neighbor, is the Holy Spirit himself." See *Summa Theologiae*, 34:11, n.d.

52. Aquinas, *Summa Theologiae*, 2a2ae.23, 2.

53. Ibid., 1a.6, 4.

54. Ibid., 2a2ae.23, 2. For more on the influence of Platonism on Thomas's thought, see Patrick Quinn, *Aquinas, Platonism, and the Knowledge of God* (Avebury: Ashgate Publishing, 1996).

55. Ibid., 2a2ae.23, 2.

56. Malebranche, *Search for Truth*, 235.

57. Ibid., 561, 245–46, 574, and 466; italics mine.

58. *The Works of George Berkeley, Bishop of Cloyne*, ed. A. A. Luce and T. E. Jessop (London: Thomas Nelson, 1948), 2:254, quoted in Lee, *Philosophical Theology of Jonathan Edwards*, 59.

59. "We move our legs ourselves," Berkeley writes in his *Philosophical Commentaries* (entry 548), "'tis we that will their movement. Herein I differ from Malebranche"—and, I would add, Edwards. See *The Works of George Berkeley*, 2:154.

60. George Berkeley, *Passive Obedience*, in *Works of George Berkeley*, 6:20–23. For more on Berkeley's moral philosophy, see Paul J. Olscamp, *The Moral Philosophy of George Berkeley* (The Hague, Netherlands: Martinus Nijhoff, 1970).

61. Augustine, *Trinity*, XV.15–25, 407–17.

62. I understand Edwards's image of the sun as primarily a means of explicating his psychological analogy. While Edwards does not unequivocally state this, at times speaking of the sun and the soul as providing "two . . . eminent and remarkable images" (H:126), as I show in the body of this chapter, Edwards conceives of the image of the Trinity in the sun within the terms of the psychological analogy. Further, Edwards also speaks of this connection explicitly (see Y13:434).

63. Tertullian, *Against Praxeas*, in *The Ante-Nicene Fathers*, ed. A. Roberts, J. Donaldson, and A. C. Coxe (Grand Rapids: Eerdmans, 1978), 3:603.

64. See Y6:219–304.

65. Fiering calls this Edwards's "grand strategy in ethical thought" (*Jonathan Edwards's Moral Thought*, 65).

66. Fiering, *Jonathan Edwards's Moral Thought*, 84.

67. For a wider discussion of Edwards's conception of the conscience in comparison to contemporaneous accounts, see Fiering, *Jonathan Edwards's Moral Thought*, 48–149. I depart from Fiering primarily in the emphasis I place on Edwards's construction of other facets and categories in his anthropology as an articulation of the conception of personhood and participation in God that is the basis of his psychological analogy. This direction, as I mention in the introduction, does not go unnoticed by Fiering, but it is left largely undeveloped by him in the interest of carrying on his work in comparative moral philosophy.

68. Here I follow Fiering's exegesis of "Miscellanies" entries 471 and 472, in *Jonathan Edwards's Moral Thought*, 62–64.

69. According to Thomas Schafer, Edwards's shift regarding the conscience is indicative of a growing dissatisfaction with the Puritan doctrine of the "preparatory" work of the Holy Spirit, which holds that the Spirit directly convicts consciences of the unregenerate in a necessary stage of humiliation before the advent of authentic regeneration. Edwards recognized, Schafer argues, that his early conception of conscience, along with the rest of the doctrine of preparation, placed undue emphasis on the individual, and therefore is an exercise of self-love and the antithesis of "true virtue." See Schafer, "Editor's Introduction," in Y13:31–32. And according to Fiering, Edwards's "early theory of conscience," evident as a form of *synteresis* in entry 471, gives way to a "mature" theory in the *Nature of True Virtue* that reiterates the obligation of the "golden rule" in the form of "natural" psychological principles. Edwards develops, Fiering believes, his "mature" theory of conscience after reading moral philosophers who accentuate the autonomy of ethics, especially Samuel Clark, Francis Hutcheson, and David Hume, and he reworks the sense of desert from 472 into an "uneasiness" of mind that follows doing unto others what one would resent others doing to oneself. See Fiering, *Jonathan Edwards's Moral Thought*, 77, 138–39.

70. These terms are what Fiering attributes to the reworking of the golden rule into a psychological principle of "sympathy" or "general benevolence" that one finds in various eighteenth-century moral philosophers. In light of both the content and time of his writings on the Trinity, however, Edwards appears to be simply reiterating his understanding of consciousness. See Fiering, *Jonathan Edwards's Moral Thought*, 138–49.

71. For the other senses of natural conscience, see Y8:595–96 (*synteresis*) and Y8:593 (*sense of desert*).

72. For example, Joseph Butler in his *Fifteen Sermons* (London: Knapton, 1726) constructs a positive account of self-love that all but identifies the dictates of self-love with virtue. Butler defines self-love specifically as a "rational desire" for one's general happiness, or a prudential concern that our lives are full and complete in terms of the different affections, desires, and passions of human nature. Armed with this definition of self-love, Butler argues that "without any prejudice to the cause of virtue and religion, that our ideas of happiness and misery are of all our ideas the nearest and most important to us." Indeed, self-love "ought to prevail over" the concerns of "order and beauty, and harmony, and proportion," in the case of "any" conceivable "inconsistence between them." Although "virtue or moral rectitude does indeed consist in affection to and pursuit of what is right and good," yet "when we sit down in a cool hour, we can neither justify to ourselves this or any other pursuit, till we are convinced that it will be for our happiness, or at least not contrary to it." See Joseph Butler, *Five Sermons Preached at the Rolls Chapel and A Dissertation upon the Nature of Virtue*, ed. S. L. Darwall (Indianapolis: Hackett Publishing Co., 1983), 56.

David Hume, in *A Treatise on Human Nature*, offers a neutral assessment of self-love as a useful principle of human artifice that is an essential component in constructing a just society. According to Hume, the conception of a "public good" derives not from a natural desire of benevolence or a straightforward concern for the common good, but from the individualistic concern to protect private property. The "rules" of justice concerning "properties, rights, and obligations" therefore are abstractions that "have in them no marks of a natural origin" but are the products of "artifice and contrivance." Hume concludes, "'Tis self-love which is their real origin; and as the self-love of one person is naturally contrary to that of another, these several interested passions are obliged to adjust themselves after such a manner as to concur in some system of conduct and behavior." The "system" comprehends "the interest of the individual" and therefore is "advantageous to the public," but it is "not intended for that purpose by the inventors." For Hume, then, self-love is a narrow concern for one's own private interest, independent of the concerns of the common good. One follows the dictates of self-interest, which declare, sometimes to the immediate objections of one's "passions," what is in the long run the best for us. Such a propensity in human nature is neither celebrated nor denigrated but accepted as a fact of life, a kind of mortar that holds the stones of society in place (Hume, *A Treatise of Human Nature*, ed. E. C. Mossner [New York: Penguin Books, 1984], 580–81).

Finally, in Western Christian theology, in both Protestant and Catholic circles, there is an understanding of self-love that is negative. Self-love, in any form, detracts from Christian love of God and neighbor as *agape*. Indeed, from this perspective, true love is defined precisely to the extent to which one denies the self and all considerations of personal happiness or self-interest. Martin Luther declares, "Blessedness is this, to will the will of God and His glory in all things, and to desire nothing of one's own either in this world or the next." (Martin Luther, *Lectures on Romans*, ed. Wilhelm Pauck, Library of Christian Classics [Philadelphia: Westminster Press, 1961], 15:163; quoted in Stephen Garrard Post, *Christian Love and Self-Denial: An Historical and Normative Study of Jonathan Edwards, Samuel Hopkins, and American Theological Ethics* [Lanham, Md.: University Press of America, 1987], 9). Luther's denigration of eudaimonistic concerns for happiness finds a corresponding, if not more intense, voice in the Roman Catholic writer Cornelius Otto Jansen (1585–1638). Jansen argues that self-love stands in radical theological opposition to the love of

God: it is incompatible with it and incapable of being compounded with it in any degree. Thus, self-love is not only to be ignored, but necessarily purged from the soul if one is to truly love as God loves. (Jansen in *French Moralists: The Theory of the Passions, 1585–1649*, ed. Anthony Levi [Oxford: Clarendon Press, 1964], 226; quoted in Fiering, *Jonathan Edwards's Moral Thought*, 155.)

73. "Miscellanies" entry 530, Jonathan Edwards Manuscripts, Beinecke Rare Book and Manuscript Library, Yale University.

74. According to Fiering, Edwards initially adheres to a positive and theocentric portrayal of self-love: "God's own self-love is thus a model of proper self-love." But ultimately, Edwards develops a neutral assessment of self-love as a result of his growing pessimism and psychological realism, along with his interaction with moral sentimentalism and encounter with "secular complacency." For this reason, Edwards's positive depiction of "compounded self-love" in "Miscellanies" entry 530 "seems to be an intermediary theory, and represents the highest possible reach of natural love." Edwards eventually determines that all self-love differs from the true love of God, even if he is "too shrewd a psychologist to accept any blanket condemnations of self-love" (Fiering, *Jonathan Edwards's Moral Thought*, 154, 157, 198). It is important to note that Fiering defines God's self-love merely in terms of the proportionate love of the most perfect being, that is, as an unaltered Neoplatonic sense of self-love. Therefore, it is a stretch to say that Fiering's interpretation of Edwards's positive attitude toward self-love bears the marks of his Trinitarian reflection. I include it in deference to Fiering's earlier intuitions regarding the Trinity in *Jonathan Edwards's Moral Thought*, 82–84.

According to Stephen Post, Edwards developed his doctrine of the Trinity "late in his career," particularly as it is found in the "Essay," to justify his long-standing "Augustinian" attitude toward happiness and self-love in opposition to the proponents of the agapeistic school of "pure" or "disinterested benevolence." As a "Puritan Augustinian," however, Edwards is unique to the extent that he tries in his ethical writings, particularly the *Religious Affections* and *True Virtue*, to develop a "real appreciation for the ideal of pure disinterested love." Thus, Edwards moves from an overtly positive to neutral, if not implicitly negative, attitude toward self-love, to the extent that in the midst of his accommodation of "pure benevolence," he would "not allow benevolence to throw all self-love to the winds" (Post, *Christian Love and Self-Denial*, 44–55).

75. Karl Rahner, *The Trinity*, trans. J. Donceel (New York: Crossroad, 1997), 22. For more on Rahner's principle in current Trinitarian theology, see LaCugna, *God for Us*, 209–41.

76. Karl Barth, *Church Dogmatics*, I/1, trans. G. W. Bromiley, ed. G. W. Bromiley and T. F. Torrance (Edinburgh: T. & T. Clark, 1995), 338–39.

77. Colin Gunton, *The Promise of Trinitarian Theology*, 2d ed. (Edinburgh: T. & T. Clark, 1997), 42–44, 54.

78. Lee, *Philosophical Theology of Jonathan Edwards*.

CHAPTER 2

1. This passage is not technically part of entry 96, but represents Edwards's summary in entry 104 (Y13:272).

2. Jonathan Edwards, "Miscellanies" entry 1182, in *The Philosophy of Jonathan Edwards from His Private Notebooks*, ed. H. G. Townsend (Westport, Conn.: Greenwood Press, 1972), 140.

3. In the interest of clarity, I have updated Edwards's spelling of "oeconomy" to "economy."

4. In this way, Edwards's use of "economy" approximates its earliest understanding in Christian theology, namely, Tertullian's "mystery of the economy" (*sacramentum economiae*), which explores how the "oneness" of God differentiates "into threeness, setting forth three, Father, Son, and Holy Spirit" (Tertullian, *Against Praxeas*, in *The Ante-Nicene Fathers*, vol. 3, A. Roberts, J. Donaldson, and A. C. Coxe, eds. [Grand Rapids: Eerdmans, 1978] 2, 595). According to George Leonard Prestige, this use of "economy" differs from the order of God's triune missions in direct relation to creation. See Prestige, *God in Patristic Thought*, 99–106. For more on the development of the word "economy" and the "Economic Trinity," as well as a review of the critical literature, see LaCugna, *God for Us*, 21–52, 209–41.

5. According to Paul Helm, the position Edwards opposes is similar to that espoused by Thomas Ridgley in his *Body of Divinity* (1731). See H:94 n. 1.

6. In the "Observations," Edwards does not offer any particular scriptural citations, but does indirectly refer to 1 Cor. 15:20–28. He probably is thinking, among others, of the relations referred to in the Gospel of John (3:16; 5:36–38; 7:28; 12:49; 14:16–26; and 17:1–5).

7. 1 Cor. 15:24–26.

8. While we develop different aspects of Edwards's appropriation of the "Covenant of Redemption," Amy Pauw's discussion of the different permutations of covenant theology is concise and helpful. See Pauw, *Supreme Harmony of All*, 91–118. For two different interpretations of covenant theology in New England Puritanism, see Perry Miller, *The New England Mind: The Seventeenth Century* (Cambridge, Mass.: Harvard University Press, 1983), 365–462; and Janice Knight, *Orthodoxies in Massachusetts: Rereading American Puritanism* (Cambridge, Mass.: Harvard University Press, 1997), 89–129. Two other important works on covenant theology are Charles Lloyd Cohen, *God's Caress: The Psychology of Puritan Religious Experience* (New York: Oxford University Press, 1986); and Michael McGiffert, "Grace and Works: The Rise and Division of Covenant Divinity in Elizabethan Puritanism," *Harvard Theological Review* 75 (October 1982): 463–502. For studies of Edwards's use of covenant theology, see Conrad Cherry, *The Theology of Jonathan Edwards: A Reappraisal* (Bloomington: Indiana University Press, 1990), 106–23, and Harry S. Stout, "The Puritans and Edwards," in *Jonathan Edwards and the American Experience*, ed. N. O. Hatch and H. S. Stout (New York: Oxford University Press, 1988), 142–59.

9. I draw this example from Prestige, *God in Patristic Thought*, 285.

10. *Epistola Papae Leonis ad Flavianum ep. Constantinopolitanum de Eutyche*, in *Decrees of the Ecumenical Councils*, ed. N. P. Tanner (Washington, D.C.: Georgetown University Press, 1990), 1:79.3–7; cited in Robert W. Jenson, *Systematic Theology*, vol. 1, *The Triune God* (New York: Oxford University Press, 1997), 131.

11. In Ephraim Chamber's *Cyclopedia* (London, 1728), a resource Edwards makes use of in writings such as the *Religious Affections* (Y2:282–83), there is the following entry under "communication": "Communication *of idioms*, in theology, the act of imparting the attributes of one of the natures in Jesus Christ, to the other. The communication of idioms, is founded on the union of two natures in person of Christ: by this communication of idioms it is, that we say, God suffered, died, &c. which

is strictly understood of the human nature; and signifies, that God suffered in his humanity, that he died as to human nature, &c. For the denominations which signify natures, or properties of nature, the schoolmen tell us, are denominations of suppositums, or persons, and are to be attributed to them: thus, the two natures only subsisting in Jesus Christ by the sole person of the word, to this person must be attributed the denominations of both natures, and of their properties. But we may not by communication of idioms attribute to Jesus Christ what would suppose him not to be God; since that would destroy the hypostatical union, which is the foundation of the communication of idioms. Thus we may not say that Jesus Christ is mere man; that he is fallible, &c."

12. Thus, in a sermon on Isaiah (51:8), Edwards explicitly states that "the divine nature is not capable of suffering," for "it is impassible and infinitely above all suffering" (Y9:295–96).

13. In "Miscellanies" entries 308 and 309, Edwards makes it clear that he understands the Logos as identical to the divine nature: "The name of the second person in the Trinity, Λογος, evidences that he is God's idea," and "the perfect idea God has of himself is truly and properly God" (Y13:393). Although Arianism flourished during the fourth and fifth centuries, it reappeared during the eighteenth century, particularly in Samuel Clarke's *Scripture-Doctrine of the Trinity* (n.p., 1712). For more on the earlier manifestations of Arianism, see Richard Patrick Crossland Hanson, *The Search for the Christian Doctrine of God: The Arian Controversy 318–381* (Edinburgh: T. & T. Clark, 1988); and Thomas C. Pfizenmaier, *The Trinitarian Theology of Dr. Samuel Clarke (1675–1729): Context, Sources, and Controversy* (New York: E. J. Brill, 1997).

14. Augustine, *Trinity*, I.iv.25, 84. Augustine's statement of the doctrine depends on his earlier discussion in I.iii.18, 77–79.

15. Aquinas, *Summa Theologiae*, 3.3.5.

16. Here I follow LaCugna, *God for Us*, 97–101.

17. Irenaeus, *Against Heresies*, III.22.3, in *Irenaeus of Lyons*, trans. and ed. R. M. Grant (New York: Routledge, 1997), 140. For my discussion of *Anakephalaiosis*, I have drawn on Robert McQueen Grant, "Rhetoric in Theology," in the same volume, 50–53.

18. Irenaeus, *Against Heresies*, III.224–25, 140–41.

19. Edwards encountered Chrysostom through John Hurrion's *The Knowledge of Christ Glorified, opened and applied in twelve sermons on Christ's resurrection, ascension, sitting at God's right hand, intercession and judging the world* (London, 1729), 196–98. The discourse was later printed in *The Whole Works of John Hurrion*, 3 vols. (London: Printed for R. Baynes by J. Henman, 1823), 2:128–32. See Y18:363 n. 3. Although Hurrion does not give the citation, "οὕτως [ἂν γένοιτο] ἀκριβὴς συνάφεια, ὅταν ὑπὸ μίαν ἅπαντα ἀχθείη κεφαλὴν, σύνδεσμόν τινα ἀναγκαῖον ἄνωθεν ἔχοντα," most likely comes from a passage at the end of St. John Chrysostum's first homily on Ephesians. See J. P. Migne, *Patrilogiae Cursus Completus; omnium SS. Patrum, Doctorum Scripturumque Ecclesiasticorum, sive Latinorum, sive Graecorum* (Turnhout, Belgium: Brepols, 1844–1963), 62:16. This passage appears in translation in *A Select Library of the Nicene and Post-Nicene Fathers*, ed. P. Schaff (Grand Rapids: Eerdmans, 1956), 13:54–55. I am grateful to both Christopher Bryan and James Dunkly at the University of the South for helping me track down this reference.

20. For more on this early articulation of the social analogy, see Prestige, *God in Patristic Thought*, 242–64, and LaCugna, *God for Us*, 66–68.

21. Augustine, *Trinity*, III.9, 132.

22. Ibid., IV.12, 161.

23. Ibid., IV.17, 165.

24. Ibid., IV.27, 172.

25. Ibid., V.12, 197.

26. Ibid., XV.31–32, 421.

27. Ibid., V.5, 191 (italics mine).

28. Ibid., V.7, 193.

29. Aristotle's depiction of friendship in books 8 and 9 of the *Nicomachean Ethics* established the paradigm of friendship in classical thought. Although the *Nicomachean Ethics* provides the most extended treatment of Aristotle's account of friendship, passages in the *Eudemian Ethics* (VII, 1234b1–1246a25), the *Rhetoric* (II.4, 1381a1–32), and the *Magna Moralia* (II.xi–xvii, 1208b1–1213b30) provide clarification and amplification. Two important essays on classical friendship are John Cooper, "Aristotle on Friendship" in *Essays on Aristotle's Ethics*, ed. A. O. Rorty (Berkeley: University of California Press, 1980), and Martha Nussbaum, *The Fragility of Goodness: Luck and Ethics in Greek Tragedy and Philosophy* (New York: Cambridge University Press, 1986), 343–72. See also Cicero, *On Old Age and On Friendship*, trans. F. O. Copley (Ann Arbor: University of Michigan Press, 1967), who provided Augustine with his knowledge of classical friendship.

30. Supporting arguments for this interpretation of Augustine on classical friendship are those of Marie A. MacNamara, *Friends and Friendship for Saint Augustine* (Staten Island, N.Y.: St. Paul Publishers, 1964); Oliver O'Donovan, *The Problem of Self-love in St. Augustine* (New Haven, Conn.: Yale University Press, 1980), 118, 125–27; John Burnaby, *Amor Dei: A Study of the Religion of St. Augustine* (London: Hodder & Stoughton, 1960), 256ff.; Robert Adams, "The Problem of Total Devotion," in *Friendship: A Philosophical Reader*, ed. Neera Kapur Badhwar (Ithaca, N.Y.: Cornell University Press, 1993).

31. Augustine, "Sermon 336.2," trans E. Hill, ed. J. E. Rotelle, in *The Works of Saint Augustine: A Translation for the Twenty-first Century*, pt. 3, vol. 9 (Hyde Park, N.Y.: New City Press, 1994), 267.

32. Augustine, "On Christian Doctrine," in *A Select Library of the Nicene and Post-Nicene Fathers of the Christian Church*, ed. P. Schaff (Grand Rapids: Eerdmans, 1993), I.iv.4, 523. Here my interpretation draws from Oliver O'Donovan, who argues that Augustine's later writings place the love of neighbor in a different category from the love of friendship, the latter being at best an instrumental good one should "use" rather than "enjoy." See O'Donovan, "Usus and Fruitio in Augustine, De Doctrina Christiana I," *Journal of Theological Studies* 23 (October 1982): 361–97.

33. Augustine, *Trinity*, VI.7, 209.

34. Pseudo-Dionysius the Areopagite, *The Divine Names*, in *The Complete Works*, trans. C. Luibheid (Mahwah, N.J.: Paulist Press, 1987), 71–96.

35. Richard of St. Victor, *The Twelve Patriarchs; The Mystical Ark; Book Three of the Trinity*, trans. G. A. Zinn (Mahwah, N.J.: Paulist Press, 1979), III.vi, 379.

36. Richard, *Book Three of the Trinity*, III.xviii, 391.

37. For more on Richard of St. Victor, and whether he can be adequately construed as positing a precursor of modern "social trinitarianism," see Nico den Bok, *Communicating the Most High: A Systematic Study of Person and Trinity in the Theology of Richard of St. Victor* (Paris: Brepols, 1996), esp. 431–75. See also Ewert Cousins, "A Theology of Interpersonal Relations," in *Thought* 45 (spring 1970): 56–82.

38. The three works are *Commentaries on the Four Books of Sentences*, the *Breviloquium*, and the *Itinerarium mentis ad Deum*, selections of which can be found in

Edmund J. Fortman, *The Triune God: A Historical Study of the Doctrine of the Trinity* (Grand Rapids: Baker Book House, 1982), 212–17. Also helpful is *Saint Bonaventure's Disputed Questions on the Mystery of the Trinity*, trans. Z. Hayes (St. Bonaventure, N.Y.: Franciscan Institute, St. Bonaventure University, 1979).

39. Fortman, *Triune God*, 210–13.

40. Bonaventure, *The Triple Way, or Love Enkindled* in *The Works of Bonaventure, Cardinal, Seraphic Doctor, and Saint: Vol. I Mystical Opuscula*, trans. J. de Vinck (Paterson, N.J.: St. Anthony Guild Press, 1960), 63.

41. Aquinas, *Summa Theologiae*, 1a.32, 1.

42. Ibid., 1a.27. Interestingly enough, in his earlier commentary on Peter Lombard's *Sentences*, Thomas did espouse a form of the social analogy, which is strikingly similar to Edwards's argument from the nature of goodness. Thomas writes that "the good is communicative of itself. But God is good in the highest degree. But he does not communicate himself in the highest degree in creatures, because they do not receive all his goodness. Therefore, there must be a perfect communication, resulting in his communicating all his goodness [with] another. But that cannot be in a diversity of essence; therefore, there must be more than one distinct [person] in the unity of the divine essence" (Thomas Aquinas, *Scriptum super Sententias*, I, d. 2, q. 1, a. 4, s.c.; quoted in Norman Kretzmann, "A General Problem of Creation: Why Would God Create Anything at All?" in *Being and Goodness: The Concept of the Good in Metaphysics and Philosophical Theology*, ed. S. MacDonald (Ithaca, N.Y.: Cornell University Press, 1991), 219. As Kretzmann notes, Thomas does not reiterate this argument in any of his major theological works.

43. Aquinas, *Summa Theologiae*, 1a.29, 3.

44. Thomas Aquinas, *Compendium Theologiae*, 226, in *Theological Texts*, ed. T. Gilby (London: Oxford University Press, 1955), 311. My analysis of Thomas on these points follows L. Gregory Jones, *Transformed Judgement: Toward a Trinitarian Account of the Moral Life* (Notre Dame, Ind.: University of Notre Dame Press, 1990), 100–108.

45. Aquinas, *Summa Theologiae*, 3a.46, 3.

46. Ibid., 2a2ae.24, 2.

47. Ibid., 2a2ae.23, 1.

48. Cotton Mather, *Blessed Unions* (Boston: B. Green & J. Allen, 1692), 47–48. For the sake of economy, I focus on Mather, though other examples in Puritan and Reformed theology are available. One other predecessor with whom Edwards is familiar is Petrus van Mastricht, *Theoretico-practica theologia*, ed. *Nova* (Utrecht, 1699). Edwards mentions van Mastricht in "Miscellanies" entry 482, noting the latter's acceptance of the social analogy as it pertains to the economic Trinity (Y13:524). But it is important to note that, like Mather, van Mastricht believes that the social analogy pertains solely to the economic Trinity. His discussion of the immanent Trinity largely follows the traditional Augustinian version of the psychological analogy with its attending substance metaphysics. See van Mastricht, *Theoretico-practica theologia*, 235–74. While Schafer refers to van Mastricht as "one of the major influences" on Edwards, it is clear that, particularly in his Trinitarian reflection, Edwards blazed new paths. See Y13:319 n. 2. On this point, Pauw and I agree. See Pauw, *Supreme Harmony of All*, 74.

49. Mather, *Blessed Unions*, 6.

50. Ibid., 23, 25.

51. Ibid., 43, 44.

52. This resemblance, Mather cautions, does not signify "equality" but "similitude" (*Blessed Unions*, 45).

53. Mather, *Blessed Unions*, 48, 49.

54. Zachary Hayes has recently argued that the proper way to interpret Bonaventure's focus on the spiritual development of the individual is not merely on the "spiritual journey of the individual person" but also the "spiritual journey of the church itself." Although this point may be valid, nonetheless Bonaventure does not view the social analogy as a model for interpersonal relations as Edwards does. See Zachary Hayes, O.F.M., *Bonaventure: Mystical Writings* (New York: Crossroad, 1999), 146.

55. Here I am indebted to Oliver O'Donovan, *Resurrection and Moral Order: An Outline for Evangelical Ethics*, 2d ed. (Grand Rapids: Eerdmans, 1994), 31–75. When viewed from the perspective of his Trinitarian writings, Edwards's theological ethics are much more in line with O'Donovan's project than O'Donovan himself believes to be the case. See O'Donovan, *Resurrection and Moral Order*, 228. Moreover, Edwards's view of the transformation of the created order adds much to O'Donovan's account, which by comparison overemphasizes the created order and underemphasizes its eschatological fulfillment.

56. Although he does not mention it, here Edwards demonstrates an awareness of the three types of friendship Aristotle identifies in the *Nicomachean Ethics*, book 8, 1156a6–1156b30.

57. Here I draw from Robert W. Jenson, "The End Is Music," in *Edwards in Our Time: Jonathan Edwards and the Shaping of American Religion*, ed. S. H. Lee and A. C. Guelzo (Grand Rapids: Eerdmans, 1999), 168–71.

58. Manuscripts, Jonathan Edwards Collection, Beinecke Rare Book and Manuscript Library, Yale University.

59. Thomas Aquinas, *De potentia* III.15c; quoted in Norman Kretzmann, "General Problem of Creation," 215. Much of what I argue concerning Edwards, Kretzmann argues concerning Bonaventure, and it appears that the two offer similar proposals regarding the relation between God's diffusive goodness and creation.

60. Although he does not directly attach his remarks in entry 679 to the social analogy, Edwards does write, "Hence we learn how all God's love may be resolved into his love to himself and delight in himself, as asserted in my *Discourse on the Trinity*. His love to the creature is only his inclination to glorify himself and communicate himself" (Y18:239).

61. As many have noted, this theme received special prominence in Irenaeus's thought, after which it became a widely accepted theological maxim. See *Against Heresies*, IV.14.1, 147. For more on Irenaeus's defense of *creatio ex nihilo*, see Gerald May, *Creatio Ex Nihilo: The Doctrine of "Creation out of Nothing" in Early Christian Thought*, trans. A. S. Worrall (Edinburgh: T. & T. Clark), 164–78.

62. Augustine, *Trinity*, V.10, 196.

63. Aquinas, *Summa Theologiae*, 1a.29, 3.

64. This concern for trithesism, it is perhaps necessary to note, is different from that identified by Helm and Pauw in the previous chapter, which concerns the idealism generated by Edwards's psychological analogy. Here the question concerns whether or not Edwards overemphasizes the individuality of the divine persons to the detriment of the principle of divine unity.

65. Here my interpretation differs from Pauw's, who holds that Edwards's social analogy, particularly in the covenant of redemption, operates with an "atomistic

view of personhood" that ascribes to the Son an "indissoluble right to self-determination." As a result, Pauw believes that Edwards's social analogy runs the risk of "succumbing to tritheism" (Pauw, *Supreme Harmony of All*, 77, 114–15).

66. Sermon on John 15:10, Beinecke Rare Book and Manuscript Library, Yale University; quoted in Pauw, *Supreme Harmony of All*, 106.

67. "Miscellanies," entry 864.

68. Ola Elizabeth Winslow, *Jonathan Edwards: 1703–1758* (New York: Collier Books, 1961), 69.

69. Patricia J. Tracy, *Jonathan Edwards, Pastor: Religion and Society in Eighteenth-Century Northampton* (New York: Hill & Wang, 1980), 149, 192.

70. Ava Chamberlain, "Brides of Christ and Signs of Grace: Edwards' Sermon Series on the Parable of the Wise and Foolish Virgins," in *Jonathan Edwards's Writings: Text, Context, Interpretation*, ed. S. J. Stein (Bloomington: Indiana University Press, 1996), 5, 7. As Chamberlain notes, her article applies an interpretation of Puritan piety by Amanda Porterfield to Edwards's sermon series on Matt. 25:1–12. By doing so, Chamberlain corrects Porterfield's own analysis of Edwards. See Amanda Porterfield, *Female Piety in Puritan New England: The Emergence of Religious Humanism* (New York: Oxford University Press, 1992), 155–56. Pauw notes some of these tensions in *Supreme Harmony of All*, 33–34.

71. Pauw, *Supreme Harmony of All*, 116.

72. For an important discussion of the difficulties surrounding the justification of hierarchy on theological grounds, see Kathryn Tanner, *The Politics of God: Christian Theologies and Social Justice* (Minneapolis: Fortress Press, 1992), 127–56.

73. LaCugna, *God for Us*, 393.

74. Margaret Farley, "New Patterns of Relationship: Beginning of a Moral Revolution," *Theological Studies* 36 (1975): 644–46.

75. Though it is true that the Pauline letters, as well as the other writings of the New Testament, contain no fully developed doctrine of the Trinity, Edwards's ascription of what we might call a "latent Trinitarianism" in the New Testament finds support in recent scholarship. See Gordon D. Fee, "Paul and the Trinity: The Experience of Christ and the Spirit for Paul's Understanding of God," in *The Trinity: An Interdisciplinary Symposium on the Trinity*, ed. S. Davis, D. Kendall, and G. O'Collins (New York: Oxford University Press, 1999), 49–72. See also David Yeago, "The Spirit, the Church, and the Scriptures: Biblical Inspiration and Interpretation Revisited," in *Knowing the Triune God: The Work of the Spirit in the Practices of the Church*, ed. J. J. Buckley and D. S. Yeago (Grand Rapids: Eerdmans, 2001), 49–93.

76. "We declare to you what we have seen and heard so that you also may have fellowship with us; and truly our fellowship is with the Father and with his Son Jesus Christ" (NRSV).

77. J. N. D. Kelly, *Early Christian Doctrines*, 5th rev. ed. (San Francisco: HarperSanFrancisco, 1978), 276.

78. Gunton, *Promise of Trinitarian Theology*, 51.

79. Moltmann, *Trinity and the Kingdom*, 172, 174. See also Gunton, *Promise of Trinitarian Theology*, 195–201; and LaCugna, *God for Us*, 243–305.

80. Karl Barth, *Church Dogmatics*, I/1, trans. G. W. Bromiley, ed. G. W. Bromiley and T. F. Torrance (Edinburgh: T. & T. Clark, 1995), 358.

81. Kathryn Tanner, *Jesus, Humanity, and the Trinity: A Brief Systematic Theology* (Minneapolis: Fortress Press, 2001), 83.

82. Rowan Williams, *On Christian Theology* (Oxford: Blackwell, 2000), 228, 231.

CHAPTER 3

1. Karl Barth, *Church Dogmatics, The Doctrine of God*, II, 2, trans. G. W. Bromiley (Edinburgh: T. & T. Clark, 1987), 543–57. See also Nigel Biggar, "Barth's Trinitarian Ethic," in *The Cambridge Companion to Karl Barth*, ed. J. B. Webster (New York: Cambridge University Press, 2000), 212–27.

2. See Hans Urs von Balthasar, *Mysterium Paschale: The Mystery of Easter*, trans. A. Nichols (Grand Rapids: Eerdmans, 1993). For an important study of von Balthasar's theological ethics, see Christopher Steck, *The Ethical Thought of Hans Urs von Balthasar* (New York: Herder & Herder, 2001). See also Anne Hunt, "Hans Urs von Balthasar: Love Alone Is Credible," in *The Trinity and the Paschal Mystery: A Development in Recent Catholic Theology* (Collegeville, Minn: Liturgical Press, 1997), 57–88.

3. For representatives of this approach as both a historical and theological thesis, see Perry Miller, "Jonathan Edwards on the Sense of the Heart," *Harvard Theological Review* 41 (April 1948): 123–45; idem, *Errand into the Wilderness* (Cambridge, Mass.: Belknap Press of Harvard University Press, 1956), 167–203; John E. Smith, "Jonathan Edwards: Piety and Practice in the American Character," *Journal of Religion* 54 (April 1974): 166–80; idem, "Testing the Spirits: Jonathan Edwards and the Religious Affections," *Union Seminary Quarterly Review* 37 (fall–winter 1981–1982): 27–37; Wayne Proudfoot, "From Theology to a Science of Religions: Jonathan Edwards and William James on Religious Affections," *Harvard Theological Review* 82 (April 1989): 149–68; idem, "Perception and Love in *Religious Affections*," in *Jonathan Edwards's Writings: Text, Context, Interpretation*, ed. S. J. Stein (Bloomington: Indiana University Press, 1996), 122–36; William Wainwright, *Reason and the Heart: A Prolegomenon to a Critique of Passional Reason* (Ithaca, N.Y.: Cornell University Press, 1995), 7–54; Daniel Walker Howe, *Making the American Self: Jonathan Edwards to Abraham Lincoln* (Cambridge, Mass.: Harvard University Press, 1997), 33–47; and James Gilman, *Fidelity of Heart: An Ethic of Christian Virtue* (New York: Oxford University Press, 2001).

4. For representatives of this approach as a historical and theological thesis, see Winslow, *Jonathan Edwards*, 182–99; Tracy, *Jonathan Edwards, Pastor*, 123–45; William Breitenbach, "Piety and Moralism: Edwards and the New Divinity," in *Jonathan Edwards and the American Experience*, ed. N. O. Hatch and H. S. Stout (New York: Oxford University Press, 1988), 177–204; idem, "Religious Affections and Religious Affectations: Antinomianism and Hypocrisy in the Writings of Edwards and Franklin," in *Benjamin Franklin, Jonathan Edwards, and the Representation of American Culture*, ed. B. B. Oberg and H. S. Stout (New York: Oxford University Press, 1993), 13–26; and Chamberlain, "Self-Deception as a Theological Problem."

5. John Smith, "Editor's Introduction," Y2:17–18.

6. It has been long noted that Edwards did not accept traditional faculty psychology. See, for example, Miller, *Jonathan Edwards*, 177ff. Compare Miller's account with Howe, *Making the American Self*, 33ff. Commentators on Edwards generally fail to notice that Edwards draws from *both* Locke and Malebranche to develop his understanding of the faculties.

7. Plato, *The Republic*, IV.439a–440d. For this description, I have drawn on Terence Irwin, *Plato's Ethics* (New York: Oxford University Press, 1995); and C. D. C. Reeve, *Philosopher-Kings: The Argument of Plato's Republic* (Princeton, N.J.: Princeton University Press, 1988), 43–53, 118–59, and 167–69.

8. John Locke, *An Essay concerning Human Understanding*, ed. P. H. Nidditch (Oxford: Clarendon Press, 1975), 236–44.

9. Malebranche, *Search for Truth*, 2, 560.

10. John Calvin, *Institutes*, quoted in Terrence Erdt, *Jonathan Edwards, Art and the Sense of the Heart* (Amherst: University of Massachusetts Press, 1980), 13.

11. In the secondary literature on Edwards, many believe that Edwards used "Miscellanies" entry 782 as a preliminary study of his argument in the *Religious Affections*. See, for example, Smith, "Editor's Introduction," Y2:52; and Miller, "Jonathan Edwards on the Sense of the Heart."

12. Robert W. Jenson, *Systematic Theology*, vol. II, *The Works of God* (New York: Oxford University Press, 1999), 53–55.

13. Obviously, the typology I offer here cannot do full justice to the permutations of virtue in the classical tradition, especially Stoic virtue theories. For a helpful survey of these virtue theories, as well as the correspondent understanding of nature and the universe, see Julia Annas, *The Morality of Happiness* (New York: Oxford University Press, 1993).

14. For more on Plato's theory of virtue see Irwin, *Plato's Ethics*; and Reeve, *Philosopher-Kings*. See also Gregory Vlastos, "The Virtuous and the Happy: Plato's Moral Theory," in *Socrates, Plato, and Their Tradition*, vol. 1 of *Studies in Greek Philosophy*, ed. D. W. Graham (Princeton, N.J.: Princeton University Press, 1995), 126–32.

15. For more on Aristotle's theory of virtue, see J. O. Urmson, *Aristotle's Ethics* (Malden, Mass.: Blackwell, 1988); William Francis Ross Hardie, *Aristotle's Ethical Theory*, 2d ed. (New York: Oxford University Press, 1980); and D. S. Hutchinson, "Ethics," in *The Cambridge Companion to Aristotle*, ed. J. Barnes (New York: Cambridge University Press, 1995).

16. As with classical accounts of virtue, my presentation of Augustine and Aquinas does not do full justice to the many accounts of virtue in Christian theology. See, for example, Rega Wood, *Ockham on the Virtues* (West Lafayette, Ind.: Purdue University Press, 1997).

17. For more on Augustine's theory of virtue, see Bonnie Kent, "Augustine's Ethics," in *The Cambridge Companion to Augustine*, ed. E. Stump and N. Kretzmann (New York: Cambridge University Press, 2001); George J. Lavere, "Virtue," in *Augustine through the Ages: An Encyclopedia*, ed. A. D. Fitzgerald (Grand Rapids: Eerdmans, 1999); and James Wetzel, *Augustine and the Limits of Virtue* (Cambridge: Cambridge University Press, 1992).

18. Aquinas, *Summa Theologiae*, 1a2ae.55–67; 2a2ae.23. For more on Thomas's theory of virtue, see Ralph McInerny, "Ethics," in *The Cambridge Companion to Aquinas*, ed. E. Stump and N. Kretzmann (Cambridge: Cambridge University Press, 1993). It is important to note that Thomas's appropriation of Aristotle only presents one part of his understanding of virtue and should not be overemphasized. See Jean Porter, "The Subversion of Virtue: Acquired and Infused Virtues in the *Summa Theologiae*," in *The Annual of the Society of Christian Ethics*, ed. H. Beckley (Washington, D.C.: Georgetown University Press, 1992), 19–41.

19. Here I draw from Lee, *Philosophical Theology of Jonathan Edwards*, 17–46. Lee himself develops what he believes is Aristotle's secondary meaning of habit as "innate tendencies" in an entity, which he believes Edwards retrieves. See Lee, *Philosophical Theology of Jonathan Edwards*, 19. In comparing Edwards's and Aristotle's moral thought, however, Edwards's repudiation of Aristotle's understanding of habit as an acquired propensity is significant, particularly in light of the importance Aristotle's moral thought has for modern virtue theory, as I argue later in this chapter.

20. With the image of the stone, Edwards seems to engage Aristotle directly. In the *Nicomachean Ethics*, Aristotle writes that a "stone" by "nature moves downwards, and habituation could not make it move upwards, not even if you threw it up ten thousand times." But the virtues "arise in us neither by nature nor against nature. Rather, we are by nature able to acquire them, and reach our complete perfection through habit" (Aristotle, *Nicomachean Ethics*, trans. Terence Irwin [Indianapolis: Hackett, 1985], 1103a20–25).

21. Here my interpretation disagrees with Ramsey's assertion that the "general picture" Thomas and Edwards paint of the "Christian moral life is the same." Given that the word "general" can mean many things, Ramsey's assertion is hard to refute. Ramsey overlooks, however, the different attitudes of Edwards and Thomas concerning the moral capabilities of the unregenerate that I argue in the body of this chapter. In addition, while noting that Thomas and Edwards both believe in infused virtues, Ramsey fails to notice that Edwards rejects the notion of acquired virtues. Further, Ramsey exaggerates misleadingly when he states that Edwards's understanding of "conscience" and Thomas's understanding of "prudence" are roughly "parallel." See Ramsey, "Editor's Introduction," Y8:55–59.

22. Though many will find Edwards's supersessionism unappealing, in comparison to his philosophical and theological contemporaries, Edwards's perspective on non-Christian faiths is strikingly open and appreciative. For more on this aspect of Edwards, see Gerald McDermott, *Jonathan Edwards Confronts the Gods: Christian Theology, Enlightenment Religion, and Non-Christian Faiths* (New York: Oxford University Press, 2000). For a suggestive proposal of "post-supersessionist" Trinitarian theology, see Bruce D. Marshall, *Trinity and Truth* (Cambridge: Cambridge University Press, 2000), 169–79.

23. Augustine, *Confessions*, trans. M. Boulding, ed. J. E. Rotelle (Hyde Park, N.Y.: New City Press, 1997), 13.9, 348.

24. This is not to say that Augustine does not appreciate, for example, the virtue of humility. As Edwards himself notes, Augustine believed that just as the three rules of rhetoric are "pronunciation, pronunciation, pronunciation," so the three rules of the Christian "philosophy" are "humility, humility, humility." Here Edwards quotes Augustine (*Letters* 113.3.22) via Calvin's *Institutes of the Christian Religion* 2.2.11. Augustine, however, often defines humility in terms of the recognition and acceptance of epistemic finitude, rather than in direct relation to the believer's recognition of his or her shortcomings and dependency regarding God's moral goodness. For more on Augustine's understanding of the virtue of humility, see Gerald W. Schlabach, "Augustine's Hermeneutic of Humility: An Alternative to Moral Imperialism and Moral Relativism," *Journal of Religious Ethics* 22 (fall 1994): 299–330.

25. For a helpful anthology of divine command morality, see Janine Marie Idziak, comp., *Divine Command Morality: Historical and Contemporary Readings* (New York: Edwin Mellon Press, 1979). For an anthology of recent work in divine command morality, see Paul Helm, ed., *Divine Commands and Morality* (New York: Oxford University Press, 1981). The most influential defender of divine command morality is Robert Merrihew Adams. See Adams, "A Modified Divine Command Theory of Ethical Wrongness," in *Religion and Morality: A Collection of Essays*, ed. G. H. Outka and J. P. Reeder (Garden City, N.Y.: Anchor Press, 1973), 318–47; idem, "Divine Command Metaethics Modified Again," *Journal of Religious Ethics* 7 (spring 1979): 66–79; idem, "Divine Commands and the Social Nature of Obligation," *Faith and Philosophy* 4 (July 1987): 262–75; and idem, *Finite and Infinite Goods: A Framework*

for Ethics (New York: Oxford University Press, 1999), 249–91. Edwards's approach to divine commands has some affinities with that offered by Richard Mouw in *The God Who Commands: A Study in Divine Command Ethics* (Notre Dame, Ind.: University of Notre Dame Press, 1990), particularly Mouw's position that commands are right-indicating more than right-making and his attempt to articulate commands from the perspective of the Trinity (22–42, 150–75). In addition, Edwards would agree with Adams's qualification in "Divine Commands and the Social Nature of Obligation" that "it matters what God's attributes are," and that God must be "beautiful" and "loving" as well as "omniscient" (272–73). In *Finite and Infinite Goods*, Adams also notes that the "character and commands of God" must satisfy the conditions necessitated of one who is in a position to give commands, specifically God's excellence and transcendence (250). Nonetheless, Edwards provides a fuller account than Adams does of divine excellence.

26. In the interest of clarity, it is important to point out that Edwards considers "trials" and "temptations" as "words of the same signification" (Y2:389).

27. Here I follow, quite generally, the interpretation of Kierkegaard offered by Gene Outka, "Religious and Moral Duty: Notes on *Fear and Trembling*" in Outka and Reeder, eds., *Religion and Morality*, 204–54. It is debatable whether Edwards would accept Outka's own "more modest" constructive position of "dispositional openness" regarding divine commands, where religious duty "can," but "need not" conflict with "ordinary antecedent judgements of right and wrong." See Outka, 250–54. But Edwards would certainly agree with Outka's point in a later article on Kierkegaard that "at a minimum," the "vindication of a direct relationship to God" lies at the heart of ethics, after which "everything else, obedience to God, the ethical, sin and so on are governed from this center." See Outka, "God as the Subject of Unique Veneration: A Response to Ronald M. Green," *Journal of Religious Ethics* 21 (fall 1993): 211. Other treatments of Kierkegaard's *Fear and Trembling* that are worthy of mention are Ronald Green, "Enough Is Enough! *Fear and Trembling* Is Not about Ethics," *Journal of Religious Ethics* 21 (fall 1993): 191–209; Brian Stiltner, "Who Can Understand Abraham? The Relation of God and Morality in Kierkegaard and Aquinas," *Journal of Religious Ethics* 21 (fall 1993): 221–45; Amy Laura Hall, "Self-Deception, Confusion, and Salvation in Fear and Trembling with Works of Love," *Journal of Religious Ethics* 28 (spring 2000): 37–61; and Adams, *Finite and Infinite Goods*, 277–91.

28. Here I am indebted to Conrad Cherry's careful review of Edwards's understanding of the connection between faith and practice in comparison to his Puritan forebears. See Cherry, *Theology of Jonathan Edwards*, 126–42.

29. Dietrich Bonhoeffer, *The Cost of Discipleship*, trans. R. H. Fuller (New York: Macmillan, 1949), 42.

30. Interestingly, few Christian ethicists have tried to tie together the renewed interest in Trinitarian theology and virtue ethics. One exception is Jones, *Transformed Judgement*. Though he addresses the relation between the Trinity and virtue, Jones's engagement with the Trinity follows a lengthy rehearsal of Aristotelian virtue ethics, so much so that one must ask whether the primary point of interpretation for his ethics is Aristotelian virtue theory or the doctrine of the Trinity. As is evident in what I argue in this chapter, Edwards offers a compelling argument that Trinitarian relations establish a very different anthropology and set of virtues than what is offered by Aristotelian virtue ethics, Thomas's synthesis notwithstanding.

31. For more on the renewed interest in Aristotelian virtue theory as well as other "particularist" accounts of ethics, see Outka, "Particularist Turn in Theolog-

ical and Philosophical Ethics." Outka's remarks also helped me see the nature of Edwards's interaction with MacIntyre's retrieval of Aristotle.

32. Here I refer generally to Kant's moral theory in *Critique of Practical Reason*, 3d ed., trans. and ed. L. W. Beck (New York: Macmillan, 1993) and *Grounding for the Metaphysics of Morals*, 3d ed., trans. J. W. Ellington (Indianapolis: Hackett Publishing Co., 1993). Along with David Hume, Kant is a popular target for criticism by proponents of Aristotelian virtue theory and other projects of particularist ethics. See Alasdair MacIntyre, *After Virtue: A Study in Moral Theory* (Notre Dame, Ind.: University of Notre Dame Press, 1981), 36–50, 273–74; Phillipa Foot, *Virtues and Vices and Other Essays in Moral Philosophy* (Berkeley: University of California Press, 1978), 1; and Bernard Arthur Owen Williams, *Moral Luck: Philosophical Papers 1973–1980* (New York: Cambridge University Press, 1981), 14, 19. Notwithstanding these assessments, in the interest of fairness one should note that, though secondary to practical reason and the categorical imperative, Kant does present a theory of virtue in *The Metaphysics of Morals* (trans. M. Gregor [New York: Cambridge University Press, 1991], 185–272). For more on Kantian virtue, see Robert B. Louden, "Kant's Virtue Ethics," in *Virtue Ethics: A Critical Reader*, ed. D. Statman (Washington, D.C.: Georgetown University Press, 1997), 286–99.

33. For a helpful anthology of recent work in virtue ethics, see Roger Crisp and Michael A. Slote, eds., *Virtue Ethics* (New York: Oxford University Press, 1997). See also Stanley Hauerwas and Charles Pinches, *Christians among the Virtues: Theological Conversations with Ancient and Modern Ethics* (Notre Dame, Ind.: University of Notre Dame Press, 1997). Hauerwas's initial work on character, *Character and the Christian Life: A Study in Theological Ethics* (San Antonio: Trinity University Press, 1985), anticipates some of MacIntyre's project, and I will return to it in chapter 5. My review of MacIntyre's retrieval of Aristotle primarily follows *After Virtue*, 146–64, 181–225. In other works, MacIntyre incorporates the theological virtues and the understanding of the *Summum Bonum* from Thomas. See MacIntyre, *Whose Justice? Which Rationality?* (Notre Dame, Ind.: University of Notre Dame Press, 1988), 88–145, 183–208; and *Three Rival Versions of Moral Enquiry: Encyclopedia, Genealogy, and Tradition* (Notre Dame, Ind.: University of Notre Dame Press, 1990), 105–48. Most of the critical literature in Christian ethics, however, focuses on MacIntyre's retrieval of Aristotle, apart from MacIntyre's Thomism. See, for example, Nancey C. Murphy, Brad J. Kallenburg and Mark Thiessen Nation, eds., *Virtues and Practices in the Christian Tradition: Christian Ethics after MacIntyre* (Harrisburg, Pa.: Trinity Press International, 1997). Two critiques of MacIntyre's Thomism are Janet Coleman, "MacIntyre and Aquinas," in *After MacIntyre: Critical Perspectives on the Work of Alasdair MacIntyre*, ed. J. Horton and S. Mendus (Notre Dame, Ind.: University of Notre Dame Press, 1994), 65–90; and John Milbank, *Theology and Social Theory: Beyond Secular Reason* (Cambridge, Mass.: Blackwell, 1994), 326–79.

34. Paul Lewis, "'The Springs of Motion': Jonathan Edwards on Emotions, Character, and Agency," *Journal of Religious Ethics* 22 (fall 1994): 276.

35. Ibid., 277, 286, 285.

36. James E. Gilman, *Fidelity of Heart: An Ethic of Christian Virtue* (New York: Oxford University Press, 2001), 7. Gilman does not propose to offer a comprehensive analysis of Edwards, but he draws on Edwards's *Religious Affections* to articulate his own constructive account of virtue, to the extent that examining his fidelity (so to speak) to Edwards is warranted.

37. Ibid., 15–68.

38. Stephen Wilson, "The Possibility of a Habituation Model of Moral Development in Jonathan Edwards' Conception of the Will's Freedom," *Journal of Religion* 81 (January 2001): 49.

39. Ibid., 72.

40. Ibid., 76.

41. See Friedrich Schleiermacher, *The Christian Faith*, trans. H. R. Mackintosh and J. S. Stewart (Edinburgh: T. & T. Clark, 1986), 12–18.

42. Here I draw from Marshall, *Trinity and Truth*, 44–49. It goes without saying that Edwards's doctrine of the Trinity, and its correlative ethics, differs from Marshall's proposal. Marshall's starting point is the depiction of the triune missions in the liturgy of the church, and Marshall prefers to construct a "coarse net" when it comes to the "inclusive power" of a Trinitarian belief system regarding the assimilation of "alien" and "novel" beliefs (156). Nonetheless, Edwards and Marshall agree on the epistemic priority of the Trinity and their understanding of the nature of the moral life with respect to this commitment (207–12).

43. See MacIntyre, *Whose Justice? Which Rationality?* 369–88.

CHAPTER 4

1. McClymond, *Encounters with God*, 6.

2. For more on classical theism, particularly in relation to Trinitarian theology, see Ted Peters, *God—The World's Future: Systematic Theology for a New Era*, 2d ed. (Minneapolis: Fortress Press, 2000), 86–128. For a helpful discussion of both classical theism and its alternatives, see Edward Farley, *Divine Empathy: A Theology of God* (Minneapolis: Fortress Press, 1996), 23–50. For a concise criticism of classical theism from the perspective of process thought, see Charles Hartshorne, *Omnipotence and Other Theological Mistakes* (Albany: State University of New York Press, 1984), 1–49. Although the criticism of classical theism originates in process thought, it is now accepted by many theologians representing a number of approaches, and appears to be one of the motivations for the renewed interest in Trinitarian thought.

3. See, for example, Richard Rice, "Divine Foreknowledge and Free-will Theism," and Bruce R. Reichenbach, "Freedom, Justice, and Moral Responsibility," in *The Grace of God, The Will of Man: A Case for Arminianism*, ed. C. H. Pinnock (Grand Rapids: Zondervan, 1989), 127–28, 283–85, 300.

4. Ramsey, "Editor's Introduction," Y2:65–69, 92–94; Holbrook, "Editor's Introduction," Y3:68–70.

5. According to Holbrook, Taylor's path to Arminianism began after he read and defended Samuel Clarke's "Arian" depiction of the Trinity in the *Scripture-Doctrine of the Trinity* (1712). See Holbrook, "Editor's Introduction," 68–70. While certainly heterodox, Clarke's long-supposed Arianism has come under recent criticism. See Pfizenmaier, *Trinitarian Theology of Dr. Samuel Clarke*, 217–20.

6. Samuel Clarke, *A Demonstration of the Being and Attributes of God and Other Writings*, ed. Ezio Vailati (New York: Cambridge University Press, 1998), 7.

7. Pfizenmaier's chapters on Clarke's intellectual context provide an excellent summary of the different currents of thought in English theology and philosophy in the seventeenth and eighteenth centuries in relation to the doctrine of the Trinity. See Pfizenmaier, *Trinitarian Theology of Dr. Samuel Clarke*, 13–85.

8. Locke, *Essay concerning Human Understanding*, IV.xiii.3, 651; quoted in J. B. Schneewind, *The Invention of Autonomy: A History of Modern Moral Philosophy* (New York: Cambridge University Press, 1998), 150. Schneewind's survey of the different authors and movements of the Enlightenment is without peer.

9. Locke, *Essay*, IV.iii.18, 549; quoted in Schneewind, *Invention of Autonomy*, 148.

10. Edwards's full title is *A Careful and Strict Enquiry into the Modern Prevailing Notions of that Freedom of Will, which is Supposed to be Essential to Moral Agency, Virtue and Vice, Reward and Punishment, Praise and Blame.*

11. In his conclusion, Edwards reaffirms all five of the articles of the synod, specifically unconditional election, limited atonement, total depravity, irresistibility of grace, and the perseverance of the saints. See Y1:430–39. For more on the Synod of Dort, see Jaroslav Pelikan, *Reformation of Church and Dogma (1300–1700)*, vol. 4 of *The Christian Tradition: A History of the Development of Doctrine* (Chicago: University of Chicago Press, 1984), 235–42.

12. For three recent articles on Augustine's understanding of the will, see Simon Harrison, "Do We Have a Will? Augustine's Way in to the Will," and Simo Knuuttila, "The Emergence of the Logic of Will in Medieval Thought," in *The Augustinian Tradition*, ed. G. B. Matthews (Berkeley: University of California Press, 1999), 195–232; and William S. Babcock, "Augustine on Sin and Moral Agency," in *The Ethics of Augustine*, ed. W. S. Babcock (Atlanta: Scholars Press, 1991), 87–113.

13. Augustine, *Contra Julianum*, 1.106; quoted in Kelly, *Early Christian Doctrines*, 365.

14. Augustine, *City of God*, in *A Select Library of the Nicene and Post-Nicene Fathers of the Christian Church*, vol. 2, trans. M. Dods, ed. Philip Schaff (Grand Rapids: Eerdmans, 1993), V.10, 92. Augustine's full account of the moral necessity of sinning occurs in XIV.1–28, 262–83.

15. Of course, there are more subtle variations among many authors that I cannot cover here. For more on these figures, as well as on the different figures and theories in modern moral philosophy, see Schneewind, *Invention of Autonomy*. Also helpful is Fiering, *Jonathan Edwards's Moral Thought*, 261–321.

16. For more on Arminianism, see Pelikan, *Reformation of Church*, 233–35.

17. As Fiering notes, another advantage to grouping several writers under the general heading "Arminianism" was that it is practical—it allowed Edwards to "charge the group as a whole with inconsistencies among themselves without necessarily exposing adequately the fallacies of each of the libertarian arguments taken alone" (Fiering, *Jonathan Edwards's Moral Thought*, 292).

18. Locke, *Essay*, II.xxi.14–21, 240–44. As Ramsey ("Editor's Introduction," Y1:53) and Schneewind (*Invention of Autonomy*, 146) point out, Locke added his comments on the will in the second edition of the *Essay* (1694). Unlike Edwards, Locke holds that personal freedom includes the liberty of suspension, that is, the ability to refrain from action while we consider the different desires and aversions we feel (*Essay*, II.xxi.47, 263). Edwards rejects the liberty of suspension, arguing that the act of suspension itself is an act of volition based on a prior consideration that determines it (Y1:209–10). See Fiering, *Jonathan Edwards's Moral Thought*, 296–98. See also Ramsey, "Editor's Introduction," Y1:60–63.

19. Clarke, *Demonstration of the Being and Attributes*, sec. X, 63–64.

20. Ibid., sec. X, 63.

21. Ibid., sec. IX, 54.

22. Ibid., sec. IX, 46.

23. Ibid., sec. X, 57.

24. Ibid., sec. X, 62.

25. Ibid., sec. IX, 49.

26. Ibid., sec. IX, 51.

27. Ibid., sec. XII, 90.

28. Here I disagree with Fiering's assessment of Edwards and Clarke on necessity. Fiering holds that Edwards used Clarke's understanding of the necessity of fitness to argue for moral necessity of the will. But the two kinds of necessity, as I argue earlier, are quite different. See Fiering, *Jonathan Edwards's Moral Thought*, 304.

29. Schneewind, *Invention of Autonomy*, 318.

30. Clarke, *Demonstration of the Being and Attributes*, sec. X, 77.

31. This is noted by Fiering, *Jonathan Edwards's Moral Thought*, 284, 291.

32. Damascene, *The Orthodox Faith*, III.6; *The Statement of Faith of the Third Council of Constantinople (Sixth Ecumenical)* in *Christology of the Later Fathers*, ed. E. R. Hardy and C. C. Richardson (Philadelphia: Westminster Press, 1954), 383.

33. Wilson, "Possibility of a Habituation Model," 61. As I mention in chapter 3, I find Wilson's reading of Edwards highly problematic, specifically in terms of the possibility that these "indirect desires" indicate the presence of a habituation model in Edwards.

34. As Allen Guelzo writes, Edwards is "in technical terms, a compatibilist," but his compatibilism is one in which "divine determinism clearly has the upper hand." See Guelzo, "The Return of the Will: Jonathan Edwards and the Possibilities of Free Will," in *Edwards in Our Time*, ed. S. H. Lee and A. Guelzo (Grand Rapids: Eerdmans, 1999), 94. The emphatic nature of what Guelzo calls the "divine determinism" of Edwards would justify referring to Edwards's position as soft determinism, but my own preference is otherwise, given his relatively expansive view of moral necessity.

35. Richard Swinburne, *Responsibility and Atonement* (Oxford: Clarendon Press, 1989).

36. Although a fitting representative of an overall approach, Swinburne of course is not alone in seeking to connect incompatibilism with Christian principles. See, for example, Eleonore Stump, "Sanctification, Hardening of Heart, and Frankfurt's Concept of Free Will," and "Intellect, Will, and the Principle of Alternate Possibilities," in *Perspectives on Moral Responsibility*, ed. J. M. Fischer and M. Ravizza (Ithaca, N.Y.: Cornell University Press, 1993), 211–62.

37. Swinburne, *Responsibility and Atonement*, 51.

38. Ibid., 164, 45–46.

39. Ibid., 51–63.

40. Harry G. Frankfurt, "Freedom of Will and the Concept of a Person," *Journal of Philosophy* 68 (1971): 5–20; idem, "Identification and Wholeheartedness," and "What We Are Morally Responsible For," in Fisher and Ravizza, eds. *Perspectives on Moral Responsibility*, 170–87; 286–95; and idem, *Necessity, Volition, and Love* (New York: Cambridge University Press, 1999). Swinburne comments on Frankfurt in *Responsibility and Atonement*, 56.

41. For more on the problems raised by Freud for ethics, particularly for the question of determinism versus free will, see Ernest Wallwork, *Psychoanalysis and Ethics* (New Haven, Conn.: Yale University Press, 1991), 49–100.

42. Swinburne, *Responsibility and Atonement*, 2, 122, 140, 184.

43. Ibid., 124.

44. Ibid., 172. As J. N. D. Kelly notes, one feature of Pelagianism is that "no room is left for any special, interior action of God on the soul," and that God's grace is limited to "purely external aids." See Kelly, *Early Christian Doctrines*, 359. Swinburne does not rule out "intervention by God into natural processes in order to forward his gracious work," but does not believe such "interventions" are necessary.

45. Swinburne, *Responsibility and Atonement*, 49, 55.

46. See Richard Swinburne, *The Christian God* (Oxford: Clarendon Press, 1994), 192–215.

47. Swinburne, *Responsibility and Atonement*, 148–49, 153, 186–87.

48. Moltmann, *Trinity and the Kingdom*, 215–16.

49. LaCugna, *God for Us*, 299, 399.

50. Edwards's full title is *The Great Doctrine of Original Sin defended; Evidences of its Truth produced, and Arguments to the Contrary Answered.*

51. The broad outlines of Augustine's doctrine can be found in his *City of God*, XIII–XIV, 245–83. See also Augustine, *The Grace of Christ and Original Sin*, trans. R. J. Teske, ed. J. E. Rotelle, in *The Works of Saint Augustine: A Translation for the Twenty-first Century*, pt. 1, vol. 23 (Hyde Park, N.Y.: New City Press, 1997), II.1–41, 434–60.

52. See Peter Brown, *Augustine of Hippo: A Biography* (Berkeley: University of California Press, 1967), 387.

53. John Locke, *The Reasonableness of Christianity*, ed. I. T. Ramsey (Stanford, Calif.: Stanford University Press, 1958), 25; cited in Philip L. Quinn, "Disputing the Augustinian Legacy: John Locke and Jonathan Edwards on Romans 5:12–19," in *The Augustinian Tradition*, ed. G. B. Matthews (Berkeley: University of California Press, 1999), 239. Although I offer a different interpretation than Quinn, his article provides an important review of the issues surrounding original sin in seventeenth and eighteenth-century philosophy and theology.

54. John Taylor, *The Scripture-Doctrine of Original Sin, Proposed to Free and Candid Examination* (London: M. Waugh, 1767), 131, 258; quoted in C. Samuel Storms, *Tragedy in Eden: Original Sin in the Theology of Jonathan Edwards* (Lanham, Md.: University Press of America, 1985), 39, 58.

55. Ibid., 70, 35, 84; quoted in Storms, *Tragedy in Eden*, 44, 42, 45.

56. Perry Miller argues that *Original Sin* was a "strictly empirical investigation, an induction, in the manner of Boyle and Newton, of a law for phenomena." See Miller, *Jonathan Edwards*, 267. Fiering challenges this interpretation, arguing that *Original Sin* presents an "interweaving of theological dogma and philosophy." See Fiering, *Jonathan Edwards's Moral Thought*, 52–61. With Fiering, I reject Miller's interpretation, both in terms of the success of this empirical strategy as well as whether it serves as the best lens through which to read *Original Sin*. See also Storms, *Tragedy in Eden*, 81–89.

57. Taylor, *Scripture-Doctrine of Original Sin*, 268–70; quoted in Storms, *Tragedy in Eden*, 59.

58. When Edwards refers to humanity's first sin, without exception he speaks of "Adam" and not "Eve." One could assign this omission to Edwards's perpetuation of the patriarchy of his milieu, but Edwards never blames "Eve" for the act of sin, which would be indicative of a patriarchal attitude. What is more likely is that Edwards uses the term collectively to refer to both of the first parents, as well as

humanity in general, consistent with the translation of the Hebrew word '*adam* in the creation narratives. When the term "Adam" appears in the body of this book it is in this latter sense that I use it.

59. See Edward A. Dowey, *The Knowledge of God in Calvin's Theology* (New York: Columbia University Press, 1965), 9–24.

60. Reinhold Niebuhr, *The Children of Light and the Children of Darkness* (New York: Charles Scribner's Sons, 1972), 16–17. For more on Niebuhr's doctrine of original sin, its connection with the Augustinian tradition, and the prospects for common morality, see Gene Outka, "Augustinianism and Common Morality," in *Prospects for Common Morality*, ed. G. Outka and J. P. Reeder (Princeton, N.J.: Princeton University Press, 1993), 129–44.

61. See Aquinas, *Summa Theologiae* 1a2ae.85, 1–6. As I point out in the previous chapters, though they agree that the Holy Spirit perfects human nature, Edwards and Thomas offer different accounts on the nature of the Spirit's indwelling and the nature of human perfection.

62. For more on this critique of Niebuhr, see Susan Nelson Dunfee, "The Sin of Hiding: A Feminist Critique of Reinhold Niebuhr's Account of the Sin of Pride," *Soundings* 65 (fall 1982): 318–24. See also Gene Outka, "Universal Love and Impartiality," in *The Love Commandments*, ed. E. Santurri and W. Werpehowski (Washington, D.C.: Georgetown University Press, 1992), 48–60.

63. Reinhold Niebuhr, *Moral Man and Immoral Society* (New York: Charles Scribner's Sons, 1960), 6.

64. Commentators have long noticed Edwards's reliance on Locke for this understanding of identity, specifically Locke's *Essay*, II.xxi.31ff. (see Wallace Anderson's note in Y6:385). But as I point out in chapter 1, Edwards's understanding of identity is equally indebted to Malebranche, specifically the notion of God's communication of ideas to created intelligent beings. Moreover, as I also argue, Edwards's point of integration for Locke and Malebranche on identity is the psychological analogy.

65. For more on the federal theory of original sin, see Geoffrey P. Fisher, "The Augustinian and the Federal Theories of Original Sin Compared," in *New Englander and Yale Review* 27 (July 1868): 468–516. Although written over one hundred years ago, this essay is without peer. As Fisher notes, elements of the federal theory of original sin were anticipated by Abelard and other nominalists in the Middle Ages. See Fisher, "Augustinian and the Federal Theories," 509.

66. For more on the following discussion of the specific arguments of Augustine, Locke, Taylor, and Edwards on Romans 5:12–19, see Quinn, "Disputing the Augustinian Legacy."

67. For example, see Storms, *Tragedy in Eden*, 120; and Quinn, "Disputing the Augustinian Legacy," passim.

68. Here I follow Christopher Bryan's translation of the passage in *A Preface to Romans: Notes on the Epistle in Its Literary and Cultural Setting* (New York: Oxford University Press, 2000), 124. Bryan broadly follows Joseph A. Fitzmyer, "The Consecutive Meaning of *eph' ho*[*i*] in Romans, 5.12," *New Testament Studies* 39, no. 3 (1993): 323–39.

69. Augustine, *The Punishment and Forgiveness of Sins and the Baptism of Little Ones*, trans. R. J. Teske, ed. John E. Rotelle, in *The Works of Saint Augustine: A Translation for the Twenty-first Century*, pt. 1, vol. 23 (Hyde Park, N.Y.: New City Press, 1997), I.10.12, 39. As Teske notes (p. 77 n. 15), Augustine is more hesitant about this

interpretation in *Two Letters of the Pelagians* (IV.4.7), but this hesitance is uncharacteristic of Augustine's usual interpretation of the passage.

70. Taylor, *Scripture-Doctrine of Original Sin*, 35–36; quoted in Storms, *Tragedy in Eden*, 42.

71. Quinn, "Disputing the Augustinian Legacy," 246–47.

72. Bryan, *Preface to Romans*, 124–27.

73. N. T. Wright, *The Climax of the Covenant: Christ and the Law in Pauline Theology* (Minneapolis: Fortress Press, 1992), 20–21.

74. William J. Wainwright, "Original Sin," in *Philosophy and the Christian Faith*, ed. T. V. Morris (Notre Dame, Ind.: University of Notre Dame Press, 1988), 53.

75. This is Wainwright's example; see "Original Sin," 44.

76. Wainwright, "Original Sin," 47.

77. Ibid., 53.

78. See, for example, 1 Sam. 16:7; Ps. 26:2; Rom. 8:27; Heb. 4:12.

79. Wainwright, "Original Sin," 54–55.

80. Alistair I. McFadyen, *Bound to Sin: Abuse, Holocaust, and the Christian Doctrine of Sin* (Cambridge: Cambridge University Press, 2000), 9–10, 26, 207, 225–26.

81. Hume's argument in the *Dialogues* sets the conditions for much of the discussion of theodicy in the twentieth century, perhaps in part because it argues for atheism. See Nelson Pike, ed., *God and Evil: Readings on the Theological Problem of Evil* (Englewood Cliffs, N.J.: Prentice-Hall, 1964). Nonetheless, Gottfried Wilhelm Leibniz wrote the first independent study of theodicy in 1710, titled *Essais de Theodicee sur la bonte de Dieu, la liberte de l'homme et l'origine du mal*. As I note below, Leibniz's theistic approach to the problem inspired Alvin Plantinga's influential free will defense.

82. David Hume, *Dialogues concerning Natural Religion*, ed. H. D. Aiken (New York: Hafner Publishing Co., 1948), 61–66, 78–81. For more on the debate over whether or not Hume's argument of logical inconsistency succeeds, see J. L. Mackie, "Evil and Omnipotence," and Nelson Pike, "Hume on Evil," in *The Problem of Evil*, ed. M. M. Adams and R. M. Adams (New York: Oxford University Press, 1990), 25–52.

83. See Alvin Plantinga, "The Free Will Defense," in *The Analytic Theist: An Alvin Plantinga Reader*, ed. J. F. Sennett (Grand Rapids: Eerdmans, 1998), 22–49. As Sennett points out, this chapter is from Plantinga, *God, Freedom, and Evil* (New York: Harper & Row, 1974), 7–64, which provides a simplified version of his argument in *The Nature of Necessity* (Oxford: Clarendon Press, 1974), 164–95. For a supporting presentation and discussion of Plantinga's "free will defense," see Stephen T. Davis, "Free Will and Evil," with comment by D. Z. Phillips, John Hick, David Ray Griffin, and John K. Roth, and reply by Davis, in *Encountering Evil*, ed. S. T. Davis (Louisville, Ky.: Westminster John Knox Press, 2001), 73–107.

84. See Richard Swinburne, "A Theodicy of Heaven and Hell," in *The Existence and Nature of God*, ed. A. J. Freddoso (Notre Dame, Ind.: University of Notre Dame Press, 1983), 37–54. See also Swinburne, *Responsibility and Atonement*, 179–200.

85. See Alvin Plantinga, *Warranted Christian Belief* (New York: Oxford University Press, 2000), 199–240, esp. 206–13; and Swinburne, *Responsibility and Atonement*, 137–47.

86. John Hick, "An Irenaean Theodicy," in Davis, ed., *Encountering Evil*, 38–52. I will also draw from Hick, *Evil and the God of Love*, rev. ed. (New York: Harper & Row, 1977), 201–40.

87. Hick, "Irenaean Theodicy," 39–42.

88. As Hick himself notes, though he calls his approach "Irenaean," it is only loosely based on Irenaeus's thought (see "Irenaean Theodicy," 41).

89. Hick, "Irenaean Theodicy," 40–43.

90. Ibid., 44–45.

91. Ibid., 48–50.

92. Ibid., 51–52.

93. It is interesting to note that in a chapter dedicated to eighteenth-century approaches to evil in *Evil and the God of Love*, Hick overlooks John Taylor's *Scripture-Doctrine of Original Sin*. This seems a strange omission given the similarity between the two.

94. Taylor, *Scripture-Doctrine of Original Sin*, 253, 354; quoted by Edwards in *Original Sin* (Y3:204).

95. Ibid., 21, 67, 70; paraphrased by Edwards in *Original Sin* (Y3:206, 209).

96. Hick, "Irenaean Theodicy," 38.

97. In *Evil and the God of Love*, 327–36, Hick admits that his Irenaean account cannot accommodate "excessive or dysteleological suffering." But he does not apparently recognize that this failure of accommodation threatens the overall plausibility (to use his terms) of his account.

98. See Augustine, *Confessions*, 7.13.19, 175.

99. Here I draw from Marilyn McCord Adams, *Horrendous Evils and the Goodness of God* (Ithaca, N.Y.: Cornell University Press, 1999), 140–41, 164–80. Adams notes that Edwards falls within the Augustinian tradition (132), but overlooks the fact that, like Bonaventure, Edwards's aesthetics are bivalent in the context of his Christology. That being said, this book represents a signal contribution to theodicy, and I could not have written the end of this chapter without Adams's deep insight into the nature of evil from the standpoint of both Christology and the Trinity.

100. Jonathan Edwards, "The Excellency of Christ," in *The Sermons of Jonathan Edwards: A Reader*, ed. W. H. Kimnach, K. P. Minkema, and D. A. Sweeney (New Haven, Conn.: Yale University Press, 1999), 164–72.

101. Here Edwards approximates the "fish-hook" simile originated by Gregory of Nyssa in his *Catechetical Oration*, an excerpt of which is found in Hardy and Richardson, eds., *Christology of the Later Fathers*, 296–301.

102. Edwards, "Excellency of Christ," 179–80, 165–66, 195.

103. Fyodor Dostoevsky, *The Brothers Karamazov*, trans. R. Pevear and L. Volokhonsky (New York: Vintage Books, 1990), 245; see also 236–64.

104. Here I draw from Adams, *Horrendous Evils*, 29–31, 39–43, 52–53, 62–85, and 129–32.

105. Edwards, "Excellency of Christ," 165, 176.

106. Ibid., 184–85, 192.

107. See also "Miscellanies" entry *n*, where Edwards argues that it is "exceeding just that God should take the soul of a new-born infant and cast it into eternal torments" (Y13:169).

108. Quoted in Clyde Holbrook, "Editor's Introduction," Y3:28 n. 1.

109. Edwards repeats this argument in "Miscellanies" entries *t*, 21, and 424 (Y13:174, 211, 478).

110. Adams, *Horrendous Evils*, 155–68. Adams's and Edwards's proposals see in the christological aesthetic more resources than many feminist and liberation theologians are willing to acknowledge. For an example of this criticism, see Rita

Nakashima Brock, *Journeys by Heart: A Christology of Erotic Power* (New York: Crossroad, 1988); and Rebecca S. Chopp, *The Praxis of Suffering: An Interpretation of Liberation and Political Theologies* (Maryknoll, N.Y.: Orbis Books, 1986). For an important discussion of this criticism, see Adams, *Horrendous Evils*, 195–98.

111. Moltmann, *Trinity and the Kingdom*, 25, 49; see also 61–128. For a comparison between Adams and Moltmann, see Adams, *Horrendous Evils*, 175–77.

112. Miller, *Jonathan Edwards*, 257, 263, 270–71.

113. Jenson, *America's Theologian*, 144, 153, 166.

114. Guelzo, "Return of the Will," 110.

115. Kant, *Critique of Practical Reason*.

116. Quinn, "Disputing the Augustinian Legacy," 247.

117. See McFadyen, *Bound to Sin*, 19–42, 107–30, 167–99; and Adams, *Horrendous Evils*, 32–55, 94–103, 157–58, 191–93.

CHAPTER 5

1. Holmes, *God of Grace*, 44–76, 241ff.

2. Francis Hutcheson, *An Inquiry into the Original of Our Ideas of Beauty and Virtue: In Two Treatises*, 4th ed. (London, 1738; reprint, Charlottesville, Va.: Lincoln-Rembrandt, 1993), xv, 107–19. For more on Hutcheson, see Schneewind, *Invention of Autonomy*, 333–42. See also Isabel Rivers, *Reason, Grace, and Sentiment: A Study of the Language of Religion and Ethics in England, 1660–1780* (Cambridge: Cambridge University Press, 2000), 153–64.

3. Francis Hutcheson, *Illustrations on the Moral Sense*, ed. B. Peach (Cambridge, Mass.: Belknap Press of Harvard University Press, 1971), 193–94.

4. Fiering holds that Edwards came to Hutcheson and the "benevolentist" school late in his life, which presented a challenge to his own project that he could not sufficiently meet. See Fiering, *Jonathan Edwards's Moral Thought*, 129–38, 322–61. Ramsey successfully demonstrates, however, that Edwards's engagement with Hutcheson occurred through much of his intellectual life, and that Edwards's attitude toward Hutcheson was appreciative but with full knowledge that "his mind was on an altogether different topic." See Paul Ramsey, "Appendix II," Y8:689–705. My own interpretation is that Edwards does try to construct an apologetic that can respond to Hutcheson in the *Two Dissertations*, but Hutcheson's challenge to Edwards is one he can only meet if he is willing to articulate his theocentrism in the context of his Trinitarian thought.

5. Many have noted the vein of Neoplatonism running through *God's End*, even those who underplay Edwards's commitment to Neoplatonism. It is clear that Edwards appeals to Neoplatonism in *God's End* in order to articulate his theocentrism in a way that would be amenable to those who would find explicit Trinitarian grammar unacceptable. Thus, the following writers are right in saying that the Neoplatonism Edwards employs in *God's End* only roughly represents Edwards's understanding of the relation between God and creation. None of the following writers, however, recognize the extent to which Edwards uses the grammar of Neoplatonism as an apologetical strategy, as I contend. See Holbrook, *Ethics of Jonathan Edwards*, 104–5; Fiering, *Jonathan Edwards's Moral Thought*, 329ff.; Douglas J. Elwood, *The Philosophical Theology of Jonathan Edwards* (New York: Columbia University Press, 1960), 12–32; Lee, *Philosophical Theology of Jonathan Edwards*, 127;

Daniel, *Philosophy of Jonathan Edwards*, 66, 127, 178; and Holmes, *God of Grace*, 59. For more on the Cambridge Platonists, see Schneewind, *Invention of Autonomy*, 194–214.

6. For more on this theme in Neoplatonism, see A. C. Lloyd, *The Anatomy of Neoplatonism* (Oxford: Clarendon Press, 1990), 98–139.

7. Although Adam Smith (1723–1790) provides the definitive statement of the ideal observer theory, it originates in the thought of Hutcheson. For more on the history and development of the ideal observer theory, see Richard B. Brant, "Ideal Observer," in *Encyclopedia of Ethics*, ed. L. C. Becker and C. B. Becker (New York: Routledge, 2001), 2:827–29. For a twentieth-century restatement of the ideal observer theory, see Roderick Firth, "Ethical Absolutism and the Ideal Observer," *Philosophy and Phenomenological Research* 12 (March 1952).

8. Hutcheson, *Illustrations on the Moral Sense*, 128.

9. Of course, Edwards in the final analysis believes that God is the ultimate ideal observer: "It belongs to him as supreme arbiter, and to his infinite wisdom and rectitude, to state all rules and measures of proceedings" (Y8:425).

10. Hutcheson, *Illustrations on the Moral Sense*, 144. Here I follow Schneewind's analysis of Hutcheson in *Invention of Autonomy*, 340–42.

11. Hutcheson, *Illustrations on the Moral Sense*, 120–21, 123–25. Hutcheson reports that he borrows the distinction he draws between justifying and exciting reasons from Grotius, *De Jure Belli et Pacis* (1625). See *Illustrations*, 121. Hutcheson also notes that he draws the distinction between ultimate and subordinate ends from Aristotle, though it is interesting to note that for Aristotle these ends form a coherent hierarchy. See *Nicomachean Ethics* 1094a1–26.

12. Here I agree with Stephen Holmes that in the "Miscellanies" entries, Edwards's Trinitarian grammar conditions his understanding of glory. See Holmes, *God of Grace*, 35–44. Other works that assert a strong correlation between Edwards's understanding of glory and the Trinity are Stephens, *God's Last Metaphor*, 1–8; Daniel, *Philosophy of Jonathan Edwards*, 118–29; Sairsingh, "Jonathan Edwards and the Idea of Divine Glory," 54–69 and passim; Richardson, "Glory of God in the Theology of Jonathan Edwards," 1–49 and passim; and Knight, "Learning the Language of God." A general shortcoming of these interpretations is that they see the Trinity as emblematic of larger themes in Edwards's thought. I argue that the Trinity *is* Edwards's major, organizing theme.

13. "Miscellanies" entry 1218; quoted in Daniel, *Philosophy of Jonathan Edwards*, 149, 154.

14. Hutcheson, *Inquiry into the Original of Our Ideas*, 117. As many have noted, in this phrase Hutcheson anticipates the moral calculus of utilitarianism, later developed by Jeremy Bentham (1748–1832), John Stuart Mill (1806–1873) and Henry Sidgwick (1838–1900). Hutcheson himself does not place this calculus at the forefront of his moral philosophy, for two reasons. First, the moral sense, rather than any discrete calculation of aggregate happiness, is sufficient. Second, Hutcheson recognizes a complexity in benevolence that the utilitarian calculus struggles to accommodate.

15. Francis Hutcheson, *An Essay on the Nature and Conduct of the Passions and Affections. With Illustrations on the Moral Sense*, 3d ed. (n.p., 1742), 51, 53; quoted in Rivers, *Reason, Grace, and Sentiment*, 209.

16. Hutcheson, *Inquiry in the Original of Our Ideas*, 119. For more on *storge*, see Rivers, *Reason, Grace, and Sentiment*, 121–24, 209–10. Fiering as well offers an impor-

tant discussion of the place of *storge* in eighteenth-century moral philosophy. See Fiering, *Jonathan Edwards's Moral Thought*, 193–99.

17. Fiering also notes this strategy. I disagree, however, that this captures "Edwards's real dispute with the benevolists concerning 'natural affections.'" See Fiering, *Jonathan Edwards's Moral Thought*, 194–95.

18. As I mention in chapter 3, the metaphor for taste was used in both Puritan theology and empiricist philosophy. Here I interpret it as an apologetical maneuver that intends to engage Hutcheson's belief that the moral sense was immediate and irreducible.

19. Thus, Hutcheson leaves open the question of whether the "Deity could not have approved one constitution more than another," for "may not the Deity have something of a superior kind, analogous to our moral sense, essential to him?" (Hutcheson, *Illustrations of the Moral Sense*, 138.) Given the incompatibility Hutcheson recognizes between speculation on the nature of God and the moral sense, it is not surprising that in 1740 Hume wrote Hutcheson to ask, "What experience do we have with regard to spiritual beings? How can we ascribe to them any sentiments at all?" (David Hume, "Two Letters to Francis Hutcheson"; quoted in D. D. Raphael, *British Moralists 1650–1800*, 2 vols. [Oxford: Clarendon Press, 1969], 2:111).

20. Miller, *Jonathan Edwards*, 285.

21. Holbrook, *Ethics of Jonathan Edwards*, 104–5.

22. Fiering, *Jonathan Edwards's Moral Thought*, 9, 322, 325–26, 361.

23. For more on foundationalism, see Jeffrey Stout, *The Flight from Authority* (Notre Dame, Ind.: University of Notre Dame Press, 1981), 228–55; and idem, *Ethics after Babel: The Languages of Morals and Their Discontents* (Boston: Beacon Press, 1988), 124–44. Even those who do hold out for "concrete universals" in human nature, such as empathy, sympathy, and benevolence, realize that these aspects of human nature operate within particular and diverse webs of belief and therefore cannot provide an independent starting point for ethics. For two examples of this perspective, see John P. Reeder Jr., "Foundations without Foundationalism," in *Prospects for a Common Morality*, ed. G. Outka and J. P. Reeder Jr. (Princeton, N.J.: Princeton University Press, 1993), 191–214; and William C. Spohn and Thomas A. Byrnes, "Knowledge of Self and Knowledge of God: A Reconstructed Empiricist Interpretation," in *Christian Ethics: Problems and Prospects*, ed. L. S. Cahill and J. F. Childress (Cleveland: Pilgrim Press, 1996), 119–33.

24. James Gustafson, *Ethics from a Theocentric Perspective* (Chicago: University of Chicago Press, 1981, 1984), 1:235–342; 2:1–22.

25. Ibid., 1:314; 2:108.

26. For example, Gustafson writes that because the "divine ordering does not have human happiness as its final end," there are "choices that have to be made which run counter to the fulfillment of human happiness" (Gustafson, *Ethics from a Theocentric Perspective*, 2:108). While Edwards would agree that God is the final end of all things, he would disagree with the implications Gustafson draws regarding human happiness, ultimately because he believes that human fulfillment and happiness through *theosis* is integral to God's end in creation.

27. While my interpretation of the *Two Dissertations* suggests that Edwards's and Gustafson's projects are discontinuous, in the interest of fairness it is important to note that Roland Delattre's two articles on Edwards's theological ethics see Edwards and Gustafson, as well as H. Richard Niebuhr, as part of one continuous project. See Delattre, "Theological Ethics of Jonathan Edwards," and idem, "Religious Ethics

Today." For further defenses of Gustafson, see Reeder, "Foundations without Foundationalism," 195–200; and Margaret Farley, "The Role of Experience in Moral Discernment," in Cahill and Childress, eds., *Christian Ethics*, 134–51.

28. Timothy P. Jackson, *Love Disconsoled: Meditations on Christian Charity* (New York: Cambridge University Press, 1999), 54. The list and definitions I provide differ from Jackson's.

29. Anders Nygren, *Agape and Eros: The Christian Idea of Love*, trans. Philip S. Watson (Chicago: University of Chicago Press, 1953), 75–81, 175–81, 208–10. For Nygren's treatment of *caritas* and self-love, see 476–558. For Nygren's treatment of *philia*, which he calls *amor amicitiae*, see 644–58. While often overlooked, Nygren also distinguishes *agape* and *nomos*, an account of the moral life defined in terms of the law; see 254–88.

30. John M. Rist, *Eros and Psyche: Studies in Plato, Plotinus, and Origen* (Toronto: University of Toronto Press, 1964), 79–80, 204–7, 213–16; Catherine Osborne, *Eros Unveiled: Plato and the God of Love* (Oxford: Clarendon Press, 1996), 52–85, 222–26.

31. Burnaby, *Amor Dei*, 15–21, 92–94, 121–22; O'Donovan, *Problem of Self-love in St. Augustine*, 137–59.

32. Stephen G. Post, *A Theory of Agape: On the Meaning of Christian Love* (Lewisburg, Pa.: Bucknell University Press, 1990), 79–105; and idem, *Spheres of Love: Toward a New Ethics of the Family* (Dallas: Southern Methodist University Press, 1994), 4–6, 17–33, 112–21, 129–46; Edward Collins Vacek, *Love, Human and Divine: The Heart of Christian Ethics* (Washington, D.C.: Georgetown University Press, 1994), 157–97, 240–59, 280–312.

33. John P. Reeder Jr., "Extensive Benevolence," *Journal of Religious Ethics* 26 (spring 1998): 47–69. See also idem, "Three Moral Traditions," *Journal of Religious Ethics* 22 (spring 1994): 75–89.

34. Gene Outka, *Agape: An Ethical Analysis* (New Haven, Conn.: Yale University Press, 1972); and idem, "Universal Love and Impartiality"; Jackson, *Love Disconsoled*. In addition to Nygren, both Outka and Jackson draw from Reinhold Niebuhr and Paul Ramsey to develop their accounts of *agape*. See Reinhold Niebuhr, *The Nature and Destiny of Man: A Christian Interpretation*, 2 vols. (New York: Charles Scribner's Sons, 1953), 2:68–97; Paul Ramsey, *Basic Christian Ethics* (Louisville, Ky.: Westminster/John Knox Press, 1993), 92–132, 234–48, 326–51.

35. For more on Outka's contribution to the discussion of love in Christian ethics, see Stephen J. Pope, "Love in Contemporary Christian Ethics," in *Journal of Religious Ethics* 23 (spring 1995): 167–97. The following outline only gives a broad depiction of Outka's proposal, and does not do justice to its richness.

36. Outka, *Agape*, 9, 12. Here I appropriate Outka's shift in a recent article from describing *agape* as "equal regard" to "unqualified regard," which "registers the depth and staying power of the other-regarding commitment and avoids conflating irreducible value with equal value." See Gene Outka, "Comment," *Journal of Religious Ethics* 25 (spring 1997): 438.

37. Outka, *Agape*, 275, 278, 21.

38. Nygren, *Agape and Eros*, 127.

39. Outka, *Agape*, 218, 220.

40. Outka, "Universal Love," 88, 73, 44.

41. Outka, *Agape*, 263–64.

42. Outka, "Universal Love," 2, 59, 53, 64.

43. Ibid., 70, 89, 91.

44. Outka, "Theocentric Agape and the Self," *Journal of Religious Ethics* 24 (spring 1996): 37–38.

45. Outka, "Universal Love," 90–91.

46. Outka, *Agape*, 7.

47. Pope, "Love in Contemporary Christian Ethics," 174–81; and idem, "Reply" in *Journal of Religious Ethics* 25 (spring 1997): 440–44. See also Post, *Theory of Agape*, 88–89; and Colin Grant, "For the Love of God: Agape" in *Journal of Religious Ethics* 24 (spring 1996): 10–14.

48. Outka, "Comment," 436.

49. Hans Frei, *The Identity of Jesus Christ: The Hermeneutical Bases of Dogmatic Theology* (Philadelphia: Fortress Press, 1975), 157–65, 75.

50. Jackson, *Love Disconsoled*, 20, 23, 25.

51. Ibid., 84, 90, 24, 9, 23.

52. Ibid., 15.

53. Ibid., 26, 62, 7, 89, 210.

54. Ibid., 229, 30, 170, 174, 167.

55. Ibid., 168.

56. Vacek, *Love, Human and Divine*, xv.

57. Ibid., 7, 21, 74, 87, 105, 147, 143.

58. Ibid., 280, 157, 162, 247, 281, 284, 301, 310, 319, 324.

59. Ibid., 149.

60. Edwards, "Excellency of Christ," 165, 183.

61. Cooey, "Eros and Intimacy in Edwards," 497. See also Post, *Christian Love and Self-Denial*, 37–55. Working from the perspective of self-love, Post's brief and suggestive analysis concurs with that of Cooey and that offered in this chapter. Unfortunately, Post does not draw on Edwards's thought in his later writings on love.

62. Edwards, "Excellency of Christ," 196.

63. Vacek, *Love, Human and Divine*, 123, 257, 105, 322–23.

64. Ibid., 166.

65. In particular, Vacek's theory of emotional development is basically that held by the object-relations school of psychoanalytic thought. Compare Vacek's account of participative love in *Love, Human and Divine*, 74–115, with that of Nancy McWilliams, *Psychoanalytic Diagnosis: Understanding Personality Structure in the Clinical Process* (New York: Guilford Press, 1994), 19–94. See also Michael St. Clair, *Human Relationships and the Experience of God: Object Relations and Religion* (New York: Paulist Press, 1994). I am grateful to R. Lawrence DePalma, M.D., for pointing out the similarity between Vacek and object-relations theory.

66. Vacek, *Love, Human and Divine*, 105, 100, 96.

67. For an interesting account of Trinitarian thought and economies of exchange and excess, see Stephen H. Webb, *The Gifting God: A Trinitarian Ethics of Excess* (New York: Oxford University Press, 1996), particularly 123–58. Webb's proposal concerning the sovereignty of God's generosity is particularly relevant to Edwards; his accommodation of freedom, and thereby reciprocity, less so.

68. See Jonathan Edwards, *Charity and Its Fruits; Or, Christian Love as Manifested in Heart and Life*, ed. Tryon Edwards (New York: Robert Carter & Brothers, 1852). As Ramsey notes, Tryon Edwards took occasional liberties with a nineteenth-century copy of Edwards's original sermons, which have now been corrected in the Yale edition. The original sermons themselves have been lost. See "Note on Texts," Y8:104–21.

69. For an example of Hauerwas's early focus on virtue, see Hauerwas, *Character and the Christian Life*. Hauerwas briefly touches on *Charity and Its Fruits* as he develops his own thought on virtue (199–201).

70. Stanley Hauerwas, *The Peaceable Kingdom: A Primer in Christian Ethics* (Notre Dame, Ind.: University of Notre Dame Press, 1983), 7–12.

71. Ibid., 102, 47, 97, 87, 94, 99.

72. For an important argument within New Testament ethics for pacifism, see Richard B. Hays, *The Moral Vision of the New Testament: A Contemporary Introduction to New Testament Ethics* (San Francisco: HarperCollins, 1996), 317–46.

73. Hauerwas, *Peaceable Kingdom*, 25–26. To be fair, in more recent writings, Hauerwas has tried to develop a more explicitly Trinitarian approach. Nonetheless, the Trinity still does not play a constructive role in his ethics. See, for example, Hauerwas, "Only Theology Overcomes Ethics: Or, What 'Ethicists' Must Learn from Jenson," in *A Better Hope: Resources for a Church Confronting Capitalism, Democracy, and Postmodernity* (Grand Rapids: Brazos Press, 2000), 117–28. See also idem, "The Church as God's New Language," in *Christian Existence Today: Essays on Church, World, and Living in Between* (Grand Rapids: Brazos Press, 2001), 47–65.

74. Harry Stout, *The New England Soul: Preaching and Religious Culture in Colonial New England* (New York: Oxford University Press, 1986), 233, 235–36.

75. For a defense of just war theory, see Paul Ramsey, *Speak Up for Just War or Pacifism: A Critique of the United Methodist Bishops' Pastoral Letter "In Defense of Creation"* (University Park: Pennsylvania State University Press, 1988).

76. John D. Zizioulas, *Being as Communion: Studies in Personhood and the Church* (Crestwood, N.Y.: St. Vladimir's Seminary Press, 1993). The following synopsis of Zizioulas's thought on personhood also relies on Zizioulas, "Human Capacity and Human Incapacity: A Theological Exploration of Personhood," *Scottish Journal of Theology* 28 (1975): 401–47.

77. Zizioulas, "Human Capacity and Human Incapacity," 408.

78. Zizioulas, *Being as Communion*, 50–56.

79. Zizioulas writes that Christology, from which he articulates his theology of baptism, "should not be confined to redemption of sin but reaches beyond that, to man's destiny as the image of God in creation. There are, therefore, two aspects in Christology, one negative (redemption from the fallen state) and another positive (fulfillment of man's full communion with God; what the Greek Fathers have called theosis)" (Zizioulas, "Human Capacity and Human Incapacity," 434).

80. Zizioulas, *Being as Communion*, 56.

81. Ibid., 46.

82. Ibid., 56–58.

83. Ibid., 21.

84. Jonathan Edwards, sermons on 1 Cor. 1:9 and 1 Cor. 10:16 (both written before 1733), Jonathan Edwards Collection, Beinecke Rare Book and Manuscript Library, Yale University. For more on Edwards's understanding of the Lord's Supper, see William J. Danaher Jr., "By Sensible Signs Represented: Jonathan Edwards' Sermons on the Lord's Supper," in *Pro Ecclesia* 7 (1998): 261–87.

85. Zizioulas, *Being as Communion*, 44, 49, 50, 57. For a similar treatment of love within Orthodox ethics, see Vigen Guroian, "Love in Orthodox Ethics: Trinitarian and Christological Reflections," in *Incarnate Love: Essays in Orthodox Ethics* (Notre Dame, Ind.: University of Notre Dame Press, 1987), 29–48.

86. Zizioulas, *Being as Communion*, 56.

87. Zizioulas, "Human Capacity and Human Incapacity," 407.

88. For further discussion on this weakness in Zizioulas's account, see Miroslav Volf, *After Our Likeness: The Church as the Image of the Trinity* (Grand Rapids: Eerdmans, 1998), 81–91.

89. Stanley S. Harakas, "Eastern Orthodox Christianity's Ultimate Reality and Meaning: Triune God and Theosis—An Ethician's View," *Ultimate Reality and Meaning* 8, no. 3 (1985): 212.

90. In *The Trinity*, Augustine explains why this tends to be the case. For if the Holy Spirit is "something common to Father and Son," then that commonality must be infinite and therefore "consubstantial." Otherwise, the Holy Spirit's equality in relation to the other persons is threatened. Further, if we define the Holy Spirit as "love," certainly the Father and Son must share this substantive designation as well. Hence, Augustine interprets 1 John 4:8, "God is love," as a statement that applies to God substance-wise, even though it is particularly appropriate to the Holy Spirit. See Augustine, *Trinity*, VI.7, 209–10. Although he does not mention Augustine, Eastern Orthodox theologian Dumitru Staniloae gives a similar reason for his rejection of the *filioque* principle. For the *filioque* entails that "divine love is no longer the love which passes between two persons, but an overflow from the common essence of the Father and the Son directed not as one person to another, but towards something else," an "explanation which confuses the persons and makes the divine essence a source of personal being" (Staniloae, "The Holy Trinity: Structure of Supreme Love," in *Theology and the Church*, trans. R. Barringer [Crestwood, N.Y.: St. Vladimir's Seminary Press, 1980], 104).

91. Zizioulas, *Being as Communion*, 48, 59.

92. Alexander V. G. Allen, *Jonathan Edwards* (Boston: Houghton Mifflin, 1889), 317, 323, 326, 335. Although written late in the nineteenth century, Allen's remarks are quite remarkable in understanding the importance of the Trinity to Edwards's thought. Unfortunately, Allen was not aware of all of Edwards's Trinitarian writings, misunderstood those he did read, and mistakenly believed that Edwards turned to the Trinity late in his life in a last ditch attempt to rectify his theology. See Allen, *Jonathan Edwards*, 338–76.

93. Holbrook, *Ethics of Jonathan Edwards*, 25–26.

94. Fiering, *Jonathan Edwards's Moral Thought*, 173.

95. Ramsey, "Editor's Introduction," Y8:81, 73.

96. The following discussion comparing Edwards and natural law is admittedly brief. For the most part, my synopsis of natural law follows Jean Porter, *Natural and Divine Law: Reclaiming the Tradition for Christian Ethics* (Grand Rapids: Eerdmans, 1999). Of the medieval natural law theorists, Thomas Aquinas figures most prominently in contemporary Christian ethics, and in another venue further comparison between Edwards and Thomas on natural law may prove fruitful. Indeed, Eugene Rogers has recently argued that Thomas's understanding of natural law articulates a "penultimate" form of knowledge that only represents our consensus regarding human nature and flourishing, and is distinct from what we come to know through grace. This position approximates the one I argue holds between Edwards's Trinitarian ethics and natural law. See Eugene F. Rogers, "The Narrative of Natural Law in Aquinas' Commentary on Romans 1," *Theological Studies* 59 (June 1998): 254–76. Nonetheless, as Porter notes, Thomas's interpretation of natural law represents only one of many such accounts in the medieval discussion, and my synopsis is meant to speak of natural law in general rather than Thomas's interpretation of it

in particular. An influential alternative account of natural law is John Finnis, *Natural Law and Natural Rights* (Oxford: Clarendon Press, 1980). Finnis's intent is not to justify the theological viability of natural law for Christian ethics, but to defend it as a legitimate means for articulating basic human goods as well as moral absolutes.

97. Porter, *Natural and Divine Law*, 98, 107.

98. Ibid., 100, 107.

99. Russell Hittinger, "Natural Law and Virtue: Theories at Cross Purposes," in *Natural Law Theory: Contemporary Essays*, ed. R. P. George (Oxford: Clarendon Press, 1995), 62. This compilation offers an important survey of the different perspectives and issues in the current discussion of natural law theory.

100. Ibid., 64.

CONCLUSION

1. Edwards Amasa Park, "The Duties of the Theologian," *American Biblical Repository* 2, no. 4 (1840): 374; quoted in Henry F. May, "Jonathan Edwards and America," in *Jonathan Edwards and the American Experience*, ed. N. Hatch and H. Stout (New York: Oxford University Press, 1988), 22.

2. As Joseph Conforti notes, Park's main theological concern was to argue for the interpretation he favored of the distinction between "natural" and "moral" necessity found in the *Freedom of the Will*. See Conforti, "Edwards A. Park and the Creation of New England Theology, 1840–1870," in *Jonathan Edwards's Writings: Text, Context, Interpretation*, ed. S. J. Stein (Bloomington: Indiana University Press, 1996), 193–207.

3. Gunton, *Promise of Trinitarian Theology*, 202.

4. John Stuart Mill, *An Examination of Sir William Hamilton's Philosophy, and of the Principal Philosophical Questions Discussed in His Writings*, 4th ed. (London: Longmans, 1872), 243, 242–64.

5. Emmanuel Levinas, *Totality and Infinity: An Essay on Exteriority*, trans. A. Lingis (Pittsburgh: Duquesne University Press, 1969), 254–85.

6. Michael Foucault, quoted in David Hardy, *The Condition of Postmodernity* (Oxford: Blackwell, 1990), 44. Hardy offers an interesting presentation of the different facets of postmodernity as a cultural phenomenon.

7. Milbank, *Theology and Social Theory*, 424.

8. Gustafson, *Ethics from a Theocentric Perspective*, 2:21.

9. Reinhold Niebuhr, "Must We Do Nothing?" *Christian Century* 49 (March 30, 1932): 417; quoted in Hauerwas, *Peaceable Kingdom*, 140.

BIBLIOGRAPHY

I. PRIMARY SOURCES

A. Edwards

Edwards, Jonathan. *Charity and Its Fruits: Or, Christian Love as Manifested in the Heart and Life*. Edited by Tryon Edwards. New York: Robert Carter & Brothers, 1852.

———. "The Equality of the Persons of the Trinity." Manuscripts. Courtesy of *The Works of Jonathan Edwards*, New Haven, Conn. Boston Public Library, Boston, Mass.

———. "The Excellency of Christ." In *The Sermons of Jonathan Edwards: A Reader*, edited by Wilson H. Kimnach, Kenneth P. Minkema, and Douglas A. Sweeney. New Haven, Conn.: Yale University Press, 1999.

———. "Justification by Faith Alone." In *The Works of President Edwards in Eight Volumes*, edited by Isaiah Thomas and Samuel Austin. Worcester, Conn.: Isaac Sturtevant, 1808–1809.

———. "Miscellanies," entry 530, Jonathan Edwards Collection. Beinecke Rare Book and Manuscript Library, Yale University.

———. "Miscellanies," entry 864, Jonathan Edwards Collection. Beinecke Rare Book and Manuscript Library, Yale University.

———. "Miscellanies," entry 1218. In *The Philosophy of Jonathan Edwards from His Private Notebooks*, edited by Harvey G. Townsend. Westport, Conn.: Greenwood Press, 1972.

———. *Treatise on Grace and Other Posthumously Published Writings*. Edited by Paul Helm. Cambridge: James Clarke, 1971.

———. *The Works of Jonathan Edwards*. Vols. 1–20. New Haven, Conn.: Yale University Press, 1957–2003.

B. Others

1. Classical

Aristotle. *Eudemian Ethics*. Loeb Classical Library. Cambridge, Mass.: Harvard University Press, 1935.

———. *Magna Moralia*. Loeb Classical Library. Cambridge, Mass.: Harvard University Press, 1936.

———. *Metaphysics*. Loeb Classical Library. Cambridge, Mass.: Harvard University Press, 1933.

———. *Nicomachean Ethics*. Translated by Terence Irwin. Indianapolis: Hackett Publishing Co., 1985.

———. *Rhetoric*. Loeb Classical Library. Cambridge, Mass.: Harvard University Press, 1947.

Cicero. *On Old Age and On Friendship*. Translated by Frank Olin Copley. Ann Arbor: University of Michigan Press, 1967.

Plato. *The Collected Dialogues of Plato*. Edited by Edith Hamilton and Huntington Cairns. Princeton, N.J.: Princeton University Press, 1987.

2. Patristic

Augustine. "On Christian Doctrine." In *A Select Library of the Nicene and Post-Nicene Fathers of the Christian Church*, vol. 2, edited by Philip Schaff. Grand Rapids: Eerdmans, 1994.

———. "Sermon 336.2." Translated by Edmund Hill. Edited by John E. Rotelle. In *The Works of Saint Augustine: A Translation for the Twenty-first Century*, pt. 3, vol. 9. Hyde Park, N.Y.: New City Press, 1994.

———. *Answer to the Pelagians*. Translated by R. J. Teske. Edited by John E. Rotelle. In *The Works of Saint Augustine: A Translation for the Twenty-first Century*, pt. 1, vol. 23. Hyde Park, N.Y.: New City Press, 1997.

———. *City of God*. In *A Select Library of the Nicene and Post-Nicene Fathers of the Christian Church*, vol. 2, translated by M. Dods, edited by Philip Schaff. Grand Rapids: Eerdmans, 1994.

———. *The Confessions*. Translated by Maria Boulding. Edited by John E. Rotelle. In *The Works of Saint Augustine: A Translation for the Twenty-first Century*, pt. 1, vol. 1. Hyde Park, N.Y.: New City Press, 1997.

———. *The Grace of Christ and Original Sin*. Translated by R. J. Teske. Edited by John E. Rotelle. In *The Works of Saint Augustine: A Translation for the Twenty-first Century*, pt. 1, vol. 23. Hyde Park, N.Y.: New City Press, 1997.

———. *The Punishment and Forgiveness of Sins and the Baptism of Little Ones*. Translated by R. J. Teske. Edited by John E. Rotelle. In *The Works of Saint Augustine: A Translation for the Twenty-first Century*, pt. 1, vol. 23. Hyde Park, N.Y.: New City Press, 1997.

———. *The Trinity*. Translated by Edmund Hill. Edited by John E. Rotelle. In *The Works of Saint Augustine: A Translation for the Twenty-first Century*. Brooklyn: New City Press, 1991.

———. *Two Letters of the Pelagians*. Translated by R. J. Teske. Edited by John E. Rotelle. In *The Works of Saint Augustine: A Translation for the Twenty-first Century*. Hyde Park, N.Y.: New City Press, 1997.

Gregory of Nyssa. *Catechetical Oration*. In *Christology of the Later Fathers*, Library of Christian Classics, edited by Edward Rochie Hardy and Cyril C. Richardson, 296–301. Philadelphia: Westminster Press, 1954.

Tanner, N. P., ed. "Epistola Papae Leonis ad Flavianum ep. Constantinopolitanum de Eutyche." In *Decrees of the Ecumenical Councils*, 1:79.3–7. Washington, D.C.: Georgetown University Press, 1990.

Tertullian. *Against Praxeas*. In *The Ante-Nicene Fathers*, vol. 3, edited by Alexander Roberts, James Donaldson, and A. Cleveland Coxe. Grand Rapids: Eerdmans, 1978.

3. Medieval

Aquinas, Thomas. *Compendium Theologiae*. In *St. Thomas Aquinas: Theological Texts*, translated by Thomas Gilby. New York: Oxford University Press, 1955.
————. *Summa Theologiae: Latin Text and English Translation, Introductions, Notes, Appendices, and Glossaries*. Translated by R. J. Batten. New York: McGraw-Hill, 1964.
Bonaventure. "The Breviloquium." In *The Triune God: A Historical Study of the Doctrine of the Trinity*, by Edmund J. Fortman. Grand Rapids: Baker Book House, 1982.
————. "Commentaries on the Four Books of Sentences." In *The Triune God: A Historical Study of the Doctrine of the Trinity*, by Edmund J. Fortman. Grand Rapids: Baker Book House, 1982.
————. "The Itinerarium mentis ad Deum." In *The Triune God: A Historical Study of the Doctrine of the Trinity*, by Edmund J. Fortman. Grand Rapids: Baker Book House, 1982.
————. *Saint Bonaventure's Disputed Questions on the Mystery of the Trinity*. Translated by Zachary Hayes. St. Bonaventure, N.Y.: Franciscan Institute, St. Bonaventure University, 1979.
————. "The Triple Way, or Love Enkindled." *The Works of Bonaventure: I Mystical Opuscula*, vol. 1. Translated by Jose de Vinck. Paterson, N.J.: St. Anthony Guild Press, 1960.
Pseudo-Dionysius the Areopagite. *The Complete Works*. Translated by Colm Luibheid. Mahwah, N.J.: Paulist Press, 1987.
Richard of St. Victor. *The Twelve Patriarchs; The Mystical Ark; Book Three of the Trinity*. Classics of Western Spirituality. Translated by Grover A. Zinn. Mahwah, N.J.: Paulist Press, 1979.

4. Modern

Ames, William. *The Marrow of Theology*. Translated and edited by John Dykstra Eusden. Boston: Pilgrim Press, 1968.
Berkeley, George. *The Works of George Berkeley, Bishop of Cloyne*. Edited by Arthur Aston Luce and Thomas Edmund Jessop. London: Thomas Nelson, 1948.
Butler, Joseph. *Fifteen Sermons*. London: Knapton, 1726.
————. *Five Sermons Preached at the Rolls Chapel and A Dissertation upon the Nature of Virtue*. Edited by Stephen L. Darwall. Indianapolis: Hackett Publishing Co., 1983.
Calvin, John. *The Institutes of the Christian Religion*. 2 vols. Library of Christian Classics. Translated by Ford L. Battles. Edited by John T. McNeill. Philadelphia: Westminster Press, 1960.

Chambers, E. *Cyclopedia: or, an Universal Dictionary of Arts and Sciences; containing definitions of the Terms and Accounts of the Things Signify'd therby, In the several Arts, Both Liberal and Mechanical, And the Several Sciences, Human and Divine: The Figures, Kinds, Properties, Productions, Preparations, and Uses, of things Natural and Artificial; the Rise, Progress, and State of Things Ecclesiastical, Civil, Military and Commercial: With the Several Systems, sects Opinions & c. among Philosophers, Divines, Mathematicians, Physicians, Antiquaries, Criticks, & c. The whole intended as a Course of Ancient and Modern Learning. Compiled from the best Authors, Dictionaries, Journals, Memoirs, Transactions, Ephemerides, & c. in several languages.* London, 1728.

Clarke, Samuel. *A Demonstration of the Being and Attributes of God and Other Writings.* Edited by Ezio Vailati. New York: Cambridge University Press, 1998.

———. *Scripture-Doctrine of the Trinity.* N.p., 1712.

Dostoevsky, Fyodor. *The Brothers Karamazov.* Translated by R. Pevear and L. Volokhonsky. New York: Vintage Books, 1990.

Hume, David. *Dialogues concerning Natural Religion.* Edited by Henry David Aiken. New York: Hafner Publishing Co., 1948.

———. *A Treatise on Human Nature.* Edited by Ernest C. Mossner. New York: Penguin Books, 1984.

Hurrion, John. *The Knowledge of Christ Glorified, opened and applied in twelve sermons on Christ's resurrection, ascension, sitting at God's right hand, intercession and judging the world.* London, 1729. In *The Whole Works of John Hurrion, Late Minister of the Gospel in London; Now First Collected; To Which is Prefixed, The Life of the Author. In Three Volumes.* Printed for R. Baynes by J. Henman, London, 1823.

Hutcheson, Francis. *Illustrations on the Moral Sense.* Edited by Bernard Peach. Cambridge, Mass.: Belknap Press of Harvard University Press, 1971.

———. *An Inquiry into the Original of Our Ideas of Beauty and Virtue: In Two Treatises.* 4th ed. London, 1738. Reprint, Charlottesville, Va.: Lincoln-Rembrandt, 1993.

Kant, Immanuel. *Critique of Practical Reason.* 3d ed. Translated and edited by Lewis White Beck. New York: Macmillan, 1993.

———. *Grounding for the Metaphysics of Morals; with, On a Supposed Right to Lie because of Philanthropic Concerns.* 3d ed. Translated by James W. Ellington. Indianapolis: Hackett Publishing Co., 1993.

———. *The Metaphysics of Morals.* Edited by Mary J. Gregor. New York: Cambridge University Press, 1991.

Locke, John. *An Essay concerning Human Understanding.* Edited by Peter H. Nidditch. Oxford: Clarendon Press, 1975.

———. *The Reasonableness of Christianity; with A Discourse of Miracles; and, part of A Third Letter concerning Toleration.* Edited by Ian T. Ramsey. Stanford, Calif.: Stanford University Press, 1958.

Luther, Martin. "The Freedom of a Christian." In *Martin Luther's Basic Theological Writings,* edited by T. F. Lull. Minneapolis: Fortress Press, 1989.

Malebranche, Nicholas. *The Search for Truth.* Translated and edited by Thomas M. Lennon and Paul J. Olscamp. New York: Cambridge University Press, 1997.

Mastricht, Petrus van. *Theoretico-practica theologia, ed. Nova*. Utrecht: N.p., 1699.

Mather, Cotton. *Blessed Unions*. Boston: B. Green & J. Allen, 1692.

Mill, John Stuart. *An Examination of Sir William Hamilton's Philosophy, and of the Principal Philosophical Questions Discussed in His Writings*. 4th ed. London: Longmans, 1872.

Schleiermacher, Friedrich. *The Christian Faith*. Translated by H. R. Mackintosh and J. S. Stewart. Edinburgh: T. & T. Clark, 1986.

Turretin, Francis. *Institutes of Elenctic Theology*. 3 vols. Translated by George Musgrave Giger. Edited by James T. Dennison Jr. Phillipsburg, N.J.: P. & R. Publishing, 1992.

5. Contemporary

Adams, Marilyn McCord. *Horrendous Evils and the Goodness of God*. Ithaca, N.Y.: Cornell University Press, 1999.

Adams, Robert Merrihew. "Divine Command Metaethics Modified Again." *Journal of Religious Ethics* 7 (spring 1979): 66–79.

———. "Divine Commands and the Social Nature of Obligation." *Faith and Philosophy* 4 (July 1987): 262–75.

———. *Finite and Infinite Goods: A Framework for Ethics*. New York: Oxford University Press, 1999.

———. "A Modified Divine Command Theory of Ethical Wrongness." In *Religion and Morality: A Collection of Essays*, edited by Gene H. Outka and John P. Reeder Jr. Garden City, N.Y.: Anchor Press, 1973.

———. "The Problem of Total Devotion." In *Friendship: A Philosophical Reader*, edited by Neera Kapur Badhwar. Ithaca, N.Y.: Cornell University Press, 1993.

Annas, Julia. *The Morality of Happiness*. New York: Oxford University Press, 1993.

Balthasar, Hans Urs von. *Mysterium Paschale: The Mystery of Easter*. Translated by Aidan Nichols. Grand Rapids: Eerdmans, 1993.

Barth, Karl. *The Doctrine of the Word of God. Church Dogmatics, I/1*. Translated by Geoffrey W. Bromiley. Edinburgh: T. & T. Clark, 1995.

———. *The Doctrine of God. Church Dogmatics, II/2*. Translated by Geoffrey W. Bromiley. Edinburgh: T. & T. Clark, 1987.

———. *The Doctrine of Creation. Church Dogmatics, III/4*. Translated by Geoffrey W. Bromiley. Edinburgh: T. & T. Clark, 1990.

Boff, Leonardo. *Trinity and Society*. Translated by Paul Burns. Maryknoll, N.Y.: Orbis Books, 1988.

Bonhoeffer, Dietrich. *The Cost of Discipleship*. Translated by Reginald H. Fuller. New York: Macmillan, 1949.

Brock, Rita Nakashima. *Journeys by Heart: A Christology of Erotic Power*. New York: Crossroad, 1988.

Cahill, Lisa Sowle. *Between the Sexes: Foundations for a Christian Ethics of Sexuality*. Philadelphia: Fortress Press, 1985.

———. "Feminism and Christian Ethics." In *Freeing Theology: The Essentials of Theology from a Feminist Perspective*, edited by Catherine Mowry LaCugna. San Francisco: HarperSanFrancisco, 1993.

Charry, Ellen T. *By the Renewing of Your Minds: The Pastoral Function of Chris-tian Doctrine*. New York: Oxford University Press, 1997.

Cousins, Ewert. "A Theology of Interpersonal Relations." *Thought* 45 (spring 1970): 56–82.

Davis, Stephen T. "Free Will and Evil." In *Encountering Evil*, edited by Stephen T. Davis. Louisville, Ky.: Westminister John Knox Press, 2001.

Farley, Edward. *Divine Empathy: A Theology of God*. Minneapolis: Fortress Press, 1996.

Farley, Margaret. "The Role of Experience in Moral Discernment." In *Christian Ethics: Problems and Prospects*, edited by Lisa Sowle Cahill and James F. Childress. Cleveland: Pilgrim Press, 1996.

Finnis, John. *Natural Law and Natural Rights*. Oxford: Clarendon Press, 1980.

Foot, Philippa. *Virtues and Vices and Other Essays in Moral Philosophy*. Berkeley: University of California Press, 1978.

Frankfurt, Harry G. "Freedom of Will and the Concept of a Person," *Journal of Philosophy* 68 (1971): 5–20.

———. "Identification and Wholeheartedness." In *Perspectives on Moral Responsibility*, edited by John Martin Fischer and Mark Ravizza. Ithaca, N.Y.: Cornell University Press, 1993.

———. *Necessity, Volition, and Love*. New York: Cambridge University Press, 1999.

———. "What We Are Morally Responsible For." In *Perspectives on Moral Responsibility*, edited by John Martin Fischer and Mark Ravizza. Ithaca, N.Y.: Cornell University Press, 1993.

Frei, Hans. *The Identity of Jesus Christ: The Hermeneutical Bases of Dogmatic The-ology*. Philadelphia: Fortress Press, 1975.

———. *Types of Christian Theology*. Edited by G. Hunsinger and W. C. Placher. New Haven, Conn.: Yale University Press, 1992.

Gilman, James Earl. *Fidelity of Heart: An Ethic of Christian Virtue*. New York: Oxford University Press, 2001.

Gunton, Colin E. *The Promise of Trinitarian Theology*. 2nd ed. Edinburgh: T. & T. Clark, 1991.

Guroian, Vigen. *Incarnate Love: Essays in Orthodox Ethics*. Notre Dame, Ind.: University of Notre Dame Press, 1987.

Gustafson, James. *Ethics from a Theocentric Perspective*. 2 vols. Chicago: Univer-sity of Chicago Press, 1981–1984.

Harakas, Stanley S. "Eastern Orthodox Christianity's Ultimate Reality and Meaning: Triune God and Theosis—An Ethician's View." *Ultimate Reality and Meaning* 8, no. 3 (1985): 209–23.

Hartshorne, Charles. *Omnipotence and Other Theological Mistakes*. Albany: State University of New York Press, 1984.

Hauerwas, Stanley. *Character and the Christian Life: A Study in Theological Ethics*. San Antonio: Trinity University Press, 1985.

———. "The Church as God's New Language." In *Christian Existence Today: Essays on Church, World, and Living in Between*. Grand Rapids: Brazos Press, 2001.

———. "Only Theology Overcomes Ethics: Or, What 'Ethicists' Must Learn from Jenson." In *A Better Hope: Resources for a Church Confronting Capitalism, Democracy, and Postmodernity.* Grand Rapids: Brazos Press, 2000.

———. *The Peaceable Kingdom: A Primer in Christian Ethics.* Notre Dame, Ind.: University of Notre Dame Press, 1983.

Hauerwas, Stanley, and Charles Pinches. *Christians among the Virtues: Theological Conversations with Ancient and Modern Ethics.* Notre Dame, Ind.: University of Notre Dame Press, 1997.

Helm, Paul, ed. *Divine Commands and Morality.* New York: Oxford University Press, 1981.

Hick, John. *Evil and the God of Love.* Rev. ed. New York: Harper & Row, 1977.

———. "An Irenaean Theodicy." In *Encountering Evil,* edited by Stephen T. Davis. Louisville, Ky.: Westminster John Knox Press, 2001.

Hittinger, Russell. "Natural Law and Virtue: Theories at Cross Purposes." In *Natural Law Theory: Contemporary Essays,* edited by Robert P. George. Oxford: Clarendon Press, 1995.

Jackson, Timothy P. *Love Disconsoled: Meditations on Christian Charity.* New York: Cambridge University Press, 1999.

Jenson, Robert W. *Systematic Theology.* Vol. 1, *The Triune God.* New York: Oxford University Press, 1997.

———. *Systematic Theology.* Vol. 2, *The Works of God.* New York: Oxford University Press, 1999.

———. *The Triune Identity: God according to the Gospel.* Philadelphia: Fortress Press, 1982.

Johnson, Elizabeth A. *She Who Is: The Mystery of God in Feminist Theological Discourse.* New York: Crossroad, 1992.

Jones, L. Gregory. *Embodying Forgiveness: A Theological Analysis.* Grand Rapids: Eerdmans, 1995.

———. *Transformed Judgement: Toward a Trinitarian Account of the Moral Life.* Notre Dame, Ind.: University of Notre Dame Press, 1990.

Jungel, Eberhard. "The Relationship between Economic and Immanent Trinity." *Theology Digest* 24 (summer 1976): 179–84.

LaCugna, Catherine Mowry. *God for Us: The Trinity and Christian Life.* San Francisco: HarperSanFrancisco, 1993.

Levinas, Emmanuel. *Totality and Infinity: An Essay on Exteriority.* Translated by A. Lingis. Pittsburgh: Duquesne University Press, 1969.

Lossky, Vladimir. *Orthodox Theology: An Introduction.* Translated by Ian and Ihita Kesarcodi-Watson. Crestwood, N.Y.: St. Vladimir's Seminary Press, 1989.

MacIntyre, Alasdair. *After Virtue: A Study in Moral Theory.* Notre Dame, Ind.: University of Notre Dame Press, 1981.

———. *Three Rival Versions of Moral Enquiry: Encyclopedia, Genealogy, and Tradition: Being Gifford Lectures Delivered in the University of Edinburgh in 1988.* Notre Dame, Ind.: University of Notre Dame Press, 1990.

———. *Whose Justice? Which Rationality?* Notre Dame, Ind.: University of Notre Dame Press, 1988.

Mackie, J. L. "Evil and Omnipotence." In *The Problem of Evil,* edited by Marilyn McCord Adams and Robert Merrihew Adams. New York: Oxford University Press, 1990.

Marshall, Bruce D. *Trinity and Truth*. New York: Cambridge University Press, 2000.

McClendon, James William, Jr. *Ethics*. Vol. 1 of *Systematic Theology*. Nashville: Abingdon Press, 1986.

McFadyen, Alistair I. *Bound to Sin: Abuse, Holocaust, and the Christian Doctrine of Sin*. Cambridge: Cambridge University Press, 2000.

McWilliams, Nancy. *Psychoanalytic Diagnosis: Understanding Personality Structure in the Clinical Process*. New York: Guilford Press, 1994.

Meilaender, Gilbert C. *Friendship: A Study in Theological Ethics*. Notre Dame, Ind.: University of Notre Dame Press, 1985.

Milbank, John. *Theology and Social Theory: Beyond Secular Reason*. Cambridge, Mass.: Blackwell, 1994.

Moltmann, Jürgen. *The Trinity and the Kingdom: The Doctrine of God*. Translated by Margaret Kohl. Minneapolis: Fortress Press, 1993.

Mouw, Richard J. *The God Who Commands: A Study in Divine Command Ethics*. Notre Dame, Ind.: University of Notre Dame Press, 1990.

Niebuhr, Reinhold. *The Children of Light and the Children of Darkness*. New York: Charles Scribner's Sons, 1972.

———. *Moral Man and Immoral Society*. New York: Charles Scribner's Sons, 1960.

———. *The Nature and Destiny of Man: A Christian Interpretation*. 2 vols. New York: Charles Scribner's Sons, 1953.

Nussbaum, Martha. *The Fragility of Goodness: Luck and Ethics in Greek Tragedy and Philosophy*. New York: Cambridge University Press, 1986.

Nygren, Anders. *Agape and Eros: The Christian Idea of Love*. Translated by Philip S. Watson. Chicago: University of Chicago Press, 1953.

Outka, Gene. *Agape: An Ethical Analysis*. New Haven, Conn.: Yale University Press, 1972.

———. "Augustinianism and Common Morality." In *Prospects for Common Morality*, edited by Gene Outka and John P. Reeder Jr. Princeton, N.J.: Princeton University Press, 1993.

———. "Comment." *Journal of Religious Ethics* 25 (spring 1997): 435–40.

———. "God as the Subject of Unique Veneration: A Response to Ronald M. Green." *Journal of Religious Ethics* 21 (fall 1993): 211–15.

———. "Religious and Moral Duty: Notes on *Fear and Trembling*." In *Religion and Morality: A Collection of Essays*, edited by Gene Outka and John P. Reeder Jr. Garden City, N.Y.: Anchor Press, 1973.

———. "Theocentric Agape and the Self." *Journal of Religious Ethics* 24 (spring 1996): 37–38.

———. "Universal Love and Impartiality." In *The Love Commandments: Essays in Christian Ethics and Moral Philosophy*, edited by Edmund N. Santurri and William Werpehowski. Washington, D.C.: Georgetown University Press, 1992.

Peters, Ted. *God—The World's Future: Systematic Theology for a New Era*. 2d ed. Minneapolis: Fortress Press, 2000.

———. *God as Trinity: Relationality and Temporality in Divine Life*. Louisville, Ky.: Westminster/John Knox Press, 1993.

Plantinga, Alvin. "The Free Will Defense." In *The Analytic Theist: An Alvin Plantinga Reader*, edited by J. F. Sennett. Grand Rapids: Eerdmans, 1998.

———. *God, Freedom, and Evil*. New York: Harper & Row, 1974.

———. *The Nature of Necessity*. Oxford: Clarendon Press, 1974.

———. *Warranted Christian Belief*. New York: Oxford University Press, 2000.

Pope, Stephen J. "Love in Contemporary Christian Ethics." *Journal of Religious Ethics* 23 (spring 1995): 167–97.

———. "Reply." *Journal of Religious Ethics* 25 (spring 1997): 440–44.

Porter, Jean. *Natural and Divine Law: Reclaiming the Tradition for Christian Ethics*. Grand Rapids: Eerdmans, 1999.

Post, Stephen G. *Spheres of Love: Toward a New Ethics of the Family*. Dallas: Southern Methodist University Press, 1994.

———. *A Theory of Agape: On the Meaning of Christian Love*. Lewisburg, Pa.: Bucknell University Press, 1990.

Rahner, Karl. *The Church and the Sacraments*. New York: Herder & Herder, 1963.

———. *The Trinity*. Translated by Joseph Donceel. New York: Crossroad, 1997.

Ramsey, Paul. *Basic Christian Ethics*. Louisville, Ky.: Westminster/John Knox Press, 1993.

Reeder, John P., Jr. "Extensive Benevolence." *Journal of Religious Ethics* 26 (spring 1998): 47–69.

———. "Foundations without Foundationalism." In *Prospects for a Common Morality*, edited by Gene Outka and John P. Reeder Jr. Princeton, N.J.: Princeton University Press, 1993.

Reichenbach, Bruce R. "Freedom, Justice, and Moral Responsibility." In *The Grace of God, the Will of Man: A Case for Arminianism*, edited by Clark H. Pinnock. Grand Rapids: Zondervan, 1989.

Rice, Richard. "Divine Foreknowledge and Free-will Theism." In *The Grace of God, the Will of Man: A Case for Arminianism*, edited by Clark H. Pinnock. Grand Rapids: Zondervan, 1989.

Schneewind, J. B. *The Invention of Autonomy: A History of Modern Moral Philosophy*. New York: Cambridge University Press, 1998.

Staniloae, Dumitru. "The Holy Trinity: Structure of Supreme Love." In *Theology and the Church*. Translated by Robert Barringer. Crestwood, N.Y.: St. Vladimir's Seminary Press, 1980.

Stout, Jeffrey. *Ethics after Babel: The Languages of Morals and Their Discontents*. Boston: Beacon Press, 1988.

———. *The Flight from Authority: Religion, Morality, and the Quest for Autonomy*. Notre Dame, Ind.: University of Notre Dame Press, 1981.

Stump, Eleonore. "Intellect, Will, and the Principle of Alternate Possibilities." In *Perspectives on Moral Responsibility*, edited by John Martin Fischer and Mark Ravizza. Ithaca, N.Y.: Cornell University Press, 1993.

———. "Sanctification, Hardening of the Heart, and Frankfurt's Concept of Free Will." In *Perspectives on Moral Responsibility*, edited by John Martin Fischer and Mark Ravizza. Ithaca, N.Y.: Cornell University Press, 1993.

Swinburne, Richard. *The Christian God*. Oxford: Clarendon Press, 1994.

———. *Responsibility and Atonement*. Oxford: Clarendon Press, 1989.

————. "A Theodicy of Heaven and Hell." In *The Existence and Nature of God*, edited by Alfred J. Freddoso. Notre Dame, Ind.: University of Notre Dame Press, 1983.

Vacek, Edward Collins. *Love, Human and Divine: The Heart of Christian Ethics*. Washington, D.C.: Georgetown University Press, 1994.

Volf, Miroslav. *After Our Likeness: The Church as the Image of the Trinity*. Grand Rapids: Eerdmans, 1998.

Wainwright, William J. "Original Sin." In *Philosophy and the Christian Faith*, edited by Thomas V. Morris. Notre Dame, Ind.: University of Notre Dame Press, 1988.

————. *Reason and the Heart: A Prolegomenon to a Critique of Passional Reason*. Ithaca, N.Y.: Cornell University Press, 1995.

Wallwork, Ernest. *Psychoanalysis and Ethics*. New Haven, Conn.: Yale University Press, 1991.

Webb, Stephen H. *The Gifting God: A Trinitarian Ethics of Excess*. New York: Oxford University Press, 1996.

Williams, A. N. "Knowledge of God in Augustine's *De Trinitate*." In *Knowing the Triune God: The Work of the Spirit in the Practices of the Church*, edited by James J. Buckley and David S. Yeago. Grand Rapids: Eerdmans, 2001.

Williams, Bernard Arthur Owen. *Moral Luck: Philosophical Papers 1973–1980*. New York: Cambridge University Press, 1981.

Williams, Rowan. *On Christian Theology*. Oxford: Blackwell, 2000.

Wright, N. T. *The Climax of the Covenant: Christ and the Law in Pauline Theology*. Minneapolis: Fortress Press, 1992.

Zizioulas, John D. *Being as Communion: Studies in Personhood and the Church*. Crestwood, N.Y.: St. Vladimir's Seminary Press, 1993.

————. "Human Capacity and Human Incapacity: A Theological Exploration of Personhood." *Scottish Journal of Theology* 28 (1975): 408.

II. SECONDARY SOURCES

A. Edwards

Allen, Alexander V. G. *Jonathan Edwards*. Boston: Houghton Mifflin, 1889.

Anderson, Wallace. "Immaterialism in Jonathan Edwards's Early Philosophical Notes." *Journal of the History of Ideas* 25 (1964): 181–200.

Brant, Richard B. "Ideal Observer." In *Encyclopedia of Ethics*, edited by Lawrence C. Becker and Charlotte B. Becker. New York: Routledge, 2001.

Breitenbach, William. "Piety and Moralism: Edwards and the New Divinity." In *Jonathan Edwards and the American Experience*, edited by Nathan O. Hatch and Harry S. Stout. New York: Oxford University Press, 1988.

————. "Religious Affections and Religious Affectations: Antinomianism and Hypocrisy in the Writings of Edwards and Franklin." In *Benjamin Franklin, Jonathan Edwards, and the Representation of American Culture*, edited by Barbara B. Oberg and Harry S. Stout. New York: Oxford University Press, 1993.

Chai, Leon. *Jonathan Edwards and the Limits of Enlightenment Philosophy*. New York: Oxford University Press, 1998.

Chamberlain, Ava. "Self-Deception as a Theological Problem in Jonathan Edwards's 'Treatise concerning Religious Affections.'" *Church History* 63, no. 4 (1994): 541–56.

Cherry, Conrad. *The Theology of Jonathan Edwards: A Reappraisal.* Bloomington: Indiana University Press, 1990.

Cooey, Paula M. "Eros and Intimacy in Edwards." *Journal of Religion* 68 (October 1989): 484–501.

Daniel, Stephen H. *The Philosophy of Jonathan Edwards: A Study in Divine Semiotics.* Bloomington: Indiana University Press, 1994.

Delattre, Roland. *Beauty and Sensibility in the Thought of Jonathan Edwards: An Essay in Aesthetics and Theological Ethics.* New Haven, Conn.: Yale University Press, 1968.

———. "Religious Ethics Today: Jonathan Edwards, H. Richard Niebuhr, and Beyond." In *Edwards in Our Time: Jonathan Edwards and the Shaping of American Religion*, edited by Allen C. Guelzo and Sang Hyun Lee. Grand Rapids: Eerdmans, 1999.

———. "The Theological Ethics of Jonathan Edwards: An Homage to Paul Ramsey." *Journal of Religious Ethics* 19 (fall 1991): 71–102.

Dwight, Sereno E. *The Life of President Edwards.* New York: G. & C. & H. Carvill, 1830.

Elwood, Douglas J. *The Philosophical Theology of Jonathan Edwards.* New York: Columbia University Press, 1960.

Erdt, Terrence. *Jonathan Edwards, Art, and the Sense of the Heart.* Amherst, Mass.: University of Massachusetts Press, 1980.

Fiering, Norman. *Jonathan Edwards's Moral Thought and Its British Context.* Published for the Institute of Early American History and Culture, Williamsburg, Va. Chapel Hill: University of North Carolina Press, 1981.

———. "The Rationalist Foundations of Jonathan Edwards's Metaphysics." In *Jonathan Edwards and the American Experience*, edited by Nathan O. Hatch and Harry S. Stout. New York: Oxford University Press, 1988.

Guelzo, Allen C. *Edwards on the Will: A Century of Debate.* Middletown, Conn.: Wesleyan University Press, 1989.

———. "The Return of the Will: Jonathan Edwards and the Possibilities of Free Will." In *Edwards in Our Time*, edited by Sang Hyun Lee and Allen Guelzo. Grand Rapids: Eerdmans, 1999.

Holbrook, Clyde A. *The Ethics of Jonathan Edwards: Morality and Aesthetics.* Ann Arbor: University of Michigan Press, 1973.

Holmes, Stephen R. *God of Grace and God of Glory: An Account of the Theology of Jonathan Edwards.* Grand Rapids: Eerdmans, 2001.

Howe, Daniel Walker. *Making the American Self: Jonathan Edwards to Abraham Lincoln.* Cambridge, Mass.: Harvard University Press, 1997.

Jenson, Robert W. *America's Theologian: A Recommendation of Jonathan Edwards.* New York: Oxford University Press, 1988.

Knight, Janice. "Learning the Language of God: Jonathan Edwards and the Typology of Nature." *William and Mary Quarterly* 48 (October 1991): 531–51.

Lee, Sang Hyun. "Edwards on God and Nature: Resources for Contemporary Theology." In *Edwards in Our Time: Jonathan Edwards and the Shaping of*

American Religion, edited by Sang Hyun Lee and Allen C. Guelzo. Grand Rapids: Eerdmans, 1999.

———. "Ethics of Jonathan Edwards." *Christian Scholar's Review* 6, no. 1 (1976): 66–69.

———. "Jonathan Edwards' Dispositional Conception of the Trinity: A Resource for Contemporary Reformed Theology." In *Toward the Future of Reformed Theology: Tasks, Topics, Traditions*, edited by David Willis and Michael Welker. Grand Rapids: Eerdmans, 1999.

———. *The Philosophical Theology of Jonathan Edwards*. Expanded ed. Princeton, N.J.: Princeton University Press, 2000.

Lewis, Paul. "'The Springs of Motion': Jonathan Edwards on Emotions, Character, and Agency," *Journal of Religious Ethics* 22 (fall 1994): 275–97.

McClymond, Michael James. *Encounters with God: An Approach to the Theology of Jonathan Edwards*. New York: Oxford University Press, 1998.

McDermott, Gerald. *Jonathan Edwards Confronts the Gods: Christian Theology, Enlightenment Religion, and Non-Christian Faiths*. New York: Oxford University Press, 2000.

Miller, Perry. *Jonathan Edwards*. Cleveland: World Publishing Co., 1964.

———. "Jonathan Edwards on the Sense of the Heart." *Harvard Theological Review* 41 (April 1948): 123–45.

———. *The New England Mind: The Seventeenth Century*. Cambridge, Mass.: Harvard University Press, 1983.

Morimoto, Anri. *Jonathan Edwards and the Catholic Vision of Salvation*. University Park: Pennsylvania State University Press, 1995.

Park, Edwards Amasa. "Remarks on Jonathan Edwards on the Trinity." *Bibliotheca Sacra* 38 (1881): 147–87 and 333–69.

Pauw, Amy Plantinga. *The Supreme Harmony of All: The Trinitarian Theology and Ethics of Jonathan Edwards*. Grand Rapids: Eerdmans, 2002.

Post, Stephen Garrard. *Christian Love and Self-Denial: An Historical and Normative Study of Jonathan Edwards, Samuel Hopkins, and American Theological Ethics*. Lanham, Md.: University Press of America, 1987.

Proudfoot, Wayne. "From Theology to a Science of Religions: Jonathan Edwards and William James on Religious Affections." *Harvard Theological Review* 82 (April 1989): 149–68.

———. "Perception and Love in *Religious Affections*." In *Jonathan Edwards's Writings: Text, Context, Interpretation*, edited by Stephen J. Stein. Bloomington: Indiana University Press, 1996.

Richardson, Herbert Warren. "The Glory of God in the Theology of Jonathan Edwards: A Study in the Doctrine of the Trinity." Ph.D. diss., Harvard University, 1962.

Sairsingh, Krister. "Jonathan Edwards and the Idea of Divine Glory: His Foundational Trinitarianism and Its Ecclesial Import." Ph.D. diss., Harvard University, 1986.

Smith, John E. "Jonathan Edwards: Piety and Practice in the American Character." *Journal of Religion* 54 (April 1974): 166–80.

———. "Testing the Spirits: Jonathan Edwards and the Religious Affections." *Union Seminary Quarterly Review* 37 (fall-winter 1981–1982): 27–37.

Stob, Henry. "The Ethics of Jonathan Edwards." In *Faith and Philosophy: Philosophical Studies in Religion and Ethics; Essays Published in Honor of W. Harry Jellema*, edited by Alvin Plantinga. Grand Rapids: Eerdmans, 1964.

Storms, C. Samuel. *Tragedy in Eden: Original Sin in the Theology of Jonathan Edwards*. Lanham, Md.: University Press of America, 1985.

Stout, Harry S. "The Puritans and Edwards." In *Jonathan Edwards and the American Experience*, edited by Nathan O. Hatch and Harry S. Stout. New York: Oxford University Press, 1988.

Tracy, Patricia J. *Jonathan Edwards, Pastor: Religion and Society in Eighteenth-Century Northampton*. New York: Hill & Wang, 1980.

Tufts, James H. "Edwards and Newton." *Philosophical Review* 49 (November 1940): 609–22.

Wilson, Stephen A. "The Possibility of a Habituation Model of Moral Development in Jonathan Edwards' Conception of the Will's Freedom." *Journal of Religion* 81 (January 2001): 49–77.

Winslow, Ola Elizabeth. *Jonathan Edwards: 1703–1758*. New York: Collier Books, 1961.

B. Others

Babcock, William S. "Augustine on Sin and Moral Agency." In *The Ethics of Augustine*, edited by William S. Babcock. Atlanta: Scholars Press, 1991.

———. "A Changing of the Christian God: The Doctrine of the Trinity in the Seventeenth Century." *Interpretation* 45 (April 1991): 133–46.

Biggar, Nigel. "Barth's Trinitarian Ethic." In *The Cambridge Companion to Karl Barth*, edited by John B. Webster. New York: Cambridge University Press, 2000.

Brown, Peter. *Augustine of Hippo: A Biography*. Berkeley: University of California Press, 1967.

———. *The Body and Society: Men, Women, and Sexual Renunciation in Early Christianity*. New York: Columbia University Press, 1988.

Bryan, Christopher. *A Preface to Romans: Notes on the Epistle in Its Literary and Cultural Setting*. New York: Oxford University Press, 2000.

Burnaby, John. *Amor Dei: A Study of the Religion of St. Augustine*. London: Hodder & Stoughton, 1960.

Burt, Donald X. *Friendship and Society: An Introduction to Augustine's Practical Philosophy*. Grand Rapids: Eerdmans, 1999.

Chopp, Rebecca S. *The Praxis of Suffering: An Interpretation of Liberation and Political Theologies*. Maryknoll, N.Y.: Orbis Books, 1986.

Cohen, Charles Lloyd. *God's Caress: The Psychology of Puritan Religious Experience*. New York: Oxford University Press, 1986.

Coleman, Janet. "MacIntyre and Aquinas." In *After MacIntyre: Critical Perspectives on the Work of Alasdair MacIntyre*, edited by J. Horton and S. Mendus. Notre Dame, Ind.: University of Notre Dame Press, 1994.

Conforti, Joseph. "Edwards A. Park and the Creation of New England Theology, 1840–1870." In *Jonathan Edwards's Writings: Text, Context, Interpretation*, edited by S. J. Stein. Bloomington: Indiana University Press, 1996.

Cooper, John. "Aristotle on Friendship." In *Essays on Aristotle's Ethics,* edited by Amelie Oksenberg Rorty. Berkeley: University of California Press, 1980.

Crisp, Roger, and Michael A. Slote, eds. *Virtue Ethics.* New York: Oxford University Press, 1997.

Cunningham, David. "Trinitarian Theology since 1990." *Reviews in Religion and Theology,* no. 4 (November 1995): 8–16.

Davies, Brian. *The Thought of Thomas Aquinas.* Oxford: Clarendon Press, 1992.

Den Bok, Nico. *Communicating the Most High: A Systematic Study of Person and Trinity in the Theology of Richard of St. Victor.* Paris: Brepols, 1996.

Dowey, Edward A. *The Knowledge of God in Calvin's Theology.* New York: Columbia University Press, 1965.

Dunfee, Susan Nelson. "The Sin of Hiding: A Feminist Critique of Reinhold Niebuhr's Account of the Sin of Pride." *Soundings* 65 (fall 1982): 316–27.

Fee, Gordon D. "Paul and the Trinity: The Experience of Christ and the Spirit for Paul's Understanding of God." In *The Trinity: An Interdisciplinary Symposium on the Trinity,* edited by Stephen Davis, Daniel Kendall, and Gerald O'Collins. New York: Oxford University Press, 1999.

Fiering, Norman. *Moral Philosophy at Seventeenth-Century Harvard: A Discipline in Transition.* Published for the Institute of Early American History and Culture, Williamsburg, Va. Chapel Hill: University of North Carolina Press, 1981.

Fisher, Geoffrey P. "The Augustinian and the Federal Theories of Original Sin Compared." *New Englander and Yale Review* 27 (July 1868): 468–516.

Grant, Robert McQueen. "Rhetoric in Theology." In *Irenaeus of Lyons,* translated and edited by Robert McQueen Grant. New York: Routledge, 1997.

Green, Ronald M. "Enough Is Enough! *Fear and Trembling* Is Not about Ethics." *Journal of Religious Ethics* 21 (fall 1993): 191–209.

Greer, Rowan A. "The Transition from Death to Life: Augustine's Theology of the Church." *Interpretation* 46 (July 1992): 240–49.

Hall, Amy Laura. "Self-Deception, Confusion, and Salvation in *Fear and Trembling* with *Works of Love.*" *Journal of Religious Ethics* 28 (spring 2000): 37–61.

Hanson, Richard Patrick Crossland. *The Search for the Christian Doctrine of God: The Arian Controversy 318–381.* Edinburgh: T. & T. Clark, 1988.

Hardie, William Francis Ross. *Aristotle's Ethical Theory.* 2d ed. New York: Oxford University Press, 1980.

Hardy, David. *The Condition of Postmodernity.* Oxford: Blackwell, 1990.

Harrison, Simon. "Do We Have a Will? Augustine's Way in to the Will." In *The Augustinian Tradition,* edited by G. B. Matthews. Berkeley: University of California Press, 1999.

Hunt, Anne. *The Trinity and the Paschal Mystery: A Development in Recent Catholic Theology.* Collegeville, Minn: Liturgical Press, 1997.

Hutchinson, D. S. "Ethics." In *The Cambridge Companion to Aristotle,* edited by Jonathan Barnes. New York: Cambridge University Press, 1995.

Idziak, Janine Marie, comp. *Divine Command Morality: Historical and Contemporary Readings.* New York: Edwin Mellon Press, 1979.

Irwin, Terence. *Plato's Ethics.* New York: Oxford University Press, 1995.

Kelly, J. N. D. *Early Christian Doctrines*. 5th rev. ed. San Francisco: Harper & Row, 1978.

Kent, Bonnie. "Augustine's Ethics." In *The Cambridge Companion to Augustine*, edited by Eleonore Stump and Norman Kretzmann. New York: Cambridge University Press, 2001.

Knight, Janice. *Orthodoxies in Massachusetts: Rereading American Puritanism*. Cambridge, Mass.: Harvard University Press, 1997.

Knuuttila, Simo. "The Emergence of the Logic of Will in Medieval Thought." In *The Augustinian Tradition*, edited by G. B. Matthews. Berkeley: University of California Press, 1999.

LaCugna, Catherine Mowry. "Current Trends in Trinitarian Theology." *Religious Studies Review* 13 (April 1987): 141–47.

Lavere, George J. "Virtue." In *Augustine through the Ages: An Encyclopedia*, edited by Allan Fitzgerald. Grand Rapids: Eerdmans, 1999.

Lloyd, A. C. *The Anatomy of Neoplatonism*. Oxford: Clarendon Press, 1990.

Loeb, Louis E. *From Descartes to Hume: Continental Metaphysics and the Development of Modern Philosophy*. Ithaca, N.Y.: Cornell University Press, 1981.

Louden, Robert B. "Kant's Virtue Ethics." In *Virtue Ethics: A Critical Reader*, edited by Daniel Statman. Washington, D.C.: Georgetown University Press, 1997.

MacNamara, Marie A. *Friends and Friendship for Saint Augustine*. Staten Island, N.Y.: St. Paul Publishers, 1964.

Mahoney, John. *The Making of Moral Theology: A Study of the Roman Catholic Tradition*. New York: Oxford University Press, 1987.

McGiffert, Michael. "Grace and Works: The Rise and Division of Covenant Divinity in Elizabethan Puritanism." *Harvard Theological Review* 75 (October 1982): 463–502.

McInerny, Ralph. "Ethics." In *The Cambridge Companion to Aquinas*, edited by Eleonore Stump and Norman Kretzmann. New York: Cambridge University Press, 1993.

Miller, Perry. *Errand into the Wilderness*. Cambridge, Mass.: Belknap Press of Harvard University Press, 1956.

Murphy, Nancey C., Brad J. Kallenburg, and Mark Thiessen Nation, eds. *Virtues and Practices in the Christian Tradition: Christian Ethics after MacIntyre*. Harrisburg, Pa.: Trinity Press International, 1997.

O'Donovan, Oliver. *The Problem of Self-love in St. Augustine*. New Haven, Conn.: Yale University Press, 1980.

———. "Usus and Fruitio in Augustine, De Doctrina Christiana I." *Journal of Theological Studies* 23 (October 1982): 361–97.

Olscamp, Paul J. *The Moral Philosophy of George Berkeley*. The Hague, Netherlands: Martinus Nijhoff, 1970.

Osborne, Catherine. *Eros Unveiled: Plato and the God of Love*. Oxford: Clarendon Press, 1996.

Outka, Gene. "The Particularist Turn in Theological and Philosophical Ethics." In *Christian Ethics: Problems and Prospects*, edited by Lisa Sowle Cahill and James F. Childress. Cleveland: Pilgrim Press, 1996.

Pelikan, Jaroslav. *Reformation of Church and Dogma (1300–1700)*. Vol. 4 of *The Christian Tradition: A History of the Development of Doctrine*. Chicago: University of Chicago Press, 1984.

Pfizenmaier, Thomas C. *The Trinitarian Theology of Dr. Samuel Clarke (1675–1729): Context, Sources, and Controversy*. New York: E. J. Brill, 1997.

Pike, Nelson. "Hume on Evil." In *The Problem of Evil*, edited by Marilyn McCord Adams and Robert Merrihew Adams. New York: Oxford University Press, 1990.

————, ed. *God and Evil: Readings on the Theological Problem of Evil*. Englewood Cliffs, N.J.: Prentice-Hall, 1964.

Plantinga, Cornelius, Jr. "Social Trinity and Tritheism." In *Trinity, Incarnation, and Atonement: Philosophical and Theological Essays*, edited by Ronald Jay Feenstra and Cornelius Plantinga Jr. Notre Dame, Ind.: University of Notre Dame Press, 1989.

Portalie, Eugene. *A Guide to the Thought of Saint Augustine*. Translated by Ralph J. Bastian. Chicago: H. Regnery Co., 1960.

Porter, Jean. "The Subversion of Virtue: Acquired and Infused Virtues in the *Summa Theologiae*." In *The Annual of the Society of Christian Ethics*, edited by H. Beckley. Washington, D.C.: Georgetown University Press, 1992.

Prestige, George Leonard. *God in Patristic Thought*. London: SPCK, 1956.

Quinn, Philip L. "Disputing the Augustinian Legacy: John Locke and Jonathan Edwards on Romans 5:12–19." In *The Augustinian Tradition*, edited by G. B. Matthews. Berkeley: University of California Press, 1999.

Ramsey, Paul. *Speak Up for Just War or Pacifism: A Critique of the United Methodist Bishops' Pastoral Letter "In Defense of Creation."* University Park: Pennsylvania State University Press, 1988.

Reeve, C. D. C. *Philosopher-Kings: The Argument of Plato's Republic*. Princeton, N.J.: Princeton University Press, 1988.

Rist, John M. *Eros and Psyche: Studies in Plato, Plotinus, and Origen*. Toronto: University of Toronto Press, 1964.

Rivers, Isabel. *Reason, Grace, and Sentiment: A Study of the Language of Religion and Ethics in England, 1660–1780*. Cambridge: Cambridge University Press, 2000.

Rogers, Eugene F. "The Narrative of Natural Law in Aquinas' Commentary on Romans 1." *Theological Studies* 59 (June 1998): 254–76.

Schafer, Thomas. "Solomon Stoddard and the Theology of the Revival." In *A Miscellany of American Christianity: Essays in Honor of H. Shelton Smith*, edited by Stuart Clark Henry. Durham, N.C.: Duke University Press, 1963.

Schlabach, Gerald W. "Augustine's Hermeneutic of Humility: An Alternative to Moral Imperialism and Moral Relativism." *Journal of Religious Ethics* 22 (fall 1994): 299–330.

Spohn, William C., and Thomas A. Byrnes. "Knowledge of Self and Knowledge of God: A Reconstructed Empiricist Interpretation." In *Christian Ethics, Problems and Prospects*, edited by Lisa Sowle Cahill and James F. Childress. Cleveland: Pilgrim Press, 1996.

St. Clair, Michael. *Human Relationships and the Experience of God: Object Relations and Religion*. New York: Paulist Press, 1994.

Stephens, Bruce M. *God's Last Metaphor: The Doctrine of the Trinity in New England Theology*. Chico, Calif.: Scholars Press, 1981.

Stiltner, Brian. "Who Can Understand Abraham? The Relation of God and Morality in Kierkegaard and Aquinas." *Journal of Religious Ethics* 21 (fall 1993): 221–45.

Stout, Harry. *The New England Soul: Preaching and Religious Culture in Colonial New England*. New York: Oxford University Press, 1986.

Teselle, Eugene. "Towards an Augustinian Politics." In *The Ethics of St. Augustine*, edited by William S. Babcock. Atlanta: Scholars Press, 1991.

Urmson, J. O. *Aristotle's Ethics*. Malden, Mass.: Blackwell, 1988.

Vlastos, Gregory. "The Virtuous and the Happy: Plato's Moral Theory." In *Socrates, Plato, and Their Tradition*. Vol. 1 of *Studies in Greek Philosophy*, edited by Daniel W. Graham. Princeton, N.J.: Princeton University Press, 1995.

Wadell, Paul. *Friends of God: Virtues and Gifts in Aquinas*. New York: P. Lang, 1991.

Wetzel, James. *Augustine and the Limits of Virtue*. New York: Cambridge University Press, 1992.

Wood, Rega. *Ockham on the Virtues*. West Lafayette, Ind.: Purdue University Press, 1997.

Wright, Conrad. *The Beginnings of Unitarianism in America*. Boston: Beacon Press, 1966.

INDEX OF NAMES

INDEX OF SUBJECTS